Veterans' Policies, Veterans' Politics

UNIVERSITY PRESS OF FLORIDA

Florida A&M University, Tallahassee
Florida Atlantic University, Boca Raton
Florida Gulf Coast University, Ft. Myers
Florida International University, Miami
Florida State University, Tallahassee
New College of Florida, Sarasota
University of Central Florida, Orlando
University of Florida, Gainesville
University of North Florida, Jacksonville
University of South Florida, Tampa
University of West Florida, Pensacola

# Veterans' Policies, Veterans' Politics

## New Perspectives on Veterans in the Modern United States

**Edited by Stephen R. Ortiz**

FOREWORD BY SUZANNE METTLER

University Press of Florida

Gainesville | Tallahassee | Tampa | Boca Raton

Pensacola | Orlando | Miami | Jacksonville | Ft. Myers | Sarasota

This book may be available in an electronic edition.

17  16  15  14  13  12   6  5  4  3  2  1

Library of Congress Cataloging-in-Publication Data
Veterans' policies, veterans' politics : new perspectives on veterans in the modern United States
/ edited by Stephen R. Ortiz ; foreword by Suzanne Mettler.
p. cm.
Includes bibliographical references and index.
Summary: An examination of the political issues and causes of veterans of the U.S. military.
ISBN 978-0-8130-4207-7 (alk. paper)
1. Veterans—United States. 2. Veterans—Services for—United States.
3. United States—Politics and government. 4. Veterans—Employment—United States.
I. Ortiz, Stephen R. II. Mettler, Suzanne.
UB357.V438 2012
362.86'5610973—dc23    2012018869

The University Press of Florida is the scholarly publishing agency for the State University
System of Florida, comprising Florida A&M University, Florida Atlantic University, Florida
Gulf Coast University, Florida International University, Florida State University, New College
of Florida, University of Central Florida, University of Florida, University of North Florida,
University of South Florida, and University of West Florida.

University Press of Florida
15 Northwest 15th Street
Gainesville, FL 32611-2079
http://www.upf.com

This book is dedicated
to the new generation of American veterans
and to those who serve them.

# Contents

# Illustrations

# Tables

# Foreword

American political and social history and state development cannot be understood apart from the role, place, and significance of veterans and the policies created for them. Yet, until recently, barely a handful of scholarly studies examined the subject of veterans in politics, and most that did treated it apart from broader questions about American political development. This volume represents a dramatic leap forward, therefore, and not only in its ability to further our understanding of the vastly neglected topic of veterans. More importantly, the dynamic research of the new generation of historians and political scientists featured in this collection considers what veterans' politics and policies illuminate about public life in the United States generally, about the contours and trajectories along which it has evolved, and the identities that have been fashioned and promoted in the process.

For decades, many scholars of American history operated on the assumption that European state development was normative; thus, they focused on what was missing in American politics by comparison. As a result, studies abound that highlight the weakness of organized labor and the late and incomplete development of European-style social welfare policies. As important as these topics are, they tell us more about what American history lacked than about what it possessed. By adding veterans to the analysis, a sparsely filled canvas suddenly becomes replete with color, highlighting political action and ideas that drove the policymaking process and informing about policies that shaped American civic identity and social life. This is illustrated by Theda Skocpol's multiple-award-winning 1992 book, *Protecting Soldiers and Mothers: The Political Origins of Social Policy in the United States*, which highlighted the development of Civil War veterans' pensions as well as "maternalist" social policies.[1] Now, two decades later, this volume continues in the same tradition, examining early and mid-twentieth century veterans' politics and probing what they indicate about the larger political context of their time and about the contours along which American life proceeded.

From the Revolutionary War onward, both American political elites and ordinary people have acknowledged the citizen soldier as an integral, defining actor in the polity. In the democratic ideals central to the nation's identity, military service represented a central obligation of masculine citizenship, and the protection of the nation by ordinary citizens rather than a standing army was regarded as essential for self-governance.[2] As George Washington explained, "It may be laid down as a primary position, and the basis of our system, that every Citizen who enjoys the protection of a free government, owes not only a proportion of his property, but even of his personal services to the defense of it."[3] In turn, these citizen soldiers gained respect and honor: the common person who served his nation became endowed with status and was viewed as the legitimate bearer of claims on his government, and he acquired a political identity that was a source of collective action and mobilization. Such dynamics prompted state development as public officials created the mechanisms and raised the resources for channeling benefits to veterans. In every era from the post-Revolutionary period down to the present, the question of how the nation should fulfill its obligations to its veterans has assumed a central role in American politics. As a result, efforts to explain American political history that omit veterans are woefully incomplete in at least four different ways.

First, veteran status has been crucial to the definition of citizenship status and stratification in the polity. Interestingly, its power operates as a double-edged sword: on the one hand, it has served to delineate who is included and who is excluded as honored and rights-bearing citizens; on the other hand, it has provided a powerful tool for expanding the bounds of the citizenry. In the nineteenth century, the United States distinguished itself from other nations by its early extension of the franchise to white men regardless of whether they owned property; military service further reinforced the privileged status of those who undertook it. While offering broad inclusive citizenship to white men irrespective of class, this cleavage institutionalized social divisions related to race and gender. Yet the legitimacy of veteran status has also made it very effective as a means of facilitating greater inclusion. By the twentieth century, the nation began—through fits and starts—to extend some social and civil rights to men who were veterans even while denying those forms of citizenship to other Americans. In this volume, Jennifer D. Keene demonstrates that for African Americans, veteran status served as an opening wedge for rights, helping to give momentum to the civil rights movement. Similarly, even in the midst of a period in which many equated government involvement in the economy with socialism, the U.S. War Department engaged in efforts to pursue reemployment for World War I veterans, as illuminated by Nancy Gentile Ford. Audra Jennings shows how disabled veterans were the first Americans to become beneficiaries of rights based on those conditions even while other disabled people remained without such status. In each case, the status afforded veterans gave them extra privileges unknown to other Americans of their social group, and it provided a model that eventually became extended to civilians as well.

Second, in a nation long associated with a slowly developed and incomplete welfare state, veterans' benefits have led the way in policy development. This theme builds on Skocpol's work on Civil War veterans' pensions by examining the veterans' benefits that followed in the early to mid-twentieth century. Nancy Beck Young, Melinda Pash, and Mark Boulton examine three generations of G.I. bills, considering the extent to which they extended social provision in the form of education and training benefits; assistance in buying homes, farms, and businesses; and unemployment insurance. Although the G.I. Bill did not mandate formal exclusions, as Young and Boulton observe, neither did it decimate those sanctioned through either informal practice or laws in local and decentralized institutions, such as racial segregation and prejudice against gays in the World War II period. It also failed to combat the rising inequality and soaring tuition that emerged in the post-Vietnam period. Nonetheless, each version granted substantial rights that were significant in the lives of many beneficiaries, granting them privileges not enjoyed by Americans who shared the same social and economic backgrounds but who lacked veteran status.

Third, veterans have played a crucial role in shaping participatory democracy. It is well known that, despite the abstract ideal of political equality, Americans vary dramatically in their rates of political participation. An individual's level of education is regarded as a crucial determinant of participation, and so too are other socioeconomic and mobilization factors. Veteran status matters too, as Stephen R. Ortiz shows in this volume. He demonstrates how veterans' organizations, competing to attract members, mobilized veterans in the pursuit of bonuses during the early 1930s and for the G.I. Bill after World War II. Veterans became activist citizens through such efforts. Veteran status can also affect political attitudes, although its impact varies by issue and by veterans' experience of military service. Jeremy M. Teigen detects few attitudinal differences among contemporary veterans and nonveterans aside from issues pertaining to military service by gays. Christopher S. Parker does find, however, that those who have suffered from posttraumatic stress because of their service experience greater political alienation and less allegiance to the nation.

Fourth, efforts to provide services to veterans have prompted the development of state capacity in the form of institutions, resources, and political affiliations. In a nation that was slow to develop its administrative state, the provision of veterans' services served as an important impetus. Carol R. Byerly shows how localities provided health services to veterans, especially those with tuberculosis, long before federal agencies were created for that purpose.

Rosemary A. Stevens explains the politics of the creation of the Veterans' Bureau in 1921, and John M. Kinder explores the architectural history of services offered to disabled veterans, analyzing the implications of different approaches for their inclusion or marginalization within society. Young's treatment of the World War II–era Congress also illustrates how politics related to veterans shaped dynamics within that institution, and Ortiz observes the political status acquired by the major veterans' organizations, the Veterans of Foreign Wars, and American Legion as they struggled to serve their constituencies by winning benefits on their behalf.

Given the overwhelming significance of veterans to American political history, one might wonder why scholars have paid so little attention to them previously. Perhaps their overwhelming presence has made us take their significance for granted rather than prompting us to examine the implications for our political life. Whatever the motivation, the neglect of this subject has left us ill poised to understand how the United States itself has developed over the course of its history. Fortunately, by placing veterans front and center, the essays collected in this volume go far to make up for omissions of past research. They provide a strong foundation on which future scholars should build, enabling us to better understand not only America's veterans but, moreover, the priorities and development of the nation they served.

*Suzanne Mettler*
*Clinton Rossiter Professor of American Institutions*
*Department of Government*
*Cornell University*

## Notes

1. Theda Skocpol, *Protecting Soldiers and Mothers: The Political Origins of Social Policy in the United States* (Cambridge, Mass.: Harvard University Press, 1992).

2. Peter Karsten, "The U.S. Citizen Soldier's Past, Present, and Likely Future," *Parameters*, Summer 2001, 61–73; R. Claire Snyder, *Citizen-Soldiers and Manly Warriors: Military Service and Gender in the Civic Republican Tradition* (Lanham, Md.: Rowman and Littlefield, 1999).

3. George Washington, "Sentiments of a Peace Establishment," in *The American Military: Readings in the History of the Military and American Society*, ed. Russell Weigley (Reading, Mass.: Addison-Wesley, 1969).

# Acknowledgments

Before embarking on this project, I heard many horror stories about the travails of editing multiple-authored collections such as this book. I am delighted to report that I have no horror story to tell. Instead, the people associated with the publication of this book have been wonderful collaborators and cheerful supporters. Foremost, I would like to thank the authors for their hard work and good-natured dedication to getting this book in print. Their shared belief in the importance of the project sustained my efforts to get it done and to get it done right. Prior to its submission, Allison L. Keane lent me astute editorial assistance. Patti J. Bower was an excellent and helpful copyeditor. Meredith Morris-Babb enthusiastically embraced the idea of this project in its earliest stages and provided a great deal of help in getting it rounded into its current form. Meredith and all of the staff members at the University Press of Florida have been consummate professionals. Finally, the book would look very different were it not for the financial support extended to me through a State University of New York faculty research grant. To all, I am extremely grateful for your efforts and assistance, and hope you share my great pleasure in seeing this book published.

# Introduction

## STEPHEN R. ORTIZ

Since the nation's founding, veterans have been a constant presence in American political life. Veterans' special claims on the state, made concrete through a broad array of entitlements (veterans' policies) and their unique role in American politics (veterans' politics), have greatly influenced partisan politics and state formation in the United States. Given this, one would assume that veterans of the modern era (1898–present), their organizations, and their role in American electoral politics and political culture are all well-studied topics. After all, during a century-plus dominated by American military intervention abroad, millions of veterans became beneficiaries of a wide range of federal entitlements, from preferential governmental hiring to the enormous level of social welfare provisioning that guarantees health care, educational and vocational benefits, and easy access to home ownership. Moreover, veterans' civic organizations such as the American Legion, Disabled Veterans of America, and the Veterans of Foreign Wars reached into the social fabric of every community and into the halls of Congress as powerful lobbyists. And yet, with one notable exception, the G.I. Bill of 1944, most topics relating to modern U.S. veterans remained underexamined.[1]

Recently, scholars have begun to turn their attention to veterans' issues more regularly and more rigorously. This anthology compiles some of the best of this new work on the formation and impact of veterans' policy, the politics of veterans' issues, and veterans' political engagement over the course of the twentieth- and twenty-first-century United States. To date, this research on veterans' policies and veterans' politics stood segregated within the various social science disciplines and their subfields. So while veteran-focused research is indeed now flowering, there has been little cross-pollination. To counter this trend, *Veterans' Policies, Veterans' Politics* brings together the work of scholars in history, the history of medicine and science, and political science to highlight veterans' issues as a field of interdisciplinary inquiry and debate unto itself.

This collection asks us to examine veterans' issues as a window into the larger topics of modern American history and to explore the continuing political implications of military service. Topics of analysis such as social welfare, health care, disability, and employment invariably come into sharper focus. But the essays also prod us into recognizing the centrality of veterans' issues and politics to modern state formation, the rise of interest group politics, understandings of citizenship, and American political culture and behavior. One key insight that informs the collection is that the debates surrounding veterans' issues nearly always turned into larger ideological battles over the nature of citizenship and the role of the federal government, two inextricably linked things. From the creation of the Veterans Bureau to the 1944 G.I. Bill to the contemporary battle over benefits to the veterans of Iraq and Afghanistan, the politics of veterans' issues was, and remains, not a site of consensus but one of ideological contestation made all the more antagonistic because the recipients of benefits and provisioning are such potent symbols in American political culture and form an important voting constituency.

Three common, broad themes emerge in this volume. The first is the way that modern liberalism and conservatism have grappled over veterans' policy. At critical junctures, veterans' issues have been viewed as vehicles for broader political agendas. During the Progressive Era, liberals sought to rationalize veterans' policy and end the corrupting influences of the Civil War pension system. After the New Deal, however, some liberals viewed veterans' policy as an avenue to expand American social welfare provisioning for all, regardless of military service. Others viewed it as an obstacle to the type of universal social provisioning being pioneered in European countries since it privileged military service as the precondition for entitlements. While early-twentieth-century conservatives sought to limit sharply the scope of veterans' entitlements and often joined with Progressive Era liberals in delineating veterans' policy, their post–New Deal counterparts tried to quarantine social welfare provisioning within the veterans' system, hoping this would derail liberals' drive for universal social provisioning. Explored by many of the essays, this larger debate and the tensions that were exposed because of it have meant that modern U.S. veterans' policy can be viewed simultaneously as an expansion of social welfare policy *and* its rejection.

A second broad theme is that modern veterans' policy was, and is, a complex policy arena with multiple actors and sites of politicization. While it is associated with the federal veteran agencies created in twentieth-century such as the Veterans Bureau, the Veterans Administration, and the Department of Veterans Affairs, other key players shown in these pages to have been important include the War Department (Department of Defense), the military service branches, Congress—especially congressional committees and subcommittees dedicated to veterans' issues—veteran organizations, and even individual veterans struggling in and against the veterans' welfare system. The contributors' diverse methodological and theoretical approaches to "the political" continually shift the focus among these institutional and cultural forces.

The essays in this volume all build upon a third theme, the importance of not viewing veterans as a monolithic power bloc, nor veterans' politics as a struggle between veterans and nonveterans. Political engagement, activism, and policy preferences have varied considerably within the veteran population. Often these differences *within* the veteran community are more pronounced than those between the veteran community and the population at large. Indeed, battles over veterans' issues often serve as proxy wars with veterans on both sides: between supporters of southern white supremacy and their critics, between the forces of labor activism and the business community, between modern liberals and conservatives, between hawkish military interventionists and noninterventionists.

The essays in this book are organized thematically, and, only incidentally, chronologically. Thematic sections are dedicated to health care, disability, the politics of race and labor, veteran entitlements such as the bonus and G.I. bills, and contemporary views of veterans' engagement and political preferences. Other very important veteran arenas such as housing and education have not been included because they have been researched and presented in the rich literature on the G.I. Bill. (Even still, there remains an unmet need to explore these arenas in the post-1944 G.I. Bill period.)

The book's opening section investigates the early origins of veterans' health care—probably the most taken for granted aspect of the veterans' entitlement system. Yet, as Carol R. Byerly and Rosemary A. Stevens describe the inception of the veterans' health care system in the early twentieth century, it was a site of bureaucratic confusion and competition, with locally autonomous actors continuing to shape policy and implementation until the creation of the Veterans Bureau. Throughout the 1900–1921 period, veterans' health care was shaped by individual veterans' agency and resistance at the local level, political mobilizations by veterans' groups, and critical congressional oversight. Byerly captures the idiosyncrasies that guided the health care of veterans suffering from tuberculosis by focusing on Fort Bayard, a hospital dedicated to serving the health care and hospice needs of military veterans prior to the emergence of the Veterans Bureau in 1921. She deftly teases out the strands of what made this local implementation of a federal matter unique and what was intrinsic to the system in this very early age of state development. Stevens crafts a counterintuitive trajectory of state development in her essay on the hospital provisioning provided to veterans of World War I. The ad hoc, makeshift care described by Byerly became swamped by the needs of the large World War I veteran cohort. In Stevens' reading, despite the antiradicalism and fears of socialism that colored the era, Congress moved to establish "socialized medicine" for veterans in the name of efficiency and in response to public outcry and mounting criticism from Congress and veterans' groups. Thus, even in the antistatist period of the 1920s, veterans' care took on many features of a strong, central administrative state.

In the second section, John M. Kinder and Audra Jennings explain the importance of veterans' disability issues to Americans' cultural understandings of disability and to the slow and constrained evolution of federal disability policies writ large. Kinder explores the experience of disability within what he calls the "architecture of disability" created through federal veterans' policy. The very spaces created for disabled veterans represented the relationship that veterans maintained both with the federal government and with the civilian population. As such, Kinder contends, these spatial arrangements materially and symbolically defined "disability" as a group identity and a social experience. Jennings investigates the ways in which federal veterans' disability policies crafted for the World War II cohort continued the veterans-only, exceptionalist approach, thus undermining the emergence of a coherent wartime and postwar disability policy for all citizens. While wartime industrial accidents produced a staggering number of severe injuries requiring rehabilitation, Congress's enshrinement of veterans' disability programs as separate, inviolable entities ensured that disability welfare would fall short of the nonveteran population's needs. Mirroring the concurrent debates over which agencies of the federal government would administer the education provisions of the 1944 G.I. Bill, the battle at the heart of Jennings' essay demonstrates the ways in which modern U.S. veterans' policy has been both a model and deterrent for broader social welfare policy.

Jennifer D. Keene and Nancy Gentile Ford delve into the politics of race and labor in the aftermath of the Great War. In each case, their essays highlight how a complex policy arena involving veterans' agencies, War Department agencies, and the private sector caused unique combinations of problems and opportunities for returning veterans. More important, the essays explain clearly how federal veterans' policies were constrained at the local, state, and federal levels. Existing social and political norms such as segregation, racial and ethnic discrimination, and intense antiradicalism worked to reshape ostensibly neutral federal policies, often to the detriment of African American, ethnic, and working-class veterans. Ford investigates the War Department's attempts to reintegrate returning soldiers into the economy following World War I. When

Congress and the business community deemed the Labor Department and its U.S. Employment Service too sympathetic to organized labor and, by implication, radicalism, the War Department became the primary federal entity responsible for veterans' demobilization and labor placement policy. Thus, even though new federal agencies such as the War Risk Insurance Bureau and Federal Board for Vocational Education were empowered to ameliorate veterans' reintegration problems, the venerable War Department successfully stepped in to address, and largely solve, the matter of economic reintegration. Keene reveals how African American veterans faced enormous obstacles to obtain the provisions to which they were entitled due to military service. Keene argues that discrimination in the implementation of veterans' policy inflicted further damage to African Americans suffering from their wartime experiences, yet discrimination also served as a rallying point for civil rights' organizations and the African American community energized by the ideological aims of the Great War and by wide African American participation in it.

Part four describes the politics behind the most notable and, indeed, controversial forms of veteran entitlements: bonuses and G.I. bills. The overarching theme in this section is the very fact that, despite substantial lip service paid to the nation's obligations to veterans, veterans' benefits were hotly contested rather than granted graciously by the government for military service provided. The first two of these essays, by Stephen R. Ortiz and Nancy Beck Young, contextualize veterans' entitlements within the politics of the Great Depression, New Deal, and World War II. Ortiz reexamines the origins of the Bonus March, focusing on the interorganizational struggle between the American Legion and Veterans of Foreign Wars (VFW) that gave spark to the 1932 Bonus crusade to explain the ways that federal veterans' policy made activist citizens out of veterans. Young describes the congressional efforts to undermine rather than advance New Deal social provisioning with the passage of the G.I. Bill. Her attention to the continued congressional power to check New Deal–style liberalism during the war and postwar years reconfirms the fact that the G.I. Bill was hardly "a New Deal for veterans," as one recent book would have it.[2] Rather, the sharply circumscribed social policy that emerged from Congress helped (many) veterans while promoting administrative decentralization and freely allowing local and state-level discrimination of racial minorities, women, and homosexuals.

Despite the circumscribed nature of the 1944 G.I. Bill, the second half of part 4 demonstrates that subsequent generations of veterans had to fight to come up with G.I. bills anywhere near as generous as the World War II cohort had won. With the corruption that riddled the original G.I. Bill, the ambiguity of Cold War–era soldiering (was stationing in West Germany or Alaska during the Cold War considered combat?), and the bureaucratic maze in which Vietnam-era veterans found their entitlements enmeshed, late-twentieth-century veterans struggled to gain the same opportunities as the "Greatest Generation." Melinda Pash details the fight for a Korean War G.I. Bill just years after the successful and popular World War II legislation. The legislation curtailed many of the provisions, Pash argues, because the Korean legislation emerged while Congress was exposed to hearings on World War II–era corruption in G.I. Bill benefits and because the solid footing of the U.S. economy in the early 1950s dampened concerns about veterans' economic reintegration. Mark Boulton examines the legislative and ideological battle over the 1966 G.I. Bill for Vietnam-era veterans. Since the bill was inclusive of all veterans regardless of stationing or whether they had seen combat, Boulton contends that the bill kept provisioning at a minimum and provoked spirited criticism for being insufficient assistance to Vietnam veterans who needed it desperately.

Finally, Jeremy M. Teigen and Christopher S. Parker explore how veterans' policy preferences and levels of civic engagement have been shaped in the early decades of the twenty-first century. In each essay, Teigen and Parker assess whether veterans have a different political make-up because of their military service and reflect on what this means for the future. Using statistical analysis of polling data from the 2004 and 2008 national elections, Teigen argues that rather than having a different set of policy preferences than the nonveteran population, veterans match up nearly entirely when other variables such as age and gender are statistically controlled. The most relevant policy difference between veterans and nonveterans, Teigen finds, is their position on the recently rescinded "Don't Ask, Don't Tell" policy for gays serving in the military. Parker uses interviews of veterans to gauge the impact of military service and combat exposure on levels of civic engagement. While a long-standing assumption has been that veterans are more politically engaged, Parker finds that combat exposure that produced feelings of alienation and mental anguish classified under the category of posttraumatic stress disorder (PTSD) led to decreased levels of civic engagement and lower levels of trust in political institutions and authority. Yet, Parker explains, combat exposure that was viewed by veterans as a positive or neutral experience led them to have high levels of civic engagement much like veterans who had not experienced combat.

When this volume began its slow movement toward publication, it seemed an opportune moment to compile new scholarship on veterans and present it in a unified manner bridging disciplines. If anything, the authors of this volume are more convinced now of the importance of doing this. And if one looks at the temporal and thematic gaps in this volume, the things not covered here could, and should, fill multiple future volumes. Yet the hope is that such a collection of essays, completed at a convenient moment for reflection and assessment, will serve as a clarion call for further research and further interdisciplinary dialogue on veterans' issues. This will build our understanding of the past impact of veterans' policies and veterans' politics, and it will aid all of us in understanding how a new generation of veterans from Iraq and Afghanistan will navigate the veterans' welfare system and American society and how they will affect policy and politics for the foreseeable future.

## Notes

1. On partisan politics, see Stuart McConnell, *Glorious Contentment: The Grand Army of the Republic, 1865–1900* (Chapel Hill: University of North Carolina Press, 1992); Richard Franklin Bensel, *The Political Economy of American Industrialization, 1877–1900* (New York: Cambridge University Press, 2000); and Mark W. Summers, *Party Games: Getting, Keeping, and Using Power in Gilded Age Politics* (Chapel Hill: University of North Carolina Press, 2004). On veteran's welfare and state-building, see Theda Skocpol, *Protecting Soldiers and Mothers: The Political Origins of Social Policy* (Cambridge: Belknap Press, 1992); and Ann Shola Orloff, *The Politics of Pensions: A Comparative Analysis of Britain, Canada, and the United States, 1880–1940* (Madison: University of Wisconsin Press, 1993). While the literature on the G.I. Bill is voluminous, the most recent works are Suzanne Mettler, *Soldiers to Citizens: The G.I. Bill and the Making of the Greatest Generation* (New York: Oxford University Press, 2005); Kathleen Jill Frydl, *The GI Bill* (New York: Cambridge University Press, 2009); and Glenn C. Altschuler and Stuart M. Blumin, *The GI Bill: A New Deal for Veterans* (New York: Oxford University Press, 2009).

2. Altschuler and Blumin, *GI Bill*.

# I

# Health Care

# 1

## Army Sanctuary For Tubercular Veterans

### Veterans' Health Care before the Veterans Bureau

CAROL R. BYERLY

### Introduction

At the dawn of the twentieth century, the United States strode onto the world stage as an economic and military power with the acquisition of colonies in the Pacific, the war with Spain, and the construction of the Panama Canal. These colonial adventures generated a growing population of sick and disabled soldiers, and the mission of the Army Hospital at Fort Bayard, New Mexico, was to care for these casualties of empire. One of them, John A. MacDonald, a veteran patient at Fort Bayard, forwarded three petitions to the governor of the Soldiers' Home in Washington, D.C., in March 1909 complaining of poor food, overly restrictive rules, disrespect, and a botched funeral. Sixty veteran-patients complained that the food was "poor in quality, insufficient in quantity, and not properly prepared" and that strict hospital rules meant "we are under a discipline more exacting than are any soldiers in Army post [sic] in the United States. This despite the fact that we are no longer soldiers and without consideration to past services." The second petition complained that an Army officer referred to the Fort Bayard hospital as a "Poor-house," and the third document alleged that a veteran had been buried unclothed in a broken casket. MacDonald claimed that more men would have signed the petitions but were afraid of the consequences because "their expulsion from the Home would be tantamount to death for many of them."[1]

The governor of the Soldiers' Home forwarded the complaints to Col. George E. Bushnell, commander of Fort Bayard, who responded swiftly with a seventeen-page letter and affidavits of his own. He countered that certain patients seemed to believe that "the government is disposed to provide bountifully for patients in this Institution and entertains a benevolent interest in their welfare, but that the Commanding Officer of this Hospital renders nugatory this benevolence by insisting upon a harsh and rigid military discipline which is unnecessary and uncalled for." He acknowledged that at times the food was poor and ordered changes in procurement and storage, but he conceded nothing regarding hospital rules. They were "regretted by no one more than myself, but that experience proved them necessary, because given complete freedom, the gamblers get together and it is almost impossible to prevent gambling." MacDonald, said Bushnell, was "one of the most experienced and successful gamblers among the beneficiaries of the Soldiers Home," and another of the signatories had been disciplined for drunkenness twelve times. Bushnell "deplored" the broken casket and ordered that each coffin be "minutely inspected before use," but he offered four affidavits maintaining that the body was clothed. He heatedly rejected MacDonald's "most unjustifiable insinuation" that he would be "so inhuman as to be capable of expelling dying men because they made complaints." He closed insisting that he be allowed to respond directly to complaints about conditions under his command.[2] The Soldiers' Home governor agreed. The Fort Bayard petitions, he told the commander, "were bundled up and sent to you without comment."[3] Bushnell consequently launched a year-long effort to clarify and even tighten the rules governing the behavior of veterans at Fort Bayard Hospital.

The Fort Bayard story includes another unseen actor—tuberculosis. All of MacDonald's petitioners were at Fort Bayard for treatment of this deadly disease at a time when the only therapy involved prolonged bed rest, fresh air, and a good diet to help the body fight the infection. This was a bitter pill for military men used to an active, robust lifestyle, so Bushnell and his staff faced continuous challenges from patients whose rowdy behavior threatened to compromise their tenuous health. While Bushnell and his officers had legal military control over active-duty patients, they had less authority over veterans who, as civilians, could discharge themselves from the hospital at any time, even against medical advice. As the veterans asserted their rights at Fort Bayard, the commanding officer asserted his authority and responsibility to care for them as a physician as well as an Army officer.

This chapter examines an army hospital from 1899 to 1920, before the creation of the Veterans Bureau in 1921, when the Army provided health care for veterans—retired and disabled soldiers, sailors, and marines—in its own institutions and developed policies to administer that care. The Fort Bayard story reveals four important points about veterans' policy during this period. The first is that while veterans' health and welfare programs presented a confusing patchwork of state and federal benefits and institutions, the system was in some ways quite simple and nonbureaucratic. Fort Bayard patients disabled by tuberculosis could move from active duty to veteran status without leaving their sick beds, thereby receiving continuous treatment. This contrasts with the more recent problems of some veterans "falling through the cracks" of government institutions and benefits.[4]

The second point is that while Congress laid out the broad lines of government funding and provision of veterans' benefits, it was up to local posts and medical officers such as Col. Bushnell to spell out specific policies governing veterans' health care, such as admission and discharge policies, length of hospitalization treatment, patient rights and responsibilities, and visiting and leave privileges. Officials in Washington often deferred to these local judgments. Third, even without a coherent set of government benefits and institutions dedicated to the care of veterans, the level of veterans' health care could be quite high. Bushnell and his colleagues were among the nation's leading tuberculosis specialists, and they provided the best care available at the time. Unfortunately, however, the incomplete understanding of tuberculosis transmission at the time and government policies that allowed veteran patients to move in and out of Fort Bayard hospital at will meant that some tubercular veterans ended up spreading the disease that Fort Bayard was dedicated to fighting. The fourth and final point is that the Army's first tuberculosis hospital was a leader in fighting a deadly disease that thrived in military conditions. By providing short-term care for military personnel who fell ill on active duty, and long-term care for aging veterans disabled by the disease, Fort Bayard represents a vivid example of the often unseen human costs of war and empire.

## Three Systems of Veterans' Benefits

Military veterans such as John MacDonald were in a privileged class—some of the first beneficiaries of federal old age and disability assistance. By the 1890s more than 40 percent of the federal budget went to pensions for veterans, including three-fourths of Union Civil War veterans.[5] Officers and enlisted men who became disabled by wounds, injuries, or illness during duty were eligible for pensions, as were career soldiers after twenty years of service in the regular Army. While lawmakers intended the pension system to obviate the need for government institutions for veterans, after the Civil War legions of disabled or impoverished former soldiers compelled the nation to cobble together a three-part system of domiciliary care for them.[6] The first part comprised the U.S. Soldiers' Home (USSH) in Washington, D.C., for poor and disabled career Army veterans, and the Naval Home in Philadelphia for disabled Navy officers, sailors, and marines, both established before the Civil War. In 1866, to accommodate thousands of needy Civil War veterans, Congress created the National Home for Disabled Volunteer

Soldiers (NHDVS) to provide food, shelter, medical care, and companion-ship for destitute or ailing veterans. By 1900 this system had eight regional branches from California to Maine. The third part emerged at the state level after 1888 legislation authorized the USSH Board of Managers to pay one hundred dollars per veteran per year to states and territories that established homes for needy veterans.[7] All of these institutions were known as "soldiers' homes" but were governed and financed separately. The USSH reported to the secretary of war, and, for purposes of funding and legal authority, Fort Bayard was considered a branch of the USSH. The NHDVS was governed by a board of managers that reported to Congress and was later incorporated into the Veterans Administration, and the state homes were subsidized by federal funds and governed by their respective states. By 1900 some 100,000 or almost 5 percent of 2.2 million Union soldiers had spent time in these facilities.[8] In 1899 alone there were about 30,000 veterans in these homes: the USSH had 1,296 beneficiaries, the NHDVS had 18,814 residents in eight regional branches, and twenty-nine state homes served 9,140 veterans.[9]

The homes were both rudimentary government medical facilities and so-cial welfare entities that offered shelter and companionship for veterans on a permanent basis and, given the infirmity of their residents, provided medical care, including tuberculosis treatment. The homes also served as respite care for families who found it difficult to care for their men and provided veterans with temporary lodging and meals if they came to the door.[10] USSH veterans were mostly career soldiers, and NHDVS veterans were largely men who had served in the Civil War or the Spanish-American War and who had an aver-age age of sixty-three by 1899.[11] Some men were eligible for both national sys-tems and moved between them, requiring Fort Bayard officers, Pension Bureau agents, and USSH and NHDVS officials to keep track of who was eligible for what benefits. For example, the USSH in Washington could send a veteran with tuberculosis to Fort Bayard for treatment, but if he recovered his health, the veteran might transfer to a branch of NHDVS. As Bushnell told one NHDVS official, "It is a very common occurrence for patients to leave here and go to the National Home in California."[12] Some veterans apparently tried to game the system because in 1909 the NHDVS Board resolved that "Soldiers who are beneficiaries of the Soldiers' Home in Washington, D.C. shall be considered as being sufficiently provided for, and will not be admitted to the National Home for Disabled Volunteer Soldiers."[13]

Contemporaries and historians alike have confused or conflated the two national systems, and it is indeed often difficult to determine under which system a veteran was a patient at Fort Bayard. Fort Bayard correspondence referred to both USSH and NHDVS patients as "beneficiaries of the Soldiers'

Home" and filed correspondence with both institutions under the same heading. Most of the surviving correspondence is between Fort Bayard and the USSH, but the hospital admitted 400 to 500 veterans a year, and the USSH reported only 100 to 150 patients at Fort Bayard annually, which suggests that many veteran patients were pensioners or beneficiaries of the NHDVS. As Bushnell unhelpfully explained to the governor of the NHDVS California branch, "beneficiaries absent from this hospital continued to be members of the Soldiers Home."[14] About three-fourths of USSH veterans received pensions; more than half were foreign-born; and a 1898 census at the home counted 41 African American residents, 400 Civil War veterans, 227 veterans of the War with Spain, and 37 old-timers from the Mexican War.[15] These aging Civil War veterans and disabled Spanish-American War veterans who crowded the homes were not only injured and poor, some were diseased, and government officials became concerned that tuberculosis in particular was an increasing threat to the residents.[16]

## Tuberculosis and the Army

Tuberculosis has been one of the most widespread and deadly pathogens in human history, attacking people of all ages across the world since ancient times. In the nineteenth century, it was the leading cause of death in much of Europe and the United States and today still infects one-third of the world's population, killing two million people annually.[17] Transmitted human to human, *Mycobacterium tuberculosis* primarily attacks the lungs but can infect virtually any part of the body. Most people's immune systems can control the invaders and wall them off into calcified lesions, but about 10 percent develop an active disease, especially people whose immune systems are weakened by hunger or other diseases associated with poverty. While some cases of tuberculosis kill people within weeks, most develop slowly and are alternately active and quiescent over the years. Antibiotic therapies developed in the 1950s cured many cases of tuberculosis and brought it under control in developed countries. But there is still no effective vaccine against tuberculosis, and today the antibiotic cures are losing power as tuberculosis bacteria develop resistance and as poverty and diseases such as HIV render millions of people vulnerable.

In 1900 tuberculosis was the single greatest killer in the country, causing 20 percent of American deaths.[18] During much of the nineteenth century, thousands of tuberculosis sufferers traveled to the West and Southwest seeking health as well as land and riches, and were often welcomed by local residents.[19] But after Robert Koch articulated the germ theory in 1882 and scientists began to identify the pathogens causing various diseases—including tuberculosis—

people began to view the sick with less sympathy and more fear.[20] By the end of the century, at least twenty-four states and many large cities had antituberculosis programs. Communities outlawed spitting, for example, authorized compulsory hospitalization or isolation for people with tuberculosis, and barred them from food-handling and teaching jobs.[21]

Physicians and the public turned to sanatoriums and tuberculosis hospitals to provide a three-fold solution of isolating patients to protect their families and the public from infection, treating the disease, and educating tuberculosis patients on how to care for themselves. Hospitals were developing as a key element in American health care at the time. New technologies such as X-rays and laboratory testing increased physicians' diagnostic capabilities, and aseptic surgery, improved sanitation, and professional nursing care made hospitals safer for patients. Hospitals increased from fewer than 200 in 1873 to more than 4,300 in 1909 with some 420,000 beds.[22] By 1916 there were more than 200 tuberculosis sanatoriums in the country.[23] The War Department's establishment of a tuberculosis hospital at Fort Bayard, New Mexico in 1899 put it in the first wave of this movement to isolate, treat, and educate tuberculosis patients.

The Army of the early 1900s was small in proportion to the national population, with fewer than one hundred thousand soldiers in a population of more than ninety-two million in 1910. It also stood on the margins of society in isolated posts that were poorly funded and held in low esteem by Americans traditionally hostile to the military.[24] In the small Army, medical officers knew each other and their families and were often well acquainted with many of their patients. Although the War Department sought to screen sick men from the ranks, each year fifty to one hundred soldiers developed tuberculosis and ten to forty died.[25] While the number of cases was small, any infection created a risk of contagion to healthy soldiers and could generate lifelong government pension obligations to disabled individuals whose lungs were so damaged they could no longer work.

The Army Medical Department was under good leadership at the turn of the century. Surgeon General George Sternberg (1893–1902) was a leader in American bacteriology as one of the first Americans to attempt to reproduce Robert Koch's famous experiments isolating tuberculosis bacteria, and he authored the first American textbook on bacteriology in 1893.[26] Sternberg would guide the Medical Department into the era of modern medicine, supporting the work of Walter Reed and William Gorgas against yellow fever in Cuba, establishing the Army Medical School, creating a special surgical hospital in Washington, D.C., and promoting professional dentistry and nursing.

As Sternberg addressed the problem of tuberculosis in the Army, he grappled with three contributing factors: the impact of war, rising rates of sexually transmitted disease and alcoholism, and aging veterans. The Spanish-American War, 1898–99, expanded the Army from 25,000 to 275,000 men, which increased tuberculosis cases from fewer than 100 annually to 547 cases in 1898. More cases developed as men serving in the tropics of Cuba or the Philippines succumbed to dysentery and tropical fevers such as malaria, which would weaken their immune systems and allow latent tuberculosis infections to become active. The 122,000 soldiers who served in the Philippines between 1898 and 1902 suffered at least 500,000 cases of illness, about four per capita.[27] So many Philippine scouts (employed by the U.S. War Department) were developing tuberculosis that the Army constructed special hospitals in country to care for them.[28]

High rates of syphilis and alcoholism also undermined soldiers' immune systems, rendering them susceptible to active tuberculosis. During the 1890s hospital admission rates for syphilis averaged 7 percent, but with the Spanish-American War the rates almost doubled to 13 percent.[29] Hospital admissions for alcoholism in the Army averaged 6 to 7 percent in the 1890s, and a standard medical text, Osler's *Principles and Practice of Medicine*, noted that "chronic drinkers are much more liable to acute and pulmonary tuberculosis."[30] In 1896 the USSH reported that 10 percent of residents suffered from alcoholism and 7.5 percent had tuberculosis.[31] That led to the third factor Sternberg faced: as Civil War veterans aged, they crowded the Soldiers' Homes, heightening the chance of spread of infectious disease.

Sternberg, a member of the USSH Board of Commissioners, recommended that it protect the other residents of the home by sending tubercular veterans to a special Army hospital for treatment. The War Department's decommissioning of Indian forts presented opportunities.[32] The Army had been caring for some tuberculosis patients at the Army-Navy hospital in Arkansas and since 1892 had transferred men in the early stages of tuberculosis to posts in Arizona, New Mexico, and Southern California "to give them the advantages of a more favorable climate."[33] After a scouting expedition reported that ninety thousand dollars could make Fort Bayard "suitable for occupation," Sternberg recommended that the Army turn it into a tuberculosis hospital and charge the USSH per capita for caring for veterans.[34] The Secretary of War and the USSH Board approved this proposal 29 August 1899.[35] For the next two decades, Fort Bayard would be home and hospital to several thousand veterans, active duty officers, and enlisted men of the Army, Navy, and Marines. Absent dedicated veterans' health care institutions or tuberculosis programs, medical officers, patients, the patients' families, and government officials would over the years negotiate the terms and conditions of their care.

## Fort Bayard

The secretary of war had established Fort Bayard in 1867, sixty miles north of the Mexican border at an altitude of 6,040 feet "to protect the miners against the Apache Indians."[36] When the first fourteen tuberculosis patients arrived in the fall of 1899 and African American regulars of the Ninth U.S. Cavalry departed, the post transformed from an Indian fort into a sanitarium. This transition reflects the broader transformation in the Army's mission from defending the nation and bringing industrial society to the American West, to extending American economic interests in the Western Hemisphere and the Pacific.

Although Fort Bayard was originally intended for veterans, the Army quickly adopted the practice of transferring all active-duty tuberculosis cases from the Philippines to Fort Bayard, and by January 1900 the hospital had forty-seven patients.[37] Comparing its new role to the former one of fighting the Apaches, Fort Bayard nurse Agnes Young wrote that the post "now shelters those who fight a fiercer, more unrelenting and insidious foe than ever before stalked these wild plains, thirsting for victims."[38]

In 1904 the Army surgeon general named George E. Bushnell, one of the most esteemed members of the Medical Corps, commander of Fort Bayard. During his tenure from 1904 to 1917, he built the hospital into a leading tuber-

Figure 1.1. U.S. Army, General Hospital, Fort Bayard, New Mexico, General View, c. 1900, showing the isolation of the post on a high mesa in New Mexico Territory. Courtesy of the National Library of Medicine, A02342.

Figure 1.2. Colonel George E. Bushnell, commander of the tuberculosis hospital at Fort Bayard, 1904–17. Courtesy of the National Library of Medicine, B03218.

culosis institution in the country. Born in Massachusetts in 1853, Bushnell went to Yale where he received an A.B. in 1876, a Ph.D. in classical languages and literature in 1878, and an M.D. in 1880.[39] He developed tuberculosis as a young man but regained his health and received his commission as a medical officer in 1881. After his tuberculosis reactivated, the Army transferred Bushnell to Fort Logan, Colorado, in 1901 following the practice of sending tubercular soldiers west. Ordered to Fort Bayard in 1903, Bushnell took command the following year. A colleague described him as "tall, thin, and rather ascetic in appearance, shy in manner, and very modest notwithstanding his learning and attainments, but very positive in his opinions."[40] Bushnell's authority to run Fort Bayard lay not only in his military position but also in his scientific and medical expertise, which he skillfully deployed within the Army's developing corporate, professional bureaucracy. In 1916 Surgeon General William Gorgas judged him "a very distinguished authority on all that relates to tuberculosis," and "one of the most efficient officers ever developed in the Medical Corps."[41] As he grappled with both tuberculosis and a confusing network of benefits and privileges, Bushnell helped craft the nation's veterans' policy from his remote post in New Mexico.

Military personnel and tuberculosis patients arriving at Fort Bayard entered a community of one thousand, including patients, Army staff and their families, and civilian laborers and trades people. Bushnell's annual report for 1911 describes an institution that would be familiar to a ship captain—an isolated, hierarchical social compound on a desert, which supplied much of its own food, supplies, entertainment, and of course, health care. The post was a collection of one hundred buildings, a greenhouse, four acres of vegetable gardens, a fruit orchard, piggery, and alfalfa and hay fields for the dairy and beef herds. The complex included laboratory and surgical facilities, a solarium, amusement hall, library, carpenter and blacksmith shops, and a nurses' residence that occupied "a commanding position on the hill west of the post."[42] Ten medical officers, an Army chaplain, ten to twenty nurses, and about one hundred enlisted men of the Hospital Corps cared for patients while noncommissioned officers managed other post duties. Bushnell recruited medical staff who had personal experience with tuberculosis—in 1906, six of the ten medical officers had the disease, one too ill to work, two on "light duty," the rest on full duty.[43] Nurses were also patients. In 1910 four of ten nurses on duty had tuberculosis, two of them on "light duty" due to their illness.[44] The nurses, many of them members of the Army Nurse Corps established in 1901, cared for the sickest patients in the enlisted men's and officers' infirmaries, feeding and bathing them, taking temperatures, giving medications, and assisting in surgeries. Members of the Hospital Corps bore the largest burden of hospital work caring for the ambulant patients. Local civilians who worked in the kitchens, dairy, stables, and construction projects included Mexicans, Mexican Americans, and members of a small Chinese community in the area.

Fort Bayard had about 400 hospital beds with a daily patient population of 220 to 380. Annually, the hospital admitted 600 to 1,000 patients, many of whom stayed six months or more.[45] They ranged in age from nineteen to seventy-one, most in their twenties and thirties; between one-third and one-half were veterans, beneficiaries of a Soldiers' Homes, or pensioners. In 1910 510 out of 1,099 admissions were veterans, and in 1916 441 out of 1,141 admissions claimed veteran status.[46] Fort Bayard documents provide little demographic information on patients, but most veterans had probably been enlisted men because officers generally had larger pensions and more economic resources to provide for their own care. Moreover, if they were like USSH and the NHDVS residents, many patients would have been foreign-born with little social or economic support.

The world they entered was familiar, based on military rhythm and order. Patients awoke to a bugle call and retired to taps. Staff took their temperatures first thing in the morning, and those with high fevers or recent lung hemorrhages stayed in bed, even for meals. Men without fevers in the ambulant wards had to rest in bed at least two hours in the morning and two in the afternoon, and retire by eight o'clock at night.

Fort Bayard became a tuberculosis hospital during a transition in tuberculosis treatment from a regime of exercise and fresh air designed to build up the body to one of complete rest to allow the body to heal. "Upon taking command here," Bushnell explained, "I changed entirely the treatment and I believe with good results."[47] His approach prevailed in the Army for the next five decades, until the development of effective antibiotic cures.[48] The premise of rest therapy was that, lacking a medical cure, bed rest could at least make the patient stronger to fight the disease. Francis Trudeau, who established one of the first and most popular private sanatoriums at Lake Saranac, New York, said it required one to "conquer fate by acquiescence."[49] But one Fort Bayard patient admitted that "the news of the treatment came as a greater shock than did my tuberculosis diagnosis."[50] One had to rest for a long time. A 1916 Fort Bayard study found that the surviving patients had been at the hospital for an average of 3.3 years, sixty-nine for at least 5 years; thirty-eight patients had been "intermittently observed" for 10 years; and the longest living veteran under Army care had been there 15.9 years.[51]

Like all sanatoriums of the time, Fort Bayard's record in treating tuberculosis was mixed. In 1908 Bushnell tried to determine how many former Fort Bayard patients from 1899 to 1904 were still alive. Checking with the Army, Navy, and the Pension Office, he found that about 45 percent were dead, 32 percent of patients were still alive, and 23 percent were unaccounted for.[52] During Bushnell's tenure, however, Fort Bayard's annual death rate dropped from 21 percent in 1904 to less than 12 percent in 1917.[53] National tuberculosis rates had declined as well. By the time Bushnell left Fort Bayard, tuberculosis had yielded first place to heart disease as the cause of death in the United States. But death still resided in the hospital, claiming on average at least one patient every week. In 1908 55 patients died; in 1914 66 died, 59 from tuberculosis.[54]

Bushnell spent the early years at Fort Bayard clarifying his authority and developing hospital policies, employing both discipline and compassion in his negotiations with officials in Washington, Soldiers' Homes, and military patients, veterans, and their families. Shortly after assuming command in 1904, he issued General Order No. 28, promulgating rules for Fort Bayard patients. In

Figure 1.3. U.S. Army, General Hospital, Fort Bayard, New Mexico, interior view of a tent ward, c. 1907. Courtesy of the National Library of Medicine, A02317.

addition to the required rest periods and reporting for weighing, temperature-taking, and roll calls, the rules forbid patients to have alcoholic beverages and firearms (except officers) or to ride horses without permission. Because a tuberculosis patient's sputum was considered dangerous and infectious, "patients must always carry spit cups, and expectorate only into them or into the large cuspidors." One of the most galling rules was that "patients are not allowed to visit other wards or tents without permission from the officer in charge of the ward which they desire to visit."[55] Bushnell settled on suspension from the hospital as a key sanction, so that a patient who failed to accept punishment, such as confinement to quarters or loss of privileges, could be dismissed from the hospital for a minimum of three months, after which he could ask for readmission. On rare occasions Bushnell permanently dismissed recalcitrant patients from Fort Bayard, effectively ending their government medical care.

While Bushnell had legal authority over active-duty Army patients, his power regarding sailors, marines, and veteran patients was less clear. In 1905, in an early example of a local Army officer crafting government policy, he set in motion a process that resulted in Congress passing a law stating that all patients at Fort Bayard "be subject to the Rules and Articles for the Government of the Armies of the United States."[56]

## Federal Funding and Local Control

A variety of federal, state, and local funding sources and benefits supported Fort Bayard veteran patients, and Bushnell administered these using both the carrot and the stick, by helping those in need secure pensions and medical care but also by extending or withholding benefits in a disciplinary manner to encourage good behavior or to punish miscreants.

An individual's path to veteran status determined his eligibility for various benefits, and veterans could become Fort Bayard patients three ways. First, 6 to 10 new veteran-patients came directly from the USSH in Washington each year, and from 1900 to 1919 the USSH reported between 50 and 175 beneficiaries under treatment at Fort Bayard annually. Second, the majority of veteran patients arrived at Fort Bayard as active-duty soldiers but became veterans when tuberculosis so disabled them that they could not continue in active service and their status changed to civilians and beneficiaries of the USSH. In 1910, for example, out of 589 active-duty patients, 260 were discharged on disability, 155 returned to duty, 20 died, and 154 remained hospitalized. In 1916, out of 588 active-duty patients, 179 were discharged on disability, 174 returned to duty, 29 died, and 206 remained hospitalized.[57] Unlike later years when the government was larger and veterans had their own hospitals, the transition from active-duty to veteran status was mostly seamless. As an inspector from the USSH explained, "in nearly all cases, when a man is discharged at Bayard for disability he is at the same time made a beneficiary of the Regular Home."[58]

The third way veteran patients came to Fort Bayard was by applying for admission themselves as beneficiaries of the USSH, the NHDVS, or as pensioners. Unlike active-duty soldiers and sailors under military authority, as civilians, veterans were free to enter and leave the hospital at will, and, as was common in all Soldiers' Homes, many rotated in and out of the hospital. Historian Patrick Kelly observes that "one of the most striking features of the NHDVS was the ability of veterans to drop in and out of the network." He calculates that between 1 July 1898 and 30 June 1899, the managers admitted 1,404 veterans and discharged 1,216.[59] The practice troubled Soldiers' Homes' managers because it caused administrative confusion and because those who left for short periods often got in trouble by drinking, fighting, or gambling. The same was true at Fort Bayard, where medical personnel worried that veteran-patients would undermine their medical treatment. Hundreds of veterans discharged themselves from Fort Bayard every year. Capt. Charles Barney was a patient and physician at Fort Bayard from 1906 until his discharge on disability in 1910, when he immediately went to Mexico. He returned to Fort Bayard for treatment for a couple of months in 1911 but then lived in Los Angeles and

Tucson until his health deteriorated again in 1917, and he requested admission to Fort Bayard.[60] Similarly, Hospital Corpsman Charles Noyes was discharged on disability in 1910 and over the next five years was in and out of Fort Bayard at least four times, working at odd jobs in New Mexico, Texas, and Louisiana between his hospital stays.[61]

The USSH, NHDVS, and the Navy paid Fort Bayard five dollars a week for patients under their jurisdiction, out of which USSH veterans received one dollar per month for tobacco and a laundry allowance of twenty-five cents per dozen pieces.[62] Pensioned veterans who were not USSH or NHDVS beneficiaries paid forty cents per day, about 40 percent of the average thirty dollar monthly pension.[63] The USSH paid transportation from Washington to Fort Bayard by rail in a sleeping car, and "a few dollars [was] given a member transferred for subsistence en route."[64] It also provided the coffins for its veterans, a supply of which Fort Bayard kept on hand.[65] The USSH did not pay transportation for patients who left the hospital at their own request, but many were eligible for the half-rate fares that rail companies extended to veterans. Fort Bayard had forms to request the special fare because, as medical officer Capt. Paul Hutton advised a Southern Pacific agent, "In reality a beneficiary of the Soldiers' Home at this hospital is an inmate of the Soldiers' Home, this hospital being a branch of the soldiers' home at Washington, D.C."[66]

Pensions were the livelihood of many veterans. Amounts ranged from six to seventy-two dollars per month, depending on a veteran's rank and level of disability, and the government assigned a portion to dependents.[67] Ambulant veteran patients, like residents of other Soldiers' Homes, could work for five to thirty dollars wages a month to supplement their pensions, and Bushnell and his officers determined who could take advantage of this opportunity.[68] The Pension Bureau issued checks quarterly, and in 1908 Congress required pensions to be paid directly to veterans, reversing an earlier, more paternalistic policy in which the USSH, the NHDVS, and institutions such as Fort Bayard paid veterans only eight dollars from their pensions each month, holding the rest until their departure from the institution.[69] Whether or not a veteran received a pension determined some of his privileges and costs, but, wrote Bushnell, "there is no way to know whether a man is receiving a pension. Many of them are evidently inclined to conceal the fact." He therefore convinced the USSH to periodically send him a list of pension beneficiaries and amounts.[70]

Fort Bayard officers at times acted as case workers, helping patients get pensions or increase their rates.[71] One medical officer supported Sgt. John J. Anderson's pension application, stating "this claimant is so disabled from chronic pulmonary tuberculosis as to be incapacitated for performing any manual labor and is entitled to thirty dollars a month."[72] In 1908 Bushnell supported increasing the pension of Navy veteran Patrick Flaherty, explaining, "Flaherty worked much beyond his strength as a Teamster because he had an insufficient pension to pay his expenses. He is now undergoing infirmary treatment and is so ill that he will probably not live to receive any increase of pension."[73] Bushnell also advised families on federal policies. After receiving a grim prognosis, Pvt. Bernard Conroy wanted to go home to die, but his mother asked Bushnell if Conroy would receive a pension if he were discharged from the Army. She wrote, "I am a poor widow and am depending on his allotment of $10.00 a month which he made over to me and I still receive." Bushnell replied that it would be better for her son to stay at Fort Bayard because, "your son is quite sick," and "he has every comfort here and his pay goes on, while if discharged he would probably have to wait some months before securing a pension."[74] Bushnell tried to protect patients in other ways. In 1908 he refused to allow a Pension Bureau examiner to interrogate several patients regarding their pension claims because the examiner did not have proper authorization. The man retreated to El Paso until he received authority from Washington to enter Fort Bayard.[75]

Fort Bayard officers tried to garnish pensions with little success because here veterans had the upper hand. When Army Chaplin Cephas Bateman tried to collect on loans the post store had extended to pensioners, the USSH told him that "the pension is not subject to levy for any purpose."[76] And in 1910, after Roy W. Osterman went AWOL with four hospital blankets, Bushnell tried to get $7.44 deducted from his pension to pay for them. The adjutant general advised against it, given the "deep solicitude on the part of Congress as to pensioners, and a determination that a pension shall pass from the government to the pensioner intact and without deduction."[77] Bushnell was more successful when the surgeon general approved his proposal that veteran pensioners who were not beneficiaries of the Soldiers' Home pay their monthly subsistence a month in advance to avoid payment defaults.[78]

The question of who should be retired on tuberculosis disability was largely determined at the local level. Fort Bayard periodically convened a medical board of three medical officers to determine if a patient was too disabled to continue to serve in the military and, if so, issued a "surgeon's certificate of disability." If the disability was certified as having been acquired during military service, Fort Bayard sent a mimeographed form to the office of the surgeon general recommending that patient's "admission to this Hospital as a beneficiary of the U.S. Soldiers' Home on his discharge from the service."[79] The War Department generally approved the local boards' recommendations. When Jewell Johnson of Lufkin, Texas, inquired as to the status of his brother, Linus Johnson, a medical officer explained, "he will shortly be discharged from the service, but can remain under treatment here without expense as long as he chooses."[80]

The War Department had different discharge policies for officers and enlisted men, keeping officers on the active list "so long as there is a fair chance for cure," but discharging enlisted men disabled by disease rather quickly, sometimes within weeks.[81] In 1907, however, Bushnell got the policy changed to keep enlisted men in the hospital at least six months to determine a patient's prognosis and thereby avoid "a possible injustice which may be committed if men of short service on admission here should be deprived of a pension and should not be admitted to the Soldiers' Home on the ground that the mode of their discharge showed them not to be disabled."[82]

Many of the men retired on disability chose to leave Fort Bayard. A study of 1,230 "completed" tuberculosis cases at Fort Bayard, 1905–7, showed that one-third of the discharged patients departed "unimproved," half left the hospital with their tuberculosis either "arrested or improved," only 6 percent were judged "apparently cured," and the rest had died. Many of those discharged, therefore, had tuberculosis bacteria in their sputum and would have been infectious.[83] Rather than fearing that they could endanger the civilian population, however, Fort Bayard medical officers worried that veterans who left treatment against doctors' orders were jeopardizing their own health. As Bushnell told the surgeon general in explaining his patient outcomes, "Since beneficiaries of the Soldiers' Home are permitted to leave the Hospital and return at their pleasure during good behavior, many cases of the foregoing tables did not receive the benefit of the continued sanatorium treatment which was desirable."[84]

Bushnell, like all physicians, understood that tuberculosis was contagious, but like most hospitals then, the Medical Department would not impose strict anticontagion controls until after World War II because of an incomplete understanding of tuberculosis transmission.

Scientists and physicians of the time believed that bacteria existed only in droplets of sputum, blood, or other tubercular material and could not be transmitted through the air. A leading textbook stated: "The germs from consumptives are carried by the sputum, not by the breath. The breath itself is harmless."[85] A 1917 military medical handbook explained, "The infection is contained in the sputum, and as long as the sputum is moist the germs cannot escape into the air."[86] Medical personnel, therefore, believed that hygienic measures, such as patients covering their mouths while coughing and properly disposing of spit cups, controlled the spread of tuberculosis. The practice of Fort Bayard and other tuberculosis institutions of allowing contagious patients—including veterans—to leave and reenter as they wished would have deadly, unintended consequences. Historians have described how legions of single men wandering throughout the West in the late nineteenth and early twentieth centuries provided labor for ranches, mines, and rail industries, fueling the industrial revolution and generating social disorder in their wake.[87] Some of these men also generated tuberculosis.

## Sanctuary or Prison?

This cycling in and out of Fort Bayard suggests that the hospital provided sanctuary to veterans, serving as home base or even a place to die for those who had nowhere else to go. Bushnell understood that role. In addition to being a hospital, he wrote, Fort Bayard "is also an asylum for discharged soldiers from the Regular Army who have tuberculosis, many of whom come and go for years and finally come back here to die."[88] Lt. Olin R. Booth may have been one who sought sanctuary. A well-educated army officer graduated from Amherst College in 1895, Booth joined the infantry and served in the Philippines during the Spanish-American War. He developed tuberculosis in 1903 and after three years of treatment was discharged on disability for tuberculosis in his entire left lung. Booth soon left the hospital but was in and out four times, spending eight years out of nine at Bayard until his death in 1914. His records indicate that he never married; the Army shipped his body to his father in Massachusetts. Fort Bayard was the closest thing Booth had to a home.[89]

Others were ambivalent about the sanctuary or resisted it outright. Fort Bayard Chaplain Bateman observed that "he who has led an active, efficient life may chafe under the confinement of a hospital and easily comes to regard an infirmary as a prison."[90] That may have been Pvt. Horace Smith's view. A twenty-year-old hospital corpsman from North Carolina, Smith had been in the Army only two years when in June 1910 he began to cough and lose weight. By the time he was admitted to Fort Bayard, he had lost 25 pounds, down to 140 from 165. Medical officers found very active lesions in his lungs and listed his condition as "unfavorable." He was discharged from the Army on 8 March 1911, admitted to Fort Bayard as a veteran patient on 9 March, and the next day, with advanced tuberculosis in both lungs, a temperature of 101, and producing two cups of sputum daily, he "left the Home at his own request."[91] Smith chose another place to die.

Fort Bayard struggled to maintain morale and fight the boredom that often overcame young, formerly active men surrounded by sickness and death. Forbidden to roam the hills, go to town, or drink alcohol, some met their new life with despair, others with rebellion.[92] Problems included promiscuous spitting, the scattering of spit cups, foul language, disrespecting officers, sexual misconduct, possession of illicit firearms, and going absent without leave.[93] One medical officer reported that one patient imitated the groans of others as they lay dying.[94] Alcohol abuse was a big problem as patients snuck to a gin mill in the nearby village of Central. Bushnell once forced the postal service to punish a mail carrier for smuggling whiskey to a patient.[95] As the officer in charge of entertainment and morale, Chaplain Bateman acquired for the hospital a movie projector, a record player and "many excellent records," a well-stocked library, and a bowling alley.[96] The amusement hall seated four hundred for religious services, theater, and orchestra performances, and Bushnell asked the USSH to fund a band. "The patients who are long under treatment here are almost exclusively Soldier's Home men," he explained, stressing "the desirability of doing everything that can be done to furnish legitimate amusement to such patients, many of whom are too infirm to leave the Hospital in search of diversion of any kind."[97]

After the 1909 MacDonald complaint, Bushnell explained to his superiors in Washington the challenges of providing health care to disabled veterans, dividing his veteran patients into three classes—older, younger, and middle-aged men. "The permanent inmates are older men whose disease runs the protracted course, and in advancing years," he wrote. "For many of them the Hospital is their only home." Therefore, he said, "I desire to make their life as pleasant as possible" and allow them to do "as they please, so long as they behave themselves." The younger veterans had the prospect of arresting their tuberculosis but needed "the rigorous treatment of the sanatoriums if they are to succeed in arresting or even temporarily checking the progress of their disease." Bushnell thought it "best to hedge them about with restrictions which are intended to prevent their taking too much exercise, and as far as practicable, to prevent indulgence in various harmful forms of dissipation." A third class of veterans (like MacDonald) was in middle life, "often spending their winters at this hospital and going elsewhere in summer." Many "remained Beneficiaries because of more or less dissipated habits," and had "thrown away the prospect of accomplishing more than a retardation of its [the tuberculosis] progress." These veterans "are apt to become morose and fault-finding, and they seek to inspire discontent in the younger beneficiaries and the enlisted patients." Some were "practically professional gamblers," while others "remain at the Institution until they become grossly intoxicated and disorderly, are then suspended and return after the period of their suspension has elapsed to repeat the same conduct." Many of these men believe that "any regulation of the Hospital that infringes upon their personal liberty is an outrage."[98] But Bushnell's view was that as government beneficiaries, they should abide by government rules.

For some veterans, however, the trial soon came to an end. Due to their relative seniority, they had higher death rates than active-duty patients. In 1910, for example, the veteran death rate was more than twice that of active duty patients, 9.6 percent to 4 percent. Most patients succumbed to tuberculosis, often in a morphine-induced haze. Chaplain Bateman ministered to them in their last days, and his monthly reports recorded the names of the deceased; their status and affiliation; date and cause of death; nearest relative or friend; and whether the person's remains were buried at the Fort Bayard cemetery or shipped home.[99] The majority of veterans were buried at the post cemetery, many of whom Bateman noted had "no relatives."

Active-duty patients were more likely to have wives or parents willing and able to pay for burial at home. As was the custom on naval vessels or at isolated Army posts, staff auctioned off unclaimed property and sent the proceeds to the USSH treasurer to distribute to any heirs. Again, local experience shaped Army policy when Bushnell suggested to the surgeon general "the desirability of giving relatives of beneficiaries of the soldiers' home an opportunity to state whether or not they desire the effects of their deceased relatives sent to them." He cited a letter from Mrs. Hettie Graham of Marion, Indiana, who asked, "I wonder why you will not send me all of John L. Graham's effects instead of selling them at auction. I am his mother, and I would love to have all of his effects." Bushnell proposed sending a property inventory to families to allow them to indicate their desires and then either ship the property to them or auction it off and send the funds to the USSH for distribution.[100] The War Department and the USSH approved Bushnell's proposal, and having held off an auction of John Grahm's effects, Bushnell was able to send one of the first property inventories to Hettie Graham. Such sensitivity to families' needs, however, would become increasingly difficult as the nation built up an army of four million to fight the war in Europe.

## World War I

Like the war of 1898, World War I would dramatically increase military tuberculosis rates and turn thousands of soldiers and sailors into disabled veterans. When the United States entered World War I in 1917, Surgeon General Gorgas called Bushnell to Washington to run the Army-wide tuberculosis program. Before the war, Fort Bayard's 400 beds were sufficient to care for an Army of 175,000. But as the nation mobilized, the growing Army required thousands of tuberculosis beds. Soldiers and recruits were not only developing tuberculosis during training and combat, but the Selective Service screening process was uncovering hundreds of young men with tuberculosis for whom the Army Medical Department assumed responsibility. Remote, isolated, and arid, Fort Bayard could not carry the load. The Secretary of War therefore established eight additional tuberculosis hospitals in the United States and designated three hospitals with the American Expeditionary Forces in France for soldiers who developed active tuberculosis in the trenches, providing a peak capacity of eight thousand beds in January, 1919.[101]

After the November 1918 armistice, the need for active-duty tuberculosis beds declined, but thousands of veteran tuberculosis patients remained. The Medical Department had greatly expanded Fort Bayard's patient capacity for the war emergency, but in considering the Army's long-term needs, its remote location was no longer considered an asset. The new tuberculosis hospitals included one in the hills of Oteen, North Carolina, and another in Denver, Colorado, locations Bushnell had chosen for their climate and easy access to railroads and supplies. These hospitals presented competition for Fort Bayard, especially after February 1919, when the aging post requested nine hundred thousand dollars to renovate existing buildings, increase the water supply, and improve the utilities.[102] Bushnell had retired and his successor in Washington, Col. Roger Brooke, recommended abandoning Fort Bayard.[103] He cited the investment in the new hospital in Denver, its modern buildings, and its central location, concluding, "It is to the interest of the Government and of our personnel and patients to give up Fort Bayard as a hospital as soon as our patients are reduced sufficiently to be cared for at Denver or Oteen."[104]

In 1920 the War Department arranged to convey the Fort Bayard facilities to the Public Health Service, which was running hospitals for World War I veterans at the time, and to transfer all USSH and NHDVS Fort Bayard patients to the Denver hospital. The secretary of war named the Denver institution the Fitzsimons General Hospital, for William Thomas Fitzsimons, a civilian surgeon serving as a medical officer and the first U.S. Army officer killed in the World War.[105] On 7 June 1920 fifty-four veterans were transferred to Denver; thirty-two veterans who refused to go to Denver "took their discharge," and the Army abandoned Fort Bayard.[106] George Bushnell was not present at the closing ceremony. During the stress of war service, his health faltered, and he retired in 1919, returning to Massachusetts to write two books on tuberculosis.[107] In 1923 he moved with his wife to Pasadena, California, where, after several pulmonary hemorrhages, he died in 1924 at age 70.[108]

The War Department's abandonment of Fort Bayard was not the end of Army Medical Department care for tubercular veterans. Throughout the 1920s, World War I veterans continued to develop tuberculosis and become eligible for hospital care or disability pensions to the point that tuberculosis became a leading cause of disability benefits in the interwar period, second only to neuropsychiatric problems. One observer calculated that from 1919 to 1940, veterans' hospitals had almost three hundred thousand tuberculosis admissions at a cost of more than one billion dollars.[109] Decreasing tuberculosis rates in the United States meant that it became less of a threat to military forces, but the Medical Department would not be able to control the disease until the development of effective antibiotic cures in the 1950s. Like their Fort Bayard forerunners, therefore, some interwar tubercular veterans would cycle in and out of hospital care, spreading tuberculosis to the outside world.

A majority of Fitzsimons Hospital's patients continued to be veterans in the 1920s—74 percent in 1924 alone.[110] But it was the end of an era. Negotiations regarding veterans' benefits would increasingly take place at the national level in Washington, D.C., due to the increasing bureaucratization of the Army Medical Department and the establishment of new institutions for veterans. With eighteen hundred beds, Fitzsimons Army Hospital was soon admitting more than three hundred patients a month, comparable to the peacetime patient population at Fort Bayard.[111] Such numbers meant that the hospital commander and his medical officers were no longer as familiar with individual patients and their families as were Bushnell and his physicians, and they had less time for casework and advocacy. Powerful new World War I veterans' interest groups such as the American Legion and the Veterans of Foreign Wars took up those roles and succeeded in expanding veterans' benefits and convincing Congress to establish the Veterans' Bureau dedicated to their care.

Over the last ninety years, the legislative expansion of benefits, such as rehabilitative care for veterans with tuberculosis and other disabilities, and the proliferation of new institutions under the Veterans Administration have offered many veterans increased support. But these changes have also created a more complex and bureaucratic government system in which some individuals, moving from one agency to another, can indeed fall between the cracks. The discovery of effective antibiotic therapies in the 1950s dramatically reduced tuberculosis rates in the United States, and medical officers can now cure most cases of tuberculosis they encounter. Other diseases, however, such as malaria and HIV, continue to take a toll on military personnel and veterans, and antibiotic-resistant strains of tuberculosis threaten to once again overwhelm medical capabilities. Disease, therefore, will continue to exacerbate the human suffering of military adventures in war and empire.

## Notes

1. John A. MacDonald to Governor of Soldiers' Home, 12 March, 1909, Record Group 112, Records of the Army Surgeon General (hereafter RG112) Entry 386, Box 25, National Archives and Records Administration (hereafter NARA).

2. George Bushnell to Governor Soldiers' Home, 5 April 1909, RG112, Entry 386, Box 25, NARA.

3. Governor Soldiers' Home to Bushnell 11 April 1909, RG112, Entry 386, Box 25, NARA.

4. See, for example, Christobal S. Berry-Cabán and Steven Lynch, "Soldiers' Experience with Medical Hold: The Case of Fort Bragg," *Military Medicine* 173 (April 2008): 349–53.

5. By 1915, 93 percent were receiving a federal pension. Theda Skocpol, *Protecting Soldiers and Mothers: The Political Origins of Social Policy in the United States* (Cambridge, Mass.: Belkap Press of Harvard University Press, 1992), 128. Veterans included those from the war with Mexico, the Indian wars, the War with Spain, and the Philippine Insurrection. For full list, see Paul R. Goode, *The United States Soldiers' Home: A History of Its First Hundred Years* (Richmond, Va.: 1957), 277–79.

6. The most concise explanation of this is found in Gustavus A. Weber and Laurence F. Schmeckebier, *The Veterans' Administration: Its History, Activities, and Organization* (Washington, D.C.: Brookings Institution, 1934), 70–75. See also Goode, *United States Soldiers' Home*; Patrick J. Kelly, *Creating a National Home: Building the Veterans' Welfare State, 1860–1900* (Cambridge, Mass.: Harvard University Press, 1997); Patrick J. Kelly, "Establishing a Federal Entitlement," in *The Civil War Veteran: A Historical Reader*, edited by Larry M. Logue and Michael Barton (New York: New York University Press, 2007); David A. Gerber, *Disabled Veterans in History* (Ann Arbor: University of Michigan Press, 2000); William A. Dobak and Thomas D. Phillips, *The Black Regulars, 1866–1898* (Norman: University of Oklahoma Press, 2001); and Trevor K. Plante, "Genealogy Notes: The National Home for Disabled Volunteer Soldiers," *Prologue* 36 (Spring 2004), http://www.archives.gov/publications/prologue/2004/spring/soldiers-home.html.

7. Kelly, *Creating a National Home*, 227.

8. Larry M. Logue, "Union Veterans and Their Government: The Effects of Public Policies on Private Lives," *Journal of Interdisciplinary History* 22 (1992): 423.

9. "Report of the Governor of the Soldiers' Home," *War Department Annual Report*, 1899, (hereafter WDAR); and "Board of Managers of the National Home for Disabled Volunteer Soldiers for the Fiscal Year Ending June 30, 1899," H. Doc. 106, U.S. Congress, 56th Cong., 1st sess. (Washington, D.C.: Government Printing Office).

10. Kelly, *Creating a National Home*, 155.

11. "Annual Report of the Board of Managers for the National Home for Disabled Volunteers Soldiers for the Fiscal Year Ending June 30, 1899," H. Doc. 106, U.S. Congress, 56th Cong., 1st sess., (Washington, D.C.: Government Printing Office).

12. Bushnell to W. E. Elwell, 16 July 1907, RG112, Entry 386, Box 7, NARA.

13. Circular No. 2, U.S. Army General Hospital, Fort Bayard, New Mexico, 17 July 1909, RG112, Entries 389, 390, 391, Box 2, NARA.

14. Bushnell to Governor, Pacific Branch, NHDVS, 12 August 1907, RG112, Entry 386, Box 8, NARA.

15. "Report of the Governor of the Soldiers' Home," WDAR, 1900, vol. 1, pt. 1, 299–301.

16. WDAR, 1899, vol. 1, pt. 1, 482.

17. "TB Today," CDC website, accessed 23 July 2009, http://www.cdcnpin.org/scripts/tb/tb.asp. Also, Michael D. Iseman, *A Clinician's Guide to Tuberculosis*, (Philadelphia: Lippincott Williams & Wilkins, 2000); and Lawrence Geiter, *Ending Neglect: The Elimination of Tuberculosis in the United States* (Washington, D.C.: National Academy Press, 2000).

18. Bureau of the Census, *Tuberculosis in the United States*, (Washington, D.C.: Department of Commerce and Labor, 1908), table 1.

19. On health seekers, see Esmond R. Long, "Weak Lungs on the Santa Fe Trail." *Bulletin of the History of Medicine* 8 (1940): 1040–54; Jake W. Spidle, "Coughing and Spitting and

New Mexico History," in *Essays in Twentieth-Century New Mexico History*, edited by Judith Boyce DeMark (Albuquerque: University of New Mexico Press, 1994); and Judith L. DeMark, "Chasing the Cure—A History of Healthseekers to Albuquerque, 1902–1940." *Journal of the West* 21 (1982): 49–50.

20. Nancy J. Tomes, "The Making of a Germ Panic, Then and Now," *American Journal of Public Health* 90, no. 2 (2000): 191–98. On the tuberculosis movement, see Richard H. Shyrock, *The National Tuberculosis Association, 1830–1910,* (New York: National Tuberculosis Association, 1957); Michael E. Teller, *The Tuberculosis Movement: A Public Health Campaign in the Progressive Era* (New York: Greenwood Press, 1988); Barbara Bates, *Bargaining for Life: A Social History of Tuberculosis, 1876–1938* (Philadelphia: University of Pennsylvania Press, 1992); and Katherine Ott, *Fevered Lives: Tuberculosis in American Culture since 1870* (Cambridge, Mass.: Harvard University Press, 1996).

21. S. Adolphus Knopf, "Public Measures in the Prophylaxis of Tuberculosis," in *Tuberculosis: A Treatise by American Authors on its Etiology, Pathology, Frequency, Semeiology, Diagnosis, Prognosis, Prevention, and Treatment*, edited by Arnold C. Klebs (New York: D. Appleton & Co., 1909), 418–20.

22. Charles E. Rosenberg, *The Care of Strangers* (New York: Basic Books, 1987), 5; Rosemary Stevens, *In Sickness and in Wealth: American Hospitals in the Twentieth Century* (New York: Basic Books, Inc., 1989); and Guenther Risse, *Mending Bodies, Saving Souls: A History of Hospitals* (New York: Oxford University Press, 1999).

23. Teller, *Tuberculosis Movement*, 82.

24. Russell Weigley, *History of the United States Army* (New York: Macmillan, 1967), 292. See also Richard W. Stewart, ed. *American Military History*, Vol. 1, *The United States Army and the Forging of a Nation, 1775–1917* (Washington, D.C.: Center of Military History, United States Army, 2005); Paul A. C. Koistinen, *Mobilizing for Modern War: The Political Economy of American Warfare, 1865–1919* (Lawrence: University Press of Kansas, 1997); and Ronald J. Barr, *The Progressive Army: US Army Command and Administration, 1870–1914* (New York: St. Martin's Press, 1998).

25. "The Army Sanatorium for Tuberculosis at Fort Bayard, New Mexico," n.d., RG112, Entry 26, Box 91, NARA; and SGAR 1892, 498.

26. George M. Sternberg, "Is Tuberculosis a Parasitic Disease?" *Medical News* 41 (July–December 1882):6–7; 87–89; 311–14; 564–66; 730–31; and George M. Sternberg, *A Manual of Bacteriology* (New York: William Wood 1892). Also John M. Gibson, *Soldier in White: The Life of General George Miller Sternberg* (Durham, N.C.: Duke University Press, 1958); and Office of Medical History, U.S. Army Medical Department, "George M. Sternberg," http://history.amedd.army.mil/surgeongenerals/G_Sternberg.html.

27. Ken DeBevoise, *Agents of Apocalypse: Epidemic Disease in the Colonial Philippines*, (Princeton, N.J.: Princeton University Press, 1995), 41–42; and WDAR, 1900,783. On tropical medicine and imperialism, see Mary C. Gillett, *Army Medical Department, 1865–1917, The Army Medical Department, 1865–1917*, Army Historical Series (Washington, D.C.: Center of Military History, 1995), 201–306; and Warwick Anderson, *Colonial Pathologies: American Tropical Medicine, Race, and Hygiene in the Philippines* (Durham, N.C.: Duke University Press, 2006).

28. Isaac W. Brewer, "Tuberculosis Amongst the Philippine Scouts of the United States Army," *Boston Medical and Surgical Journal* 163 (1910): 940–42.

29. WDAR, 1901, Vol. 1, pt. 2, 709.

30. WDAR, 1899, Vol. 1, pt. 1, 275, and William Osler, *The Principles and Practice of Medi-*

*cine* (New York: D. Appleton, 1901), 382; and Thomas J. Mays, "Alcohol as a Factor in the Causation of Pulmonary Consumption," *Journal of the American Medical Association* 48 (2 February 1907): 398–99. On alcoholism and tuberculosis, see Barron H. Lerner, *Contagion and Confinement: Controlling Tuberculosis along Skid Row* (Baltimore: Johns Hopkins University Press, 1998). On alcoholism in the Army, see Edward M. Coffman, *The Old Army: A Portrait of the American Army in Peacetime, 1784–1898* (New York: Oxford University Press, 1986); and James Marten, "Nomads in Blue: Disabled Veterans and Alcohol at the National Home," in *Disabled Veterans in History*, edited by David A. Gerber (Ann Arbor: University of Michigan Press, 2000).

31. WDAR, 1896, Vol. 1.

32. Parker W. Thorton, "A National Sanatorium for Consumptives," *Journal of the American Medical Association* 26 (1896): 570–72; and "An Army Sanitarium for Tuberculosis," *Boston Medical and Surgical Journal* 141 (7 September 1899), 248–49. In 1899 the Public Health and Marine Hospital Service established the first federal sanatorium for Merchant Marine seamen and others at Fort Stanton, New Mexico; in 1906 the Navy assumed Fort Lyon, Colorado, for care of its tuberculosis personnel and veterans; and in 1915 the government established the Navajo Agency Sanatorium at Fort Defiance, Arizona.

33. "An Army Sanitarium for Tuberculosis," 248; and Gillett, *Army Medical Department, 1865–1917,* 339.

34. M. I. Ludington to Quartermaster General, 18 August 1899, RG112, Entry 26, Box 359, NARA.

35. WDAR, 1899, Vol. 1, pt. 1, 482. See also Eve E. Simmons, "It Took Blood, Bravery to Make Ft. Bayard History," *El Paso Times*, 20 January 1963.

36. War Department, Surgeon General's Office, *A Report on Barracks and Hospitals with Descriptions of Military Posts*, (Washington, D.C.: GPO, 1870), 240. On the establishment of Fort Bayard, see Daniel M. Appel, "The Army Hospital and Sanatorium for the Treatment of Pulmonary Tuberculosis at Fort Bayard, New Mexico," *Journal of the American Medical Association* 39 (1902): 1373–79. In 2004 Congress designated Fort Bayard a National Historic District. See Public Law 108–209, "Fort Bayard National Historic Landmark Act," 108th Cong., 2nd sess.

37. WDAR, 1900, Vol. 1, pt. 2, 784 and 538.

38. Agnes G. Young, "Notes from Fort Bayard, New Mexico," *American Journal of Nursing* 6 (1906): 370.

39. Information on Bushnell's life is drawn from "Efficiency Report," George E. Bushnell, Record Group 94, Records of the Adjutant General (hereafter RG94), ACP, Box 715, NARA; Earl H. Bruns, "Colonel Bushnell: The Estimate of his Character and Work," *American Review of Tuberculosis* 11 (June 1925): 275–91; James M. Phalen, "George Ensign Bushnell: Colonel, Medical Corps, U.S. Army," *Army Medical Bulletin* 50 (1939): 130–33; "Obituary: George Ensign Bushnell," *Military Surgeon* 55 (September 1924): 423–24; and *Yale University Doctors of Philosophy, 1861–1960* (New Haven, Conn.: Yale University, 1961).

40. "Obituary: George Ensign Bushnell," *Military Surgeon* 55 (September 1924): 424.

41. Efficiency Report, George E. Bushnell, RG94, ACP, Box 715, NARA; and SGAR, 1916, Vol. 1, 469.

42. Bushnell to Surgeon General, 18 February 1912, RG112, Entry 26, Box 919, NARA.

43. J. L. Chamberlain, Inspection Report, 22 October 1906, RG112, Entry 386, NARA.

44. Howard Priest to the Adjutant, 25 February 1910, RG112, Entry 386, Box 29, NARA.

45. Surgeon General and War Department Annual Reports, 1904 to 1917.

46. Fort Bayard Annual Reports (hereafter FBAR), 1910 and 1916, RG112, Entry 26, Box 919, NARA.

47. Bushnell to Surgeon General, 4 April 1908, RG112, Entry 386, Box 12, NARA.

48. The actual effectiveness of rest therapy was unclear at the time and is still debated today. Bates, *Bargaining for Life*, 318–21; and Thomas Dormandy, *The White Death: A History of Tuberculosis* (New York: New York University Press, 1999), 149.

49. Quoted in Bruns, "Colonel Bushnell," 275.

50. Bruns, "Colonel Bushnell," 275. The boredom and difficulty of the rest cure is vividly described in tuberculosis memoirs such as Betty MacDonald, *The Plague and I* (Philadelphia: J. B. Lippincott, 1948); and novels such as Thomas Mann, *The Magic Mountain* (New York: Knopf, 1924).

51. Thomas H. Johnson, "Diseases Complicating Chronic Pulmonary Tuberculosis," unpublished paper, 1916, RG112, Entry 26, Box 466, NARA.

52. United States Army General Hospital, Fort Bayard, New Mexico. "Record of Completed Cases of Tuberculosis, 1899–1907." Fort Bayard, New Mexico, 1908, RG112, Old Entry 399, NARA.

53. FBAR, 1900 to 1917; and "Record of Complete Cases of Tuberculosis, 1899–1907, United States Army Hospital, Fort Bayard, New Mexico," RG112, Old Entry 399, NARA.

54. "The U.S. Army General Hospital, Fort Bayard, New Mexico, 1908," report, RG112, Entry 31K, Box 16, NARA; and FBAR, 1914.

55. General Orders, No. 28, U.S. General Hospital, Fort Bayard, New Mexico, 17 October 1904, RG112, Entry 26, Box 359, NARA.

56. Bushnell to Surgeon General, 15 June 1909, and Bushnell to Adjutant General, 8 September 1909, RG112, Entry 386, Box 25, NARA.

57. FBAR 1910 and 1916.

58. "Report of the Board of Commissioners of the Soldier's Home," WDAR, 1902, vol. 2, pt. 8, 83.

59. Kelly, *Creating a National Home*, 154–55.

60. Medical Record, Charles Barney, RG112, Entry 390, NARA.

61. Medical Record, Charles H. Noyes, RG112, Entry 390, NARA.

62. General Orders, No. 28.

63. Correspondence between Inspector General and U.S. General Hospital, Fort Bayard, N.M., October 1910, RG1112, Entry 386, Box 24, NARA; and Bushnell to Surgeon General, 23 March 1907, RG112, Entry 386, Box 5, NARA.

64. "Beneficiaries Soldiers' Home," Letters Received, 1904, RG112, Entry 380, Box 1, NARA; and Goode, *United States Soldiers' Home*, 165.

65. Correspondence between Fort Bayard and U.S. Soldier's Home, September 1910, RG112, Entry 386, Box 34, NARA.

66. Paul Hutton to Charles S. Fee, Southern Pacific Company, 14 May 1907, RG112, Entry 386, NARA.

67. "Report of the Board of Commissioners of the Soldiers' Home," WDAR, 1899, 481.

68. Kelly, *Creating a National Home*, 160.

69. Public Law 148, 28 May 1908

70. Bushnell to H. M Kendall, 15 August 1906, RG112, Entry 380, Box 3, NARA; and H. M. Kendall to commanding officer, 18 December 1908, RG112, Entry 386, Box 18, NARA.

71. "Pensions" forms, RG112, Entry 380, Box 1, NARA.

72. E. C. Jones to Adjutant General, 6 June 1980, RG112, Entry 386, Box 14, NARA.

73. Bushnell to Adjutant General, 7 March 1908, RG112, Entry 386, Box 12, NARA.

74. Bushnell and Ellen A. Conroy correspondence, RG112, Entry 386, Box 3, NARA.

75. Bushnell to Adjutant General, 19 December 1908 and endorsements, RG112, Entry 386, Box 19, NARA.

76. Cephas C. Bateman to Adjutant General, Fort Bayard, 30 March 1909, and endorsements, RG112, Entry 386, Box 21, NARA.

77. Bushnell to Adjutant of the Army, 13 May 1910, and endorsements, RG112, Entry 386, Box 32, NARA; and "Examiners, Pension Bureau," RG112, Entry 380, Box 2, NARA.

78. Bushnell to Surgeon General, 23 March 1907, and endorsements, RG112, Entry 386, Box 5, NARA.

79. Numerous forms can be found in RG112, Entry 386, Box 1, NARA.

80. George P. Peed to Jewell Johnson, 8 September 1905, RG112, Entry 380, Box 1, NARA.

81. Document File # 62565, RG112, Entry 23, NARA.

82. Bushnell to Surgeon General, 16 September 1907, RG112, Entry 386, Box 3, NARA; and Bushnell to Charles M. Mason, 22 November 1904, RG112, Entry 26, NARA.

83. United States Army General Hospital, Fort Bayard, New Mexico. "Record of Completed Cases of Tuberculosis, 1899–1907." Fort Bayard, New Mexico, 1908, RG112, Old Entry 399, NARA; and "Record Of Completed Cases of Tuberculosis at the United States Army General Hospital, Fort Bayard, New Mexico," (Washington, D.C.: GPO, 1917), RG112, Entry 26, Box 919, NARA.

84. FBAR, 1911.

85. Arnold C. Klebs, ed. *Tuberculosis: A Treatise by American Authors on Its Etiology, Pathology, Frequency, Semeiology, Diagnosis, Prognosis, Prevention, and Treatment* (New York: D. Appleton & Co., 1909), 805.

86. Charles Field Mason, *A Complete Handbook for the Sanitary Troops of the U.S. Army and Navy and National Guard and Naval Militia*, 4th ed. (New York: William Wood and Company, 1917), 256.

87. David Courtwright, *Violent Land: Single Men and Social Disorder from the Frontier to the Inner City* (Cambridge, Mass.: Harvard University Press, 1996); and David F. Musto, *The American Disease: Origins of Narcotic Control*, 3rd ed. (New York: Oxford University Press, 1999).

88. Bushnell to Guy Hinsdale, May 1908, RG112, Entry 386, NARA.

89. Efficient Record, Olin R. Booth, RG94, #224422, Box 1417, NARA.

90. Cephas C. Bateman, "The Army Hospital at Fort Bayard: Fort Bayard, New Mexico," n.p., n.d., Lawrence: Kansas Collection, University of Kansas Libraries, c. 1911, p. 9.

91. Horace E. Smith, Medical Chart, RG112, Entry 396, NARA.

92. Jeffrey Reznick has shown that during World War I, British soldiers and veterans resented being confined to bed and other restrictions of hospitalization; see Jeffrey S. Reznick, *Healing the Nation: Soldiers and the Culture of Caregiving in Britain During the Great War* (Manchester, UK: Manchester University Press, 2004), 83. On discipline and the coercion of tuberculosis patients see Lerner, *Contagion and Confinement*; Barron H. Lerner, "New York City's Tuberculosis Control Efforts: The Historical Limitations of the 'War on Consumption.'" *American Journal of Public Health* 83 (1993): 758–66; and Richard Coker, *From Chaos to Coercion: Detention and the Control of Tuberculosis* (New York: St. Martin's Press, 2000).

93. Numerous records of discipline problems can be found in RG112, Entry 380, NARA. On the AWOL issue, see Charles A. Byler, *Civil-Military Relations on the Frontier and Beyond, 1865–1917* (Westport, Conn.: Praeger Security International, 2006).

94. Paul Hutton to commanding officer, 20 January 1905, RG112, Entry 381, NARA. Numerous records of discipline problems can be found in RG112, Entry 380, NARA.

95. Simmons, "It Took Blood "; and Bushnell to Walter M. Murphy, 26 December 1905, RG112, Entry 380, NARA.

96. J. L. Chamberlain, Inspection Report of General Hospital at Fort Bayard, New Mexico, 22 October 1906, RG112, Entry 386, Box 1, NARA; and Bateman, "Army Hospital at Fort Bayard."

97. Bushnell to Surgeon General, 24 July 1907, RG112, Entry 386, NARA.

98. Bushnell to Adjutant General, 9 September 1909, RG112, Entry 386, Box 25, NARA.

99. Cephas C. Bateman, Monthly Reports, RG94, Box 1283, NARA.

100. Bushnell to Surgeon General 21 January 1911 and 10 April 1911, RG112, Entry 386, Box 38, NARA.

101. Carol R. Byerly, *Good Tuberculosis Men: The Army Medical Department's Struggle with Tuberculosis in the Twentieth Century* (Fort Detrick, MD: Borden Institute, forthcoming).

102. "U.S.A. General Hospital, Ft. Bayard, N.M., 1918," RG112, Entry 31-K, Box 16, NARA.

103. Roger Brooke, "Reply to Report of Sanitary Inspection of General Hospital, Fort Bayard, N.M., on 19, 20, and 21 February 1919, by Col. J. B. Clayton," RG112, Entry 31-K, Box 20, NARA.

104. Roger Brooke, "Memorandum for the Secretary of War," 11 December 1919, RG112, Entry 31-K, Box 16, NARA.

105. G.O. No. 40, War Department, 26 June 1920.

106. USSH Annual Report, 1920, 3. Under provision of Public Act 326, Section III, dated 3 March 1919. See congressional inquiries in NARA RG112, Entry 31-K, Box 16; and Adjutant General memos, 12 May 1920, RG112, Old Entry, 399, NARA.

107. George E. Bushnell, *A Study of the Epidemiology of Tuberculosis with Especial Reference to Tuberculosis of the Tropics and of the Negro Race* (New York: William Wood and Company, 1920); and Joseph H. Pratt and George E. Bushnell, *Physical Diagnosis of Diseases of the Chest* (Philadelphia: Saunders, 1925).

108. Gerald B. Webb, "Colonel E. Bushnell, M.C., U.S.A: An Appreciation," *Journal of the Outdoor Life* 21 (September 1924): 521–22.

109. Benjamin Goldberg, "Presidential Address: War and Tuberculosis," *Diseases of the Chest* (October 1941): 322–24.

110. "Monthly Per Diem Operating Expenses for Period January 1 to March 31, 1924," RG112, Entry 29, Box 172, NARA.

111. "Annual Report for the year ending December 31, 1924," RG112, Fitzsimons General Hospital, Annual Reports, 1918–1930, Box 4, NARA.

# 2

## The Invention, Stumbling, and Reinvention of the Modern U.S. Veterans Health Care System, 1918–1924

ROSEMARY A. STEVENS

Why did the United States create a major government agency dedicated to services for veterans in 1921? And how did a "socialized" hospital and medical system for veterans come about in the years after World War I, a time of heightened concerns about socialism and the dangers of a strong state? The answers to these two questions are interconnected. Two parallel forces influenced the creation of a new, independent Veterans Bureau, the forerunner of today's Department of Veterans Affairs. The first reflected social and political dissatisfaction with the implementation of benefits for World War I veterans. The bureau's establishment on 9 August 1921, almost three years after the armistice, followed widespread frustration among veterans and veterans' groups, legislators, and the popular press with problems ranging from excessive red tape and the slow processing of claims to an appalling lack of services and unfair determinations of eligibility. Clashes among the different federal agencies that were initially responsible for veterans' benefits added to the unrest. A strong political response to veterans' complaints was particularly important to counter simultaneous demands from veterans for a special payment recognizing the higher pay earned by civilians in the booming war economy: the hotly contested so-called soldiers' bonus.[1] However, complaints alone did not dictate the invention of a brand-new, independent federal entity. The movement to reform federal government agencies under the banner of business efficiency acted as a second, concurrent force.

This chapter describes social policies that emerged from an environment of conflicting congressional goals, strong veteran lobbying, and battling bureaucracies. Some of the themes apply to all aspects of veterans' entitlements: disability benefits; life insurance; vocational training; and medical, dental, and hospital care. But the chapter's focus is hospital provisioning for disabled veterans because it was central to the Veterans Bureau's creation. Hospital service became the special target of a major Senate investigation of the bureau in 1923, providing fodder for both political parties as they geared up toward the 1924 presidential election. Indeed, allegations of improprieties in hospital location and construction and in the handling of supplies led to the conviction and imprisonment of the first director of the bureau, Charles R. Forbes, for conspiracy to commit fraud. In turn, this highly publicized scandal—the first major scandal of the Harding administration—inspired the reinvention of the Veterans Bureau as a stable, all-American institution.

## Veterans' Benefits for Hospital Care

During World War I, the U.S. Treasury Department assumed responsibility for disabled veterans' medical conditions as part of a broader public commitment to define war damage as an insurable risk. On September 2, 1914, Congress passed the War Risk Insurance Act (Pub. L. 63–193), on which veterans' benefits were later to be based. The act empowered the Treasury to set up its own Bureau of War Risk Insurance (BWRI) to insure American vessels, freight, and cargoes against loss or damage from risks of war. Highlighting its commercial purpose, this insurance was only extended to the lives of officers and crew on merchant ships in mid-1917, after the United States entered the war. A mere twenty workers seated in four rooms of the Treasury Department coped with the task of running the bureau.[2] Marine war insurance proved profitable; the Treasury reported excess income over payouts of $17.5 million during the period of war. More important perhaps, as noted by the BWRI director in 1920, the success of this venture "resulted in stabilizing the commerce of the entire country, as well as causing renewed confidence in the government."[3]

American entry into World War I in April 1917, followed by congressional approval of military conscription in May, raised urgent questions of how to deal with future veterans' benefits. Disabled veterans of earlier wars received pensions, and many lived as pensioners in national or state-supported soldiers' and sailors' homes. In 1917 these older methods were out of tune both with Progressive beliefs in the superiority of contributory social insurance over noncontributory pensions and with newly acquired business expertise in selling private life insurance.[4] President Woodrow Wilson's Treasury secretary, William G. McAdoo, remarked that the pension system was "as unscientific as the distribution of prizes from a Christmas tree . . . mechanical, inequitable, and unjust."[5] The planned enormity of effort for the Great War also raised questions of scale. In August 1914 there were only 785,000 living veterans, about half of whom had served in the Spanish-American War.[6] Providing disability entitlements to four or five million mostly young Americans could burden the federal treasury for decades. Fortunately for policymakers of the time, expertise was available by 1917 to craft an alternative to pensions based on commercial and social insurance principles.

A small group of experts on insurance and the family, under federal auspices and supported by Columbia University, crafted the new package of benefits for future veterans during the summer of 1917. True to prevailing Progressive ideas, the focus was on readjustment, rehabilitation, and family protection in the context of absent or incapacitated fathers and sons.[7] War risk insurance for veterans was, conceptually, workers' (specifically workmen's) compensation, a concept widely accepted by 1917 through programs in the states for workers in industry and in the federal government for civilian employees. These programs typically paid for associated medical services provided by local hospitals and physicians. The insurance proposals also fell neatly into contemporary market rhetoric. A Treasury official noted in 1918 that war risk insurance used "business methods with which the people of the United States are already familiar in nearly every department of their life."[8] Enlisted men with dependents were subject to specified, compulsory family contributions. Besides compensation entitlements for death and disability, the bureau offered life insurance on a voluntary basis.

The development of a vast new system of public insurance policies rapidly transformed the BWRI. The bureau set up an active office in Paris and, later, other offices throughout France. About a hundred million dollars' worth of insurance was sold before insurance application forms and instructions had even arrived. One soldier reportedly wrote his application on the wall of his dugout before going to his death. His application was photographed, sent to the bureau, and accepted. By June 1918 BWRI had about thirteen thousand employees, 90 percent of them women recruited from all over the United States. The bureau's new ten-story building on Vermont Avenue in Washington, D.C., was ready for partial occupation in February 1919, filling the entire block between H and I streets. By January 1920, the building overflowed, with staff spilling over into other buildings. A banking magazine noted in 1918 that in a few short months the BWRI wrote insurance equivalent to more than half the value of all life insurance sold in the United States.[9] Although more than three-quarters of the four million policyholders stopped paying their premiums by July 1919, their experiences with war risk insurance reportedly proved to be a huge postwar boon to the private life insurance industry.[10]

Beside the provision for compensation to disabled soldiers and sailors through BWRI, medical and vocational rehabilitation benefits were included in the amendment of the War Risk Act of 6 October 1917. Section 302 of the legislation provided hospital and medical care to the "injured person" with such services to include "such reasonable governmental medical, surgical, and hospital services and with such supplies, including artificial limbs, trusses, and similar appliances, as the director [of BWRI] may determine to be useful and reasonably necessary." Section 303 provided for medical examinations to determine disability. Section 304 provided for vocational training. This latter function was removed from BWRI to the new Federal Board for Vocational Education in June 1918. For BWRI beneficiaries, compensation and medical care were to be provided to those who could show disability of 10 percent or more from disease or injury "incurred in or aggravated by military or naval service in the World War."[11] Beneficiaries must have been honorably discharged from the military and must not have caused or contributed to their own injuries.

The easily discernible definitional and organizational troubles that lay ahead ensured that any director of the bureau would receive constant criticism. For example, what was an "injured person"? One person's definition was often different from another's, as revealed in subsequent congressional hearings. Why did eligibility include someone who was inducted into the military via a local draft board and its cursory medical examination but then discharged with tuberculosis, mental illness, or some other disabling condition after only a few weeks at an Army base or cantonment? What was "reasonable" and "useful" care? Did this care assume first-rate specialized service given in well-built modern institutions? Did it mean lifelong care? What was to stop veterans from abusing the system? Was someone eligible for government-supported care if he had latent tuberculosis or mental illness or a manageable physical problem before induction into the Army or Navy but claimed it was exacerbated in the service? Who was to write the manuals for doctors to use in making disability ratings? Would there be a right to appeal a negative disability rating? The BWRI was an insurance organization. Who would organize the doctors and hospitals needed for veterans? Where would they come from? The list of unanswered questions seemed endless.

The lack of specific attention to the details of veterans' hospital care carried long-term repercussions. In theory, hospital care needed for discharged soldiers and sailors could be provided through contractual arrangements between the BWRI and private hospitals, sanatoria, and doctors throughout the United States. It could also be accomplished through preexisting government facilities such as federal military hospitals; civilian U.S. Public Health Service hospitals; and state, county, or city institutions, where these existed—or through a mixture of public and private methods. In reality, the lack of immediate, decisive measures plagued hospital care. The national commander of the American Legion, representing 1.6 million veterans, stated the problem in January, 1921:

"When we mobilized our wealth and our manpower the nation went to war; there was one fundamental which we overlooked and for which we are now paying, and that is there was no hospital building program. We seemed, with the other things, of which there were many, to have forgotten that in a great war these men, broken derelicts, were coming back, and the hospital building program, which should have been adopted at the time, was not adopted, and practically no hospitals were built, even civilian hospitals for the needs of the civilian population." He concluded, "Everything was subservient to the war, the successful prosecution of the war."[12]

For the duration of the war at least, it was also expected that injured and sick men would remain in the service until they had reached maximum improvement since the Army was setting up reconstruction hospitals for this purpose.[13] This was both a logical view and the expert one. Leading American medical schools and teaching hospitals representing the elite of American scientific medicine had set up huge, high-quality base hospitals in France, which clearly provided better care than hospitals in the United States. However, at home, outside of a mixed bag of military facilities, there were grossly inadequate hospital services for the conditions disabled veterans faced: tuberculosis, mental illness, physical rehabilitation, and long-term care. Most American private nonprofit hospitals were building up profitable surgery and maternity care to a growing clientele of middle-class patients but had little interest in welcoming a socially diverse group of young men who might pollute their pristine institutions with ex-soldiers' vices and unpleasantries.[14] Veterans and their families had their own concerns. They did not want to be labeled paupers by going to urban county hospitals or confined in state institutions for the insane.

Although Army hospitals were to provide service to many veterans both during and after the war (particularly for tuberculosis), military hospitals had no legal duty to veterans who were by definition no longer soldiers but civilians. What is more, veterans used them reluctantly. The Army had a hospital bed capacity of 147,636 beds in the United States on 11 November 1918, including beds in 89 new hospitals, while Army procurement officers were scouring U.S. cities to look for more hospitals and sites.[15] Congress had been generous to the military, appropriating more than $242 million for Army hospitals between 12 May 1917 and 11 July 1919.[16] The Army had also built up substantial expertise in hospital design, organization, statistical reporting, construction, and staffing in its huge base hospital system in France. Here was a modern hospital system in the making.[17] But military hospitals required military discipline of patients, such as obeying orders from superiors, confinement to barracks as ordered, and other irksome conditions, which veterans often vigorously rejected. "Discipline" also became a problem in some veterans' hospitals, as tuberculosis and mentally ill patients headed off into town, or even took their own discharge at will.

The domestic hospital problem was compounded when veterans complained through the newly formed American Legion or their congressional representatives that the hospital services they expected—and were entitled to by law—were not available to them at home. The already bad situation was exacerbated when military medical leaders rapidly reduced military hospital beds in the United States after the war on the reasonable grounds that they were no longer needed for military purposes. By 18 August 1919 the Army had reduced the general hospital beds under its control in the United States to 33,414; and by 30 October 1920 to 3,750.[18] As late as 1921 some veterans continued to be treated in military hospitals, including Walter Reed Hospital in Washington, D.C. The Army would care for a veteran on a space-available basis if he happened to be a dependent of a serving soldier and allowed veterans to reenlist for rehabilitation.[19] But these were exceptions. Generally, the chasm between military and veterans' services was clear, for they had different missions.

The U.S. Public Health Service (PHS), a medical, research, and public health agency housed in the Treasury Department, was the obvious place to provide or designate federal civilian hospitals for veterans. Like the military, the PHS was in the hospital business, though on a relatively small scale. In April 1917 there were twenty-two PHS Marine Hospitals scattered along the coasts and major rivers of the United States. Marine hospitals, as their name indicated, were originally established for members of the merchant marine. But the PHS was also heavily vested in other aspects of veterans' medical care. In April 1917 President Woodrow Wilson had mobilized the PHS as part of the nation's military forces, with all PHS stations opened to sick and wounded men during the war.[20] After October 1917 the BWRI established its own medical division with PHS doctors detailed to it, including a senior medical adviser to the bureau. PHS officers and PHS-designated doctors provided medical and dental evaluations for disability and were responsible for health services for BWRI recipients across the United States. On paper at least, the structure existed for a workable insurance function for veterans (BWRI) complemented by a medical service function (PHS).

Both BWRI and PHS were located in the Treasury. Toward the end of the Wilson administration an assistant secretary was made responsible for both these agencies, thus suggesting future policy coordination for veterans' services as a whole, although vocational rehabilitation services were housed in an independent government organization, the Federal Board for Vocational Education (FBVE).[21] The assistant secretary under Wilson, and then briefly under Harding, was Ewing Laporte, a Yale-educated lawyer from Pittsburgh who was one of the most concerned and knowledgeable people in Washington on veterans' services. Unfortunately, he appeared less a coordinator than a banger of truculent heads. "It was just as if I were a brigadier general and they [the directors of BWRI and PHS] were colonels under me," he recollected, "I earned the enmity of all of them."[22]

Between 6 October 1917 and 30 June 1920, the PHS was responsible for overseeing hospital services for veterans declared eligible by BWRI, a truly thankless task. Both PHS hospitals and leased facilities were used, together with available beds in other public hospitals, such as the psychiatric wards at St. Elizabeth's Hospital (a federal institution in Washington, D.C.). After 1 July 1920 hospitals operated by the independent National Home for Disabled Soldiers and of the Army and Navy could also be used by BWRI beneficiaries if beds were available. By the fall of 1921 the PHS was operating sixty-two hospitals, including twenty-one Army and cantonment hospitals, twenty-one Marine hospitals, one naval home, two hospitals it had bought, and a variety of other hospitals set up in leased facilities.[23] To give some idea of the scope of these patched-together medical operations, in fiscal year 1921, the BWRI spent $5 million on medical services it provided directly while reimbursing PHS more than $38 million, with another $590,000 to the War Department, and $5,000 to the National Home.[24] The PHS remained the focus of hospital care for BWRI until the Veterans Bureau (VB) was established, and only formally dissociated itself from veterans' hospital service when PHS hospitals serving veterans were transferred to the VB as of 1 May 1922.

Yet PHS hospitals were far too small to cope with thousands of new veteran beneficiaries. In March 1918 the PHS reported only 1,704 beds in its Marine hospitals, of which 1,171 were occupied, leaving a sparse 533 available for war risk patients—and these were not necessarily located in places veterans would want to go. PHS officials were also understandably reluctant to assume the political hassle of choosing which private hospitals would be accepted on contract as participants for war risk beneficiaries, and which not. The PHS crisis rapidly became acute. In July 1918 the BWRI director requested accommodations for 14,000 discharged tuberculosis patients. On top of this, a committee of Army, Navy, and PHS medical officers estimated in September 1918, while the war was still raging, that an additional 20,000 men would be rejected on medical grounds in 1918 after having been inducted into the military—and thus automatically and immediately be entitled to war risk insurance benefits.[25]

Postwar congressional hearings rang with questions as to why military hospitals in the United States could not fully meet the needs of veterans. One senator pointed out an obvious if frustrating truth that three branches of government, the Army, PHS, and BWRI, all claimed they needed more hospitals—yet one branch did not know what the other was doing.[26] A critical set of questions emerged during the congressional hearings: how many hospitals in the United States, and which ones, would the Army and Navy cede to the Treasury, or be willing to open to patients on a contract basis? Were those that were offered actually suitable for the medical treatment of veterans? Were they appropriately located to suit veterans' needs?

Drawing on experiences in their own constituencies, the prevailing view in Congress was that existing military beds were unsatisfactory for veterans' care. They were located on military posts or cantonments that were distant from centers of population, housed in temporary wooden structures (and thus neither permanent nor fireproof), or were in insufficient supply in the states where veterans actually lived. A senior government official described the "depressing effect of a large number of rough, empty buildings situated out in the country" in dreary "nothing more or less than deserted villages," to which veterans simply would not go.[27] While fiscally conservative representatives favored using available military stock wherever it might be located, or saw no need to take any action on hospitals at all, a consensus developed that reform was necessary.[28] But congressional reformers faced lines of organizational and individual confrontation with the Army as one power bloc in a contested policy domain.

After considerable debate, Congress made a de facto, if tentative, decision on how to address veterans' health care in legislation passed on 3 March 1919 (Pub. L. 65 326). This act recognized the strapped PHS as the agency responsible for disabled veterans' hospital care, and enabled the Army to turn over to the PHS fourteen of its unwanted hospitals containing more than thirteen thousand beds. The largest of these, with more than two thousand beds, was at Camp Beauregard, Louisiana. None of the fourteen hospitals was located in the Rocky Mountain or western states.[29] The 1919 legislation appropriated $9.05 million for the PHS to improve these and other facilities, a puny sum compared with military hospital expenditures. The appropriation was also designed to build two new hospitals (in Chicago and Norfolk, Virginia) and to buy a hospital in Washington, D.C. Whereas in June 1919 the PHS operated twenty Marine hospitals and one sanitarium for tuberculosis, one year later the agency maintained 11,639 beds in fifty-two hospitals including facilities specifically designated for veterans.[30]

In 1919, as discharged soldiers flocked homeward batch by batch, the lack of acceptable veteran hospital provision at the local level was made visible in towns and cities across the United States. Veterans received hospital care in overcrowded PHS hospitals, in demobilized or contracted Army and Navy hospitals typically attached to bases and cantonments in the United States, and in civilian hospitals ranging from the excellent to the terrible. Moreover, a huge backlog of pending cases existed. A congressional study estimated that 204,000 U.S. soldiers had been "wounded not mortally," while an uncounted number suffered from tuberculosis and neuropsychiatric conditions. A PHS report estimated that perhaps 300,000 or more veterans would need further hospital care.[31] But estimates whirled around in profusion, with different sources producing different figures. Hospital provisioning appeared overwhelmed in the chaos of demobilization.

Clear policy directions had yet to emerge because the major civilian and military bureaucracies serving veterans were often at loggerheads. The BWRI, PHS, and Army were drawn from different professional cultures and were suspicious of each other's motivations. Army medical experts could boast of their specialized medical expertise developed in base hospitals in France and elsewhere. Leading experts in the PHS were the mandarins of public health. The BWRI was both a huge public insurance enterprise and the voice of disabled veterans. Finally, vocational rehabilitation experts moved an agenda within the broader field of education. Efforts to cross the boundaries of these different professional cultures were readily labeled as bureaucratic encroachment. For example, Richard G. Cholmeley-Jones, BWRI director in 1920, was a dedicated, hard-working public servant who allegedly offended the PHS because he tried "to take over this hospital job, virtually to acquire control of the Public Health Service, and they resented it." With the federal agencies at odds, veterans' health care catapulted into the political arena.[32]

## Hospitals and Politics

As veterans' health care entered into the larger political milieu, three issues emerged. The most pressing concern was increasing the supply of hospital beds and distributing them equitably across the country. A second concern was to get existing agencies to work together, and a third was a political concern—specifically, how to keep federal money appropriated for any new veterans' hospitals from being bandied around in an unseemly free-for-all in Congress, where legislators sniffed the air for pork-barrel deals.

Congressional action on veterans' hospitals between 1918 and 1921 illustrated only too clearly the problems of having Congress design a national hospital program. Squabbling over the location of a new hospital for veterans marked hearings in the House of Representatives in October 1918, when an enterprising group of private citizens in Dawson Springs, Kentucky, offered the U.S. government a piece of land, provided that a veterans' hospital was constructed there. Kentucky Democrats supported this proposal while Republicans in the House rallied against it. The Dawson Springs hospital was built, funded under

Pub. L. 65–326, but its success invited the question: was the United States to have a pork-barrel system of tax-supported hospitals located, one by one, according to the relative clout of individual legislators?[33]

Two other special deals in the works before Warren G. Harding took office on 4 March 1921 exemplified the informal, hands-on, sometimes vitriolic style of hospital policy, marked by political pull, bureaucratic confusion, and occasional chicanery. The first deal was in Missouri, where prominent Republican lawyer E. L. "Liv" Morse offered to sell the federal government his large house in Excelsior Springs for use as a hospital. The idea, Morse reported later, was suggested to him in 1920 by a "Mr. Fardell" from the PHS and three men from the American Legion on a visit to the area.[34] Morse sent a telegram to Assistant Secretary of the Treasury Ewing Laporte at their suggestion. Laporte rammed through a deal and pressed PHS Surgeon General Hugh Cumming to prepare a lease because there was no money appropriated at the time to buy the house.[35] Laporte testified later that he pushed the project through rapidly because he felt the urgency of veterans' care: "These men were out on the streets."[36] But there was political urgency too: the lease was signed on the last day of the Wilson administration.[37] Excelsior Springs ultimately got its hospital for veterans, although the project remained mired in confusion, mixed signals, and administrative neglect. Embarrassingly, among other contractual problems and suspicions of fraud, the plans for renovation omitted a kitchen, and the hospital was still not finished in late 1923.[38]

The second illustrative case involved a potential hospital in Chicago. Lumber magnate Edward Hines owned a 320-acre racetrack near Chicago, which he proposed to give to the Army as a site for a huge military hospital in honor of his son, Lt. Edward Hines Jr., who died of disease in Flanders. The Broad View (Speedway) hospital was to be both his father's memorial to him and a center for the best possible hospital care for soldiers. In August 1918 Hines thought he had an agreement with the Army Quartermasters Office to construct a military hospital on the site, with construction to be done by the Shank Construction Company. Work began on the site on the strength of contract approval at all relevant government levels except for that of Secretary of War Newton Baker, who departed for Europe in September 1918 without giving the final signature. At this point, according to Hines, an unnamed man appeared purporting to be a government official and demanded one hundred thousand dollars from the president of the construction company as payment for the signed contract.[39] Shank and Hines refused to deal. On 27 September 1918 the Shank Corporation, which had eight hundred men already on the job, received notice that the contract would not be signed. Negotiations reopened with the Army, with new specifications. Still without a contract, the Hines group continued to build a huge brick and concrete building, initially designed to have 3,500 beds and billed as the "largest hospital building in the world."[40]

The Speedway project was finally resolved by turning it over to the beleaguered PHS. In the legislation of 3 March 1919 (Pub. L. 65–326), Congress authorized three million dollars for the hospital's construction. This time the secretary of the Treasury was unwilling to sign the contract. More disagreement followed in Congress and elsewhere, but political pull prevailed. After all, Hines, a prominent Republican, had contributed more than a million dollars of his own money to the project. President Harding personally approved its special name, the Edward Hines Junior Memorial Hospital.[41]

As the preceding examples show, politics was a continuing presence with the prospect of federal money in view. President Harding was not immune. Two weeks after his inauguration, his office received a letter from the Chamber of Commerce from his hometown of Marion, Ohio, lobbying for a veterans' hospital in that city: "Would appreciate any information you can give us and will be glad to follow out any plans suggested by yourself to make successful the location of a hospital here."[42] Likewise, Sen. John W. Harreld (R-Okla.) demanded a hospital as a political quid pro quo. He argued that Republicans in Oklahoma had roundly criticized the Wilson administration for failing to deal with the needs of veterans during the 1920 political campaign, and that this issue had been instrumental in swinging the state to the Republican party, but now Democrats were flexing their muscles, and Oklahoma deserved a veterans' hospital as an entitlement and "vote of confidence."[43]

Political claims were not confined to elected officials. World War I veterans became a political force. The American Legion, formed in Paris in 1919 with a patriotic, law, and order agenda and dedicated to the concept of "100 percent Americanism," joined the Veterans of Foreign Wars, and the Disabled American Veterans as highly effective lobbyists for veterans' benefits. Cries of "equity" and "national obligation" focused political interest and provided a running refrain to debates about veterans' services. In 1919 alone, fifty-five bills were introduced in Congress to "adjust" the rates of pay servicemen had received during the war up to the levels they might have received had they stayed at home and profited from the boom in wartime industry.[44] Providing vocational training and better hospital services to sick and disabled veterans offered less expensive, more politically palatable alternatives to doling out money to all veterans whether they seemed to need it or not.[45]

Meanwhile field investigations made by the American Legion reported stories of deplorable hospital conditions. Legion officials found shell-shocked veterans sent to hospitals for feeble-minded children where they were forced to sit on infants' chairs, and tuberculosis patients directed to marshy districts detrimental to their health.[46] Approximately 20,000 eligible veterans were in hospital in the fall of 1920, many in facilities that medical experts considered undesirable. About 7,900 veterans were in hospital for tuberculosis, 5,200 for mental illness, and 6,800 for general medical and surgical conditions. The last group was the easiest to place in PHS, military, or civilian facilities. According to expert opinion, however, 30,000 beds would be needed within the year as latent and looming medical problems came to light. There were especially urgent needs for beds for mental illness (mostly for war-induced or aggravated insanity rather than "shell shock") and tuberculosis.[47]

Central to congressional and veteran organization frustrations, a large number of veterans encountered problems getting the benefits to which they were entitled. Congressional representatives such as Rep. John Jacob Rogers (R-Mass.), a strong advocate for organizational reform of veterans' services, reported that he spent much of his time interceding with the different agencies on behalf of veterans, taking up specific cases directly with the BWRI and PHS. Veterans, their families, and others bombarded the BWRI with inquiries, requests, and complaints. The BWRI reportedly received about 25,000 letters a day, plus telegrams and phone calls. Meanwhile, about 75,000 men had entered vocational training through the FBVE, including 5,000 in training at 130 hospitals that employed 400 teachers. These vocational rehabilitation decisions continued to be made separately. By the spring of 1921 two and a half years after the armistice, the hospital program for veterans was a nightmare of red tape, inefficiency, confusion, and neglect.[48]

Members of Congress continued to have difficulty understanding what different government agencies did and rated them according to their own preconceptions. Rep. James R. Mann (R-Ill.) opined in 1919: "As to the Public Health Service, I was going to say it is a grasping body, but that is true of all Government functions. It is very rare that any bureau or department of the government does not seek to increase its authority and jurisdiction rather than decrease it." Rep. Royal Johnson (R-S.D.) thought the BWRI should not be entrusted with hospitals for reasons of "competence and efficiency." Others considered the Army and Navy to be efficient but were distressed at hearing that the military was willing to give its worst facilities, not its best, to other departments for veterans. In any event, this did not solve the problem of veterans' hospitalization.[49] It is easy to see how, by 1921, reorganization of veterans' services into a single organization, the Veterans Bureau, had become the conservative, efficient, consensus solution—even a panacea—that might (perhaps) stop prevailing rivalries and wrangling.

Attempts to grapple with hospital policy in the Wilson years culminated in the establishment of an expert committee to make hospital location and construction decisions, thus formally removing the process from the sphere of congressional politics. President Wilson, seriously weakened by illness, signed this potentially transforming law (Pub. L. 66–384, most likely designed by Ewing Laporte) in his last hours in office, on 4 March 1921.[50] The act appropriated $18.6 million for hospital facilities for veterans. A new committee was to serve without pay as "consultants in hospitalization" and report directly to the Treasury secretary, thus operating above the level of BWRI and PHS. Laporte, remaining in place for a few weeks after the presidential transition, made a list of the "very best men in the country," for the new Republican secretary of the Treasury, millionaire banker Andrew W. Mellon.[51] Mellon sent for the well-known tuberculosis specialist, Dr. William Charles White, to chair the committee.[52]

Displacing decisions to an expert committee could be seen either as a progressive, top-down, prescriptive response to social policy or as a convenient political sleight of hand. The White committee and its team of expert advisers acted more in the Wilson than the Harding style: as an elite group of professionals producing scientific facts for the nation. Warren Harding's style of governing blended business assumptions with practical politics. However, the White committee provided a useful transition in the veterans' hospital debates. In the two years it was active, beginning in March 1921, the consultants conducted hearings with more than a hundred public and private groups, visited hospitals across the country, sought advice from major hospital associations and philanthropic foundations, and produced copious, detailed maps of where all hospitals were across the United States. They published standards for construction, equipment, and personnel, and rated hospitals in different areas as satisfactory or unsatisfactory. The consultants even attempted to set up machinery for federal oversight and federal standards for all hospitals in the United States so that "uniform care of the citizens of the United States" could be achieved, rather than relying on the "influence of individual or local interests."[53]

Agreeing with the American Legion and others that veterans should be served, where possible, in federal rather than local hospitals on grounds of quality of care, the consultants allocated the $18.6 million to buildings and acquisitions. This allocation eventually produced more than six thousand beds, many of them in hospitals built or acquired by the PHS. At the same time, the committee relinquished unsatisfactory beds in leased hospitals. The consultants' least bold act was to act as broker and decision maker for the building of a segregated national hospital for black veterans at Tuskegee, Alabama, to respond to what they called "Problems of Race."[54]

The work of the White committee strengthened the idea that permanent federal hospitals were the proper approach to veterans' hospitalization. The legislation of 4 March 1921 also moved the agenda toward a larger administrative structure for veterans' policy and management. One of the committee's first acts was to endorse the idea of a single veterans' bureau, although there remained diverse views of where this bureau should be located: in the Treasury, in the Interior Department, or elsewhere. The White committee considered it should be a new government department, headed by a cabinet member. The vigorous efforts of the Harding administration to reform the organization of the federal government by business methods buttressed the committee's endorsement. By the end of April 1921 the course was set toward a new federal veterans' agency.

## The Veterans Bureau

As far as veterans were concerned, Warren G. Harding came to office with two conflicting organizational reforms in view. The more sweeping was his endorsement of a department of public welfare that would bring multiple health, education, and welfare agencies together in a single department "where their interrelationships could be properly appraised" for "increased effectiveness, economy, and intelligence of direction."[55] Although this idea was not new—it had been endorsed by a growing clan of experts in public administration as well as reform-minded legislators—this was a naïve proposal politically. Not surprisingly, it foundered on the reefs of sectional interests including, among others, advocates for an independent department of education, or a department of health, or for assurance that the cabinet officer in charge would be female, while veterans' supporters, a lusty band of increasingly powerful lobbyists, fought for their own special interests.[56]

The proposal is relevant here for the role played by Harding's personal representative on organizational reform: homeopathic physician, sanatorium operator, and presidential doctor Charles E. Sawyer. Harding made Sawyer a brigadier general with a federal administrative portfolio. At joint Senate and House hearings on the proposed department of public welfare on 11 May 1921, Sawyer had a prominent opening role. His tone was visionary and upbeat. Veterans' services would be coordinated—and "soldier interests will be best cared for," he affirmed—as one administration in this huge new department.[57] Although the larger proposals failed, Sawyer consistently sought to coordinate federal activities in health above the level of veterans' services, both as Harding's trusted emissary and as de facto surgeon general. As a brigadier general he acquired offices in the War Department, adding offices in the Veterans Bureau after its creation. Sawyer was not in favor of a truly independent veterans' agency and continued to propose a larger department of public or social welfare through at least 1923.

Harding's second proposal was to combine existing veterans' services into a veterans' bureau. Harding did not specify where this would be placed: under a secretary as a cabinet-level department; as a division headed by an assistant secretary within the Treasury, Interior, or some other department; or as an independent federal entity with a director reporting to the president. To make specific recommendations, Harding appointed a committee headed by Charles G. Dawes, a highly respected banker who, as a general, had run the entire supply service in Europe for the U.S. Army during the war. Known as General "Hell 'n' Maria" Dawes for colorfully expressed frustration before a congressional committee, he liked to get things done. For veterans, Dawes wanted someone to cut though bureaucratic inertia—"someone with a meat ax."[58]

The Dawes committee met on 5 April 1921, worked through the next day, and reported out on 7 April, relying in part on the plan of organization given to them by the White committee. Dawes thought the director of the new organization should not be a cabinet member but be administratively responsible directly to the president, and that recommendation was included, without reference to General Sawyer's position.[59] The Dawes committee plan was to transfer the whole of BWRI, those PHS services that were dedicated to veterans, and vocational rehabilitation services (then housed in the FBVE) to a new federal veterans' organization. That organization would operate outside of cabinet departments and thus be beyond the supervision of a cabinet member. This became the model for the Veterans Bureau. Existing organizational structures had been identified as the stumbling block to change.

Events moved quickly between the Dawes committee report in April 1921 and the establishment of the Veterans Bureau in August. On April 19 PHS medical functions for veterans (except for hospitals) were transferred to the BWRI, thus strengthening its position as the central veterans' organization. On 28 April Charles R. Forbes, a friend and protégé of Harding, became the director of BWRI—Forbes's first entry into this long-conflicted scene. Less than three years later, when his own life was unraveling, Forbes remembered a warning he received from the battle-scarred, departing director of BWRI, Cholmeley-Jones: "Colonel Forbes, you are coming into a job that will bring you only grief and sorrow. I have done everything within my power to build up this institution and make it really worth while. It is politically stagnant, and I do not believe that you or any other man will ever be able to put it over." The "first difficulty" Forbes would face, he said, was the PHS.[60]

Forbes brought new energy to BWRI in the fourteen weeks he served as its director. He worked well with the new assistant secretary of the Treasury to whom he reported, Edward Clifford, and he received, as an ultimate accolade, Sawyer's praise in a letter to Dawes: "The two new young chaps who are now in charge of the Assistant Secretary of the Treasury Secretary's Office and the War Risk are certainly making good. I do not know whether you know Forbes or not, but Forbes is a real man, just your type. He delivers every day from the bat and makes home runs."[61] In the summer of 1921, Forbes and his staff at BWRI worked with FBVE to consolidate its field offices with those of BWRI functions at the local level, anticipating the transfer of vocational rehabilitation functions to the Veterans Bureau in August.[62] Indeed, administrative coordination seemed already to be under way even before official consolidation.

When Senate finance subcommittee hearings on the establishment of a veterans' bureau began in July 1921, Forbes was a skilled and influential presence. Sen. Reed Smoot (R-Utah), chair of the subcommittee, seemed to assume that Forbes would get the job as director of the new bureau. Pressed for his own views, Forbes agreed that a bureau reporting directly to the president would be "more advantageous" than one operating within the Treasury.[63] On 8 August 1921 the act to establish the Veterans Bureau as an independent federal organization was signed (Pub. L. 67–47), taking effect the following day. President Harding immediately appointed Forbes as director. Pressed by veterans' concerns, the legislation was passed with almost unseemly haste, as was Forbes's appointment. Harding simply shoehorned him into the job.[64]

Yet old conflicts do not disappear when organizations are reshuffled. Melding disparate groups with a total of more than thirty thousand employees into an organization that is both a national enterprise and a service to clients at the local level, required an extraordinarily capable leader. The new bureau needed someone of impeccable status, a rock-hard reputation, first-rate professional credentials, and superb people skills. Forbes had none of these attributes. He came from an unproven background; his management experience had been in the Army and as a project manager in the construction industry, both of which emphasized top-down command-and-control rather than the political finesse and consensus-building that the VB needed at this early stage. His highest rank in the Army was lieutenant colonel in the Signal Corps. Among many management problems, he had an early run-in with his eminent medical adviser, Haven Emerson, who resigned (or was fired) in September 1921, and who became an outspoken critic.[65] A second potential ally, Arthur R. Dean of Columbia University, whom Forbes appointed as assistant bureau director for vocational training, resigned in January 1922 after a disagreement with Forbes over the centralization of vocational training in a few national centers. Dean, who believed adamantly that veterans should receive training near their homes, reportedly complained that the VB was "dominated by the War Risk Insurance group."[66] And this was true. In short order, Forbes had lost the services of major representatives from the PHS and vocational educational communities.

Dr. Charles E. Sawyer, who was much more politically and diplomatically skilled than Forbes, soon also became a foe. Less than three months into the Veterans Bureau first year, Sawyer became chief coordinator of a new Federal Board of Hospitalization—part of a network of coordinating committees for the new (and first) U.S. Bureau of the Budget, created and directed by Dawes. Forbes was vice-chair of the hospitalization board, which brought together leading representatives of the Army and Navy, PHS, the VB, and other federal organizations with hospital responsibilities. The board sought bureaucratic efficiencies: coordination and standardization of federal hospitals, and the elimination of redundancies and waste across departmental lines. Antagonism developed because of the confusion over Forbes's and Sawyer's roles, the former seeing himself in sole charge of the VB and its hospitals, the latter as the government's overall hospital and public health coordinator and as Harding's emissary for government efficiency.[67]

Despite the bureaucratic obstacles, consolidation was hailed as an important reform. "The day of divided authority in the Government's dealing with ex-service men is over," proclaimed the New York Times a few weeks after the Veterans Bureau's creation. It also noted that the Bureau was "one of the largest organizations in the world in terms of money controlled." Forbes was responsible for average expenditures of a million dollars a day. As in "any well-organized business institution," power was vested in one man. Forbes drew praise for decentralizing and consolidating decision making for veterans' care at the local level. His enlargement of the hospital for tuberculosis patients at Fort Bayard, New Mexico, his progress with other hospital projects, and his pledge to provide hospital treatment to ex-servicemen and -women even without completed paperwork for eligibility were all viewed favorably.[68] Yet he was more often singled out for his failures than successes.

Hospital construction and supplies managed by the VB were soon to be the center for political scandal. New legislation (Pub. L. 67–216) had transferred the PHS veterans' hospitals to the VB and provided the VB for the first time with money of its own—$17 million—for hospital construction and renovation. The White committee was meanwhile working on its own $18.6 million program separately within the Treasury Department, mostly for beds for neuropsychiatry and tuberculosis, and turning over new beds to the VB as they were completed. Forbes argued unwisely at the hearings that preceded Pub.

L. 67–216 that he could build hospitals less expensively than the consultants, which turned out to be incorrect.

This new responsibility for hospital provision came on top of Forbes's attempts to make eligibility evaluations and other services more effective and timely at the district level. Despite his efforts, though, more than 51,000 active life insurance claims were still pending as of 30 June 1922, including the death benefits of veterans who had died after discharge. Almost 352,000 disability claims had so far been allowed, with many more left to evaluate.[69] Rehabilitation services and successful job placement for veterans were major headaches. And members of Congress continued to press the interests of individuals in their constituencies through a flood of letters to the VB, expecting immediate attention, and provoking criticism that the VB was too "political."

Most important, the hospital construction program provided a new opportunity for contractors, lobbyists, and fixers seeking lucrative federal contracts, and it raised concerns about the effects of political pressure, shady deals in the purchase of sites, and sugarcoated payments to government officials. As new federal hospitals came online, leased and contract hospitals were phased out. In October 1920, for example, 71 percent of VB psychiatric patients who were hospitalized were in contract hospitals. In January 1923 this declined to 44 percent.[70] Such hospitals, however, took time to build. By February 1924 only thirteen projects had been started under the Pub. L. 67–216 appropriation, and only two hundred new beds were actually in service.[71] Running criticisms about construction delays thus added to understandable concerns about administrative inefficiency and corruption. Putting responsibility for construction into the VB, it was argued, "did not make for speed or economy, but did afford an opportunity for the consummation of conspiracies to defraud the government."[72]

By the end of 1922 the VB was a mess, with tales of inefficiency, political influence, and irregularities sweeping through Washington's renowned rumor mills. Staff morale was low. There seemed to be a never-ending cavalcade of problems and complaints. The coup de grâce was discovery of gross mismanagement, if not outright corruption, in the handling of supplies at the VB depot in Perryville, Maryland. Vast quantities of new sheets, floor wax, and other materials as well as numerous train carloads of wartime surplus were being sold for twenty cents on the dollar to a Boston consignment firm. Forbes's critic Sawyer and PHS officials blew the whistle. At a time of major government commitment to efficiency, the Perryville decision was, at best, egregiously inefficient—maybe crooked. Forbes resigned. The first phase of the Veterans Bureau was over by the spring of 1923.

## Reinvention of the Bureau, plus "Socialized Medicine"

Reinvention began with a major political and organizational cleansing. By resolution on 2 March1923 the Senate created a three-man bi-partisan committee of investigation of the Veterans Bureau: Senators David A. Reed (R-Pa.) as chair, Tasker L. Oddie (R-Nev.), and David A. Walsh (D-Mass.). Senate Resolution 466 of the 67th Congress, fourth session, listed four reasons for the investigation: delay in the adjustment of veterans' claims; delay in hospital construction; excessive overhead and staffing; and improper sales of surplus property. Taken together, these represented a major investigation of the VB as an organization, how it worked, and how it had been run, with the ultimate goal of revealing its faults and correcting them through managerial reforms.

Veterans' health care reform once again moved quickly. On 3 March 1923, President Harding's appointee as the second director of the VB, Brig. Gen. Frank T. Hines, was sworn in. On 8 March the Senate investigating committee announced the appointment of Maj. Gen. John F. O'Ryan (a Democrat) as the committee's counsel, to take charge of investigations and gather facts before and during the Senate hearings. O'Ryan, both a lawyer and professional soldier, had built up the New York National Guard before the war, taken it to war as an Army division, and returned home a national hero. In 1922 he had become a transit commissioner for New York State. He was successful, ambitious, and skillful, if sometimes unorthodox in his methods. No "political considerations" would affect his work, O'Ryan affirmed. He announced that the investigation would be "disinterested and complete." O'Ryan proceeded "without the distractions of publicity" (that is, in secret), concentrating first on the "worthy claims of needy veterans," then on hospitalization and rehabilitation, and, finally, on the effectiveness of the bureau itself. Mere complainers, he said, were avoided.[73]

O'Ryan quickly wrote to every senator and member of Congress, asking for volunteer service from leading attorneys, preferably veterans. He sought examples of "dereliction on the part of the Government service" and suggestions for improvement. Letters went to national and state commanders and district rehabilitation committee chairs of the American Legion, Disabled American Veterans, and Veterans of Foreign Wars; to presidents of Chambers of Commerce in cities with VB activities (almost five hundred cities); and to Kiwanis clubs. Bar associations of each state were asked to produce pro bono lawyers, "men of the highest character and preferably veterans of the war," to conduct local investigations. The letter to medical associations noted that already a corps of about 300 lawyers has been established throughout the country, and asked for medical cooperation. Finally, requests were made via the War Department Judge Advocate General and Medical Corps. These methods elicited the volunteer services of 596 lawyers and 541 physicians, nearly all World War I veterans. O'Ryan warmly praised them and their efforts; their work was an "inspiration" to him, he wrote.[74] Thus equipped, he embarked upon a moral quest, an efficiency sweep, and incomparable national and regional buy-in for the investigation. In the process, the investigation developed and refined public opinion. Publicly, the VB problem was being solved.

Concurrently, VB Director Hines worked with O'Ryan through the late spring and summer of 1923 to reduce staff and fix problems as they were identified. During the war, Hines had run the nation's complex and essential embarkation service, getting troops organized, mobilized, and shipped to France. He had spent time on foreign government missions and in the shipping industry, and was diplomatic and savvy in public relations. Where O'Ryan could be judgmental, Hines gave the devil his due: "In fairness to the Bureau and those who located and purchased the present hospitals," he noted at the hearings in the fall, "the pressure upon Congress for immediate relief of the men was great, and that has resulted in the purchase of some institutions that should not have been purchased . . . the only advantage being that of having something immediately available to answer the great emergency which existed when they started."[75] Hines defined his task as twofold: to "solve a peculiarly human problem," and to "head up a gigantic business enterprise." The first required "building up the right kind of personal relationship in the organization and between the organization and those for whom it exists;" the second, "guiding the organization along business lines."[76]

The combination of the two generals, their staff, and hundreds of volunteers, accompanied by interviews with VB and other government personnel (but not with Forbes, who was identified as part of the problem and consigned to the past) gave the VB an extraordinary top-to-bottom, future-oriented management evaluation. The hearings publicized both problems and solutions. The evaluation supported the new management of the bureau by fostering organizational unity, building better working relationships across VB units and among VB staff, assuring all constituencies that professional rationality was now in charge, and emphasizing the efficacy of business methods. These were general themes of the Senate hearings, which ran from 22 October through 21 November 1923. In the first morning of the hearings it was established that the VB had been in disarray, but now it was being effectively and rapidly cleaned up.

By the time of the hearings the political world had taken a major turn. President Harding died in San Francisco on 2 August 1923. Vice President Calvin Coolidge became president but would be up for election in November 1924. Meanwhile political scandals were brewing. In March 1923 the VB's former general counsel, Charles F. Cramer, committed suicide. In May, Jess Smith, close friend of the attorney general, killed himself. Senate hearings on the oil lease scandal (Teapot Dome) began in October 1923, running concurrently with hearings on the VB investigation. That same month, Senator Reed announced that the VB committee's files would go the Department of Justice for criminal investigation of alleged fraud. In December 1923 attorney general Harry M. Daugherty decided on prosecution of Forbes and others after visiting President Coolidge. The Justice Department appointed a special assistant attorney general as lead prosecutor. In February 1924 a special grand jury met in Chicago (where Forbes had allegedly taken a bribe in a bathroom at the Drake Hotel) and indicted Forbes and a contractor on several counts, including conspiracy to commit fraud. In April a second grand jury indicted Forbes and two associates in Baltimore with respect to the Perryville case. While the trial was deferred until after the 1924 elections, Forbes and contractor J. W. Thompson were ultimately convicted. Forbes entered the federal penitentiary at Leavenworth, Kansas, in March 1926.

With blame for the VB's woes now assigned to leadership—not organization or mission—and a failed leader toppled, the VB could move ahead with administrative reforms without further organizational upheavals. The experimental first stage of its career was visibly over, replaced by a stabilizing second stage. The "Veterans Bureau scandal" played an important role in this, by legitimating the bureau and its services through public excoriation, house cleaning, and redemption. The rhetoric of business efficiency eased the wheels of change. Disaffected veterans' groups were at least partially mollified. Federal hospital construction continued apace.

Veterans' medical benefits and hospitals had become facts of political life, as had an independent federal Veterans Bureau. Veterans' hospital needs were defined as long-term governmental medical commitments, rather than as a quick, postwar, postmilitary response to a short-term demand for rehabilitation. Indeed, when 1924 legislation extended veterans' medical benefits to conditions previously deemed non-service-connected, the American Medical Association charged "socialized medicine" to no avail. The acceptance of veterans' hospitals as a national, governmental system had fallen into place. In the terms of the day, these were "normal" and "American." But veterans' health services were also clearly differentiated from other government health agencies, and they, like other veteran benefits, remain independently administered to this day.

# Notes

My appreciation to Carol Byerly and Sanders Marble for very helpful comments on an earlier draft. Research for this chapter forms part of a larger study of veterans' health policy and politics 1918–30, funded by the DeWitt Wallace Fund, Department of Psychiatry, Weill Cornell Medical College. Initial work was funded under a Robert Wood Johnson Foundation Investigator Award in Health Policy Research.

1. For discussion of the bonus bill in the early 1920s, see Robert K. Murray, *The Harding Era: Warren G. Harding and His Administration* (Minneapolis: University of Minnesota Press, 1969), 185–88, 308–14.

2. Robinson E. Adkins, "Medical Care of Veterans." Report prepared for the House Committee on Veterans Affairs. 90th Cong., 1st sess. Committee Print 4, 1967, p. 95. I draw on this source for general background in this chapter; also on Gustavus A. Weber and Laurence F. Schmeckebier, *The Veterans' Administration: Its History, Activities and Organization*. Service Monographs of the United States Government No. 66 (Washington, D.C.: Brookings Institution, 1934); William P. Dillingham, *Federal Aid to Veterans 1917–1941* (Gainesville: University of Florida Press, 1952); and K. Walter Hickel, "Medicine, Bureaucracy and Social Welfare," in *The New Disability History: American Perspectives*, edited by Paul K. Longmore and Lauri Urnanski, 236–67 (New York: New York University Press, 2001). See also Rosemary Stevens, "Can the Government Govern? Lessons from the Formation of the Veterans Administration," *Journal of Health Politics, Policy and Law* 16, no. 2: 281–305.

3. Richard G. Cholmeley-Jones, War Risk Insurance. *Scientific Monthly* 12, no. 3 (March 1921): 229.

4. There were 49 million private life insurance policies in effect in the United States by 1917, up from 25 million in 1907. U.S. Bureau of the Census, *Statistical Abstract of the United States, 1919* (Washington, D.C.: Government Printing Office, 1920), 645.

5. William G. McAdoo, *Crowded Years. The Reminiscences of William G. McAdoo* (Boston: Houghton Mifflin Company, 1919), 428.

6. Adkins, "Medical Care of Veterans," 87.

7. See Theda Skocpol, *Protecting Soldiers and Mothers: The Political Origins of Social Policy in the United States* (Cambridge, Mass.: Harvard University Press, 1992); and Sarah Frances Rose, "No Right to be Idle: The Invention of Disability" (Ph.D. diss. University of Illinois at Chicago, 2008).

8. Thomas B. Love, "The Social Significance of War Risk Insurance." *Annals of the American Academy of Political and Social Science* 79 (September 1918): 46.

9. Adkins, "Medical Care of Veterans," 96–99; and "The Greatest Insurance Business in the World." *Bankers Magazine* 96, no. 5 (May 1919): 550.

10. C.O.H., "Conversion of War-Risk Policies." *Journal of Political Economy* 27, no. 8 (October 1919): 718–21; and McAdoo, *Crowded Years*, 435.

11. For the relations of WRIB and PHS Health Service, see Laurence F. Schmeckebier, *The Public Health Service: Its History, Activities and Organization*. Institute for Governmental Research, Service Monographs of the United States Government, No. 10 (Baltimore: Johns Hopkins University Press, 1923); and L. B. Rogers, "The War Risk Act and the Medical Services Created under It," *Journal of the American Medical Association*, 76, no. 1081 (1921).

12. Statement of Col. F. W. Galbraith Jr., U.S. Congress, House, Committee on Interstate and Foreign Commerce, "Bureau of Veteran Reestablishment." Hearing . . . on HR 14961, 66th Cong. 3rd sess., 7 January 1921, 28.

13. See Sanders Marble, "Rehabilitating the Wounded: Historical Perspective on Army Policy." U.S. Army, Office of Medical History, Office of the Surgeon General, Washington, D.C., June 2008, ch 1 and 2.

14. See Rosemary Stevens, *In Sickness and in Wealth: American Hospitals in the Twentieth Century*, 2nd ed. (Baltimore: Johns Hopkins University Press, 1999), 105–31.

15. *The Medical Department of the United States Army in the World War*, Volume V., *Military Hospitals in the United States*, (Washington, D.C.: Government Printing Office, 1923), 112. I am grateful to Carol R. Byerly for the point about tuberculosis treatment in military institutions.

16. These are appropriations, not actual expenditures; see ibid., 54.

17. For a congressional discussion, see 65th Congress, 3rd sess., House Report No. 879. "Hospital and Sanatorium Facilities for Discharged Sick and Disabled Soldiers and Sailors," 21 December 1918. "Report from the Committee on Public Buildings and Grounds . . . to accompany H.R. 13026," 1.

18. *Medical Department*, 190.

19. For discussion of Army policy at the time, see Marble, "Rehabilitating the Wounded."

20. For the PHS in historical context, see Robert Straus, *Medical Care for Seamen: The Origin of Public Medical Services in the United States* (New Haven, Conn.: Yale University Press, 1950); Harry S. Mustard, *Government in Public Health* (New York: The Commonwealth Fund, 1945); Beth Furman, *A Profile of the United States Public Health Service, 1798–1948* DHEW Pub. No. (NIH) 73–369 (Washington, D.C.: National Library of Medicine, 1973).

21. On the FBVE, see W. Stull Holt, *The Federal Board for Vocational Education: Its History, Activities and Organization*. Institute for Governmental Research, Service Monographs of the United States Government, No. 6 (New York: D. Appleton and Company, 1922).

22. Laporte had been drafted and inducted, then discharged from the military for disability. Testimony of Ewing Laporte, U.S. Senate, Select Committee on Investigation of Veterans' Bureau, [hereafter Senate Hearings on VB] "Hearings . . . pursuant to S. Res. 466 Authorizing the Appointment of a Committee to Investigate the Leases and Contracts Executed by the United States Veterans' Bureau, and for Other Purposes." 67th Cong., 4th Sess., 22 October to 7 November 1923, 491.

23. Dillingham, *Federal Aid to Veterans*, 60 (he cites 66th Cong., House Document 481.)

24. Schmeckebier, *Public Health Service*, 67–68.

25. Ibid, 59–60.

26. U.S. Senate, Committee on Public Buildings and Grounds, Hearings. . . . Pursuant to S. Res. 386. *Military Hospitals*. 65th Cong., 3rd sess. Sen. Joseph L. France of Maryland, (Washington, D.C.: Government Printing Office, 1919), 18.

27. U.S. Congress. House. Committee on Public Buildings and Grounds. *Hearings on HR 13026*, 65th Cong., 3rd. sess., 1918, 7. Assistant PHS surgeon general, Dr. W. D. Stimpson.

28. See, e.g., U.S. Congress. House. 65th Cong., 3rd sess. House . . . Report No. 879. *Hospital and Sanatorium Facilities for Discharged Sick and Disabled Soldiers and Sailors*, 21 December 1918. Report from the Committee on Public Buildings and Grounds . . . to accompany H.R. 13026, 1.

29. Ibid, 190.

30. See Adkins, "Medical Care of Veterans," 104, 106.

31. Ibid., 102–4; and Hugh S. Cumming, "The Work of the Public Health Service in the Care of Disabled Veterans of the World War." *Public Health Reports* 36 (1921): 1893–1902.

32. Senate Hearings on VB, Testimony of Ewing Laporte, 496.

33. See Stevens, "Can the Government Govern?"

34. Senate Hearings on VB, Testimony of E. L. Morse, 319.

35. Testimony of Ewing Laporte, 474.

36. Ibid., 477.

37. For a good review, see "Veterans Hospital Doomed as Unfit, Kept through Pull." *New York Times*, 31 October 1923, 1.

38. Senate Hearings on VB, Testimony of Frank T. Hines, 414.

39. The man was later identified as Milton J. Trainer, who was connected in an unspecified way with the real estate division of the War Department. U.S. Senate, Committee on Public Buildings and Grounds, Hearings . . . Pursuant to S.Res. 386, *Military Hospitals*. 65th Cong., 3rd sess. Testimony of William S. Bennet, Esq., 22 January 1919, 7, 11. Trainer was apparently not prosecuted.

40. Ibid., 10.

41. The correspondence is included in Warren G. Harding Papers [hereafter HP], Ohio Historical Association (microfilm edition, Roll 210, file 862, folder 1). How times can change events! Hines VA hospital is now an eminent patient care, research, and teaching institution.

42. Harry F. Palmer to George B. Christian, 22 March 1921. HP Roll 176. Veterans' Affairs. File 95, folder 16. Applications for Hospitals.

43. Senator J. W. Harreld et al. to Charles E. Hart, The White House, 9 April 1921. HP Roll 176. Veterans' Affairs. File 95, folder 16, "Applications for Hospitals."

44. For discussion, see Murray, *The Harding Era*, 185–88, 308–14.

45. "Selfish or Unselfish Heroes." *World's Work*, April 1921, 538.

46. Robert D. Leigh, *Federal Health Administration in the United States* (New York: Harper and Brothers, 1927), 192–93.

47. U.S. Congress, HR, Committee on Interstate and Foreign Commerce, Bureau of Veteran Reestablishment. Hearing . . . on H.R. 14961, 7 January 1921, 46.

48. Ibid., 71–110.

49. *Congressional Record*—House, 25 January 1919, 2049–60 and 27 January 1919, 2150–72. Debate on HR 13026. Mann's quote is at 2155; Johnson's, 2059.

50. Senate Hearings on VB. Testimony of Ewing Laporte, 486.

51. Ibid., 478–79, 485.

52. White was a prominent member of the National Tuberculosis Association and had directed the wartime hospital program for tuberculosis for the Red Cross in France and Italy.

53. See U.S. Department of the Treasury, *Report of the Consultants on Hospitalization Appointed by the Secretary of the Treasury to Provide Additional Hospital Facilities under Public Act 384* (Washington, D.C.: Government Printing Office, 1923).

54. Ibid., 18. See Pete Daniel, "Black Power in the 1920s: The Case of Tuskegee Veterans Hospital." *Journal of Southern History* 36, no. 3 (August 1970), 368–88.

55. WGH special message to Congress April 12, 1921, quoted in James A. Tobey, *The National Government and Public Health* (Baltimore: Johns Hopkins University Press, Institute for Government Research, 1926), 30.

56. See Murray, *Harding Era*, 124–27. For President Harding's correspondence on the issues, see Warren G. Harding Papers, Ohio Historical Society (microfilm edition), Roll 196.

57. U.S. Senate and House of Representatives, Committee of Education of the United States Senate, Committee of Education, House of Representatives, "Department of Public Welfare," Transcript of Hearing, 11 May 1921. Harding Papers, Roll 196, folder 312:2.

58. Dawes Committee proceedings, included as Exhibit 2 in U.S. House of Representa-

tives, Committee on Interstate and Foreign Commerce, Subcommittee on Consolidation of Government Agencies for the Benefit of Disabled Ex-Service Men, Hearings . . . 67th Cong., 1st sess., on H.R.3, Part 1, 29 April 1921, 44–130, at 49.

59. Charles G. Dawes to Charles E. Sawyer, 26 April 1921. Harding Papers. Roll 196, folder 312:1. Dawes had not checked out the governance recommendation with Sawyer and later tried to change the location of the proposed bureau to the Treasury Department with an assistant secretary in charge, as Sawyer requested. Charles G. Dawes to Milton J. Foreman, 26 April 1921, and Charles G. Dawes to F. W. Galbraith Jr., 26 April 1921. Harding Papers, Roll 196, folder 312–1. Leaders of the American Legion were not prepared to deal.

60. Senate Hearings on VB. Forbes testimony, 913.

61. Charles E. Sawyer to Charles G. Dawes, 7 May 1921. Dawes papers, Northwestern University, Box 93, folder 33.

62. Annual Report of the Director, United States Veterans' Bureau, for the Fiscal Year Ended 30 June 1922 (Washington, D.C.: Government Printing office, 1922), 6.

63. U.S. Congress, Senate Committee on Finance. Subcommittee. "Establishment of a Veterans' Bureau." Hearings on H.R. 6611 [Sweet Bill]. 67th Cong. 1st sess. 5 and 7 July 1921, 61.

64. Gen. John F. O'Ryan, running the investigation of the VB for the Senate in 1923, looked hard and unsuccessfully to find a letter of appointment for Forbes. The Senate approved the appointment in November 1921.

65. It is beyond the scope of this chapter to review the tumultuous eighteen-month career of the Veterans Bureau under Forbes, that is, from 9 August 1921 to 30 January 1923, when he went on sick leave and then resigned under pressure. See Haven Emerson, "Taking Stock of Veterans' Service." *Outlook* 130 (5 April 1922): 542–46.

66. "Practical Veteran Relief," *New York Times*, 17 January 1922, 13.

67. For discussion of this board in the context of Harding efficiency reforms, see Tobey, *National Government and Public Health*, 381–82; and, more broadly, Charles G. Dawes, *The First Year of the Budget of the United States* (New York: Harper and Brothers, 1923), particularly 92, 122–28. Quote from Dawes, 127.

68. "Veterans' Bureau at Work, Colonel Forbes Clearing up the Tangle of Service Men's Relief." *New York Times*, 25 September 1921, 77.

69. Annual Report, VB 1922, 18.

70. U.S. Senate, Committee on Investigation of United States Veterans' Bureau, Third Preliminary Report, (pursuant to S. Res. 466, 67th Cong., 4th sess.) 68th Cong., 1st sess. Report No. 103, Part 3, 6 June 1924, 23.

71. O'Ryan Report. U.S. Senate, Committee on Investigation of United States Veterans' Bureau, Second Preliminary Report, (pursuant to S. Res. 466, 67th Cong., 4th sess.) 68th Cong., 1st sess. Report No. 103, Part 2, 7 February 1924, 18.

72. Ibid., 18.

73. Ibid., 4.

74. Ibid., 4–8.

75. Senate Hearings on VB, 20.

76. Frank T. Hines, "Placing the War Veteran in Industry." *Nation's Business*, 5 June 1923, 11, 7.

# Disability

# 3

## Architecture of Injury

### Disabled Veterans, Federal Policy, and the Built Environment in the Early Twentieth Century

JOHN M. KINDER

Since the mid-nineteenth century, when modern war first emerged as a total
izing force in Western societies, military conflict has transformed the built
environment in profound and unexpected ways.[1] To be sure, war has left behind a legacy of unparalleled destruction. The landscape of war is scarred with
bombed-out cathedrals, ruined cities, and other architectural casualties. Indeed, as critic Robert Bevan recently argued, the intentional devastation of
public spaces and cultural landmarks has become a defining feature of modern
warfare. From the firebombing of Dresden in World War II to the shelling of
the Stari Most bridge in the Bosnian War, clashing armies have deliberately
targeted the built environment as a means of terrorizing civilian populations
and erasing cultural patrimony.[2]

Yet war's impact on the built environment is by no means limited to material
trauma. On the contrary, the prosecution of modern warfare inevitably sparks
massive building projects, both in theater and at home. Waging war, even on a
limited scale, requires the construction of a wide array of utilitarian building
types—supply depots, administration offices, barracks, and the like—without
which military operations quickly grind to a halt. With a few notable exceptions, such as the Pentagon, the vast majority of the structures erected to meet
wartime exigencies are dismantled within a half-decade of war's end. Those
that persist typically have one of two aims: commemorating the conflict (military cemeteries, monuments, war memorials) or helping war's survivors transition to civilian life (pension offices, veterans' halls, military hospitals, clinics).

This chapter explores the relationship between one particular set of structures, which I call the architecture of injury, and federal veterans' policy in late-
nineteenth- and early-twentieth-century America. I use this term to describe
the myriad architectural constructions, spatial organizations, and built envi-

ronments that emerged in response to the "problem of the disabled veteran," a perceived crisis about the social legacies of war disability between the Civil War and World War II.[3] As Americans' anxieties about the fate of disabled ex-soldiers reached new heights, the U.S. military, the federal government, and veterans' groups experimented with a number of built "solutions" to mitigate the long-term effects of war-produced trauma—from work camps and charity houses to federally funded residential hospitals and asylums. Taken together, this architecture of injury represented an unprecedented expenditure of public and private resources to house, care for, and rehabilitate the United States' disabled veterans. Equally important, it reflected a growing tendency among policymakers to craft veterans' policy in spatial terms, wedding specific policy aims to the construction of specific built environments.

Unfortunately, scholars of U.S. veterans' policy have paid scant attention to the spatial politics of federal disability policy.[4] To date, much of the literature on U.S. veterans' policy has been written by economic and political historians, many of whom highlight the monetary and legal dimensions of disabled veterans' relief while ignoring the ways federal disability policy has been incorporated within and expressed through the built environment.[5] In this chapter, I offer a different approach to the architecture of injury, one that is guided by two interrelated premises. The first premise is that there is a close connection between the spaces people traverse, the buildings they inhabit, and the ways they come to understand the world. Spatial arrangements—from the scale of a single building to that of an entire built environment—are rarely if ever ideologically neutral. Rather, they exist within a complex interplay of factors (legal systems, cultural attitudes, professional practices) that shape social relations and produce individual and collective identities.[6] In the case of the United States' architecture of injury, built structures such as demobilization centers and military hospitals served as much more than useful locations for introducing disabled veterans to state aid. The buildings themselves—and the ways veterans interacted within them—constituted the material and experiential articulations of federal veterans' policy.

The second premise is that spatial arrangements play an important role in the construction of "disability" as both a group identity and social experience.[7] Disability is the product of a complex set of interactions between people with physical and mental impairments and the sociocultural and architectural environments they inhabit.[8] Historically, such environments have resulted in what Robert Wilton has described as the "spatial exclusion of disabled people from everyday life."[9] Despite long-standing patterns of economic deprivation and social marginality, however, the experience of disability and the social meanings ascribed to disabled people are seldom static or uniform. In fact, disabled veterans have been quite adept at using spatial arrangements—from separate parade floats to veterans-only camp grounds—to carve out a privileged social status for themselves and their families, above that afforded to other veteran groups or civilian disabled populations.

Although this essay touches on several built environments, three veterans' institutions receive special attention: the National Home for Disabled Volunteer Soldiers (NHDVS), federal reconstruction hospitals and vocational schools, and disabled veterans' farm colonies. I have chosen these particular institutions because they collectively reflect the three most common spatial strategies the federal government used to solve the problem of the disabled veteran in the decades between the Civil War and World War II. Built to house disabled Union veterans, the NHDVS was governed by a spatial strategy of institutional domestication, establishing group homes for disabled veterans set apart—socially and geographically—from the rest of the American body politic. World War I–era reconstruction hospitals and vocational schools, by contrast, pursued a spatial strategy of reintegration. Unlike soldiers' homes, they were not designed to permanently concentrate disabled veterans into institutional settings; instead, their primary aim was to help disabled vets assimilate into the public sphere as productive and normatively masculine citizen-workers. I conclude with a brief look at a group of disabled veterans' farm colonies established in rural Minnesota in the early 1920s. An experiment in communal living, farm colonies ultimately reflected a spatial strategy of marginalization, relegating disabled veterans—individually and collectively—to the fringes of U.S. society.

Examining soldiers' homes, rehabilitation centers, and veterans' farm colonies can shed new light on the various ways the federal government conceived of and responded to the social and material consequences of military engagement. As we shall see, the spatial politics of late-nineteenth- and early-twentieth-century veterans' policy was intimately bound up with broader concerns about gender, work, and the "place" of disabled veterans in postwar American society. Ultimately, I suggest that one cannot fully understand the implications and consequences of federal disability policy without considering the built environments in which such policies are enacted, contested, and experienced.

## Domesticating Disabled Veterans: The National Home for Disabled Volunteer Soldiers

Of all the built environments constructed to care for sick and disabled veterans, none inspired greater praise—and greater condemnation—than the soldiers' home. From the 1860s until the early 1900s, federally funded soldiers' homes were the gold standard against which other architectural models of veterans' care were measured. To many observers, they appeared both luxurious and orderly—the ideal sanctuary for men who bore the scars of battle. Not all Americans agreed that building permanent residential institutions represented the best solution to the nation's disabled veteran problem, however. As the United States' premier architecture of injury, federal soldiers' homes provided war-injured men with shelter and security, but at what price?

The underlying principles of the federal soldiers' home date back to the early modern period, when the rise of national armies radically transformed the relationship between disabled veterans and the state. Prior to that time, most disabled vets in Western Europe and the North American colonies were geographically and socially dispersed, reliant upon private charities and religious monasteries for their daily survival. Beginning in the 1500s, however, European governments began to enact their own measures to care for the men injured in wartime service. Such measures typically came in the form of monetary pensions and, by the mid-1600s, soldiers' homes—the twin pillars of federal disability policy from the early modern period to World War I. Part of a broader pattern of disciplinary internment, government efforts to resettle indigent and disabled veterans into state-sponsored infirmaries, asylums, and residential homes left two long-standing legacies. On the one hand, they placed the welfare of war-injured soldiers—increasingly viewed as public menaces—under the authority of government officials. On the other hand, bringing disabled veterans together within a delimited space encouraged a sense of shared political consciousness among veteran internees. Indeed, in the century leading up to American independence, the collective identity of disabled veterans was as much a product of the soldiers' home as it was of the battlefield.[10]

The most prominent veterans' institution to emerge from Enlightenment-era Europe was France's Hôtel des Invalides, a massive veterans' hospital and retirement facility built in central Paris in the 1670s. Renowned for its architectural splendor, L'Hôtel housed more than four thousand sick, disabled, and aged veterans in a complex of buildings just outside the city center. Once admitted, men received food, shelter, and medical care. In return, they were treated as virtual prisoners, their behavior and movement regulated according to a strict set of military guidelines. Although critics charged that the Hôtel des Invalides consigned its wards to lives of unmanly idleness, the home helped establish the principle of institutional segregation, the cornerstone of the spatial politics of disabled veterans' policy in the West for the next three centuries. In effect, it sent the message that the proper "place" for disabled veterans was (within) a state institution, set apart from other dependent populations.[11]

Although the U.S. federal government quickly adopted the European principle of pensioning disabled veterans, it did not construct ex-soldiers' homes of any significance until the mid-nineteenth century.[12] The delay can be attributed to several factors. In the eyes of many political elites, lavish institutions like the Hôtel des Invalides were not only too expensive but out of step with the democratic ethos and aesthetics of the fledgling republic. Furthermore, throughout the first six decades of U.S. history, it was common practice to reward disabled veterans—indeed all ex-soldiers—with public land, a policy that both relocated disabled veterans to the hinterlands and helped tighten the United States' grasp on the North American continent. By 1850 disabled veterans' need for some kind of permanent institutional assistance proved impossible to ignore, and Congress established the United States Soldiers' Home in Washington, D.C., for veterans of the Regular Army and the expansionist campaign in Mexico. However, the federal government did not take steps toward building the United States' first "comprehensive system of veterans' institutional care" until fifteen years later, as the Civil War drew to a bloody close. As the system's centerpiece, the National Home for Volunteer Disabled Soldiers would shelter nearly one hundred thousand disabled and indigent Union veterans by the century's end.[13] It would also serve as a model for countless state and local institutions designed to house the nation's disabled veterans.

The decision to build the National Home was inspired as much out of social necessity as public sympathy. Arguably the first modern war, the Civil War ushered in a frightening new age of industrialized slaughter. Besides rifled muskets—standard issue in the North by 1861—Civil War soldiers wielded a diverse arsenal of weapons, including Gatling machine guns, breech-loading and magazine arms, exploding artillery shells, and canister shot (tin cans filled with grape-sized bullets). While viewed as something of an "aberration" by many Americans, the Civil War proved how effectively the machinery of industrial capitalism and the modern state could be mobilized in the dissemination of organized violence.[14] The integration of new technologies of communication and transportation, such as telegraphs, railroads, and steam engines, enabled both sides to equip and deploy men to the battlefield with unprecedented speed. The fact that so many men could be mobilized at a single time—up to 1 million for the North and 464,500 for the South—virtually ensured that casualty rates would be high.[15] By war's end, more than a million soldiers had been wounded in action, many with injuries so devastating in function and horrific in appearance that they had little hope of resuming their prewar lives. Among the permanently disabled, tens of thousands of veterans returned home missing a limb, while untold numbers suffered undiagnosed psychological trauma for the rest of their lives.[16]

What would happen to such men? Throughout much of the war, the answer was not immediately clear. The U.S. Soldiers' Home in the nation's capital had room to house only 250 residents, a tiny fraction of the veteran population in need of long-term institutional care. As casualty rolls mounted, female philanthropists set up small soldiers' homes and halfway houses in major cities across the United States. Working out of storefronts or private residences, volunteers provided food, temporary shelter, and medical assistance to thousands of indigent and wayward veterans, including many en route home. But these facilities proved to be stopgap measures at best, and in March 1865 Congress passed the National Asylum for Disabled Volunteer Soldiers Act. In an era that championed laissez-faire government and heroic individualism, the act signaled a dramatic expansion of the social contract between disabled veterans and the American state, one that continues to set disabled veterans apart as a privileged class of U.S. citizens. With the stroke of Lincoln's pen, it was no longer enough to reward disabled veterans with pensions or other forms of monetary assistance; now the federal government had to provide them with food, shelter, and a chance to live out their lives in dignity.[17]

Originally known as the National Asylum for Disabled Volunteer Soldiers (the word "Asylum" would be replaced with "Home" in 1873), America's Invalides was not a single institution but a network of four regional branches serving thousands of veterans every year. At the start, NHDVS admission standards were highly restrictive, with entrance granted only to honorably discharged Union veterans with service-connected disabilities or illnesses. Eventually, however, the National Home became a refuge for a wide range of down-and-out Union veterans, including seemingly healthy men with nowhere else to go. Although the mission of the NHDVS would evolve over time, its board of managers originally designed the network with four goals in mind. First, it was built to provide disabled veterans with "comfort," a Victorian concept that encompassed a state of material and social well-being beyond the mere satisfaction of bodily needs. Second, planners hoped to use the homes to bolster their residents' "sense of manly independence" through "active employment."[18] In addition to living and dining quarters, each branch of the NHDVS contained a central workshop where disabled veterans supplemented their pensions by making shoes, binding books, coopering barrels, and knitting uniforms. Third, the NHDVS was designed to demonstrate the nation's deep gratitude toward its wounded warriors. Writing in 1875, J. C. Gobrecht, author of an early guidebook to the Central Branch, offered a typical assessment: "The Soldiers' Home is a 'living monument'; one upon which the war-worn veteran may gaze with pleasurable emotion as he proudly contemplates it and exclaims: 'I live in the hearts of my countrymen!'"[19]

Finally, and most importantly, the NHDVS was designed to provide disabled Union veterans with a *home*. During the mid-nineteenth century, the home emerged as the key site in the reproduction of bourgeois social relations and behaviors. In addition to serving as a sanctuary from the masculine world of competitive work, the Victorian home came to be idealized as a "seat of moral, aesthetic, and cultural stability" and the spatial center of family life.[20] Within this cultural milieu, homelessness conveyed more than a lack of shelter; it suggested a dangerous and potentially pathological declension from mainstream values and social structures. As Patrick J. Kelly has shown, references to "home" not only saturated NHDVS planning and public discourse but also provided the "conceptual framework within which a generous institution for the care of veterans could be built and governed." Officials at the National Home routinely invoked domestic metaphors to distinguish soldiers' homes from asylums, poorhouses, and other increasingly stigmatized models of institutional care. Equally important, Kelly argues, "By designating veterans' establishments as 'homes' . . . the Board of Managers signaled the state's intention to assume the same domestic responsibilities for veterans, offering food, shelter, clothing, and medical care, as mothers and wives assumed for their families in the nineteenth century household economy."[21] As a result, virtually everything about the National Home—from its architecture to its institutional rituals—was situated within a gendered discourse of domesticity, even if the built environment in its entirety bore little resemblance to the single-family dwellings that epitomized Victorian home life.[22]

Aside from their shared commitment to institutional domesticity, individual branches of the NHDVS were remarkably different in design. Built on a failed health resort in Togus Springs, Maine, the Home's Eastern Branch initially resembled a European square with four reconverted, Second Empire–style buildings surrounding an elegant piazza. After a fire damaged the main living quarters in 1868, the branch expanded dramatically, adding a new barracks, a barn, and eventually an opera house (Figure 3.1).[23] At the Northwestern Branch, near Milwaukee, Wisconsin, architect Edward Townsend Mix followed the "linear plan" favored by Thomas Story Kirkbride, the noted mental health professional and author of several influential works on asylum design.[24] The bulk of the home's activities took place within a grand Gothic-style structure, five stories high and three hundred feet long, with a central tower overlooking Lake Michigan. Designed to centralize living, administrative, and treatment spaces beneath one roof, the main building's wings contained workshops, a three-story hospital, and sleeping quarters for more than six hundred men. The Southern Branch in Hampton Roads, Virginia, was by far the most humble institution in the original NHDVS network. Intended as a sanctuary for African American veterans, the home was located on the former site of a small

EASTERN BRANCH NATIONAL HOM
TOGUS, KENNEBE

COPYRIGHTED BY WM H. PRINCE

Figure 3.1. Formerly a health resort, the Eastern Branch of the National Home for Disabled Volunteer Soldiers at Togus Springs, Maine, was organized around a formal quadrangle made up the residents' barracks and the branch hospital. As it expanded, the campus began to take

ISABLED VOLUNTEER SOLDIERS.
OUNTY, MAINE.

SKETCHED & DRAWN BY WM. H. PRINCE
TOONS. ME.

on a more decentralized design, with smaller residences, workshops, and recreational facilities spread out across the 1,900-acre property. Library of Congress Prints and Photographs Division, Washington, D.C. LC-DIG-ppmsca-08307.

women's college on the shores of Chesapeake Bay.[25] When it opened in 1870, the Southern Branch had room to house only about 350 residents; within the following decade, however, the facility had erected a number of new structures, including a large multipurpose hall containing a library, a bakery, a bowling alley, and a soap factory.[26]

The Central Branch, built a few miles outside of Dayton, Ohio, was the flagship of the NHDVS network. It exemplified a "decentralized model" of asylum construction that would become the hallmark of American soldiers' homes throughout the late nineteenth century. Designed by architect C. B. Davis, the compound's main administrative and residential buildings were organized along a military-style grid. The remaining buildings were spread out over five hundred acres of landscaped gardens and parkland, providing residents with the freedom of movement thought necessary for stimulating physical and mental health. During the mid-1870s, the Central Branch housed more than 2,500 Union veterans, more than the other three branches combined.[27] Residents were responsible for much of the home's daily maintenance, a reflection of NHDVS planners' belief in the moral and salutary benefits of physical labor. Veterans butchered cattle, laundered clothes, upholstered furniture, and erected new buildings, while the Home's workshops—which included a saw-house, various metal shops, a cigar manufactory, and a printing office—employed more than 1,500 men at any given time. In return for their efforts, residents received a modest wage (between thirty and forty cents per day), which they used to purchase goods not provided by the institution itself.

Perhaps the most striking aspect of the Central Branch was not its industrial efficiency but the relative splendor of the home's built environment. Residents enjoyed access to recreational facilities—including a sumptuous music hall—that would have been beyond the reach of many Americans of their era. Moreover, although NHDVS officials were critical of what they perceived as the aesthetic excesses of European veterans' homes, the Central Branch displayed a similar fondness for architectural grandeur, a quality evidenced in everything from the frescoed ceilings of the library to the pinnacled roof and Corinthian columns of the three-story hospital. The home's picturesque landscape, laid out by Thomas Budd Van Horne, a chaplain at the Central Branch, was particularly noteworthy. Described by one commentator as a "paradise of beauty and grace," the grounds were an irregular patchwork of flower gardens, manicured lawns, and secluded groves, interspersed with four small lakes and thick plantings of wild foliage.[28] A popular tourist attraction with picnickers and Civil War enthusiasts, the home featured a grotto, a deer-park, and a conservatory of tropical palms and other exotic plants. The Central Branch even boasted a small menagerie, where visitors and residents alike could spend their afternoons admiring the home's collection of bears, antelopes, and alligators.

Despite their somewhat opulent surroundings, residents could not ignore the institutional nature of their daily lives. Like all branches of the NHDVS network, the Central Home was deliberately located outside of the city, a measure its administrators hoped would not only isolate veterans from the "temptations of urban life" but also prevent sick, disfigured, and otherwise disturbing men from violating the public sphere with their presence.[29] Indoors, privacy was a scarce commodity (each 125 by 56 foot barracks sheltered up to forty men), and residents had little space to call their own. Throughout their stay, the men wore uniforms and were expected to adhere to military discipline. Activities such as eating, working, and attending chapel were highly regimented. Indeed, the home's strict regulations limited many of the social freedoms veterans assumed to be their male birthright. While men were free (and even encouraged) to drop out of the NHDVS network, they could not come and go as they pleased. Veterans who left the home without permission could be fined, and NHDVS officials enforced strict measures to curtail any behavior—such as swearing, drinking excessively, and squandering money—that threatened to disrupt institutional hierarchy or cast the National Home in bad light.

At the same time, the home's policy toward dependent family members made it nearly impossible for residents to fulfill their masculine roles as fathers and heads of households. Because only male veterans were allowed to take up permanent residence in the National Home, men were physically separated from their wives and family, sometimes for years on end. In short, although NHDVS officials were no doubt sincere in their efforts to create a "pleasant, comfortable, and happy HOME" for their residents, the price of institutional domestication—and the social and spatial segregation it seemed to require—was too high for many disabled veterans.[30] As a result, men who could often chose to forgo the relative "comforts" of institutionalized living and strike out on their own.[31]

In spite of such tensions, the NHDVS system continued to expand throughout the late nineteenth and early twentieth centuries. Economic depression and old age forced tens of thousands of Union veterans to seek shelter in federal veterans' homes, where disabled veterans of the Spanish-American War and World War I eventually joined them. In the early 1930s, when the National Home was absorbed within the Veterans Administration system, the network was home to more than 22,500 men (roughly 700 of whom were Civil War vets). In addition to eleven major branches, the NHDVS oversaw thirty-one residential and treatment facilities in cities across the United States.[32]

Nevertheless, the National Home's dominance as the architectural standard for disabled veterans' care was relatively short-lived. Well before the start of World War I, federal veterans' relief in general—and soldiers' homes in particular—began to draw serious criticism from across the political spectrum. Sheltering disabled veterans was notoriously expensive, even when veterans themselves provided much of the labor. Patrick J. Kelly has calculated that the total cost of the NHDVS system between 1866 and 1930 topped $250 million, a staggering sum at the time.[33] Worse still, many Americans believed that federal veterans' homes encouraged unhealthy idleness and dependency in their residents. In an era that conflated economic independence with manliness and good citizenship, critics argued that soldiers' homes transformed disabled veterans into social parasites with little initiative to pursue economic reward. Furthermore, Progressive reformers charged that soldiers' homes—with their military uniforms, hierarchies, and rituals—fostered an unhealthy atmosphere of veteran solidarity, with disabled veterans more concerned about recounting battles past than engaging the issues of the day. In the eyes of many Americans, permanently "entombing" disabled veterans in soldiers' homes was antimodern, wasteful, and cruel. Writing in *The Red Cross Magazine* in May 1919, Progressive reformer Samuel Hopkins Adams announced that the age of the soldiers' home was over. Americans were "no longer content to accept for our maimed and crippled a future which will commit them to the life of fungi. A place in the social and economic world must be found for them."[34]

## Reintegrating Disabled Veterans: Federal Reconstruction Hospitals and Vocational Schools

If the Civil War ushered in a period of institutionalized domestication, the architecture of injury to emerge from World War I would reflect a far different set of policy aims. As Americans increasingly saw it, the soldiers' home was an anachronism, a relic of an era in which the federal government's primary obligation to disabled veterans was to provide them with a monetary pension and a roof over their heads. Beginning in late 1910s, however, American policymakers opted for a decidedly "modern" solution to the problem of the disabled veteran, one that continues to serve as the backbone of federal disability policy to this day: rehabilitation. With it would come an entirely new set of built environments—reconstruction hospitals, vocational schools, among others—all designed to ease disabled veterans' return to civilian life.

Instituted in varying degrees by all of the Great War's belligerent nations, rehabilitation was an integrated program of occupational therapy and vocational training combining orthopedics, physical reconstruction, psychological counseling, and industrial discipline. Its goal was to help disabled veterans reintegrate into peacetime society as productive and economically independent citizen-workers. As both a social ideal and set of medico-vocational practices, rehabilitation was not entirely new. Reform-minded physicians had experimented with rehabilitation techniques (with limited success) in the immediate aftermath of the Civil War. In subsequent decades, European and American charity groups established a number of small training asylums for "congenital cripples" and victims of industrial accidents or disease. Models for later institutions, they provided students with specialized training in basket weaving, shoe repair, and other occupations considered well suited for the bodily impaired.[35]

Western governments did not fully embrace rehabilitation efforts on a national scale until World War I, a conflict of unprecedented human and material destruction that left more than eight million veterans disabled because of injury or disease.[36] Although U.S. troops were spared the worst of the carnage, more than 224,000 doughboys were seriously wounded in combat, including large numbers from German artillery and weaponized gas.[37] Tens of thousands more suffered the lingering effects of accidents, disease, and "shell shock," a neuropathological condition whose debilitating symptoms were said to stem from the "stress and special horrors of modern warfare."[38] Rapid advances in wound treatment and military psychiatry allowed many war-wounded doughboys to recover from their injuries. Even so, roughly 200,000 U.S. servicemen returned from the Great War with permanent physical and mental impairments.[39]

As had been the case following the Civil War, it was initially unclear what would become of the latest generation of disabled vets. Throughout the war years, Progressive reformers, politicians, military officials, and veterans themselves forecast a number of different scenarios—nearly all bad. Some predicted that the high cost of veterans' care would drain the public coffers, sending the U.S. economy spiraling into depression. Others worried that disabled veterans' impairments and dependencies—on the state, their families, and female caregivers—would prevent them from meeting the rigorous demands of normative masculinity.[40] Still others conjured nightmarish visions of armies of "war cripples" begging on the streets and menacing the civilian population. Whatever the scenario, all parties agreed on two things: first, that veterans' homes on the order of the NHDVS were no longer a viable solution; and second, that the problem of the disabled veteran would not go away on its own. The federal government had to take action, and it had to do so, critics argued, without the sentimentality and hero worship that had reduced Civil War veterans to lives of "idleness and dependency."[41]

On this final point, the soldiers' rehabilitation movement was typical of a number of Progressive era reform projects. It was undergirded by an abiding faith in the power of science and rational planning to confront (and eventually resolve) the social problems of industrial modernity.[42] Moreover, the ideological underpinnings of rehabilitation were highly normative, reflecting the social, economic, and gender ideals of the middle- and upper-class reformers who made up its most vocal champions. Though the primary goal of rehabilitation was to provide disabled veterans with the skills necessary to secure long-term employment, the movement also sought to inculcate trainees in the values Progressives considered to be the building blocks of national health: efficiency, independence, social responsibility, and gender normativity. As one supporter enthused in September 1918, rehabilitation would transform the war-disabled into "almost perfect men again—useful citizens, who despite their handicaps of missing legs and arms and eyes, [would] walk and work among their fellows again, shave themselves, roll their makin's unassisted, and pile up their savings until they own (and drive) their flivvers back among the home folks."[43] At their most optimistic, the movement's supporters believed that rehabilitated veterans would be more socially and economically viable than when they had entered service. Indeed, some predicted that rehabilitation—once expanded to civilian populations—would eventually bring about the "end" of disability in modern life.[44]

The federal government did not wait until the end of World War I to put its plans into action—or to start building architectural structures meant to promote disabled veterans' smooth reintegration into civilian society. In June 1918 Congress passed the Vocational Rehabilitation Act, which authorized extensive medical treatment and job training for all disabled veterans. The act divided the rehabilitation process (or, in military euphemism, the "career of the disabled soldier") into two stages—physical reconstruction and vocational education—each centered on a specific set of spatial environments. The goal of the first stage, which began the moment a soldier was injured, was the restoration of bodily function and, to a lesser extent, appearance. Military physicians and "reconstruction aides" employed a wide array of treatment methods and specialized apparatuses (e.g., hydrotherapy, radiant light therapy, skin grafts) to rebuild the bodies and minds of America's wounded warriors. Much of this work took place on hospital ships and at large reconstruction hospitals stateside, where recovering soldiers remained under military supervision.

In an effort to boost morale, it was common practice to segregate certain classes of disabled men—usually those with the most stigmatized impairments—from the rest of the hospital population. Blind patients, for example, convalesced at General Hospital #7, a converted plantation just outside of Baltimore, Maryland. "Shell-shocked" soldiers, on the other hand, were typically sent to General Hospital #30 in Plattsburgh Barracks, New York, where their disturbing symptoms remained invisible to the vast majority of their fellow patients.[45] No matter where they recovered, all patients were expected to engage in some kind of "curative work" during their stay. At General Hospital #28, located on an old Army post in suburban Chicago, patients wove baskets, built furniture, learned telegraphy, and printed their own newspaper, *The Fort Sheridan Recall*.[46] According to the surgeon general's office, such activities not only hastened patients' physical recovery but also inspired the men to "qualify [themselves] for future occupation." By the start of 1919 the U.S. military was carrying out physical reconstruction work at forty-five hospitals, including the nation's largest facility, Walter Reed Hospital in Washington, D.C.[47]

Once their physical reconstruction was deemed complete, disabled veterans were mustered out of service, at which point tens of thousands of men chose to abandon their rehabilitation "careers" altogether. The rest began a stint—sometimes as long as five years—at a federally approved training facility. In an effort to cut costs, the Federal Bureau for Vocational Education, the agency initially in charge of the second stage of the rehabilitation process, decided to outsource nearly all of veterans' training to the private sector. Within three years of the Great War's end, the federal government secured contracts with more than 3,500 commercial schools, correspondence programs, and universities, as well as with 30,000 individual businesses, to provide academic and vocational education to disabled veterans. When these proved inadequate, the newly formed U.S. Veterans Bureau (USVB) established the first of forty-nine vocational schools for disabled veterans in November 1921.[48] Federal vocational schools came in three types—civilian rehabilitation centers, nonresidential schools, and residential schools—each differing in both function and design.

Civilian rehabilitation centers were located in Public Service Hospitals and typically reflected the clinical settings of their home institutions. As with the "curative work" programs found in Army reconstruction hospitals, their central aim was to provide ailing veterans with occupational therapy and limited vocational training during their convalescence. Much of this training took place in the soldiers' individual beds or in small classroom environments, where a half-dozen or more patients might spend a few hours each day making crafts and building up their bodily strength. Like other federal vocational schools, civilian rehabilitation centers offered vets an opportunity to socialize, learn basic job skills, and gain self-confidence. However, civilian rehabilitation centers were unique in one regard: they were established within preexisting medical facilities. Thus, patients were expected to eat, sleep, and train on the hospital grounds—all under the watchful gaze of medical authorities.

Nonresidential schools, by contrast, were stand-alone institutions. Founded in urban areas and small residential communities where trainees had easy access to private housing, they were largely designed to provide "try-out" courses to help veterans determine their future career objectives. Many offered day and evening classes as well as opportunities for students to pursue independent academic work related to their vocational interests. In addition, some schools administered terminal training programs in such varied trades as photography, sign painting, and music.[49] Unlike NHDVS soldiers' homes, nonresidential vocational schools emphasized functionality over ornament. Most facilities were small and drab, with few of the material "comforts" of the National Home (this is partly due, of course, to the fact that students were not expected to live on campus).

The USVB vocational school in Atlanta was typical in this regard. When Florence A. Egan, a Veterans Bureau field officer, first visited the school in April 1922, she discovered more than 130 students crowded into a single, inadequate room (180 by 165 feet) on the second floor of a rundown commercial building. The floors were covered in grime, and due to poor ventilation and the constant use of electric lights, the temperature inside the school was stifling. For all its faults, however, the Atlanta vocational school was hardly the worst of its kind. Although the facility lacked key equipment, its instructional staff was top-notch—something that could not be said about many schools within the USVB network. Nonresidential schools were notoriously underfunded, and because the work was meant to be temporary (the last nonresidential school shut its doors in 1925), they had a difficult time attracting qualified teachers.[50]

In turn, even the best nonresidential schools seemed to send mixed messages to their students about the "place" of disabled veterans in postwar society. On the one hand, as with all USVB vocational schools, their educational mission was to transform disabled vets into independent, economically viable, and socially "normal" citizens—men who saw themselves as Americans first, disabled veterans second. On the other hand, in their attempts to address the psychological and recreational needs of their students, USVB schools (somewhat inadvertently) cultivated a sense of community and shared identity among their disabled trainees. Once again, the Atlanta vocational school was characteristic of many nonresidential schools. In addition to its other activities, the school sponsored a Saturday morning speakers' series, a literary society, dances, and athletic events for disabled veterans and their families.[51]

Although federal residential schools made up only sixteen of the forty-nine educational facilities in the USVB network, in both their goals and architectural environments, they represented the greatest long-term challenge to the soldiers' home model of veterans' care. Originally, residential schools were meant to function like halfway houses for discharged veterans—mainly tubercular and neuropsychiatric cases—who were not yet healthy enough to meet the demands of fulltime training. Quickly, however, they opened their doors to broader populations of Great War veterans, including men with little need of therapeutic care. Offering an alternative to both soldiers' homes and private training facilities, federal residential schools allowed disabled veterans to engage in comprehensive vocational training for years on end—all on Uncle Sam's dime. Upon their "rehabilitation," Great War vets would graduate with the job skills necessary to lead an independent life and, policymakers hoped, escape the institutionalized fate of their Civil War forbearers.

The first and largest vocational school was Camp Sherman, a sprawling 4,800-acre complex established on a former military barracks and P.O.W. camp near Chillicothe, Ohio. The camp was reserved for men whose injuries were of a "general medical and surgical nature" (shell-shocked men, veterans with pulmonary disease, and other "undesirables" were sent elsewhere), and very few of the trainees exhibited obvious signs of disfigurement. In its built environment and landscape design, Camp Sherman shared little of the picturesque splendor of the Central Home, located about seventy-five miles to the northwest. At best, the camp resembled a cross between a military installation and a rural agricultural college, which essentially was what it was. One-half of the campus was devoted to farming, with large pens teeming with cattle, chickens, and hogs. Leftovers from the war years, most of the buildings were constructed of rough-hewn wooden planks, giving the entire camp an air of martial utilitarianism.

Upon his first inspection in January 1921, Robert S. Marx, national commander of the Disabled Veterans of the World War, declared Camp Sherman a "farce and a fraud," a reference in part to the camp's poor living, training, and medical facilities.[52] Early on, rehabbing vets bedded down in barracks, barns, and wherever else they could find room. Eventually, married trainees moved into small, sparsely furnished apartments (two to six families per building) while single men bunked together in two-story dormitories in the middle of campus.[53]

When they were not eating or performing chores, residents spent most of their waking hours in one of Camp Sherman's twelve workshops. The camp offered courses in twenty-seven lines of work, including tire repair, carpentry, and beekeeping. Outside of class, students occupied their time with a host of specially approved amusements. Convinced that idleness bred immorality and dissent, Camp Sherman's directors relied heavily upon athletics and other body-wearying activities to keep the men busy from morning until night. To this end, the camp boasted a swimming pool, a rifle range, and a massive recreational hall complete with a dance floor, six bowling alleys, and an after-hours canteen.[54]

Despite such amenities, friction between students and staff remained a constant source of tension throughout the USVB system. Now civilians, veterans bristled at the strict rules imposed at federal facilities, particularly as rehabilitation ideology stressed the importance of personal independence. In June 1921 students at the government rehabilitation center in Pascagoula, Mississippi, staged a two-day strike to protest poor living conditions and ill treatment from the staff.[55] For their part, USVB instructors complained that most veteran-students lacked the discipline and intelligence necessary to pursue all but the most menial of trades. According to E. G. Dexter, Camp Sherman's commander, "The morale problem in Vocational School No. 1 was not unlike that in other institutions where a considerable number of physical adults, who are at the same time mental semi-adults, are congregated."[56] Such attitudes reflected the paternalism inherent in many Progressive reform projects; they also highlighted a significant difference between Great War–era rehabilitation schools and post–Civil War veterans' homes. At the National Home, veterans themselves occupied key positions of authority. In federal rehabilitation facilities, on the other hand, those roles were typically filled by civilian "experts"—teachers, psychologists, counselors, orthopedists—whose professional and ideological agendas did not necessarily align with those of the men in their charge.[57]

Federal vocational schools such as Camp Sherman differed from soldiers' homes in several other ways as well. For one thing, all USVB training facilities, even residential schools, were meant to serve as little more than transitional environments for disabled veterans. At most, the federal government expected disabled veterans to stay a few years, and many rehab facilities actively encouraged their students to spend as much time off campus as possible. Furthermore, because the ultimate goal of rehabilitation was to help ex-servicemen assimilate as "normal" citizens, USVB vocational schools had little interest in nurturing a culture of veteran solidarity among their students. Rehabilitationists believed that former soldiers would never be able to readjust fully to peacetime society until they rid themselves of their wartime identities and allegiances. As a result, many rehab facilities preached a gospel of "demilitarization," urging their students to put the Great War behind them as soon as possible.

Most important of all, there was little sense that this latest architecture of injury would remain a permanent part of the national landscape. Once the problem of the disabled veteran had been solved, policymakers predicted, government-sponsored rehabilitation schools would be shut down or reconfigured for alternative uses, as had been the case for many temporary structures built to meet wartime exigencies. As it turns out, the Veterans Bureau did not wait long before dismantling its network of vocational schools. Most schools went out of business within the first two years, well before the work of rehabilitation was complete. When Camp Sherman closed shop in 1924, only 341 of its 1,250 students had received a diploma. The rest had transferred to a private facility, terminated their work, or, in the case of one student, died.[58]

## Marginalizing Disabled Veterans: Disabled Veterans' Farm Colonies

No matter how you look at it, rehabilitation's architecture of injury—including civilian rehabilitation centers, nonresidential schools, and residential training facilities—reflected a profound shift in the spatial politics of federal disability policy. From an architectural perspective, it challenged the long-standing link between federal veterans' facilities and an aesthetics of comfortable domestication. Just as significant, it signaled a growing consensus among disability policymakers that the best "place" for disabled veterans was not in a gender-segregated group home but rather in their own private residences, where they would cast off their veteran identities and take up their lives as "normal" men. Despite rehabilitation's widespread appeal, however, not all Americans believed that social and spatial reintegration represented the best strategy for solving the problem of the disabled veteran after World War I. A small yet vocal group of political figures favored rewarding disabled ex-servicemen with rural homesteads, a practice that dated back to the Revolutionary War.

Leading the way was Secretary of the Interior Franklin K. Lane, a California politician with a penchant for outdoor life. Lane worried that the pleasures and economic opportunities of urban America would lure many returning veterans away from their prewar homes, setting the stage for demographic unrest for decades to come. As early as 1918, he drew up extensive plans to resettle former doughboys in small cooperative farm colonies on unimproved public lands. The following year, the U.S. War Department distributed more than a million copies of "'The Rube's Day is Done': Forward to the Farm—Why Not?" (1919), a sixteen-page pamphlet outlining the civic virtues of agricultural life. Among other misconceptions, the pamphlet sought to dispel the stereotype that farmers were uneducated "rubes," cut off from modern technological society. Today's farmer, the pamphlet argued, was "apt to be a scientific expert who has been to the State agricultural college. He receives frequent bulletins from the United States Department of Agriculture. He reads high-class magazines devoted to the farm and country life."[59] Although the back-to-the-farm movement gained extensive support throughout the Great War era, Lane's specific plan to establish cooperative colonies of veteran-farmers proved much more controversial. Critics charged that that the idea "smacked of 'socialism,'" and due to a shortage of tillable land and congressional support, the secretary's resettlement schemes were soon abandoned.[60]

The one major exception was an experimental program, sponsored by District #10 of the Veterans Bureau and the University of Minnesota School of Agriculture, to establish farm colonies for rehabilitated veterans in the upper Midwest. On paper, disabled veterans' farm colonies combined the best elements of both institutional domesticity and rehabilitation. Like soldiers' homes, they promised disabled veterans a sense of community often missing in the competitive world of the capitalist marketplace. At the same time, they offered disabled veterans an opportunity to avoid the stigma of dependency and to achieve a semblance of economic (and masculine) autonomy. While no one expected individual veterans to get rich, the plan's supporters believed that cooperative farming would allow war-wounded men a chance to live out the American Dream with minimal government expense.

In 1922, after an extensive search for suitable locations, the Veterans Bureau established five small farm colonies—Argonne Farms, Veteransville, Silver Star, Onamina, and Moose Lake—in rural Minnesota, home to the largest number of disabled agricultural trainees in the nation. In an effort to accommodate the diminished health of the colonists (the men suffered from psychological trauma, arrested tuberculosis, and various other ailments), planners modeled the individual properties on the small, intensive farms that doughboys had encountered in wartime France. Although residents cooperated regularly on clearing land and erecting communal buildings, veteran farm colonists did not share living quarters, as had been the case at federal soldiers' homes and residential rehabilitation schools. Rather, each man was responsible for building his own home, according to a standard design—a policy that both ensured a sense of uniformity to the built environment and reaffirmed the colonists' commitment to the value of private property. By April 1923, 138 disabled veterans and their families were living in Minnesota farm colonies.[61]

Conditions at the colonies were far from luxurious. At Veteransville, located about ninety miles north of Minneapolis, the land was studded with thousands of hardwood stumps, which the colonists had to remove by hand. Farmers and their families lived in simple log cabins, and when they were not clearing fields, they earned money selling poultry and vegetables in towns nearby (Figure 3.2). Life at Argonne Farms, Minnesota's most populous farm colony, was little better. The colony was situated on 160 acres of partly timbered swampland about twenty miles south of Saint Paul. The property had been collectively purchased and then divided into small plots, between three and seven acres apiece. The Veterans Bureau hired a landscape architect and a master carpenter to give the colony a coherent design, with clusters of homes, garages, and other buildings spread out across a picturesque landscape of bogs and gentle inclines. In the early weeks, a number of colonists camped out on the ground or sought temporary shelter in chicken coops, some of the first structures to be erected on the property. Eventually, Argonne Farms' thirty-plus families settled into identical four-room bungalows (24 by 32 feet) without electricity, plumbing, or insulation against the harsh Minnesota winters.[62]

Despite the rough conditions, both residents and Veterans Bureau officials were initially optimistic about the colonies' long-term success. At Argonne Farms, colonists specialized in raising poultry and growing raspberries, while individual farmers harvested small crops of celery, onions, and pickling cucumbers. As the population increased, colonists dug community wells, built a cooperative school and union church, and established the Argonne Farms Egg and Berry Association, a trade group that marketed the colonies' products. The Disabled American Veterans of the World War, the nation's premier disabled veterans' service organization, even established a colony post.[63]

Yet only a few months elapsed before the colonies began to exhibit signs of trouble. In 1923 investigations by the American Legion and the Veterans Bu-

Figure 3.2. This man is building a small log cabin on the Veterans Bureau farm colony of Veteransville, Minnesota. The colony was situated on a large tract of cutover land, much of which had to be cleared before residents could build their homes. Unlike the homesteads at the more densely populated Argonne Farms, the farms at Veteransville averaged sixty acres apiece, large enough to plant corn and raise dairy cattle. Veterans Veteransville, 1922. Minnesota Historical Society, Saint Paul, Minnesota.

reau detailed numerous complaints among residents about inadequate training, inflated property prices, and poor soil quality.[64] Due to a shortage of available farmland, the colonies were located in swampy or cutover areas, which the government had failed to improve prior to the veterans' arrival. For many disabled men, the backbreaking work of pulling stumps, clearing brush, and readying their farms for cultivation proved physically impossible. At Veteransville, four men suffered physical and mental breakdowns within the first year (one man died, another suffered fits of epilepsy, and the remaining two were institutionalized for tuberculosis). Moreover, although all of the men received training at the Minnesota School of Agriculture, few had any real experience managing a farm. During the colonies' early years, most families were able to bankroll their farms by selling produce or using the veterans' training stipends to pay down high interest rates. But after the government appropriations for agricultural rehabilitation ended in 1926, a wave of foreclosures and sellouts emptied the colonies of their original inhabitants.[65] By 1930, when the Farmer's Rural Credit Administration assumed control of the colonies, 75 percent of the farms had been abandoned.[66]

In retrospect, many involved with Minnesota's farm colonies came to believe the experiment in collective living had been doomed from the start. E. L. Holton, dean of vocation at Kansas State Agricultural College and director of farm instruction in Minnesota, claimed that the "theory of group settlements" prevented disabled veterans from rubbing shoulders with "real farmers." Holton further criticized the decision to locate the colonies on unimproved land. Clearing cutover land "was a job for the able-bodied," he argued, "and not for those who were in physical distress."[67] For their part, many veterans believed unscrupulous real estate operators had swindled them into purchasing poor land at inflated prices. In 1925 Dr. Roy Benham, a Minneapolis real estate agent, was indicted for committing grand larceny and fraud at Argonne Farms. When charges were dropped following the death of the complaining witness, the bitterness of disabled veterans and their neighbors became palpable.[68] "Any man with farm experience over the road through Argonne Farms would know that the land there never was or would be worth $204 an acre for farming purposes," observed one outraged neighbor. He concluded, "Uncle Sam's arm of justice must be palsified if it cannot reach out and punish the perpetrator of this tragic joke on veterans."[69]

Today, the Great War's disabled veterans' farm colonies have faded from public memory. Argonne Village, a suburban strip mall in Lakeville, Minnesota, is all that remains of the settlement that once shared its name. Yet the failure of Minnesota's disabled veterans' farm colonies was by no means preordained, as Holton and others would claim. With proper funding, management, and implementation, the "theory of group settlement" might very well have proven successful, particularly if limited to disabled veterans with strong backgrounds in agriculture. Theoretically, collective farming offered disabled veterans not only the communal structure of institutionalized living but also the personal autonomy necessary to fulfill their culturally prescribed roles as husbands, fathers, and economic actors. Unfortunately, due to poor planning and execution, Minnesota's farm colonies produced an entirely different result: the social and spatial marginalization of disabled veterans and their families. Instead of helping disabled veterans reintegrate into peacetime society, the USVB relocated them to land of little monetary or agricultural value. Once there, most residents found themselves both literally and metaphorically out of place, cut off from the familiar surroundings and communal ties they knew prior to their injuries. Given such circumstances, it is somewhat amazing that Minnesota's veteran-pioneers stuck it out as long as they did.

## Conclusions

Soldiers' homes, federal vocational schools, and disabled veterans' farm colonies were not the only built environments constructed in response to the problem of the disabled veteran. In the seventy-five years between the end of the Civil War and the start of World War II, Americans built a wide array of structures to shelter, house, and heal the nation's disabled vets. Besides hospitals, psychiatric asylums, and tuberculosis colonies, the United States' architecture of injury included summer camps, clubhouses, and canteens—intimate spaces where war-wounded men could seek the community and understanding necessary to ease their transition to civilian life. In many respects, the existence of such structures testifies to the ways in which disabled veterans—indeed, all disabled people—found themselves increasingly isolated in modern American society. Put another way, for all of the government's efforts, disabled veterans remained (and continue to remain) a "problem" population, whose very presence disrupts normative ideals about the body and public space.

Taken together, soldiers' homes, federal vocational schools, and disabled veterans' farm colonies are especially significant because they represented the three most common spatial strategies late-nineteenth- and early-twentieth-century Americans used to fulfill the nation's social compact with disabled vets. The NHDVS implemented a strategy of institutional domestication, providing disabled veterans with permanent homes in comfortable, albeit socially segregated, settings. Federal vocational schools urged a strategy of social reintegration, returning disabled veterans to civilian life as rehabilitated workers. Disabled veterans' farm colonies tried to do both (e.g., segregate and reintegrate), yet for all their fine intentions, they wound up further marginal-izing disabled veterans and their families. Despite their significant differences, however, soldiers' homes, rehabilitation schools, and disabled veterans' farm colonies shared at least one thing in common: all three highlighted disabled veterans' individual and collective resistance to the built environments con-structed in their name. From the architectural splendor of the National Home to the drafty log cabins at Veteransville, disabled veterans routinely disrupted the smooth rhetoric of design and function, reconstructing the architecture of injury (and their relationship to it) to meet their needs and desires.

For scholars of federal veterans' policy, soldiers' homes, rehabilitation schools, and disabled veterans' farm colonies offer additional lessons. First, they remind us that the "discursive support for military conflict" is not limited to words, images, and ideas.[70] The built environment also plays an important role in making modern warfare appear reasonable, survivable, and worthy of mass support. In turn, the United States' architecture of injury reveals not only different philosophies of disabled veterans' relief but competing social visions of modern war's impact on American life. Soldiers' homes (and, to a lesser extent, disabled veterans' farm colonies) indexed what might be described as a traumatic vision of modern war, one in which the effects of military conflict continue to linger—in the bodies of disabled veterans and in the built environ-ment—for decades to come. Federal rehabilitation schools, on the other hand, sent a far less troubling message. They implied that war was ultimately a transi-tory phenomenon, one that could be easily reconciled with the nation's needs and international ambitions. Thanks to the benefits of science and technology, rehabilitation's supporters argued, disabled men would be able to "return to normalcy" (to quote Warren G. Harding's famous 1920 presidential slogan) within a handful of years. Indeed, I would suggest that the much of the appeal of soldiers' rehabilitation—both in the aftermath of World War I and today—stems from its promise of trauma-free warfare.

Finally, it is my hope that the architecture of injury will prompt scholars to think carefully about how the ideologies (and effects) of federal veterans' policy are incorporated within the built environment. To borrow a phrase from Melanie McAlister, veterans' policy "is a semiotic activity, not only because it is articulated and transmitted through texts but also because the policies themselves construct meanings."[71] I contend that scholars can gain a richer understanding of U.S. veterans' policy by examining a set of spatial "texts"—hospitals, military bases, communal homes, veterans' halls—that have been largely overlooked by political and architectural historians alike. Only then can we begin to appreciate how the politics of veterans' policy shapes (and is shaped by) the practices of everyday life.

# Notes

1. I employ a flexible understanding of modern war, one that foregrounds the application of instrumental rationality to questions of warfare and logistics; the use of techniques of industrial production; the blurring between civilians and combatants; and the tension between war's role in the construction of racial or national identity and its capacity to undermine, disturb, or dismantle political and social institutions. Furthermore, because modern war depends heavily on the active participation of the population at large, it is characterized by an increased investment in technologies of mass communication and commemoration (the printing press, radio, film, architecture) to mobilize public support and to concretize war's memory.

2. Robert Bevan, *The Destruction of Memory: Architecture at War* (London: Reaktion Books, 2006).

3. The rise of the disabled veteran as a national "problem" can be attributed to a host of factors, chief among them the expanding population of disabled veterans within the broader body politic. Thanks to new developments in emergency transportation, wound treatment, and antisepsis, casualty survival rates rose steadily in the decades between the Civil War and World War II. By the 1910s upward of four-fifths of U.S. casualties could expect to survive their injuries, although often with debilitating pain or physical impairments. In addition, Americans' rising concerns about disabled veteran were rooted in shifting ideas about the role of federal veterans' policy in mitigating the high cost of war-related disability. By the end of World War I, there was a growing sense that the "problem of the disabled veteran" had reached a boiling point. Unless the federal government embraced new solutions, disabled veterans would threaten the nation's social, economic, and moral health for decades to come. On the evolution of veterans' disability policy between the Civil War and World War II, see Theda Skocpol, *Protecting Soldiers and Mothers: The Political Origins of Social Policy in the United States* (Cambridge, Mass.: The Belknap Press of Harvard University Press, 1992); and Richard K. Scotch, "American Disability Policy in the Twentieth Century," in *The New Disability History: American Perspectives*, edited by Paul K. Longmore and Lauri Umansky (New York: New York University Press, 2001), 375–92. For more on the "problem of the disabled veteran" in late-nineteenth- and early-twentieth-century America, see John M. Kinder, "Encountering Injury: Modern War and the Problem of the Wounded Soldier" (Ph.D. diss., University of Minnesota, 2007).

4. Notable exceptions include Patrick J. Kelly, *Creating a National Home: Building the Veterans' Welfare State, 1860–1900* (Cambridge, Mass.: Harvard University Press, 1997); James Marten, "Nomads in Blue: Disabled Veterans and Alcohol at the National Home," in *Disabled Veterans in History*, edited by David A. Gerber, 275–94 (Ann Arbor: University of Michigan Press, 2000); and R. B. Rosenburg, *Living Monuments: Confederate Soldiers' Homes in the New South* (Chapel Hill: University of North Carolina Press, 1993).

5. For example, see William H. Glasson, *Federal Military Pensions in the United States* (New York: Oxford University Press, 1918); John Maurice Clark, *The Costs of the World War to the American People* (New Haven, Conn.: Yale University Press, 1931); and Richard Severo and Lewis Milford, *The Wages of War: When America's Soldiers Come Home—From Valley Forge to Vietnam* (New York: Simon and Schuster, 1989).

6. See David Atkinson, Peter Jackson, David Sibley, and Neil Washbourne, eds., *Cultural Geography: A Critical Dictionary of Key Concepts* (London: I. B. Tauris, 2005); Henri Lefebvre, *The Production of Space*, trans. D. Nicholson-Smith (Oxford: Blackwell, 1991); and Mona

Domosh and Joni Seager, *Putting Women in Place: Feminist Geographers Make Sense of the World* (New York: Guilford, 2001).

7. For detailed discussions of the relationship between disability and space, see Brendan Gleeson, *Geographies of Disability* (London: Routledge, 1999); and Ruth Butler and Hester Parr, eds., *Mind and Body Spaces: Geographies of Illness, Impairment and Disability* (London: Routledge, 1999).

8. Paul K. Longmore and Lauri Umansky, "Disability History: From the Margins to the Mainstream," in *The New Disability History: American Perspectives*, edited by Paul K. Longmore and Lauri Umansky (New York: New York University Press, 2001), 19.

9. Robert Wilton, "(Dis) ability," in *Cultural Geography: A Critical Dictionary of Key Concepts*, edited by David Atkinson Peter Jackson, David Sibley, and Neil Washbourne (London: I. B. Tauris, 2005), 120.

10. On the emergence of federal disability policy in early modern Europe and North America, see Geoffrey L. Hudson, "Disabled Veterans and the State in Early Modern England," in *Disabled Veterans in History*, edited by David A. Gerber, 117–44 (Ann Arbor: University of Michigan Press, 2000); and Douglas C. McMurtrie, *The Disabled Soldier* (New York: Macmillan, 1919).

11. Henri-Jacques Stiker, *A History of Disability*, trans. William Sayers (Ann Arbor: University of Michigan Press, 1999), 99–101. Stiker argues that the Hôtel des Invalides operated according to the logic of "internment" described by Michel Foucault, in which the principle goal of seventeenth century hospitals and asylums was not to cure deviant subjects but to manage their behavior through discipline and confinement.

12. There were a few domiciliary institutions established for disabled ex-servicemen prior to the 1850s; however, these tended to be small and lacking the institutional infrastructure of later soldiers' homes. See Kelly, *Creating a National Home*, 205n10.

13. Ibid., 2–3.

14. John Whiteclay Chambers II, "The American Debate over Modern War, 1871–1914," in *Anticipating Total War: The German and American Experiences, 1871–1914*, edited by Manfred F. Boemeke, Roger Chickering, and Stig Förster (Cambridge: Cambridge University Press, 1999), 245.

15. Allan R. Millet and Peter Maslowski, *For the Common Defense: A Military History of the United States of America*, rev. and exp. ed. (New York: Free Press, 1994), 163.

16. Lareann Figg and Jane Farrell-Beck, "Amputations in the Civil War: Physical and Social Dimensions," *Journal of the History of Medicine and Allied Sciences* 48, no. 4 (1993): 454. On the Civil War's legacy of psychological trauma, see Eric T. Dean Jr., *Shook over Hell: Post-Traumatic Stress, Vietnam, and the Civil War* (Cambridge, Mass.: Harvard University Press, 1997).

17. Kelly, *Creating a National Home*, 13, 32; and Leslie E. Miljat, ed., *Admission Applications 1867–1872: National Home for Disabled Volunteer Soldiers, Northwestern Branch, Milwaukee Wisconsin* (Wauwatosa: State Historical Society of Wisconsin, 1991), ix–xi.

18. J. C. Gobrecht, *History of the National Home for Disabled Volunteer Soldiers: with a Complete Guide-book to the Central Home, at Dayton, Ohio* (Dayton, Ohio: United Brethren Printing Establishment, 1875), 33.

19. Ibid., 18.

20. Domosh and Seager, *Putting Women in Place*, 7. For more on the home and the Victorian cult of domesticity, see Peter G. Filene, *Him/Her/Self: Gender Identities in Modern America*, 3rd ed. (Baltimore: Johns Hopkins University Press, 1998).

21. Kelly, *Creating a National Home*, 90, 94.

22. See Jessica H. Foy and Thomas J Schlereth, eds., *American Home Life, 1880–1930: A Social History of Spaces and Services* (Knoxville: University of Tennessee Press, 1992).

23. Suzanne Julin, "National Home for Disabled Volunteer Soldiers: Assessment of Significance and National Historic Landmark Recommendations," United States National Parks Service, http://www.nps.gov/history/nhl/Downloads/NHDVS/NHDVS%20Draft%20Two.pdf, 40 (accessed 15 June 2009).

24. Kelly, *Creating a National Home*, 113. On Thomas Story Kirkbride and nineteenth-century asylum design, see Nancy Tomes, *The Art of Asylum-Keeping: Thomas Story Kirkbride and the Origins of American Psychiatry* (Philadelphia: University of Pennsylvania Press, 1994).

25. Although all of the National Home branches accepted veterans of the U.S. Colored Troops, facilities were internally segregated, with African American residents living in separate barracks and dining at separate tables. Yet even at Hampton Roads, African Americans represented a minority of the resident population. Kelly, *Creating a National Home*, 98; and Julin, "National Home for Disabled Volunteer Soldiers," 16–17, 47.

26. Julin, "National Home for Disabled Volunteer Soldiers," 47; and Gobrecht, *History of the National Home*, 62.

27. Gobrecht, *History of the National Home*, 60.

28. Ibid., 84.

29. Kelly, *Creating a National Home*, 108.

30. Lewis B. Gunckel, resident manager of the Central branch, quoted in Gobrecht, *History of the National Home*, 48.

31. Kelly, *Creating a National Home*, 155.

32. Ibid., 198; Julin, "National Home for Disabled Volunteer Soldiers," 34.

33. Kelly, *Creating a National Home*, 50.

34. Samuel Hopkins Adams, "The Miracle of Reeducation," *Red Cross Magazine* 14, no. 5 (May 1919): 44.

35. On the history of rehabilitation prior to World War I, see Stiker, *History of Disability*, 115–18; Brad Byron, "A Pupil and a Patient: Hospital-Schools in Progressive America," in *The New Disability History: American Perspectives*, edited by Paul K. Longmore and Lauri Umansky (New York: New York University Press, 2001), 133–56; C. W. Hutt, *The Future of the Disabled Soldier* (London: John Bale, Sons and Danielsson, 1917); and McMurtrie, *Disabled Soldier*.

36. Deborah Cohen, "Will to Work: Disabled Veterans in Britain and Germany after the First World War," in *Disabled Veterans in History*, edited by David A. Gerber (Ann Arbor: The University of Michigan Press, 2000), 295.

37. Clark, *Costs of the World War*, 182.

38. U.S. Office of the Surgeon General, *The Medical Department of the United States Army in the World War*, Volume 10 (Washington, D.C.: GPO, 1927), 1.

39. David A. Gerber, ed., *Disabled Veterans in History* (Ann Arbor: University of Michigan Press, 2000), 19.

40. On the feminization of dependency in modern America, see Nancy Fraser and Linda Gordon, "A Genealogy of *Dependency*: Tracing a Keyword of the U.S. Welfare State," *Signs: Journal of Women in Culture and Society* 19, no. 2 (Winter 1994): 309–36.

41. War Department Office of the Surgeon General, "Introductory," in Bulletin of *Abstracts, Translations, and Reviews of Recent Literature on the Subject of the Reconstruction and Reeducation of the Disabled Soldier and Sailor* 4 (25 May 1918): 1.

42. On the history and ideologies of American Progressivism, see Alan Dawley, *Changing*

*the World: American Progressives in War and Peace* (Princeton, N.J.: Princeton University Press, 2003).

43. Frank Ward O'Malley, "Home Comers from France," *Carry On*, September 1918, 7.

44. "The Passing of the Cripple," *Outlook*, 3 October 1917, 166.

45. A. J. Dekker to Assistant Director, Rehabilitation Division, United States Veterans' Bureau (26 April 1922), Folder: San Antonio, TX, Box 11, RG 15, National Archives Building, Washington, D.C. [hereafter NAB].

46. *U.S.A. General Hospital, No. 28* (Fort Sheridan, IL: c. 1920); Ford Motor Company, *The Reawakening* (1920), 200FC-2478, National Archives Motion Picture Collection, National Archives, College Park, Maryland [hereafter NACP].

47. Colonel E. D. Warfield to Inspector General of the Army (May 1919), Box 232, RG 112, NACP.

48. In addition to vocational schools, the federal government established a number of small rehabilitation centers and training programs. The latter tended to focus on veterans with arrested tuberculosis. "The Vocational Rehabilitation Program and its Administration," RG 15, National Archives Research Room, NAB.

49. On nonresidential schools, see "The Vocational Rehabilitation Program and its Administration."

50. Report from Florence A. Egan (8 April 1922), Folder: Atlanta, GA, Box 1, RG 15, NAB.

51. Ibid.

52. "Judge Declares School Farce," *Indianapolis Sunday Star*, 29 January 1922, 8.

53. E. G. Dexter to Director of the U.S. Veterans' Bureau (5 July 1924), Folder: Camp Sherman, Chillicothe, OH, Box 2, RG 15, NAB.

54. In their equation of immorality and idleness, Camp Sherman's managers reiterated a key tenet of the recently demobilized Commission on Training Camp Activities, the federal agency responsible for ensuring the moral and spiritual health of doughboys in training. See Nancy K. Bristow, *Making Men Moral: Social Engineering during the Great War* (New York: New York University Press, 1996).

55. "Remarks of E. H. Hale Delivered before the Assembled Trainees at Pascagoula," F: Pascagoula, Mississippi, Box 8, Rehabilitation Historical File, RG 15, NAB.

56. E. G. Dexter to Director of the U.S. Veterans' Bureau.

57. On the professionalization of rehabilitation, see Glenn Gritzer and Arnold Arluke, *The Making of Rehabilitation: A Political Economy of Medical Specialization, 1890–1980* (Berkeley: University of California Press, 1980).

58. E. G. Dexter to Director of the U.S. Veterans' Bureau.

59. Arthur C. Woods, "'The Rube's Day is Done': Forward to the Farm—Why Not?" (Washington, D.C.: Government Printing Office, 1919), 7.

60. Dixon Wecter, *When Johnny Comes Marching Home* (Cambridge, Mass.: Riverside Press, 1944), 379.

61. On the founding of Minnesota's disabled veterans' farm colonies, see John S. McClain, "Making Farmers of Ex-Soldiers," *American Review of Reviews* 66 (July–December 1922): 519–24; and Bill G. Reid, "Colonies for Disabled Veterans in Minnesota," *Minnesota History* (Summer 1965): 241–51. One should note Veteransville residents did rent a community center to serve as a barracks for a few single men. See Reid, "Colonies for Disabled Veterans," 244.

62. "War Vets Hold Farm Exhibit," *Hastings Gazette*, 5 October 1923; "Disabled Soldiers Making Good at Argonne Farms," *Dakota County Tribune* (hereafter *DCT*), 25 January 1924; "'Argonne Farms' Valuable Asset to World War 'Vets,'" *DCT*, 26 January 1923; "Argonne

Farms," *Over the Years*, January 1985, 5; clippings in Argonne Farms File, Dakota Country Historical Society, Lakeville, Minnesota [hereafter DCHS].

63. On residents' initial optimism, see McClain, "Making Farmers of Ex-Soldiers," 522.

64. "Veterans' Farm Enterprise on a Wobbly Basis," 18 June 1923, clipping in Argonne Farms File, DCHS.

65. "4 Argonne Farms Vets to Be Ousted," *DCT*, 16 September 1927; "Start Foreclosure Proceedings on 4 Veterans' Farms," *DCT*, 20 August 1926; clippings in Argonne Farms File, DCHS.

66. Reid, "Colonies for Disabled Veterans in Minnesota," 250.

67. "Disabled Soldiers on Farms Will Be Cut Off From Government Financial Help June 30," *St. Paul Dispatch*, 21 May 1926, 2; clipping in Folder: Argonne Farms Situation, Box 1, Edwin G. Dexter File, Rehabilitation Division Historical File, 1919–1925, RG 15, NAB.

68. "Court Dismisses Dr. Benham Case," *DCT*, 7 January 1927; "Benham Faces Larceny Charge," *DCT*, 18 September 1925; "Benham to Return and Face Charges," *DCT*, 2 October 1925; clippings in Argonne Farms File, DCHS.

69. Editorial, *Northfield Independent*, 12 May 1927; clipping in Argonne Farms File, DCHS.

70. Daniel Pick, *War Machine: The Rationalisation of Slaughter in the Modern Age* (New Haven, Conn.: Yale University Press, 1993), 16.

71. Melanie McAlister, *Epic Encounters: Culture, Media, and U.S. Interests in the Middle East, 1945–2000* (Berkeley: University of California Press, 2001), 5.

# 4

## "An Emblem of Distinction"

### The Politics of Disability Entitlement, 1940–1950

AUDRA JENNINGS

In September 1945 Capt. Frank P. Kreuz of the U.S. Navy Bureau of Medicine and Surgery testified before a subcommittee of the House of Representatives Committee on Labor. His testimony, part of a massive, two-year investigation of disability services in the United States, pointed to the need for better prosthetics for sailors.[1] It was far from clear, however, that veterans would have these needs met, at least in the immediate future. In the realm of artificial limbs, Kreuz noted that available prosthetics fell short in six areas: appearance, utility, weight, durability, noise, and texture. For Kreuz, the veteran's prosthetic should be viewed "as an emblem of distinction," but as with the failings of prosthetic technology itself, this sentiment represented a yet unattained goal.[2]

The demobilization of World War II veterans created intense fears about the nation's social and economic stability.[3] As the war came to a close, a variety of social commentators gave voice to this unease. Some of these commentators focused on the threat that disabled veterans posed to the economy, the family, and the social order. All of them tended to emphasize the debt owed to the nation's protectors by individual Americans and by American society as a whole. This debt, they argued, could only be repaid by easing soldiers' transitions to peacetime employment, family, and home.[4] If Americans fixated on the sacrifices and worried about the difficulties all veterans would face, the injuries of disabled veterans magnified both the sense of obligation and fears about adjustment.[5]

The 670,846 American military personnel who sustained nonfatal injuries proved to be very visible reminders of the public's responsibility to its defenders. Aware of their visibility, these men pushed to redefine the contours of the welfare state and demanded protection from uncertainty in exchange for their service.[6] In partnership with disabled and able-bodied veterans, Congress set new terms for the repayment of the debt owed to veterans. The Vocational

Rehabilitation Act of 1943 codified a set of new responsibilities of the state to disabled veterans. Combined with the Servicemen's Readjustment Act of 1944, or the G.I. Bill of Rights, this legislation placed the weight of the federal government behind guaranteeing veterans—at least straight, white, males—access to jobs, higher education, medical care, and homes. Taken together, the laws that defined this new category of entitlement represented a dramatic expansion of the state and the entitlements connected to military service.[7]

Despite this development, significant gaps in the veterans' welfare system prevented disabled veterans from sharing the same entitlements as their able-bodied brethren. Consequently, disabled veterans, veterans' organizations, and policymakers pushed for change that acknowledged the sacrifice and special status of disabled veterans and honored their disabilities. By focusing on the battles fought over national amputation and prosthetic programs, this essay will show that during and immediately after World War II, the American welfare state developed a new category of elevated benefits  those earned by the men who had sacrificed for the nation.[8] I argue that veterans not only pushed to expand the benefits of this new category; they also worked to maintain their separate and special status as deserving welfare recipients. By policing the boundaries of disability policy, veterans rejected attempts to create a universal disability policy, stymieing civilian disability activists' and liberal policymakers' hopes to leverage the wartime necessity of employing disabled workers to create a broader social safety net for all Americans.[9]

The roots of the debates over the national amputation and prosthetic programs extended to the beginning of the war. Only days after the attack on Pearl Harbor, President Franklin D. Roosevelt called on the Federal Security Agency (FSA), a forerunner to the Department of Health, Education and Welfare, to develop a stronger vocational rehabilitation program that could ready greater numbers of disabled Americans for the workforce faster. Paul McNutt, acting administrator, and the FSA worked with the president and the Bureau of the Budget to develop a new program.[10] In August 1942 Rep. Graham Barden (D-N.C.) and Sen. Robert La Follette (R-Wisc.) introduced bills in the House and Senate to codify the administration's plans for the rehabilitation program. In its earliest incarnation, the plan outlined in these bills would have placed the administrative responsibility for an expanded rehabilitation program for both veterans and civilians in the FSA.[11]

Throughout 1942 and 1943 Congress debated various incarnations of the administration's new rehabilitation plan. Veterans, their organizations, and their supporters in Congress railed against the plan that would take services for disabled veterans out of the Veterans Administration (VA) and instead create a program that addressed the needs of civilians and former soldiers with few distinctions. In response to this outcry, Congress considered a compromise measure that left the VA in control of veterans' rehabilitation but encouraged the VA's administrator to send veterans to the civilian program. This overlap still proved to be too much for veterans, who argued that the bill mixed "the special rights of the veterans" with the government's responsibility to civilians. In the end, Congress dramatically expanded rehabilitation for veterans and civilians in 1943. At the insistence of veterans, however, it did so in two different bills, through two different agencies, and at two different levels. Veterans emerged from the debates receiving a higher level of support justified by their service and sacrifice.[12]

These tensions between pushing for a broad, national disability policy and meeting veterans' demands for a policy that recognized their "special rights" flared repeatedly during the war and immediate postwar years. From the need to employ disabled workers to the desire to aid disabled veterans, the war made disability public, and it created an opening for disability activism. Veterans, of course, stepped into this opening, but they were not the only disability activists of the day. The American Federation of the Physically Handicapped, a group of largely civilian disability activists, demanded an expansive federal program to end employment discrimination and ensure access to education, jobs, and health care. As policymakers, veterans, and civilians pushed to redefine disability policy, veterans again and again demanded separate programs. Veterans' demands for separate and "special" entitlements shaped the establishment of a long-term prosthetic development policy. To fully understand veterans' concerns, one must examine the amputation/prosthetic programs of the Army, Navy, and the VA. Just as prostheses left much to be desired, these programs, particularly those of the Army and VA, did not provide veteran amputees with the kind of care to which, they believed, their service entitled them.

Servicemen in the Army were more likely to suffer catastrophic injuries that required amputations. While roughly 70 percent of U.S. military personnel served in the Army during World War II, Army casualties constituted 86 percent of all military amputations. The Army Medical Corp reported that it performed successful amputations on approximately 14,000 soldiers during the war, a figure that excluded "minor" amputations of digits. Moreover, of these amputation cases, some 1,057 soldiers lost two or more limbs.[13]

By mid-1945 the Army had developed a complex system for handling amputation cases. In many regards, this system closely resembled World War I–era care. On the front lines, the Surgeon General of the Army mandated that surgeons use the "open circular," or "guillotine," method for all emergency cases requiring amputation. A technique widely practiced during World War I, the open amputation required surgeons to remove the limb at the lowest possible point that still allowed for the removal of tissue that was beyond repair. Instead of surgically closing the wound, Medical Corp personnel applied skin traction and prepared the soldier for transport. On the one hand, this procedure allowed surgeons to preserve as much tissue as possible and generally increased an individual's chances of successfully adapting to prostheses. Because the wound remained open, the technique also helped to reduce the risk of serious infection. On the other hand, the use of this procedure meant that soldiers almost always had to endure at least one more operation to prepare the limb for a prosthetic.[14]

While the Army mandated the use of the same surgical technique preferred during World War I, other medical advances contributed to a greatly improved survival rate. Not only had the Army placed more surgeons at the front, but these surgeons now could also use sulfa drugs and penicillin to treat infections. Additionally, they had a blood bank system that made whole blood and plasma available to wounded soldiers. In real numbers, these advances allowed the Technical Information Division of the Office of the Surgeon General of the Army to report in May 1945 that some sixty thousand men had already survived injuries that would have certainly proved fatal in 1918.[15]

Medical advances tell only a small part of the story. While the ability to preserve life had improved dramatically, the capacity to cause grave harm had also increased exponentially, and many more Americans served in harm's way for longer periods. Amputation cases are telling in this regard. During World War I the Army recorded 2,635 amputations, 52 of which were double amputation surgeries. These cases represented .06 percent of the soldiers who served in the Army during the war. In contrast, .12 percent of World War II–era personnel survived amputations. All told, 3.4 times as many men served in World War II, and 3.3 times as many men returned home after nonfatal wounds. Taken together, these factors meant that many more injured soldiers would survive to become disabled veterans, needing postoperative care, rehabilitation, prostheses, and training.[16]

The system could not handle the increase. Early in the war the Army cared for amputees immediately following the injury and then transferred them to the VA, which was charged with their further treatment, rehabilitation, and training. In 1943, when the tremendous influx of patients overwhelmed the VA, Army officials decided that they had no choice but to offer "definitive" care for all of its casualties. In March 1943 the Army established five amputation centers in existing Army hospitals: Washington, D.C.; Atlanta, Georgia; Battle Creek, Michigan; Temple, Texas; and Brigham City, Utah. Each of these facilities could house up to 500 amputees.[17]

By September 1944 it was clear that the 2,500 spaces in the existing centers could not meet the demand, and the Army established two more amputation centers in Atlantic City, New Jersey, and Richmond, Virginia. As fighting intensified in Europe in 1944 and 1945, each of these seven centers cared for up to 1,600 patients at a time, well beyond the planned 500-bed limit. The admission rate reached 412 new patients per month in a single center.[18]

Each of the Army's amputation centers provided surgical and medical care and rehabilitative therapy, worked to boost patients' morale, and operated limb shops. Beyond meeting the physical and emotional needs of the wounded soldiers in their care, the Army envisioned these centers as training facilities, where surgeons could learn military amputation techniques and technical staff could learn to make and fit prosthetics.[19]

Medical staff surgically prepared recently amputated limbs, or "revised stumps," for prosthetic wear and supervised the healing process. Physical and occupational therapists helped patients to gain strength and trained them to use their new limbs. In addition to providing entertainment and leisure activities, the Army sought to improve morale by introducing patients to amputees skilled in the use of prosthetics.[20]

To facilitate rapid adjustment, the Army provided temporary limbs to all of its amputees as soon as the stump had healed. These limbs, designed to be malleable as the stump changed during early recovery, were far from ideal. The plan was that the VA would provide soldiers with commercially manufactured limbs after their discharge. Because the Army needed thousands of limbs, the Army's limb shops tended to emphasize quantity and standardization over quality and individualization.[21]

This push toward mass manufacturing was constrained by a lack of skilled personnel. The Army had not kept a list of prosthetic technicians in the service. Therefore, to find trained staff, the Army had to contact civilian limb makers to obtain the names of soldiers with the skills to work in the Army's limb shops. After the creation of its amputation centers, all trained limb makers and technicians were transferred to one of the centers. The Army launched a three-month training program to meet the growing need. Despite these efforts, the Army did not have enough trained people, and production line methods were adopted to allow unskilled workers to contribute to the process and to preserve skilled workers for more complicated tasks. Finally, the Army focused its efforts on assembling purchased parts and then fitting the limb to the individual. By purchasing joints, hooks, and other parts, the Army was able to produce standardized limbs with a shortage of skilled workers.[22] The Army's failure to plan ahead and its emphasis on quantity created considerable problems for the veterans who would need these services, setting the stage for outraged critiques and political activism.

While the Army's amputation program pushed for standardization in re-sponse to the growing numbers of casualties, the Navy's Bureau of Medicine and Surgery instituted a program of research, development, and team care shortly after the attack on Pearl Harbor. These programs differed not only in vision and implementation but also in mission. The Army handled far more amputation cases than the Navy. However, the Army came to the realization that it would need an in-depth amputation program relatively late in the game, well over a year after Pearl Harbor. As a result, Army medical officials were constantly reacting, expanding into new facilities, increasing patient capacity beyond planned limits, and searching for doctors, limb makers, and techni-cians. The Navy launched its amputation program immediately. The Surgeon General of the Navy established a limb shop at the Navy hospital in Mare Is-land, California, staffing the facility with medical officers experienced in am-putation techniques and care. Navy physicians worked closely with the limb makers, and limbs were constantly altered based on a dialogue between the patient, physician, and limb maker until an optimal fit had been achieved. The Navy limb shop experimented with materials, design, and fitting techniques. In large measure, the small numbers cared for by the Navy made this individual-ized care possible.[23]

Navy amputations paled in comparison to Army casualties. While the Ar-my's seven amputation centers fitted approximately 1,000 limbs per month in the final push of the war, the Navy program cared for roughly 2,200 amputees during the entire war. In fact, because it was created early and the bulk of am-putations occurred later in the war, the Navy program could develop over time without the same pressing need experienced by Army officials. Navy casualty rates are instructive here. Seven sailors lost limbs in 1942, 41 in 1943, and 155 in 1944.[24]

In response to increased casualties in the Pacific Theater, the Navy instituted some critical changes in its amputation program. In April 1944 the Navy ex-panded its care for injured sailors to include a rehabilitation program, which significantly increased the level of care and training provided to injured sailors. Initially the Navy, much like the Army, had addressed the more immediate needs of its injured servicemen. The Navy's general policy on casualties, ac-cording to Kreuz, centered on "prevention, immediate emergency medical at-tention in the battle areas, expeditious evacuation, and expert definitive treat-ment in special hospitals designated for the various types of casualties." The issue for the Navy, however, was that what constituted "definitive treatment" was in flux during the war. In the early years of the war, "definitive treatment" meant preserving life and as much tissue as possible through judicious surgical techniques and new treatments such as sulfa drugs, penicillin, and plasma. It meant stabilizing the individual, evacuating him to a hospital or hospital ship, healing the wound, and fitting a prosthetic device. During the war, however, physicians began to contemplate a new definition of "definitive treatment" that expanded medical care beyond the physical mechanics of healing a wound into the realm of physical, social, emotional, and economic adjustment. Coping with the staggering number of war casualties had opened the door for the field of rehabilitation medicine, which gained official recognition as a distinct specialty from the American Medical Association in 1947.[25]

The Navy's rehabilitation program emphasized physical and mental preparation for life after an amputation. Physical training involved strengthening muscles and developing basic skills using the prosthetic. Injured sailors received educational and vocational guidance, and some even began an educational or vocational course of study while in the hospital, through either onsite training or correspondence classes. By focusing on life after the injury, the Navy's rehabilitation program sought to ease the "mental shock" and depression common among its patients.[26]

While both the Army and the Navy developed elaborate programs for the care of amputees, the VA retained significant responsibilities in the maintenance of these servicemen. Both the Army and the Navy provided their amputees with surgical and medical treatment, artificial limbs, and training in the use of those limbs, but once discharged from military service all future care fell to the VA. The VA allowed veteran amputees to purchase a second artificial limb in case of damage to the primary prosthetic. Additionally, the VA provided maintenance and repair for damaged or ill-fitting limbs and replaced unsalvageable limbs. If problems developed with the amputation stump, veterans could also receive medical and surgical care through the VA. The VA maintained 12 amputation centers for difficult cases that required surgery or special fitting. Unlike the Army and Navy, the VA purchased the vast majority of its limbs from private manufacturers. Each year the VA took bids on artificial limbs and established contracts with fixed prices for the year. In 1945 the VA had contracts with 140 limb manufacturers, and in most cases, veterans had to select from specific limbs made by these companies. To receive any of these services, however, veterans had to apply at the nearest VA field station.[27]

Soldiers and sailors benefited from numerous programs designed to speed their healing and adjustment to an artificial limb. Still, serious deficiencies in the limbs themselves stymied the creation of a program that would truly satisfy the needs of these servicemen. An official Army report concluded that the quality of prosthetics available through private industry was "not of sufficiently high standards" for use in the Army program. In fact, the report noted that prosthetic development "had not kept pace with other modern manufacturing."[28]

Serious deficiencies surrounded the appearance, utility, weight, durability, noise, and texture of artificial limbs. For instance, arm amputees faced a choice between a not very functional cosmetic or "dress" hand, or a far more functional but certainly far from life-like mechanical hook prosthetic. In the case of arm prosthetics, the struggle was to create a limb that was both functional and life-like, but utility was a major issue for all artificial limbs. Limbs available to the average soldier offered a severely limited range of motion and were prone to malfunction. As with the tension between appearance and utility, soldiers faced a trade-off when it came to weight and durability—lighter limbs tended to be less durable, and heavier limbs were less functional. Artificial joints lacked the full utility of natural joints, and they were also the least durable parts of prosthetic limbs. Various joint mechanisms tended to create noise, and none of the prosthetics available were life-like in texture.[29]

The quality of prosthetic appliances had real-world implications for the soldiers and veterans who wore them. In 1945 Army lieutenant Sol Rael expressed his extreme dissatisfaction with his prosthesis—a dissatisfaction he believed was near universal among his fellow amputees. He reported, "There was no question in my mind when I received my prosthesis that I was greatly disappointed and disillusioned in seeing what a hackneyed article it really was." Rael contrasted the very modern weapons and medicine used by the Army to his artificial arm, which he believed was the best available but still "crude and out-moded and definitely a throw-back to horse-and-buggy days." Artificial arms like the one he wore had so little practical value that he and his friends at Walter Reed Hospital called this type of prosthetic "the 'pros-useless.'"[30]

Captain Kreuz admitted that the heaviness of artificial limbs was a common complaint. However, he also downplayed the significance of the issue compared to other concerns such as function and strength. But the weight of Lt. Howard Morse's limb made it impossible to use. Having had an above-the-elbow amputation while in the Army, Morse had very little stump, leaving him with far fewer muscles to put his prosthetic to work. Though he had "pleaded" for a lighter limb, he had been told that there was nothing lighter to give him. Meanwhile, the best available limb, he said, "just fills out my sleeve."[31]

Veterans also had substantial complaints about the utility and fit of their new limbs and the process they had to go through to get assistance from the VA. Eugene F. Trainor, who was discharged in July 1945 after having recovered from a below-the-knee amputation, reported that his "GI leg," or standard Army prosthetic, caused his amputation stump to break open, forcing him to miss work. Trainor went to the VA when his stump first opened up; he was told to soak it with Epsom salts and that the wound was caused by his Army-issued prosthetic. Trainor made application to the VA for a new limb, which he received, but it required repeated adjustments because of the tenderness of his stump after having worn a "GI leg."[32]

In the end, Trainor had to visit his limb maker for adjustments and travel to a VA facility for care of his stump. His opinion of the care that he received at the VA was quite low. According to Trainor, "You have to wait around there a half a day before you get to see a doctor," and the doctor that he finally saw was no orthopedic specialist. Given time away from work and the constant travel, this was a costly prospect for Trainor, who feared that he would be set back in his physical progress with his leg and his economic progress with his job.[33]

As desperate as Trainor's situation was, Robert L. Rogers experienced greater trials. After losing a limb in an explosion in northern Africa in July 1943, he was shipped home to receive treatment at Walter Reed Hospital. Rogers' leg was amputated about five inches below the knee, but like Trainor, once he began walking with his prosthetic, his stump opened up. After four surgeries and more than a year in Walter Reed, Rogers still had constant troubles with his leg and was waiting for a new socket and a new leather foot to give him greater function. He argued that the Army's legs were improperly fitted and made of poor quality materials so cheap that a limb maker had told him that his leg was not worth "two hoots in hell."[34]

Rogers argued that a man who came "from a special family who has enough money" would not have to deal with the same problems. But for men like Rogers, who depended on their earnings to make ends meet, replacing an ill-fitting or low-quality limb with personal funds was out of the question. Taking time away from work to travel to the VA for repairs and to apply for a new limb had costs as well. The VA had determined that Rogers' artificial leg should be repaired and not replaced; consequently, Rogers had to go to the VA repeatedly and wait. He had to wait for repairs, wait for the VA to decide that he was eligible for a new limb, and he even had to wait for new crutches. When his Army-issued "sticks," as veteran amputees sometimes called their crutches, broke, he went to the VA to request a new pair. Fortunately, Rogers was able to borrow a pair from the dispensary at his job because it took more than two months for his VA crutches to arrive. All of the waiting had profound consequences for Rogers. He had difficulty working, shifting from job to job in hopes of finding something that would not set off the pain, and as a result, he had difficulty making a living. Describing the pain, he said, "I started hunting around for a toothache because I would rather have a toothache than to have this leg on when it is paining me."[35]

Like many other veterans, Rogers said that he was not alone in his troubles and that he had "yet to find [a veteran amputee from Walter Reed] who is satisfied." At least four of his friends had stumps break open like his did, one of which did not just open up but instead "rip[ped]." According to Rogers, men were tired of waiting and tired of having their situation ignored. He said that the public face of Army amputation centers was a farce. When they photographed men walking and dancing, he claimed it was after only a few steps. But, Rogers said, "They do not take his picture after he had walked 20 steps." Nor did they show the man after the dance when "he has hopped . . . into the corner or goes hopping downstairs to get his crutches." Just as the pain made Rogers "hate to walk," it made him and others like him question the government that had sent them to battle. "These derned [sic] legs," he cried, "I do not know what is wrong, the Government is supposed to be trying to do so much for us, and they are not doing a darned thing."[36]

Veterans' criticisms reached a fever pitch at the end of the war, but veterans' organizations had advocated for change from almost the beginning of the war. In September 1942 at the Twenty-fourth Annual National Convention of the American Legion in Kansas City, Missouri, veterans adopted a resolution demanding government action to improve the quality of prosthetics available to veterans. Legion members argued that thousands of World War I veterans had lost limbs in service to the nation and that many more would "make similar sacrifices" during World War II. The authors of the resolution noted, "Improvement in the manufacturing of artificial limbs had not kept pace with mechanical progress shown in many other phases of engineering." Given this lack of momentum, the Legion demanded that government agencies sponsor research on the development of better prosthetics "so that victims of this World War can be the immediate beneficiaries of this much needed service."[37]

Despite veteran activism, corporate interests and VA apathy colluded to obstruct any real advancement in research. T. O. Kraabel, national director of the American Legion's rehabilitation committee, forwarded the resolution to Gen. Frank Hines, administrator of the VA and noted anti–New Dealer, asking the VA to launch such a program.[38] Hines shared the resolution with Chester C. Hadden, president of the Association of Limb Manufacturers of America (ALMA), asking for his opinion and commenting that he "was not aware" of any lack of progress.[39]

Hadden indignantly denied the allegation that prosthetic makers had failed to keep apace with modern development, claiming that the members of his organization not only possessed "the finest equipment in the land" but also produced prostheses that "exceeded mechanical progress shown in a great many fields." Moreover, Hadden noted that many members of ALMA had "spent many thousands of dollars year after year in research." He concluded, given that his members already conducted research and that they produced high quality, modern appliances, "there is absolutely no necessity for the allocation of any Federal funds for research in this field."[40]

On the surface, Hadden's absolute refusal of federal dollars might seem puzzling. But admitting that there was indeed a problem at best would have implied that artificial limb makers did not have the resources to make sure that their products were in touch with the times and at worst would have suggested that greed or ineptitude had prevented improvement. Additionally, these manufacturers, like most at the time, actively sought federal contracts—in this case with the VA, Army, and Navy, and perhaps, they feared that federal research would endanger these contracts and cut off a valuable source of business.

Regardless of their motivations, the stance of ALMA leaders effectively halted the VA's contemplation of launching a research campaign. Hines informed American Legion leaders of his decision in December, and the issue was dropped, at least temporarily.[41] While the VA had decided that private manufacturers should be in charge of research, Army officials reported that they had "assumed that the responsibility for a development program lay with another Government agency, namely, the Veterans Administration."[42] From the perspective of the VA, launching a research program did not make sense because the VA did not make limbs but instead contracted with private companies. In the early years of the war, only the Navy put forth a concerted effort to improve the situation. But the Navy handled only a fraction of the nation's amputation cases, and its program did little to meet the overwhelming need.[43]

More than a year after the American Legion passed a resolution calling for research, ALMA launched the Research Institute Foundation in consultation with the National Research Council (NRC), a division of the National Academy of Sciences. While the foundation's efforts were to be guided by a host of government agencies and private organizations, including the Army, Navy, and VA, the foundation was, at least according to the Army, very much controlled by the manufacturers and their organization, ALMA. The Army criticized not only the foundation's direction but also its efforts, arguing that it "lacked funds and personnel" and failed to address immediate or long-term needs.[44]

With the VA passing responsibility to private organizations and the foundation stumbling, Army Medical Corps officials decided that inaction was no longer an option. Colonel Peterson and other officials determined that the "considerable emphasis . . . placed on the techniques and skill of limb fitting" had undermined "progressive development in the mechanics and engineering of prostheses." Late in 1944 these officials called a meeting with the NRC. In January 1945 some seventy individuals—officials from the NRC and the Army and representatives of the limb manufacturers, orthopedic surgeons, and various plastic and metal producers—met in Chicago where the Army asked for assistance in its efforts to improve and standardize artificial limbs. Participants discussed problems and possible solutions identified by each of the Army's amputation centers. From this meeting, the Committee on Prosthetic Devices developed. The committee brought engineers together with orthopedic surgeons to study the situation. Its members represented some of the nation's most prosperous and inventive corporations and prestigious universities: Goodyear Tire & Rubber, Henry Ford Hospital (Ford Motor Company), General Motors, Columbia University, and Northwestern University. The committee installed as its research director Dr. Paul E. Klopsteg of Northwestern Technological Institute and the NRC, and based its operations at Northwestern.[45]

With funds from the National Academy of Sciences and staff at Northwestern, the committee began its work, emphasizing the needs of wounded servicemen. It established a short-range program in conjunction with Army, Navy, and government rehabilitation agencies "to meet the present emergency" and a long-range program of continued development designed to provide "the best possible artificial legs and arms, particularly for those who have sustained loss of these members in war." The committee and the various companies that conducted research on the committee's behalf worked with the amputation centers of both the Army and Navy, testing improvements and studying defects. Orthopedic surgeons on the committee developed "a bill of complaint against" existing prosthetics. Moreover, the committee contracted various pieces of the needed research out to major companies and universities. For example, the committee hired Northrop, a leading manufacturer of aircraft, to study the problem of improving the knee joint, which could not bear weight when flexed. Another contract went to Goodyear Tire & Rubber to study the ankle mechanism, which was too heavy for optimal function. With its numerous projects, the committee attempted to break major issues into pieces, harness the inventive spirit of engineers and researchers working in manufacturing powerhouses and universities, and draw scientific benefit from the thousands of patients at the Army and Navy amputation centers.[46]

In the end, the Army's efforts came too late. Significant results from the research begun in 1945 were years away, and wounded soldiers and the American public expected better. Throughout 1945 American newspapers repeatedly ran stories scandalizing the plight of America's servicemen who had sacrificed limbs in protection of the nation. These articles highlighted the negative consequences of VA policies and the shortcomings of the prostheses issued to soldiers and veterans. The first and perhaps most widely circulated of these stories was splashed across Drew Pearson's nationally syndicated column, "The Washington Merry-Go-Round," in February 1945. Pearson reported that in Washington, D.C., "several hundred amputation cases have been confined for months, many of them disgusted with the treatment they have received." He attacked the quality of both the Army's temporary limbs and the limbs purchased by the VA. According to Pearson, one soldier left a D.C. hospital on furlough to Rochester, New York, and had to be returned in an ambulance because both of his prosthetic legs broke. The soldier was issued new prostheses, but these too broke, leaving the man "to drag himself by his hands for half a city block." Pearson noted that the Army legs were not only heavy and cheaply made but also inflexible, which for many veterans meant that they would have to learn to walk all over again when they got a commercially manufactured limb with bendable joints.[47]

Pearson also lambasted the VA, arguing that the agency "so far [had] refused to pay for the best artificial limbs." He reported that Army amputees who wished to stay in the service and take on clerical work received permanent limbs purchased from high quality manufacturers. While the Army paid high prices for its permanent limbs, between $225 and $275 for full legs and between $150 and $175 for below-the-knee prosthetics, the VA, Pearson wrote, refused to pay for quality, capping payouts for full legs at $205 and below-the-knee models at $125. He also noted that the quality of VA limbs forced many veterans to purchase their own prosthetics. Merging immediate concerns about prosthetics with wider fears about reintegration, Pearson concluded, the "result of all this discomfort and insecurity regarding both the temporary and permanent legs is that the men are far from their best during the difficult readjustment period when they should be getting used to normal life."[48]

Pearson would not have the last word on the situation. In March 1945, *The Nation* covered this "first-class scandal," one it argued was fueled by "sabotage" on the part of the limb-making industry and "governmental indifference." Even the article's title, "Should Veterans Have Legs?," was incendiary. The article featured not only the American Legion's 1942 resolution calling for research but also quoted from the correspondence between General Hines and Chester C. Hadden of the ALMA. In response to Hadden's claims that limb manufacturers invested thousands of dollars in research, *The Nation's* reporter pointed out that there were "no regular scientific reports embodying the results of their costly research." Moreover, he noted that ALMA's recently founded Research Institute represented a true about face, most likely instigated by the NRC. The reporter wryly observed the "grim humor in the prospectus of the new institute," which declared the need for research in the field of prosthetics long to have been "apparent" and stated that its research would be funded by a variety of sources including "federal and state funds." The article concluded, "Improvement in the design of artificial limbs is too vital to the happiness and well-being of our disabled veterans to be left to any private group of this kind, however well-intentioned."[49]

Dorothy Dunbar Bromley, a columnist for the *New York Tribune*, also took up the cause. After interviewing recently discharged veterans and Charles C. McGonegal, national field secretary for the American Legion, she concluded that the future for Army amputees was "not bright." McGonegal told Bromley that before 1945 almost no research had taken place in the field and that it was commonplace for limbs to break down, especially among new amputees who had yet to become accustomed to the limits of their prostheses. But in her interviews Bromley uncovered evidence that pointed to deeper problems than the greenness of new users. One technician told her that scarcity of supplies had forced Army limb makers to use undersized knee joints in the place of hip joints. He also noted that the parts used by the Army were "cheap" and could not withstand the strain of use. Another employee said that half of the men experienced some kind of mechanical failure in the first month of use. A third said that joints and belts routinely broke. Like *The Nation*, Bromley emphasized that the manufacturers had not made significant improvements and that the American Legion had called for a program of research in 1942. Unlike *The Nation*, she reported that the Army and the NRC had launched a campaign of research—research that, at least at Northrup, was beginning to show some results. Still, she warned, the current situation set veterans up to be "humiliated" and "discouraged" as they attempted to settle into civilian pursuits.[50] Taken together, these articles demonstrate the public's serious concerns about demobilization in general and the well-being of disabled veterans in particular. Moreover, the repeated references in news stories to the American Legion's demand for research in 1942 and the critical comments by Legion representatives reveal the organization's hand in directing media attention to the plight of amputees. Finally, these stories reflect veterans' ability to capture and harness public concern in this period of transition.

The image of the veteran, particularly the disabled veteran, proved to be a powerful political motivator. These very public exposés pushed both the House of Representatives and eventually the Federal Bureau of Investigation (FBI) into action. For seven days in September and October, the House Subcommittee on Aid to the Physically Handicapped listened to the testimony of thirty-nine individuals, including soldiers, veterans, and representatives of the Army, Navy, VA, NRC, Disabled American Veterans (DAV), and American Legion. Veteran amputees shared their disappointment, anger, and suffering and demanded action. The Army and Navy provided the committee with an overview of their amputation programs and the research they had and were sponsoring.

The VA explained the benefits it offered to veteran amputees and how veterans could access those benefits.[51]

While representatives of the Army and Navy freely discussed the shortcomings of artificial limbs, Dr. Charles M. Griffith, medical director of the VA, took a defensive position. He claimed that "complaints have been relatively few" and suggested that the expectations of amputees for "nearly perfect restoration" were unreasonable. Other witnesses mentioned the exaggerated expectations of patients, but veterans and committee members might have perceived the VA's statement as an expression of indifference. This assumption of indifference was no doubt reinforced by the VA's stance on research. Dr. Griffith argued that the NRC's work would "keep the civilian manufacturers on their toes," expressing very little concern that the effort be maintained by the government.[52]

Veterans' organizations took a careful approach at the hearings, emphasizing positive change but still demanding more. Evidence suggests that the American Legion helped to focus media attention on the problems veteran amputees faced. At the same time, Legion efforts had begun to produce results: the joint effort between the NRC and the military services. Moreover, the Legion needed to remain on good terms with the military and VA because its program of bringing veteran amputees to the hospitals to encourage patients depended on access to the patients. Taken together, the Legion's conciliatory testimony perhaps suggested less about the organization's judgment on the progress of the NRC research and more about the organization's unwillingness to lose hard-won ground.[53]

Still, the American Legion's representatives at the hearing did not miss the opportunity to offer at least a muted critique. Charles McGonegal, who led the Legion's morale-building program in the amputation centers, pointed out how little had changed. He noted that "there has been no real improvement in appliances for the upper extremities for the last 25 years," the entire time that he had been wearing one. His testimony further stressed the critical need for research and development when he thanked Medical Corps officers who had pushed for research, affirmed the insistence on research by medical leaders such as Colonel Peterson, and emphasized the positive good of the NRC's research, insisting that it not be allowed to lapse.[54]

The DAV took a much more direct approach. Dr. Harry Malisoff, chairman of the DAV Committee for Scientific Research and Development Programs for Handicapped Veterans, set forth a clear agenda, reacting to the NRC's work and demanding that research efforts be refocused to attend to veterans' immediate needs. According to him, DAV members had pushed the organization to form a committee to fight "for the improvement and renovation of the archaic prosthetic devices now available." Malisoff criticized the NRC's Committee on

Prosthetic Devices for failing to include DAV representatives, or even a representative from any veterans' organization. Worse, he argued, it was "distressing to note the apparent absence of recognition of both the urgency and priority of the World War II disabled veterans' needs." Fitting with ongoing veteran-led efforts to police veterans' special entitlements, the DAV argued veterans' policy, not even research into prosthetics, should not be confused with civilian policy.[55]

In reaction to civilian disability activism and lingering tensions from earlier policy debates, Malisoff argued that veterans leading the way was the only way. He maintained, "After every victorious war of the democracy, veterans' benefit legislation has extended the frontiers of social legislation, setting precedents and creating practical models that inspire similar civilian benefits for the nonveteran population." Hinting at the American Federation of the Physically Handicapped's relatively unsuccessful campaign to expand the benefits available to disabled civilians, Malisoff argued that because disabled civilians had yet to win government support, including their needs in a research program would make it difficult to fund and slow the progress.[56]

Malisoff and the DAV built on past successful arguments of veterans' special status and the dangers of mixing civilian and veteran policy. Malisoff concluded that progress in artificial limbs was absolutely necessary to pay back "an undischarged war debt." In contrast to a program that lumped the needs of civilians and veterans together, as had been suggested in 1942, he argued that a research program focused on addressing the needs of disabled veterans "would stand second to no item on the postwar agenda."[57]

The pressure veterans and their organizations had mounted for change forced action on several fronts. Responding to the testimony it had heard, the Committee on Aid to the Physically Handicapped issued a scathing report, condemning the "shocking examples" they had seen of low quality prostheses, poor methods of providing and fitting those appliances, and unnecessary bureaucracy that veterans had to navigate to receive a working, well-fit, quality prosthetic. Committee chair Augustine B. Kelley (D-Pa.) laid into the VA, arguing that the limitations it set on how often, where, and at what cost veterans could obtain prostheses "condemn[ed] the veteran who is badly fitted to needless and inexcusable pain and inconvenience." VA regulations, he maintained, concentrated on the prevention of fraud at the expense of ensuring that veteran amputees received proper limbs. The committee urged the VA to relax its strict regulations in relation to prostheses, making it easier for men to obtain better prosthetics and repairs on the ones that they already had. Kelley scoffed at the idea that a man with no real complaint would take off work to demand unnecessary repairs or willy-nilly request new limbs, given that breaking in a new artificial limb was an extremely painful process. On the critical topic of research, Kelley deviated from the veterans' first principle. He concluded, "Because the Veterans' Administration has no tradition of successful research or scientific excellence," the research under way in the Committee on Prosthetic Devices should be taken up by the U.S. Public Health Service.[58]

The VA was not the only organization to take a hit in the committee's report. Kelley also focused considerable attention on the artificial limb industry, maintaining that there existed "little substantial difference in the limbs being made and furnished veterans now and those made at the close of the Civil War." He pointed out that the artificial limb industry faced less regulation than barbers and beauticians. He reported that the committee had induced the Federal Trade Commission to develop a trade-practice code for the industry and encouraged the FBI to investigate the industry's violations of antitrust laws.[59]

The committee's call to action produced results. The Justice Department indicted approximately three-quarters of the artificial limb industry for antitrust violations, claiming that members of the ALMA had fixed prices. The Justice Department charged that these manufacturers had agreed to submit identical, artificially inflated prices to the VA when it collected its annual bids and to charge higher prices to veterans who approached them directly. Finally, the indictment alleged that the manufacturers of artificial limb parts had refused to sell to government agencies that provided limbs for free. The Justice Department secured convictions, but the U.S. Court of Appeals reversed these convictions.[60] Despite this reversal, the investigation and prosecution brought attention to the industry and demonstrated that veterans, the public, and the government would not tolerate abuses of the nation's former and current servicemen.

The public lashing in Congress and in the press also pushed the VA into action. The VA chaffed at the committee's characterizations of its policies and at the notion of the Public Health Service taking over research. It requested a second opportunity to talk with the committee and sent Maj. Gen. Paul R. Hawley, surgeon general of the VA, to make its case. While careful not to malign the Public Health Administration, Hawley pointed out that under the new leadership of Gen. Omar Bradley things had changed in the VA. While the VA might have appeared to be unconcerned before, he argued that that was no longer the case. Hawley said that the VA had been so impressed with the work of the Committee on Prosthetic Devices that it had arranged to funnel existing research monies within the VA into the committee. Additionally, the VA had hired Walter Bura, an outstanding engineer who happened to be an amputee, to run its revamped prosthetic program. Moreover, Hawley reported progress in simplifying the repair process by negotiating maintenance and upkeep into all of its new contracts with manufacturers. The VA also would be pushing manufacturers to agree to offer repairs on limbs made by other companies. Further, the VA planned to open orthopedic shops in each of its general hospitals to service veteran amputees and to pay for their travel expenses to one of these shops. Finally, he concluded that of all the government agencies involved in prosthetics, the VA was "more concerned than the Public Health Service."[61]

While the VA's actions were no doubt encouraged by a desire not to lose ground to another agency, veterans and their organizations played an integral role in creating the threat. In the end, the VA altered its policies, invested a million dollars a year in research, and instituted a policy of veteran participation in its administration. In fact, a committee of veteran amputees would consult with the VA in its research program, and by 1948, this new program of research became a permanent fixture in VA policy when it succeeded in winning congressional approval of an annual prosthetic research budget of one million dollars.[62]

Ultimately, veterans and their organizations had focused national attention on the plight of servicemen with amputations and leveraged this national attention to force the VA into action. With federal research dollars being funneled through the VA, veterans ensured first and special access to prosthetic development. Veteran amputees had succeeded in turning prosthetics into "emblem[s] of distinction." Prosthetics developed through this research would most certainly eventually become available to civilians, but veterans, because of their service, received the fruits of the combination of federal dollars, modern technology, and industry at no cost and before they were available to civilians.

While civilians, industry, and lawmakers pushed for the universal in disability policy, veterans insisted that distinctions be made. Throughout the war and early postwar years, veterans and their organizations demanded recognition of their special status within the polity as payment for their service to the nation. By claiming and policing the boundaries of the benefits connected to service, veterans actively shaped a new channel in the maze of the U.S. welfare state. This category of entitlement linked service with a new and higher, guaranteed standard of living supported and maintained by the federal government. Like policies that linked industrial work to programs such as Social Security, these were earned benefits—earned though sacrifice and service to the nation. By policing the boundaries between veteran and civilian disability policy, veterans tended to emphasize the distance between their earned benefits and the benevolent aid that might be bestowed on the nation's unfortunate disabled citizenry.

# Notes

1. U.S. Congress, House, Committee on Labor, Subcommittee to Investigate Aid to the Physically Handicapped [hereafter APH], *Hearings*, Parts 1–25, 78th–79th Cong. (Washington, D.C.: G.P.O., 1945–46).

2. Testimony of Captain Frank P. Kreuz, Medical Corps, Bureau of Medicine and Surgery, U.S. Navy, U.S. Congress, House, Committee on Labor, Subcommittee to Investigate APH, *Hearings*, Part 15, Amputees, 79th Cong., 1st sess. (Washington, D.C.: G.P.O., 1945), 1586–95.

3. For a general history of the New Deal and World War II era, see David M. Kennedy, *Freedom from Fear: The American People in Depression and War, 1929–1945* (New York: Oxford University Press, 1999). For the postwar period, see James T. Patterson, *Grand Expectations: The Unites State, 1945–1974* (Oxford: Oxford University Press, 1996).

4. See David A. Gerber, "Heroes and Misfits: The Troubled Social Reintegration of Disabled Veterans in *The Best Years of Our Lives*," in *Disabled Veterans in History*, edited by David A. Gerber (Ann Arbor: University of Michigan Press), 70–95; and Susan M. Hartmann, "Prescriptions for Penelope: Literature on Women's Obligations to Returning World War II Veterans," *Women's Studies* 5 (1978): 223–39.

5. For histories of the welfare state and the drive for security in this uncertain time, see Jill Quadagno, *One Nation Uninsured: Why the U.S. Has No National Health Insurance* (Oxford: Oxford University Press, 2005); Edward D. Berkowitz, *Robert Ball and the Politics of Social Security* (Madison: University of Wisconsin Press, 2003); Colin Gordon, *Dead on Arrival: The Politics of Health Care in Twentieth-Century America* (Princeton, N.J.: Princeton University Press, 2003); Jennifer Klein, *For All These Rights: Business, Labor, and the Shaping of America's Public-Private Welfare State* (Princeton, N.J.: Princeton University Press, 2003); Alice Kessler-Harris, *In Pursuit of Equity: Women, Men, and the Quest for Economic Citizenship in 20th-Century America* (Oxford: Oxford University Press, 2001); Edwin Amenta, *Bold Relief: Institution Politics and the Origins of Modern American Social Policy* (Princeton, N.J.: Princeton University Press, 1998); Edward D. Berkowitz, *Mr. Social Security: The Life of Wilbur J. Cohen* (Lawrence: University Press of Kansas, 1995); and Alan Derickson, "Health Security for All? Social Unionism and Universal Health Insurance, 1935–1958," *Journal of American History* 80 (March 1994), 1333–56.

6. Figure taken from Patterson, *Grand Expectations*, 4. For a discussion of civilians' role in this redefinition of the welfare state, see Audra Jennings, "With Minds Fixed on the Horrors of War: Liberalism and Disability Activism, 1940–1960" (Ph.D. diss., Ohio State University, 2008).

7. Surprisingly few scholars have studied veteran politics in the New Deal and postwar periods. Much of the existing work focuses on the G.I. Bill. Stephen R. Ortiz's recent book contextualizes this major policy gain by examining the relationship of veterans to the New Deal. See Stephen R. Ortiz, *Beyond the Bonus March and GI Bill: How Veteran Politics Shaped the New Deal Era* (New York: New York University Press, 2010). For a study of the G.I. Bill and its impact on civic participation, see Suzanne Mettler, *Soldiers to Citizens: The G.I. Bill and the Making of the Greatest Generation* (Oxford: Oxford University Press, 2005). Many scholars have examined the ways that the G.I. Bill excluded gay and lesbian soldiers, African Americans, and women; see Margot Canaday, "Building a Straight State: Sexuality and Social Citizenship under the 1944 G.I. Bill," *Journal of American History* 90 (December 2003): 935–57; Robert F. Jefferson, "'Enabled Courage': Race, Disability, and Black World War II Veterans in Postwar America," *Historian* 65 (September 2003): 1102–24; and Susan M. Hartmann, *The*

*Home Front and Beyond: American Women in the 1940s* (Boston: Twayne Publishers, 1982). For a celebratory history of the G.I. Bill, see Michael J. Bennett, *When Dreams Came True: The G.I. Bill and the Making of Modern America* (Washington, D.C.: Potomac Books, 1996). For more on the social response to veterans, see Hartmann, "Prescriptions for Penelope." For disabled veterans, see Gerber, *Disabled Veterans in History*.

8. Katherine Ott skillfully traces the contours of the literature on the cultural meanings of prosthetics in her coedited collection on the history of prosthetics. See Katherine Ott, "The Sum of Its Parts: An Introduction to Modern Histories of Prosthetics," in *Artificial Parts, Practical Lives: Modern Histories of Prosthetics*, edited by Katherine Ott, David Serlin, and Stephen Mihm, 1–42 (New York: New York University Press, 2002). This collection moves to uncover the concrete lives of the individuals who used prosthetics in different times and places. See also David Serlin, *Replaceable You: Engineering the Body in Postwar America* (Chicago: University of Chicago Press, 2004).

9. Historians have written much about the divided nature of the welfare state, arguing that the mechanisms of the welfare state divided benefits into two categories: entitlement and aid. In this dichotomy of welfare, workers earned benefits while dependents received aid because of their familial relationships to workers or through the beneficence of the state. Much recent scholarship on the welfare state has built upon this "two-channel" model. This scholarship reveals the way that prevailing social constructions of race, gender, class, and sexuality shaped these channels, determining who qualified for benefits and who would receive aid. See Robyn Muncy, "Coal-Fired Reforms: Social Citizenship, Dissident Miners, and the Great Society," *Journal of American History* 96 (June 2009): 72–98; Ira Katznelson, *When Affirmative Action Was White: An Untold History of Racial Inequality in Twentieth-Century America* (New York: W. W. Norton, 2005); Canaday, "Building a Straight State"; Kessler-Harris, *In Pursuit of Equity*; Suzanne Mettler, *Dividing Citizens: Gender and Federalism in New Deal Public Policy* (Ithaca, N.Y.: Cornell University Press, 1998); Linda Gordon, *Pitied but Not Entitled: Single Mothers and the History of Welfare, 1890–1935* (New York: Free Press, 1994); and Linda Gordon, ed., *Women, the State, and Welfare* (Madison: University of Wisconsin Press, 1990).

10. See Memo, 8 April 1942; Memo for the President from Harold Smith, 22 April 1942; Memo for the Director of the Budget, 12 March 1942, Paul McNutt to the President, 27 February 1942; and Memo for the President from the Director of the Bureau of the Budget, 17 July 1942, Franklin D. Roosevelt Papers, Official File 504, Advisory Committee on Vocational Education, 1941–45, box 2, Franklin D. Roosevelt Presidential Library, Hyde Park, N.Y. [hereafter, Roosevelt Papers]. Memo from Paul McNutt to the President, 30 March 1942, Franklin D. Roosevelt Papers, OF 836, Physically Handicapped Persons, box 2, Roosevelt Papers; Memo about Director of the Bureau of the Budget's Position, 17 July 1942, Franklin D. Roosevelt Papers, OF 3700, Federal Security Agency, box 1, Roosevelt Papers.

11. Congress, Senate, Senator La Follette of Wisconsin introducing S. 2714, 77th Cong., 2nd sess., *Congressional Record* [hereafter CR] 88, pt. 5 (13 August 1942): 6819–20; Congress, House, Representative Barden of North Carolina introducing H.R. 7484, 77th Cong., 2nd sess., CR 88, pt. 5 (13 August 1942): 6853.

12. Congress, Senate, Senator La Follette of Wisconsin introducing S. 2714, 77th Cong., 2nd sess., CR 88, pt. 5 (13 August 1942): 6819–20; Congress, House, Representative Barden of North Carolina introducing H.R.7484, 77th Cong., 2nd sess., CR 88, pt. 5 (13 August 1942): 6853; Congress, House, Representative Barden of North Carolina introducing H.R. 699, 78th Cong., 1st sess., CR 89, pt. 1 (6 January 1943), 24; Congress, Senate, Senator La Follette of Wisconsin introducing S. 180, 78th Cong., 1st sess., CR 89, pt. 1 (7 January 1943), 36; Congress, Senate,

Remarks of Senator Wheeler of Montana on Vocational Rehabilitation, 78th Cong., 1st sess., CR 89, pt. 2 (5 March 1943), 1568–69; Congress, Senate, Debate over S. 180 and S. 786, 78th Cong., 1st sess., CR 89, pt. 2 (5 March 1943), 1580–95, 1605–12; Congress, House, Debate over S. 786, 78th Cong., 1st sess., CR 89, pt. 2 (15 March 1943), 1986–88; Congress, Senate, Message from the President, 78th Cong., 1st sess., CR 89, pt. 2 (25 March 1943), 2447–48; Congress, House, Debate over H.R. 2536, 78th Cong., 1st sess., CR 89, pt. 4 (10 June 1943), 5654–79; Congress, Senate, Debate over H.R. 2536, 78th Cong., 1st sess., CR 89, pt. 5 (22 June 1943), 6253–64; Congress, Senate, Amendment of Vocational Rehabilitation Act—Conference Report, 78th Cong., 1st sess., CR 89, pt. 5 (29 June 1943), 6726; Congress, House, Vocational Rehabilitation Act Amendments, 1943, 78th Cong., 1st sess., CR 89, pt. 5 (29 June 1943), 6750–56; and Congress, House, Message from the President, 78th Cong., 1st sess., CR 89, pt. 6 (14 September 1943), 7550. The veteran rehabilitation bill became the Vocational Rehabilitation Act of 1943, and the civilian bill became the Barden–La Follette Act of 1943.

13. Scott Sigmund Gartner, "Military Personnel and Casualties, by War and Branch of Service: 1775–1991," Table Ed1–5 in *Historical Statistics of the United States, Earliest Times to the Present: Millennial Edition*, edited by Susan B. Carter, Scott Sigmund Gartner, Michael R. Haines, Alan L. Olmstead, Richard Sutch, and Gavin Wright (New York: Cambridge University Press, 2006). Available online at http://dx.doi.org.proxy.lib.ohio-state.edu/10.1017/ISBN-9780511132971.Ed1–145 (accessed 19 September 2009); Testimony of Colonel Leonard T. Peterson, Chief of Orthopedic Branch, Office of the Surgeon General, Army Medical Corps, House, APH, *Hearings*, Part 15, 1571.

14. Peterson, House, APH, *Hearings*, Part 15, 1571–84; Leonard T. Peterson, "Medical History of World War II: Surgery-Amputations-ZI," folder Surgery-Amputations-ZI, Medical Hist WWII-Amputations-ZI, box 454, Record Group 112, Office of the Surgeon General of the Army, WWII Administrative Records [hereafter, RG 112], National Archives and Records Administration, College Park, MD [hereafter, NARA II].

15. Technical Information Division, Office of the Surgeon General, U.S. Army, "The Physically Disabled," *Annals of the American Academy of Political and Social Science* 239 (May 1945), 10–19; and Albert E. Cowdrey, *Fighting for Life: American Military Medicine in World War II* (New York: Free Press, 1994), 165–69.

16. Leonard T. Peterson, "Medical History of World War II: Surgery-Amputations-ZI," folder Surgery-Amputations-ZI, Medical Hist WWII-Amputations-ZI, box 454, RG 112, NARA II; and Gartner, "Military personnel and casualties," Table Ed1–5.

17. Peterson, House, APH, *Hearings*, Part 15, 1571; and Leonard T. Peterson, "Medical History of World War II: Surgery-Amputations-ZI," folder Surgery-Amputations-ZI, Medical Hist WWII-Amputations-ZI, box 454, RG 112, NARA II.

18. Peterson, House, APH, *Hearings*, Part 15, 1571–72; Peterson, "Medical History of World War II."

19. Peterson, House, APH, *Hearings*, Part 15, 1571–86; and Peterson, "Medical History of World War II."

20. Peterson; Testimony of T. O. Kraabel, National Director of Rehabilitation, The American Legion; Testimony of Charles McGonegal, National Field Secretary, American Legion, House, APH, *Hearings*, Part 15, 1575, 1570, 1595–1603; and Peterson, "Medical History of World War II."

21. Peterson, House, APH, *Hearings*, Part 15, 1572–73; and Peterson, "Medical History of World War II."

22. Peterson, House, APH, *Hearings*, Part 15, 1572–80; and Peterson, "Medical History of World War II."

23. Kreuz, and Peterson, House, APH, *Hearings*, Part 15, 1571–95; Leonard T. Peterson, "Medical History of World War II: Surgery-Amputations-ZI," folder Surgery-Amputations-ZI, Medical Hist WWII-Amputations-ZI, box 454, RG 112, NARA II.

24. Kreuz, and Peterson, House, APH, *Hearings*, Part 15, 1580, 1586–95.

25. Kreuz, House, APH, *Hearings*, Part 15, 1586–89; Glenn Gritzer and Arnold Arluke, *The Making of Rehabilitation: A Political Economy of Medical Specialization, 1890–1980* (Berkeley: University of California Press, 1985), 86–122.

26. Kreuz, House, APH, *Hearings*, Part 15, 1588–89.

27. Testimony of Dr. Charles M. Griffith, Medical Director, Veterans' Administration, House, APH, *Hearings*, Part 15, 1607–8.

28. Leonard T. Peterson, "Medical History of World War II: Surgery-Amputations-ZI," folder Surgery-Amputations-ZI, Medical Hist WWII-Amputations-ZI, box 454, RG 112, NARA II.

29. Kreuz, House, APH, *Hearings*, Part 15, 1591–92.

30. Testimony of Lt. Sol Rael, U.S. Army, House, APH, *Hearings*, Part 15, 1654–58.

31. Testimony of Lt. Howard Morse, U.S. Army, and Rael, House, APH, *Hearings*, Part 15, 1656–63.

32. Testimony of Eugene F. Trainor, A Veteran, House, APH, *Hearings*, Part 15, 1667–71.

33. Ibid.

34. Testimony of Robert L. Rogers, Sparrows Point, MD, House, APH, *Hearings*, Part 15, 1709–15.

35. Ibid.

36. Ibid.

37. American Legion Resolution, Twenty-fourth Annual National Convention, Kansas City, MO, September 1942, folder 422 Prosthetic Appliances-Artificial Limbs, box 374, Record Group 15, Records of the Veterans Administration, Policy and General Administration Files [Hereafter, RG 15], National Archives and Records Administration, Washington, D.C. [Hereafter, NARA I].

38. T. O. Kraabel to Gen. Frank T. Hines, 21 October 1942, folder 422 Prosthetic Appliances-Artificial Limbs, box 374, RG 15, NARA I; and Canaday, "Building a Straight State," 939.

39. Gen. Frank T. Hines to Chester C. Hadden, 14 November 1942, folder 422 Prosthetic Appliances-Artificial Limbs, box 374, RG 15, NARA I.

40. Chester C. Hadden to Gen. Frank T. Hines, 30 November 1942, folder 422 Prosthetic Appliances-Artificial Limbs, box 374, RG 15, NARA I.

41. Gen. Frank T. Hines to T. O. Kraabel, 14 December 1942, folder 422 Prosthetic Appliances-Artificial Limbs, box 374, RG 15, NARA I.

42. Peterson, "Medical History of World War II: Surgery-Amputations-ZI," folder Surgery-Amputations-ZI, Medical Hist WWII-Amputations-ZI, box 454, RG 112, NARA II.

43. Kreuz, and Peterson, House, APH, *Hearings*, Part 15, 1571–95

44. Peterson, "Medical History of World War II: Surgery-Amputations-ZI," folder Surgery-Amputations-ZI, Medical Hist WWII-Amputations-ZI, box 454, RG 112, NARA II.

45. Ibid.; and Testimony of Dr. Paul E. Klopsteg, Chairman, Committee on Prosthetic Devices, National Academy of Sciences, House, APH, *Hearings*, Part 15, 1616–28.

46. Ibid.

47. Drew Pearson, "The Washington Merry-Go-Round," *Washington Post*, 10 February 1945, 5.

48. Ibid.

49. Edward M. Maisel, "Should Veterans Have Legs?" *The Nation*, 10 March 1945, 271–72.

50. Dorothy Dunbar Bromley, "Army Amputees' Lives Not Bright as Pictured," *Washington Post*, 17 June 1945, B2.

51. House, APH, *Hearings*, Part 15.

52. Griffith, Medical Director, House, APH, *Hearings*, Part 15, 1607–9.

53. Kraabel, and McGonegal, House, APH, *Hearings*, Part 15, 1595–1603.

54. McGonegal, House, APH, *Hearings*, Part 15, 1596–1603.

55. Testimony of Dr. Harry Malisoff, Chairman, Disabled American Veterans Committee for Scientific Research and Development Programs for Handicapped Veterans, House, APH, *Hearings*, Part 15, 1703–7.

56. Ibid.; for more on the American Federation of the Physically Handicapped, see Jennings, "With Minds Fixed."

57. Malisoff, House, APH, *Hearings*, Part 15, 1703–7.

58. Report of Rep. Augustine B. Kelley, U.S. Congress, House, Committee on Labor, Subcommittee to Investigate APH, *Hearings*, Part 15a, Amputees, 79th Cong., 1st sess. (Washington, D.C.: G.P.O., 1945), 1–7.

59. Ibid.

60. "Artificial Limb Price-Fixing Charged to 45 Firms by Federal Indictment," *New York Times*, 15 November 1945, 8; "Limb Firms Indicted for Price Fixing," *Washington Post*, 15 November 1945, 1; and "Court Reverses Convictions of Artificial Limb Makers," *Washington Post*, 28 January 1947, 3.

61. Testimony of Maj. Gen. Paul Hawley, Surgeon General, VA, House, APH, *Hearings*, Part 15a, 9–24.

62. Congress, House, Message from the President, 80th Cong., 2nd sess., CR 94, pt. 8 (26 July 1948), 9365–66; Charles Hurd, "Veterans to Pass on Artificial Limbs," *New York Times*, 3 November 1945, 4; Charles Hurd, "Engineer, Who Lost Leg, Named Chief of Prosthetics for 'Vets,'" *New York Times*, 14 November 1945, 8; and "$1,000,000 For Help to War Disabled," *New York Times*, 27 October 1945, 13.

# III

## The Politics of Race and Labor

# 5

# "Put Fighting Blood in Your Business"

## The U.S. War Department and the Reemployment of World War I Soldiers

NANCY GENTILE FORD

The demobilization of some four million American soldiers at the end of World War I occurred simultaneously with widespread social unrest, rising unemployment, and economic hardship characterized by frequent labor strikes and the nation's first Red Scare. Successful solutions to combat the political and economic crisis did not come from Progressive reforms, the U.S. Labor Department, Congress, or the White House but from an unlikely source—the U.S. War Department. In an effort to reestablish soldiers into civilian life and keep the young men out of the "clutches" of Bolshevism, the War Department created a massive campaign to convince American employers to "put fighting blood" in their businesses. The War Department's Emergency Employment Committee for Soldiers, Sailors and Marines of the Council of National Defense gathered together leading economists and well-educated officers to formulate inventive reemployment strategies including specialized employment services, creative publicity campaigns, citation awards, and public works projects. In doing so, the War Department exerted unprecedented—and largely unexamined—control over veterans' policy.

## Bring the Boys Home

Although demobilization was under way by January 1919 (mostly men stationed on the home front), some two million men still anxiously waited abroad for their homecoming and a return to the job market. According to a War Department report, "with labor conditions already bad and with . . . many men yet to be demobilized . . . the situation was extremely uncomfortable."[1] Demobilization was not an easy task. The secretary of War, Newton D. Baker, emphasized that it was important to return the men "back into the normal life of the country without filling the country with unemployed men."[2] Yet the U.S. Army chief of staff, Gen. Peyton C. March, explained the difficulty of returning millions of men into the postwar civilian society. March concluded, "There was no precedents afforded by experience of our former wars," since in past conflicts soldiers generally returned in much smaller numbers and often to an improved economy due to "economic and territorial expansion of the nation."[3] As Col. (and former president) Theodore Roosevelt noted at a meeting of the Brooklyn Chamber of Commerce, "after the Civil War we still had a frontier. We absorbed a great many of the restless people on the frontier. We have no frontier now."[4]

Slowing the demobilization process was not an option, especially considering that the citizen-soldiers and their families demanded an immediate return home. Cost was another key issue. Assistant Secretary of War Benedict Crowell estimated that the price tag for the conflict had reached "about $50,000,000 day" by 11 November 1918. Crowell added, "Everyday of indecision in adopting" and implementing demobilization "added tremendously to the burden of taxation . . . for generations to come."[5]

The War Department planners came up with four options: demobilize by prewar trades or occupations, by length of service, by original point of induction, or by military units. Although returning soldiers by trade or occupation may have helped prevent a sudden rise of unemployed men, it would have required the massive regrouping of soldiers before the discharge process. It would also necessitate a clear understanding of the labor market and industrial situations not readily available. After some discussion, General March agreed the best plan was to return soldiers with their units. This was important since, as one military report put it, there was "strong sentiment among the men" who had fought together to come home together and "perhaps have a parade before the home folks."[6] However, this decision, although considered to be the best for the morale of the soldiers, would worsen an already growing economic recession.[7]

Most divisions did return to American de-embarkation centers together and were then divided into groups based on home territory. Each group was sent to one of thirty-three demobilization camps located throughout the United States, which placed soldiers in "close proximity" to their homes. There, soldiers were deloused, bathed, and inspected before receiving back pay; a bonus of sixty dollars; and a new uniform, shoes, and a coat. Social welfare volunteers took soldiers directly to railroad stations so the men could buy tickets home (at reduced prices). "This encouraged men to return directly to their homes instead of squandering their money and lingering in large urban area," Colonel Doe explained the problem.[8]

The military demobilization process had its share of critics in Congress and the press. Communities suffering from the closing of munitions factories "protested" the return of soldiers that would escalate their economic crisis. Production that once flowed quickly eroded in most industrial areas, and cities that lost war contracts faced escalating unemployment. In early January 1919 the U.S. Department of Labor conducted a survey of 122 U.S. cities and reported that 39 percent had an "oversupply" of workers. This number would rise rapidly in coming months.[9] To add to the crisis, in early 1919 more than one hundred thousand men a month began arriving back in the United States. Shortly, the number rose to ten thousand a day. The statistical branch of the General Staff noted that the number of doughboys out of work grew from 16 percent in February to 33 percent in March 1919. By April 1919 unemployment rates for returning soldiers rose to 41 percent. A War Department investigation indicated that in parts of the country more than a million former soldiers could not find employment.

The unemployment in the nation's major cities also reached critical levels. Woods reported, "In some of the larger cities and manufacturing centers, hundreds of discharged men, most of them still in uniform, were walking the streets looking for work."[10] In early 1919 U.S. labor statistics estimated that discharged men made up 25 percent of the unemployed in New York City. Labor experts expected this number to double by April 1919 with the continued demobilization of the Twenty-seventh and Seventy-seventh divisions. Other government investigations indicated, "returning soldiers added to the labor tension" in Seattle and Portland, and soldiers could be found "among the waterfront workers [causing] continuous unrest."[11] Reports from around the nation also told of former soldiers, still in uniform, who were "peddling and panhandling" to make a living.[12]

Although a number of social welfare agencies and veteran organizations such as the Red Cross, YMCA, National Catholic War Council, Salvation Army, Jewish Welfare Board, and American Legion were graciously trying to help soldiers find jobs, they had limited success. The War Department found the agencies' reemployment efforts were often hampered by "factional jealousies and local animosities" from the groups who did not coordinate their efforts and had a limited knowledge of the workplace. The result was "wasted effort, useless expense" and "duplication."[13]

## Crisis in the Department of Labor

Problems in the U.S. Department of Labor made the postwar situation worse. Influenced by reformers during the Progressive Era, Congress created the Department of Labor in 1913 "to foster, promote, and develop the welfare of the wage earners of the United States, to improve their working conditions [and] to advance their opportunities for profitable employment by maintaining a national system of employment offices."[14] President Woodrow Wilson appointed William B. Wilson (no relation) as the first secretary of Labor. William Wilson, a former secretary-treasurer of the United Mine Workers of America and a former member of Congress, oversaw the establishment of the U.S. Employment Service during the war as an emergency agency.

Although Congress approved the original financing of the U.S. Employment Service, the agency was struggling by 1919. The service's newly created Bureau for Returning Soldiers, Sailors, and Marines was in place in many cities but proved ineffective due to financial constraints. To make matters worse, many local chambers of commerce across the nation refused to work with the federal employment service since they associated the agency with the hiring of "labor men," and therefore, with unionization.[15]

In March 1919 Congress refused to provide additional funding to the employment agency, further reducing its effectiveness. A few months later, Rep. Thomas Lindsay Blanton (D-Tex.) shouted down another attempted appropriation to the U.S. Employment Service, declaring it "unauthorized by law." Frustrated supporters of the agency predicted it would soon "be forced to curtail its operations even more strictly . . . or disband completely."[16]

The debate over the effectiveness of the U.S. Employment Service continued through the spring, summer, and fall of 1919. In June 1919 the Senate began to debate a possible Labor Department appropriation of four hundred thousand dollars. Those who supported the appropriation argued that the employment office needed to be equipped to assist some four million returning soldiers. But the opposition alleged that the office was securely in the hands of organized labor and charged the agency with corruption and blatant misspending. Those who opposed funding the U.S. Employment Service ruled the day, and eventually its ability to assist civilians and discharged men was reduced by 80 percent.[17]

Making matters worse, the U.S. Congress did not promptly address the rapidly growing economic crisis. Surely Congress was inundated trying to "unscramble much of the wartime legislature," including returning the railroads, telegraphs, and telephone systems back to private control.[18] On the first day of the session in the House, more than "600 measures" materialized. Postwar fears of radicalism brought forth Americanization and immigrant restriction legislation. Taxes, women's suffrage, and prohibition also made the agenda. Although Congress immediately discussed the repeal of the wartime Espionage Act, the Senate—now caught up in the Red Scare—was busy adopting a number of resolutions calling for the investigation of "radical intellectuals" and checking "the spread of bolshevism." Members of Congress vowed to uncover organizations thought to be "planning to overthrow the American government by violence."[19] There were also long, heated debates over the League of Nations and the country's movement toward isolationism. Debates over federal versus state responsibility also crippled Congress. Congressional discussions on how best to help with problems associated with demobilization quickly stalled in a quagmire of investigating commissions that tended to print findings in "volumes very rarely read." The U.S. Employment Service became trapped in the intense debates.[20]

## The War Department Steps In

The nation clearly faced a major crisis. Secretary of War Newton Baker "foresaw that, unless something was done and done quickly, the results of the breaking-down of the [federal] employment Service would be both far-reaching and of untold danger." Baker declared that "it was obviously up to the War Department to step into the breach," and he approved of a massive campaign to find jobs for returning doughboys.[21] To expedite the process, Baker created the Office of Assistant to the Secretary of War on 3 March 1919. (This would eventually develop into the Service and Information Branch of the War Plans Division of the General Staff.)

In the lead was Col. Arthur D. Woods, the new assistant to the secretary of War. A graduate of Harvard College and the University of Berlin, Woods's civilian life included work as a schoolmaster, reporter, businessman, New York police commissioner, and associate director of foreign propaganda for the Committee on Public Information (CPI). He was commissioned in the Army's Aviation Section in March 1918, and after his honorable discharge from his position as the assistant director of Military Aeronautics in January 1919, Woods took on the project of finding jobs for the returning troops.[22]

Woods saw the War Department's reemployment efforts "not as a charity, or even as a kindness, but as a duty that rests on everybody with power and opportunity to assist the Government in meeting its moral as well as its technical obligation to those who have served it so heroically."[23] Colonel Woods believed that the War Department's ethical responsibility for returning doughboys extended beyond the sixty dollar bonus and free transportation home, especially considering the sacrifices of the American soldiers who did their patriotic duty but now returned home to a poor economy that offered little opportunity. In addition, Woods noted, "If no legal responsibility, at least a moral one rested upon the Government, which had taken these men out of civil life."[24] Despite the language of patriotism and moral obligation, however, it was the postwar return of intense labor and capital hostility that spurred military leaders to act.

The rapid onset of the Red Scare served as the key motivation for the War Department's involvement in finding jobs for doughboys. Prior to World War I, many Progressive reformers and union leaders opposed unregulated capitalism that resulted in a sharp disproportion of wealth and left much of the urban and rural poor living and working in unsafe, dangerous, and disease-ridden squalor. Workers' wartime gains brought on by labor shortages and lucrative government war contracts temporarily improved conditions and inadvertently helped fuel the rise in labor union membership. However, the sudden end of the war brought about the hasty cancellation of profitable war contracts. Workers' demands to hold on to economic advances made during the conflict and the rapid rise of inflation led to widespread labor agitation. Faced with reduction of wages and hours, mounting economic uncertainty, and increasing job competition, workers reacted. At war's end, strikes plagued postwar America. In 1919 alone, more than 3,300 strikes involving some four million workers (one in every five) shook the nation as laborers joined the fight for better wages and working conditions in bitter disputes. The U.S. Labor Department reported strikes in twenty-four different states as the economy worsened.[25]

This widespread labor unrest collided with postwar social stress and the lingering super-patriotic hysteria stemming from the war that demanded total conformity and an end to radicalism. While the American Federation of Labor (AFL), the leading trade union, sought to soften the disparages of capitalism, the Industrial Workers of the World (IWW), founded by socialists, radical trade unionists, and anarchists, stood firm against the abuses of a system that exploited the workers and left so many Americans trapped in the underclass. In reality, American Socialist, Anarchist, and Communist organizations fragmented over conflicting ideology and had relatively low membership. However, the harsh and prolonged reaction of the American public and government to the 1917 Bolshevik Revolution in Russia left no room for radicalism, perceived to be on a rapid rise in America. By 1919 radicalism had become synonymous with unionism. The acute tension in the nation mounted as Atty. Gen. A. Mitchell Palmer arrested thousands of suspected communists and deported some 250 foreign-born radicals in the legendary "Palmer Raids."

Assistant Secretary of War Col. Arthur Woods feared that the outcome of labor strikes created an unstable work place that would prevent the assimilation of soldiers back into American society. As labor unrest spread and strikes grew more frequent, governors called out the National Guard to suppress the strikers. Although not specifically stated in their reports, the War Department was surely aware that the growing labor unrest increasingly pitted the National Guard against ex-soldiers. With the growing antagonism between capital and labor, Woods also warned against "the crucial danger of discontented soldiers" being tempted by radicals. Woods told his staff, "The soldier is unsteady. . . . He is wayward and impatient and unsettled. . . . We cannot let them alone to wander about the streets and listen to the Bolsheviki."[26] Colonel Woods reminded his men that the key to locking out radicalism was to assist the returning soldiers in readjusting to civilian life, since the soldiers' sympathies would be determined by how they were treated.[27]

Former army chief of staff Maj. Gen. Leonard Wood, who fought hard to improve the military in the prewar years, joined the voices warning against the danger of radicalism. Wood told the *New York Times* that without jobs soldiers could become "more susceptible to the influences of Bolshevism."[28] After a new union made up of returning service members called the Soldiers, Sailors, and Marine Council joined the American Federation of Labor, the general asked the new unionists in Chicago to "disband their organization." They refused. The general also alerted business leaders about another group of "radical units" consisting of unemployed discharged soldiers who created problems in Chicago. As soon as the men received help finding jobs, the situation became "much healthier."[29] In an Associated Press dispatch, General Wood called discharged men "potential reds," declaring it was "absolutely essential" for the federal government to find jobs for returning soldiers in order to "combat Bolshevism." He added, "many of the men who have returned are sick, both physically and mentally, and waiting with nothing to do and finding on every hand radical orators only too willing to sow the seeds of discontentment."[30]

Early in 1919 the *Infantry Journal* also warned against the spread of communism: "The millions in the Army must be reabsorbed into industry. Prices will fall and wages will fall with prices, but more slowly. . . . The problem of unemployment will again thrust up its head. . . . Bolshevism will be quick to make capital out of maladjustment and discontent."[31] The solution, according to the journal, was to instill the "spirit" of Americanism and good citizenship in all soldiers, especially in the many foreign-born soldiers who served in the American army. An editorial in the *Infantry Journal* warned its readers about the dangers of unions by focusing on the police strike in Boston and the "Bolshevik attitudes of policemen." The editor asked the reader to imagine a union of "soldiers, and officers, seamen and officers. . . . Pretty picture, isn't it? It is then but a step to the reddest spot of Russia, the soviet, an American Lenine [sic], and a Disunited States of America."[32]

## Emergency Employment Committee

In March 1919 Col. Arthur Woods took charge of the demobilization crisis by creating the "Emergency Employment Committee for Soldiers, Sailors and Marines of the Council of National Defense." The *New York Times* announced the new committee, "composed of some of the ablest men in Washington," and explained that its creation was necessitated by the "radical curtailment" of the U.S. Employment Service.[33] According to the *Times*, because Congress refused to allocate funds, the federal Employment Service would be "forced to order the closing of all of its branch offices except those in fifty-six important industrial centers."[34]

Woods began by sending an investigation team of military officers to inspect the economic situation throughout the United States. The group met on 11 April 1919 to share information in a brainstorming session in Chicago, Illinois. Gen. Leonard Wood joined the discussion with Colonel Woods's team which consisted of sixteen military career officers. Most of the officers had worked in the business field prior to enlistment.

Woods divided the nation into four districts and selected district chiefs to head each area. Four officers, with experience in the business field, led each district. In March Woods sent Maj. John Bateson Reynolds to Camp Lee, Virginia, to select thirty-five officers to serve as field representatives from the pool of "emergency officers desiring Regular Army commissions." These officers coordinated the employment efforts in each state and reported to their area's district chiefs. A number of naval officers also served with Woods. The team soon reached 172 members divided among the publicity section, public works section, service and information section, employment section, and personnel and office management section. Almost all of the men selected by Woods and Reynolds were well-educated, well-trained officers. Almost all held university, college, or business school degrees, and many had earned graduate or law degrees. Many officers received their education from top universities in the nation including Columbia, Cornell, Dartmouth, Harvard, Princeton, Yale, MIT, Rensselaer, and others. While some members of Wood's emergency team went into the service directly from college, others worked in a variety of fields prior to the war. This included advertising, business, construction, engineering, health inspection, law, management, news reporting, law enforcement, sales, social welfare, and teaching. Woods carefully selected soldiers from the American Expeditionary Force (AEF) because the servicemen would understand the experience of the returning doughboys and their desire to better themselves.[35]

The Emergency Employment Committee also received assistance from the Department of Labor, the Department of Agriculture, the Department of Interior, the U.S. Post Office, and social welfare leaders. Eventually, more than twenty-four thousand field representatives "stationed at reemployment centers throughout the country" came under Woods's "command." In addition, Secretary of Interior Franklin K. Lane volunteered fifteen thousand Interior employees to help Woods's team as needed.[36]

In March the War Department estimated that some three million discharged men needed assistance securing work. To help ease economic conditions and reestablish soldiers into the workplace, the War Department team developed a number of innovative solutions. First, the military allowed officers and rank-and-file men to remain in the service (if desired) until the economic situation improved. Secretary of War Baker telegraphed commanding officers telling them to make it "clear to every soldier that where he would normally be discharged under orders for demobilization, he may remain temporarily in the military service at his own written request until such time as he can secure employment."[37] Baker made this decision not only to help the soldier but also to help the economy of the nation.

## Helping Soldiers Adjust

To help veterans readjust to civilian employment, the Emergency Employment Committee's service and information section distributed three million copies—equal to six train carloads of paper—of the booklet, *Where Do We Go From Here?* The booklet, handed out on returning ships and debarkation ports, encouraged soldiers to take the first job they found, instead of waiting "indefinitely" for the right job, and provided a list of welfare organizations that offered help. The booklet also acknowledged that "the soldier's point of view was considerably changed by his service, that he returned to civil life with different ideas about what he should do, and that many changes moreover had come over the civil surroundings he had formerly known and to which he must be adjusted afresh."[38] Colonel Woods took the next step in solving the unemployment situation by taking over the operation of Employment Service's deteriorating Bureau for Returning Soldiers, Sailors, and Marines. In an official report, Woods noted that the U.S. Employment Service was crippled by financial problems, suffered from a low "esprit de corps," and had lost the confidence of business leaders throughout the United States. The bureaus were already located in more than two thousand cities and towns but not efficiently operated due to its small staff and lack of congressional funding. Therefore, Woods sent field representatives to direct each bureau with the help of available Labor Department employees and social welfare agencies. Maj. William Hoffman Kobbe served as the director of field activities. Kobbe graduated from

Yale University and worked as a forester and later in the oil business in both the Philippines and Turkey. Dozens of field representatives (active and discharged captains and lieutenants) worked under Major Kobbe and took their place in bureaus for returning soldiers throughout the United States.[39]

The War Department's Emergency Employment Committee also implemented an employment card system, rewarded citations to businesses that rehired soldiers, retrained servicemen for skilled industrial jobs, and created an intense patriotic propaganda campaign to educate the public about the demobilization crisis. Perhaps the War Department's most ambitious program was its attempt to promote public works projects. The War Department also established employment service offices in demobilization camps.

To match specific soldiers with specific jobs, the War Department asked men aboard ships returning from Europe and in Demobilization Centers to fill out employment cards noting their previous experience. Detailed instructions accompanied the cards, and officers helped the servicemen as needed. Woods advised that "each soldier on a transport should be talked to, preferably in private, and made to understand that in the United States there is a great government enterprise at work solely toward assisting him to connect with the job for which he is best fit."[40]

Because many men were returning after a two-year absence and were now unfamiliar with the nation's economic changes, the War Department suggested that the discharged men go directly to the Bureau for Returning Soldiers, Sailors, and Marines near their home (where the cards were sent) to meet with field representatives. The bureau helped untrained, technically trained, and destitute ex-soldiers by matching each soldier's job cards with available employment opportunities. In addition to bureau field representatives, personnel officers also assisted in finding jobs for soldiers.[41]

The War Department distributed millions of copies of *That Job—Your Rights*, which provided soldiers with information on the bureau and details about allotments, insurances, and bonuses. The booklet advised soldiers to be on their best behavior and show up for work. It also asked the men not to quit without notice since employers would stop cooperating with the bureau if the discharged men gave the War Department agency a bad reputation. An inspiring message told servicemen to look good for the job interviews: "Spruce up— look like a winner," look the interviewer "straight in the eye, Don't flinch . . . do your best for your employer. . . . 'Go over the top' as you did in France."[42]

Discharged military officers received special attention in finding jobs from Capt. Edwin L. Holloway, the director of placement of technical men. Holloway was a personnel manager in a Pittsburgh lumber company before serving in the Twenty-seventh Division of the AEF and as a liaison officer between Wood's office and the chief of staff. After Holloway's resignation from the Emergency Employment Committee, Woods's executive assistant, Edward S. Gardner, a Yale-trained engineer and former member of the First Marine Aviation Force, took over the task. Gardner and his staff continued the job of finding skilled positions for ex-officers, even "hunting up" jobs by visiting companies throughout the United States.[43]

## "Put Fighting Blood in Your Business"

Woods's staff also sent out two thousand letters a week to companies throughout the nation educating them about the bureau, and they personally contacted executives of big businesses. Letters from the War Department went to post office workers instructing them to direct all unemployed soldiers to the bureau, and Woods sent letters to mayors of "principal cities" to ask for help in finding jobs for discharged service members. When learning of a civil service job opening, Woods representatives directed the unemployed men to the Civil Service Department since the agency gave preference to veterans.[44]

Knowing that chambers of commerce throughout the country held a negative view of the U.S. Employment Service, Colonel Woods attempted to bring them on board by sending personal letters to chambers throughout the country asking them to work with the Bureau for Returning Soldiers, Sailors, and Marines. The letter noted the power of the chambers, called the effort to find jobs for soldiers a "privilege," and asked for the national organizations' assistance. After some discussion, the president of the U.S. Chamber of Commerce, Harry Wheeler, agreed to set up a special committee for "soldier and sailor employment" to help in the economic crisis and established a "bureau for expediting and clearing this work."[45] Wheeler also instructed local chambers to work with the War Department or to create their own committee to find job openings. Woods reported success after receiving positive responses from several hundred chambers and the promise of assistance from over 150 more. To help in the process, Woods assigned Maj. Harry Taylor as his "special representative" to act as liaison between the War Department and the U.S. Chamber of Commerce.[46]

The Emergency Employment Committee clearly understood that publicity was their "most important weapon" in achieving their goals. With firsthand experience from his days working with the CPI, Colonel Woods knew the value of a creative and passionate propaganda campaign. Therefore, Woods and his team stepped up their efforts by using the same high-pitched, super-patriotic propaganda machine used by the CPI during the war. Col. Reginald L. Foster, a graduate of Yale and a former journalist, served as Woods's director of publicity. Foster's publicity subsection was staffed with a number of military officers including 1st Lt. Bryon Philip Spry, who once served as the publicity manager for Paramount Pictures. Woods and Foster believed "if the entire country could read about jobs for soldiers, it would think about jobs for soldiers."[47]

The publicity section used automobile stickers, movie picture-slides, and posters, along with Liberty Loan workers, "Four-minute men," and school children to help spread a strong message that ex-servicemen should be rehired as soon as possible. More than thirteen thousand newspapers were identified and bombarded with daily press releases and photographs educating the public about the scope of the War Department's new role. Field representatives also visited editors of national papers to ask for their cooperation. Articles appeared in the *Women's Home Companion*, *McClure's*, *Leslie's*, *The Old Colony Magazine*, and *Life*. Soldiers' journals such as *Treat 'Em Rough*, *As You Were*, *National Service*, and the *American Legion Magazine* also helped out by publicizing the cause. This included articles titled "The Returning Soldier and a Job," "The Employer's Opportunity," "Jobs for Cripples," "Teaching Discharged Soldiers Mining," and "The Land and the Soldier." A War Department report announced, "Practically every magazine of standing in the United States gave generous space."[48]

Woods's team also focused on newspapers, magazines, Sunday supplements, and front-page stories. Articles and "ad columns" in major newspapers notified returning soldiers that the War Department was there to help them. Newspapers in New York City, including the *New York World*, *New York Times*, and *Evening Globe*, offered to assist. Woods attempted to "sell" the ex-soldiers as an "excellent buy" since the returning men were "animated by an elevated spirit of citizenship," trained by army discipline, and in top physical condition. In a front-page article of the *Times*, the colonel appealed to American industries to do their share by hiring the returning soldier—"a full sized, red blooded, two fisted man, a real American." Woods supplied nine reasons to hire ex-servicemen including the men's loyalty, mental and physical endurance, and commitment to give 100 percent. According to the colonel, the army helped develop the soldier's "skill to the highest efficiency" and taught the men to obey orders "to the best of his ability without grumbling." Newspaper articles told the stories of gallant deeds of soldiers going "over the top" and tied their return to the need to help find jobs for the young heroes. Woods also gave public speeches to emphasize that a job for ex-soldiers meant "industrial peace to our country."[49]

The War Department, the Department of Labor, and the Department of Agriculture used posters to convince employers to hire ex-soldiers and distributed them with the help of social welfare agencies and the chambers of commerce. The Red Cross donated the money needed for the War Department to produce 550,000 copies of a magnificently designed poster, "Put Fighting Blood in Your Business." The colorful, dramatic image showed American soldiers charging the battlefield. The artist located a shield listing the names of important battles in the upper left corner. The poster also read, "Here's His Record! Does He Get a Job?" Included among the more than 17,500 lantern slides developed by the War Department was a slide show titled "Put Fighting Blood in Your Business."[50]

A similar message came in another colorful poster financed by the American Red Cross and designed by a well-known artist, Dan Smith. It showed a soldier carrying his honorable discharge paper into the Bureau for Returning Soldiers and Sailors. The message was clear, "Jobs for Fighters: If You Need a Job. If You Need a Man." The American Library Association, Chambers of Commerce, Methodist Episcopal Church, U.S. Post Offices, Department of Interior, War Camp Community Service, U.S. Railroad Administration, U.S. Department of Agriculture, and the Jewish Welfare Board all assisted in distributing the poster. This poster also noted the new connection between the U.S. Employment Service and the War Department's Council of National Defense. Another government poster showed a man standing at attention as he was applying for a job. The boss noted, "I can tell you've been a soldier by the way you stand—Report for work tomorrow morning." A different poster showed an ex-soldier and a civilian walking down the street. Unlike the civilians, the soldier stood tall in his clean, pressed clothing. The caption read, "The Soldier in 'Cits.' Pick him out." Posters also reminded soldiers to "spruce" themselves up when interviewing for a job.[51]

The advertising campaign proved to be a success and soon letters poured into the government from servicemen seeking assistance. In one week alone, the War Department received 1,209 letters from soldiers, including a letter from a soldier writing to "Square-Deal Woods." The moniker also appeared in national newspapers. Woods appreciated the "Square Deal" label and said, "It would be hard to imagine a better evidence of appreciation."[52]

Churches also offered help with the War Department's new mission. The Methodist Episcopal Church designated 4 May 1919 as "Employment Sunday" and asked churches throughout the nation to join in the effort to find jobs for soldiers. President Wilson endorsed the project by adding his "voice" to the appeal. The General War Times Commission, with a membership of some 150,000 churches, pledged to help along with the National Catholic War Council and the Knights of Columbus. In sermons and statements to the press, religious leaders urged the public to support the soldiers employment effort. New York Monsignor M. J. Lavelle declared that "no more important work" existed before the public than finding jobs for returning servicemen, and Bishop David H. Greer called it "a patriotic duty."[53]

## Citation Awards

Articles, posters, slides, speeches, and sermons, no matter how compelling or imaginative, were not enough. To get industries on board, the War Department team designed an award program directed at "patriotic" employers. Any business that took back their former workers seeking reemployment after being discharged from the military received a "War and Navy Department Citation." Signed by Newton D. Baker and Arthur Woods, the certificate praised the employer who "assured the War and Navy Department that he will gladly re-employ everybody who formerly worked for him and left to serve in the army or navy during the Great War."[54] The citations, designed like shields, could be displayed in store and office windows or on service flags. Employers received one shield for each soldier they took back at war's end. Similar to the "patriotic" symbols used during the war, this shield showed the public that this employer was doing his duty. Each "citation" company or retail merchant also received newspaper publicity—a special thank you from the War Department.[55]

To advertise the citation awards, the War Department sent out thousands of letters to leading magazines, trade journals, manufacturers' associations, companies, retail merchants, and mayors of cities with populations over 5,000. Over 12,600 letters went to newspapers alone. A lantern slide show, shown at local picture houses, also drove home the patriotic reemployment message. More than 18,000 Boy Scout troops helped to advertise the awards by personally delivering citation application forms. The Emergency Employment Committee also asked more than 1,200 chambers of commerce to publicize the government's citation awards in their magazines. To celebrate the success of the program, the Fifth Avenue Association of New York City sponsored a day for all stores and offices to "simultaneously display" their citation awards on 14 July 1919. The War Department followed suit when Secretary Baker announced a "Citation Week" beginning 1 September 1919. By the end of the year the War Department had distributed some seventy thousand citations.[56] While the citation award system was not intended to displace civilian workers and replace them with discharged men, it was not immune from the prominent antiradical and anti-immigrant sentiments of the era. According to a report filed by Maj. J.C.R. Peadbody, chief of the northeastern district, in at least one section employers were asked to replace "slackers, aliens, or conscientious objectors with the 'original' soldier-employee."[57]

## Relocating Soldiers

Relocating soldiers to available jobs in rural America was another option to solve the employment crisis. In fact, during a congressional hearing, New York farmers pleaded for the continuation of the U.S. Employment Service because of the "alarming labor shortage in farming districts."[58] After cutbacks in the federal employment agency, the War Department's Emergency Employment Committee surveyed the farm situation in New York, Pennsylvania, New Jersey, Delaware, and Connecticut along with Midwest states and confirmed a critical need for labor. However, although farming opportunities were much more readily available than industrial jobs, the Emergency Committee soon discovered that returning soldiers "exhibited generally no keen desire to go to farming."[59]

With the help of a well-crafted publicity campaign, the War Department was able to "stimulate interest in so wholesome" an occupation with the help of eight hundred thousand copies of the booklet "Forward to the Farm, Why Not?" The booklet, which provided a discussion of modern agricultural method along with farming photographs, was distributed to Demobilization Centers, the remaining U.S. Employment Service offices, and the Bureau for Returning Soldiers, Sailors, and Marines. Woods's team also came to the aid of Department of Agriculture with the recruitment of some fifty thousand men for the Kansas wheat harvest in danger of being lost. In addition, the Emergency Employment Committee sent telegrams to the American Federation of Labor, the U.S. Chamber of Commerce, and various welfare agencies reporting the Kansas agricultural openings. Despite the fact that discharged men had to pay for their railroad tickets, the response from ex-soldiers was so great that within a month the Kansas crisis passed.[60]

## Industrial Retraining

Even with the success of the War Department's Emergency Employment Committee, new attitudes of the returning soldiers complicated the reemployment efforts. Military discipline, physical conditioning, and war experiences left many with a desire for improvements in their civilian lives. Perhaps even more importantly, the war experience left ex-soldiers with the belief that they now deserved career advancement and increased wages. According to a War Department report on the psychology of the servicemen, this new attitude was "due not to selfishness, lack of patriotism, or ignorance, but rather to the fact that immense experiences had supervened" and had changed "the disposition, the ambitions and the habits" of the men.[61] At a dinner meeting with the New

York Furniture Exchange Association, Colonel Woods told the story of a decorated former elevator man who did not want to return to his former position to run "an elevator up a shaft only to bring it down again. . . . He felt the war had equipped him for better things."[62] Money was another issue. As soldiers returned home, it became clear that while risking their lives for thirty dollars a month, war industry workers had benefited with substantial economic gains. Labor Department reports confirmed that with higher wages and overtime pay, the incomes of many families "had doubled, tripled, and even quadrupled" during the war.[63] Ex-soldiers now wanted to make up for financial losses and be paid higher wages to counter the rising cost of living.

Understanding the desire for advancement, the War Department began to oversee an "on the job" industrial retraining program to help turn unskilled soldiers into skilled workers since "lack of skill . . . was as much an economic disability as the loss of a hand or of eyesight."[64] During the war, the Department of Labor's U.S. Training Service had headed up a program to train civilians for much needed industrial war work. But at war's end, it could not maintain the program due to financial constraints. In July 1919, when the Department of War took over the retraining program, it convinced participating companies to continue the on-the-job training and the "vestibule schools" (training schools that duplicated shop conditions for trainees before putting them on the shop floor). Frances O. Perkins (who would later became the first woman secretary of Labor in 1933) assisted the War Department in organizing the programs. Industrial retraining classes for ex-soldiers took place in more than three hundred plants throughout the country that allowed the men to earn a living while learning a new skill. Many other companies expressed interest in hosting a training program. Woods argued that stimulating interest in retraining programs was an economic necessity in an industrial nation. It benefited both the soldier and the company since turnover decreased and production increased with "the efficiency and loyalty of workers."[65]

## Public Works Projects

Perhaps the most challenging postwar effort was the War Department's attempt to create new construction jobs and promoting public works projects to "stimulate" employment. The Emergency Employment Committee publicized a "Spruce-up Campaign" designed to encourage "individual householders, merchants, and manufacturers" to make repairs or improvements.[66] Sprucing-up in turn created jobs. The *Saturday Evening Post, Collier's, Review of Review, Independent, Scientific American, World's Work, Women's Home Companion, National City, U.S. Bulletin, Industry, McClure's Metropolitan, Leslie's, Life,*

*American*, and hundreds of other magazines, trade, and military journals published articles about the "Spruce-up Campaign." The Labor Department assisted by flooding the country with inspirational and patriotic posters calling for remodeling and new construction. Posters targeted homeowners and businesses to do their part to help the economy. Colonel Woods and his staff gave speeches to advertise the campaign, and Woods became the honorary chair of a New York Jewish Building Fund to help inspire construction. In October 1919 John D. Rockefeller Jr. and Sr. donated $75,000 to the fund.[67]

Invigorating the economy through public works projects was also a way of creating jobs for discharged soldiers. According to a 1919 General Staff report, "it was felt that the Government, particularly through the War Department, could consistently endeavor to stimulate public works and to preach the gospel of building."[68] Capt. Alfred Hoyt Granger (a trained architect) served as the chief of the War Department Public Works Section. Woods also created the Emergency Employment Committee's Federal Aid & Works Section with Otto T. Mallery in charge. Mallery became well known during the war as a member of the American Association for Labor Legislation. In 1917 Mallery wrote an act that provided funding for statisticians to help the Department of Labor "to observe the employment situation," he and authored the article "A National Policy—Public Works to Stabilize Employment" for the American Academy of Political and Social Science in January 1919.(Mallery eventually became a member of Herbert Hoover's Economic Advisory Committee in 1921. He remained a well-known authority in government economics.[69]) With a dedicated team of twenty-one staff members, Granger, Marlow, and Mallery worked diligently to handle the "many troubled projects needing Federal aid of one kind or another" and to expedite "the release of large quantities of material from the War Department to the Department of Agriculture and its delivery to the State Highway Commission for highway construction work."[70]

With an appropriation of more than three billion dollars pending congressional approval, Marlow divided his "small field force" into districts set up to stimulate public works and get public works contracts signed. Marlow received assistance from men trained in economics, engineering, and construction. For example, Maj. Charles Welsh, a civil engineer, served as the chief of the highway subsection of the War Department public works section. The section also included Capt. James Armstrong (who studied economics at the University of Chicago and Stanford University) and Capt. John Parker Hill (who studied at Princeton University and had experience working on military construction).[71] Marlow's officers secured architectural draftsmen and engineers along with other men needed to finish public works projects. The officers also helped expedite paperwork for river and harbor improvements and for road and state highway construction. To keep public works projects on track, Marlow's men (with the assistance of the Labor Department) arbitrated with building trade unions in Youngstown, Ohio; Jersey City, New Jersey; and Syracuse, New York, and helped with the completion of various local and state public works projects that became stalled. The military officers worked with community leaders in various districts to help raise funds, get contracts signed, and solve problems associated with public works projects as they arose. Marlow's team provided "double service" by stimulating public works thus creating jobs for discharged soldiers.[72]

With the return of laissez-faire economic philosophy, the federal government eventually pulled the plug on the planned railroad reconstruction programs that would have helped "absorb" returning soldiers. Congress refused to approve a U.S. Emergency Public Works Board or appropriate the $1.1 million needed to run the projects. However, the government eventually authorized $1.4 million in public works money, made $1.1 million available, and, by April 1919, issued $575 million worth of contracts. The War Department's Public Works Branch claimed success after helping to contract $260 million (of $575 million) public works projects after their officers' "direct visits."[73]

In August 1919 Woods discontinued the Public Works Branch because "it [had] served its purpose" by overcoming an economic crisis. Even with its short existence, the War Department's public works efforts should not be dismissed. In Woods's final report, the assistant secretary concluded it "was able, not only to overcome the unfavorable factors which had threatened to obstruct the execution of public works throughout the country, but also to speed up many new public projects together with accompanying private projects, an provide means of employment both directly and indirectly through the building trades manufacturers for a very large number of unemployed included discharged soldiers."[74] Colonel Woods strongly advocated the future use of public works during periods of "industrial depression" or unemployment crisis.[75]

## Solving Problems

Even with the success of its innovative employment strategies and well-crafted advertising efforts, the War Department faced problems with labor unrest, panhandling, language problems, and racial tensions. Moreover, disabled veterans needed special attention. Labor unrest and strikes sometimes hampered the War Department's employment efforts. This was especially true in the Western District where prewar and wartime strikes were more prevalent. The situation in the West was critical due to the large migration of unemployed ex-servicemen, the decline in shipbuilding, and the "danger" from the radical union, the

Industrial Workers of the World. The Central District also reported problems. Captain Scott, a field representative in Cleveland, Ohio, telegraphed the War Department about radicals from the Soldiers, Sailors, and Marines Union who were soliciting subscriptions for their *National Weekly News*. Scott also sent a copy of other "Bolshevik" newspapers to Colonel Wood's office including *Rebel Worker: Organ of Revolutionary Unionism* and *The Melting Pot: An Exponent of International Communism*. The central chief, Major Reynolds, reported that strikes in the steel and coal industries "were an ever-present problem." Reynolds and his field representatives attempted to dodge the problem by relocating and finding jobs for ex-servicemen in areas not plagued by strikes. Although the War Department understood the urgency of finding jobs, they realized that frequent labor unrest throughout the nation complicated the employment situation. Therefore, field representatives were instructed to tell applicants to use their judgment when applying for jobs in plants that were on strike.[76]

Radicalism continued to concern the War Department. According to the director of the Western District, Capt. Edwin Copely Wemple, radical organizations "were putting forth a supreme effort to convert" ex-soldiers by greeting soldiers at train stations and providing them with free meals, money, and clothing. Wemple reported that his field officers worked with the U.S. Intelligence Bureau and the American Legion to break up the "powerful" soldiers and sailors union, "pro-Bolshevik ex-soldier organizations," and other radical groups. After an investigation of growing radicalism in Spokane, Washington, the War Department arranged for "Four-Minute Men" speakers to counter radical propaganda in movie picture houses, theaters, churches, and on street corners.[77]

In August 1919 Secretary of War Baker asked Colonel Woods to deal with soldiers who were begging or peddling on the streets of America. To stop returning soldiers from peddling, field representatives asked local authorities "to refuse licenses" to men in uniform and encouraged the passing of local and state laws outlawing peddling in uniform since it exploited military service. The Emergency Employment Committee also contacted the local posts of the American Legion to assist with the panhandling problem. The Legion sent veterans out to have a "heart to heart talk" with the "work slacker." In addition, Woods sent letters to police chiefs throughout the nation requesting the police redirect any peddling ex-servicemen to the closest Bureau of Returning Soldiers. If the situation continued, Colonel Woods asked police to place the ex-servicemen on probation with the American Legion instead of placing them in jail. He asked the police chiefs to watch out for fraud, including the "cooties" that employ discharged soldiers to panhandle in uniform in order to "play upon the public sympathy which the uniform arouses"; Woods estimated that 80 percent of the men who were panhandling and peddling on the streets never served in the military. Woods urged newspapers to expose "peddlers in uniform" who were "imposters."[78]

## Immigrant and African American Soldiers

The War Department also produced employment materials in foreign languages for soldiers who spoke little English. The massive migration from Southern and Eastern Europe in the late nineteenth and early twentieth centuries brought millions of immigrants to the United States. During the war, the American military was stunned to find that more than 18 percent of the soldiers in their ranks were foreign-born who spoke little or no English, but they soon became proficient in training and educating immigrant soldiers. To assist with finding jobs for discharged immigrant soldiers, the Emergency Employment Committee supplied job information to ethnic newspapers throughout the United States including Italian, Jewish, Bohemian, "Czecho-Slav," and German language papers. Woods's team also produced the *Jobs for Soldiers* booklets, press releases, and other employment information in many different languages and sent letters to mayors throughout the United States telling them "we must not forget, also, the large number of foreign-speaking men who have served our colors with the greatest loyalty and often with extraordinary courage and enthusiasm."[79]

Northern postwar racial tension made finding jobs for black soldiers more difficult. From 1910 to 1920 the Great Migration brought more than one million African Americans from the South to new industrial opportunities in the North and to escape the horrors of Jim Crow Laws, voting restrictions, and open violence by white supremacists. Employment opportunities for African Americans expanded greatly during the war. As servicemen returned from overseas, Jesse O. Thomas, the state supervisor of Negro Economics in the Department of Labor, encouraged the rehiring of black soldiers. Thomas reminded religious leaders that the reemployment "campaign [was] intended to reach, affect, and benefit every race or nationality in our common country."[80]

The employment situation became more complex when many black soldiers, originally from the South, headed to the North on their return from Europe. With jobs remaining in short supply in the industrial areas of the Midwest, the War Department's Central District Field Representatives worked with black social welfare agencies to help find jobs for African American soldiers who "refused to return to their old homes in the South" at the end of the war.[81] However, as the economic crisis worsened and racial tension accelerated, the employment representatives began to encourage southern black ex-servicemen to return home. District Chief Reynolds argued that this was needed "so as not to arouse any race hatred." Although Central District's report did not specifically mention increasing racial tensions that developed into the tragic Chicago race riots that shook the city during the summer of 1919, this may have played a part in the decision. The War Department also looked in the South for employment opportunities and asked Southern commercial organizations to pay for the transportation costs of all African American soldiers they hired.[82]

## Disabled Soldiers

Disabled soldiers offered another challenge. Although an act of Congress put the care of disabled men in the hands of the Federal Board for Vocational Education, the War Department continued to assist whenever possible to "lighten the burden" of the wounded soldier.[83] During their work, it became clear to Colonel Woods that the Federal Board was not meeting the needs of disabled soldiers. In response, Woods and his men were in constant touch with the board and "as tactfully as [they] could, brought to their attention miscarriages of policy and lapses in administration."[84]

Woods also assigned Edward Leo Holl, the assistant to the director of placement for technical men, to find jobs for disabled servicemen. Holl, who graduated from the University of Pennsylvania and had experience as an employment manager, was assisted by other field representatives in the four districts, along with volunteers from social welfare organizations. One field representative, Maj. Carl Clyde Rutledge (chief of the Eastern District), had previous experience as a social welfare executive in the public sector. Rutledge used his knowledge and connections to expedite vocational training and compensation claims and worked closely with welfare agencies to meet the particular needs of injured ex-soldiers. Frederick Orville Perkins (who had substantial experiences in the business world as both a vice president and a company director) studied the problems of rehabilitating the disabled and explored the potential of industrial training. In June 1919 Woods announced courses for disabled men who would be paid during training and sent out bulletins providing important information about various federal, civic, and fraternal agencies that provided help to disabled veterans. To help reach "crippled men" panhandling on the streets in their uniforms, Woods asked civilians to inform the disabled men "of provision made for them by the government."[85]

After the Federal Board for Vocational Education stopped hospital visits on 1 July 1919 (due to financial constraints), the War Department's Emergency Employment Committee representatives filled the void and went to hospitals. There they made sure that wounded and disabled men knew where to go for employment help when they recovered. Woods team arranged to have "captains of industry," especially those "who overcame disabilities in life," visit the injured servicemen. Colonel Woods also wrote letters to commanding officers of military hospitals announcing plans to send successful business leaders to inspire wounded soldiers and lift their spirits.[86]

## Conclusion

With the armistice of 11 November 1918, the United States looked forward to a new and brighter future. But rising unemployment, relentless labor conflicts, and a Red Scare coincided with the return of some four million soldiers, sailors, and marines. Postwar cutbacks by the federal government and charges of pro-unionism all but paralyzed the Department of Labor's U.S. Employment Service's efforts to address the crisis. Fearful that radicalism would poison returning soldiers and motivated by a sense of moral obligation to help young men who served their country, the War Department responded to the growing employment problem with a surprisingly energetic program.

The War Department's Emergency Employment Committee for Soldiers, Sailors, and Marines of the Council of National Defense helped find jobs through industrial retraining classes, "spruce-up" campaigns, public works efforts, citation awards, and an effective employment card service. To combat the overall economic crisis, the War Department sent military officers to head up the U.S. Employment Service's Bureau for Returning Soldiers, Sailors, and Marines. The new assistant to the secretary of War, Col. Arthur Woods, gathered the best and the brightest military officers who had pertinent prewar experience and relied on economic experts for assistance. From his war experience with the CPI, the government's wartime propaganda machine, Woods understood the need for an effective publicity campaign to convince employers of their "patriotic duty" to hire Uncle Sam's fighting men.

In September 1919 Col. Arthur Woods stepped down from his duties, but not before recommending that the vital work conducted by his "office be discontinued only as the need for it disappears."[87] Maj. Gen. William George Haan became the new head of the Emergency Employment Committee. Lt. Col. Mathew Smith of the War Plans Division assisted Haan with the Emergency Employment Committee. Haan and Smith continued policies established by Colonel Woods and increased assistance to disabled ex-servicemen.

In December 1919, as the economy began to improve, the War Department phased out the Emergency Employment Committee. According to reports submitted by military officers from the Bureau for Returning Soldiers, Sailors, and Marines, 1,322,494 discharged men registered for assistance, and the Emergency Employment Committee found jobs for 949,901 by the end of 1919.[88] In a final report, Capt. C. B. Hammond, chief of the service and information section under General Woods, summarized the War Department's employment work as "of the utmost value and importance not only to the discharged servicemen of the Great War but as well to the country at large, and in which it has been a matter of the greatest satisfaction and inspiration to have assisted."[89] In doing so, the War Department carried out a veterans' employment agenda every bit as large in scope as later efforts to assist veterans through the emergent veterans' bureaucracy. The fact that the War Department dissolved the program was a testament to its success, not to its lack of ambition or to the military's disregard for veterans' welfare.

## Notes

This chapter is reprinted with some minor changes from Nancy Gentile Ford, *The Great War and America: Civil-Military Military Relations During World War I* (Westport, Conn.: Praeger Security International/Greenwood Publishing Group, 2009). Reproduction with permission of Greenwood Publishing, Inc., Westport, Conn.

1. "An Account of the Work of Colonel Arthur Woods, Assistant to the Secretary of War, in Aiding the Return to Civil Life after the Great War of Soldiers, Soldiers, and Marines, March—September 1919," 2, Records of the War Department General and Special Staff, War College Division, RG 165, National Archives Records Administration II, College Park Maryland. [Hereafter WDGSS, RG 165, NARA]; Stella Stewart, *Demobilization of Manpower, 1918–1919* U.S. Department of Labor, Bureau of Labor Statistics report (Washington, D.C.: U.S. Government Printing Office, 1944), 51–54; Note: Strikes were reported in Arizona, California, Connecticut, Georgia, Illinois, Indiana, Iowa, Kentucky, Massachusetts, Minnesota, Missouri, Montana, New York, North Carolina, Ohio, Oklahoma, Pennsylvania, South Carolina, Texas, Utah, Virginia, Washington, West Virginia, and Wisconsin.

2. W. E. Haseltine, "Demobilization, Reparation and Rehabilitation of Army Personnel 1918–1919," (Carlisle, PA: Prepared in the Historical Section, Army War College, 1943), 2.

3. Gen. Peyton C. March quoted in John C. Sparrow, *History of Personnel Demobilization in the U.S. Army* (Washington, D.C.: Center of Military History, United States Army, 1994, original printed by Department of the Army, 1952), 12.

4. "Say Soldiers See World in New Light: Col. Roosevelt and Arthur Woods Discuss Job Finding with Brooklyn Employers," *New York Times*, 30 March 1919, 9.

5. Haseltine, "Demobilization, Reparation and Rehabilitation of Army Personnel," 2.

6. Ibid., 3.

7. Lt. Col. Mathew C. Smith, "Report of the Activities of the Service and Information Branch for the Year 1919," Report for period from 11 November 1918 to 31 December 1919, Records of the War Department General and Special Staffs, Service and Information Branch, 165.8.2, War Plans Division, RG 165, National Archives Record Administration, College Park, Maryland, 7–10. [Hereafter WDGSS, SIB, RG 165, NARA.] Note: On 20 September 1919, Lt. Col. Mathew Smith and Major General Haan succeeded Woods as the head of the War Department's Emergency Employment Committee; also see Stewart, *Demobilization of Manpower*.

8. Sparrow, *History of Personnel Demobilization in the U.S. Army*, 16; and Henry Hossfeld and Charles H. Collins, "Demobilization of Manpower in the United States Army, 1918–1919," (Carlisle, PA: Prepared in the Historical Section, Army War College, 1942), 60–61, 119.

9. Stewart, *Demobilization of Manpower*, 28, 33.

10. "An Account of the Work of Colonel Arthur Woods," 6.

11. Stewart, *Demobilization of Manpower*, 49.

12. Ibid., 42, 59; "To Get Jobs for Soldiers," *New York Times*, 17 April 1919, 6; Sparrow, *History of Personnel Demobilization in the U.S. Army*, 17; Stewart, *Demobilization of Manpower*, 59; and "Woods's Nine Points: Assistant to Secretary of War Presents His Reasons for Giving Jobs to Soldiers," *New York Times*, 27 June 1919, 1.

13. "An Account of the Work of Colonel Arthur Woods," 4, 6.

14. U.S. Congress, *Congressional Record*, 66th Cong, 1st sess., Senate, V.58, pt 3–5, 1 July 1919, 2154.

15. "Fight Employment Service," *New York Times*, 8 May 1919, 27.

16. "Employment Service Hit," *New York Times*, 30 May 1919, 7.

17. *Congressional Record*, 66th Cong., 1st sess., Senate, V.58, 2169; and Stewart, *Demobilization of Manpower*, 60.

18. "Flood of Bills in New Congress," *New York Times*, 20 May 1919, 4.

19. "Senate Acts to Purge U.S. of Bolshevism," *Chicago Tribune*, 5 February 1919, 1.

20. "Employment of Returning Soldiers and Sailors," *Infantry Journal* 15, no. 7 (January 1919), 589; and "Flood of Bills in New Congress," *New York Times*, 20 May 1919, 4.

21. Haseltine, "Demobilization, Reparation and Rehabilitation of Army Personnel," 10–11.

22. "An Account of the Work of Colonel Arthur Woods," September 1919, Biographical appendix, 1.

23. "Much Can Be Done by Mayors," *New York Times*, 15 March 1919, 14.

24. See Letter to Mayors attached to "An Account of the Work of Colonel Arthur Woods," September 1919; and "Woods Issues Plea to Employment Soldiers: Sends a Letter to Mayors Asking Active Co-operation in the Movement," *New York Times*, 14 March 1919, 9.

25. Stewart, *Demobilization of Manpower*, 51–54, and "An Account of the Work of Colonel Arthur Woods," 2.

26. George F. Fitzgerald, "Stenographic Report of the Emergency Employment Committee Meeting Report," 11 April 1919, 6 [WDGSS, RG 165, NARA].

27. "An Account of the Work of Colonel Arthur Woods," September 1919, 11–12.

28. "Wood Sees Danger in Idle Soldiers: General Says Lack of Work Makes Discharged Men Susceptible to Racial Views," *New York Times*, 15 June 1919, 13.

29. Ibid.

30. *Congressional Record*, 66th Cong., 1st sess., Senate, 1 July 1919, 2156, 2157, 2160.

31. "Bolshevism," *Infantry Journal* 15, no. 7 (January 1919): 604.

32. "Union Affiliation," *Infantry Journal* 16, no. 5 (November 1919): 427.

33. "The Emergency Committee," *New York Times*, 17 March 1919, 14; and "Council of Defense to Aid Employment: Agency Formed Under Colonel Woods to Offset Curtailment of Federal Service," *New York Times*, 15 March 1919, 5.

34. "Council of Defense to Aid Employment," 5.

35. Ibid.; "The Solder and His Job: Government Has Mobilized Many Agencies to Make Sure They Will Get Together," *New York Times*, 22 June 1919, 11; "An Account of the Work of Colonel Arthur Woods," Biographical appendix, 1–19; and "To Find Jobs for Soldiers: Woods Organizes Advisory Committee of Ex-Service Men," *New York Times*, 12 June 1919, 18.

36. Smith, "Report of Activities of the Service and Information Branch," 11 November 1918 to 31 December 1919, 21.

37. "All Enlisted Men Allowed to Stay in Army Until They Find Civilian Employments," *New York Times*, 25 January 1919, 1.

38. "An Account of the Work of Colonel Arthur Woods," 18.

39. Ibid., 4, 12; "Tell Employment Plans: Governors and Mayors inform Council of National Defense," *New York Times*, 16 April 1919, 16; "States Aid in Job Hunting: Offer Support to Army Officers Who Are to Help Soldiers Find Work," *New York Times*, 6 April 1919, 14; Haseltine, "Demobilization, Reparation and Rehabilitation of Army Personnel," 13–14; and "The Emergency Committee," *New York Times*, 17 March 1919, 14.

40. "Hasten Listing Soldiers for Work: Woods Announces that Applications Will Be Made Out on Transports," *New York Times*, 27 May 1919, 17.

41. Smith, "Report of Activities of the Service and Information Branch," 7, 15, 20, 25–26, appendix 6, 9; Haseltine, "Demobilization, Reparation and Rehabilitation of Army Personnel," 11–15; Edward L. Bernays, "The Soldier and His Job," *New York Times*, 22 June 1919, 11; and "An Account of the Work of Colonel Arthur Woods," appendix, 1–19.

42. "An Account of the Work of Colonel Arthur Woods," 10; and Smith, "Report of Activities of the Service and Information Branch," 19.

43. "An Account of the Work of Colonel Arthur Woods," appendix, 1–19.

44. Smith, "Report of Activities of the Service and Information Branch," 79.

45. "Call on Business to Furnish Jobs: National Chamber of Commerce, at Wood's Request, Makes Plea for Aid," *New York Times*, 24 March 1919, 3.

46. Letter to the Chamber of Commerce from Arthur Woods, Assistant to the Secretary of War, 21 March 1919, attached to "An Account of the Work of Colonel Arthur Woods"; also see 27–28 and appendix 16.

47. "An Account of the Work of Colonel Arthur Woods," 19.

48. Smith, "Report of Activities of the Service and Information Branch," 31, 41.

49. "Tell the Story of 77th First Fight: Major Weaver Reports 2,000 More Jobs Available," *New York Times*, 31 March 1919, 6; "Col. Woods's Nine Points: Assistant to Secretary of War Presents His Reasons for Giving Jobs to Soldiers," *New York Times*, 29 June 1919, 1; and Smith, "Report of Activities of the Service and Information Branch," 41.

50. Smith, "Report of Activities of the Service and Information Branch," 36. Military posters are found on various Web sites; see, e.g., Library of Congress, http://www.loc.gov/pictures/collection/wwipos/, and University of Georgia, Poster Collection, http://fax.libs.uga.edu/ww-post/iwwp.html.

51. Smith, "Report of Activities of the Service and Information Branch," 37.

52. "An Account of the Work of Colonel Arthur Woods," 15, 16, 19.

53. "Churches to Aid Soldiers" *New York Times*, 23 March 1919, 18; "Col. Wood's Nine Points," *New York Times*, 27 June 1919, 1; "Wilson Asks Work for Men from War," *New York Times*, 20 April 1919, 20; and "Churches Help Find Jobs for Soldiers," *New York Times*, 4 May 1919, 1.

54. "Citation for Giving Fighters' Jobs Back: Woods Announces Government Will Recognize Employers' Patriotism with Certificate," *New York Times*, 4 May 1919, 11.

55. Ibid., 21; Smith, "Report of Activities of the Service and Information Branch," 37–39.

56. Smith, "Report of Activities of the Service and Information Branch," 37–39.

57. "Lt. Colonel Jacob C. R. Peadbody, "History of Northeastern District," 9 January 1920, 5. This report attached is to Smith, "Report of Activities of the Service and Information Branch."

58. "Appeal for Farm Labor," *New York Times*, 17 June 1919, 9; and "Need Men for Farm Work: 2,000 Jobs Open at Good Pay in This State Alone," *New York Times*, 24 June 1919, 25.

59. "An Account of the Work of Colonel Arthur Woods," 39; Smith, "Report of Activities of the Service and Information Branch," 87.

60. Smith, "Report of Activities of the Service and Information Branch," 87.

61. Ibid., 11.

62. "Furniture Dealers Dine: Col. Arthur Woods Says Unemployment Problems Are Being Met," *New York Times*, 9 April 1919, 6.

63. Stewart, *Demobilization of Manpower*, 28; "An Account of the Work of Colonel Arthur Woods," 6; and "Woods Issues Plea to Employ Soldiers," 9.

64. Smith, "Report of Activities of the Service and Information Branch," 26; and "An Account of the Work of Colonel Arthur Woods," 14–15.

65. "An Account of the Work of Colonel Arthur Woods," 14–15.

66. Ibid., 25; and Smith, "Report of Activities of the Service and Information Branch," 43.

67. Smith, "Report of Activities of the Service and Information Branch," 39–40; and "Rockefellers Give $75,000," *New York Times*, 8 October 1919, 24.

68. "An Account of the Work of Colonel Arthur Woods," 21.

69. Udo Sautter, "Government and Unemployment: The Use of Public Works before the New Deal," *Journal of American History* 20, no. 4 (December 1992): 65. Sautter's article does not discuss Otto Mallery's 1919 role as head of the War Department's Federal Aid and Works Section.

70. "An Account of the Work of Colonel Arthur Woods," 22.

71. Ibid., appendix, 22, 1–28.

72. Ibid., appendix, 1–28; and Smith, "Report of Activities of the Service and Information Branch," 47.

73. Smith, "Report of Activities of the Service and Information Branch," 22, 46–48.

74. "An Account of the Work of Colonel Arthur Woods," 24.

75. Ibid.

76. Colonel John B. Reynolds, "A History of the Central District," undated but probably submitted in December 1919 or January 1920, 7; and Peadbody, "History of Northeastern District," 4. Both reports attached to Smith, "Report of Activities of the Service and Information Branch;" "An Account of the Work of Colonel Arthur Woods," appendix, 17, Note: Copies of *Rebel Worker: Organ of Revolutionary Unionism* and *The Melting Pot: An Exponent of International Communism* in file with telegram sent to Col. Arthur Woods signed by Captain Scott, Cleveland, Ohio, 13 June 1919.

77. Capt. Edwin Copely Wemple, "History Western District," 31 December 1919, 2–3, 6–7, 11. This report is attached to Smith, "Report of Activities of the Service and Information Branch."

78. Letter from Secretary of War Baker to Col. Arthur Woods, War Department, 28 August 1919; and Letter to Police Chiefs from Arthur Woods, Assistant to the Secretary, undated, attached to "An Account of the Work of Colonel Arthur Woods"; Smith, "Report of Activities of the Service and Information Branch," 22, 92–93; and "Bars Uniform to Fakers: Col. Woods Calls Them 'Cooties' and Asks Police to Stop Them," *New York Times*, 29 April 1919, 7.

79. Letter to Mayors from Colonel Arthur Woods, 13 March 1919, attached to "An Account of the Work of Colonel Arthur Woods"; also see 20. For detail on the training and treatment of foreign-born soldiers in the American Army, see Nancy Gentile Ford, *Americans All: Foreign-*

*Born Soldiers in World War I* (College Station: Texas A&M Press, 2000); and Smith, "Report of Activities of the Service and Information Branch," 36.

80. "Churches Help Find Jobs for Soldiers," *New York Times*, 4 May 1919, 1.

81. Reynolds, "A History of the Central District," 8, attached to Smith, "Report of Activities of the Service and Information Branch."

82. Ibid.

83. Smith, "Report of Activities of the Service and Information Branch," 30.

84. "An Account of the Work of Colonel Arthur Woods," 13.

85. Ibid., 3–14; Maj. Carl Clyde Rutledge, "History of the Eastern District," undated but probably submitted in December 1919 or January 1920, 5, attached to Smith, "Report of Activities of the Service and Information Branch," 30; and "Tells How U.S. Aids Disabled Fighters: Col. Woods Urges All Crippled Ex-Service Men to Take Free Courses," *New York Times*, 8 June 1919, 2.

86. Letter to Commanding Officers of Hospitals from Arthur Woods, Assistant to the Secretary, undated, attached to "An Account of the Work of Colonel Arthur Woods"; also see 13–14; and Smith, "Report of Activities of the Service and Information Branch," 25, 30.

87. Smith, "Report of Activities of the Service and Information Branch," 30, 33.

88. Ibid., 70, 59–69.

89. Sautter, "Government and Unemployment," 65; and "An Account of the Work of Colonel Arthur Woods," 35.

# 6

# The Long Journey Home

## African American World War I Veterans and Veterans' Policies

### JENNIFER D. KEENE

> It is not an exaggeration to say that the return of the Negro soldier to civil life is one
> of the most delicate and difficult questions confronting the Nation, north and south.
>
> *George E. Hayes, Director of Negro Economics, Labor Department, November 1918.*

After World War I, federal aid to black veterans became a key battleground in the ongoing struggle to advance civil rights. By forcing the federal government to become a benefactor, albeit a limited one, on behalf of black veterans, this generation of African American veterans and activists breathed new life into a civil rights strategy that had proven successful during the Reconstruction Era when the federal government actively protected African American civil rights. Foreshadowing the unrelenting pressure that civil rights activists would put on the federal government in the 1950s and 1960s to spearhead the end of Jim Crow, black veterans and their advocates successfully argued that Washington, D.C., could not turn a blind eye to discrimination directed against African American veterans. The ensuring struggles over veterans' benefits served as a key milestone in the broader civil rights movement, turning veterans' personal readjustment to civilian life into a collective racial struggle for social justice.

Individual ex-servicemen, however, did not see themselves simply as foot soldiers of the civil rights movement. Reducing the disabled veteran experience simply to a story of veterans' relationship with the state or the civil rights movement obscures the collective identities that the wartime generation developed and maintained.[1] Preserving their distinctive identity as survivors of the world war, both within and without the African American community, also informed black veterans' efforts to influence veterans' policies.

In the aftermath of World War I, the federal government created several new agencies to handle the problem of reabsorbing veterans into civilian society. The U.S. Employment Service, a part of the Department of Labor, and the War

Department offered all returning veterans some help in finding a job, while the Federal Board of Vocational Education initiated an ambitious scheme to retrain wounded men so that they could lead self-sufficient and productive lives. In many respects these agencies raised expectations of federal support that were never fully realized for either white or black veterans. The government's determination to preserve the class, ethnic, and racial status quo meant that black veterans were not the only ones to suffer discouragement when trying to obtain government-sponsored rehabilitation services. And, like their white counterparts, black veterans did not suffer in silence. Many turned to civil rights organizations such as the National Association for the Advancement of Colored People (NAACP), veterans' organizations, or the federal agents appointed to manage their care to press their claims forward.

Bureaucratic delay and inefficiency certainly accounted for some of the problems that veterans encountered in accessing employment and rehabilitation services. Far more important, however, were the competing ways that veterans and officials measured success for these programs. For veterans, these programs offered not just a chance to regain a useful occupation but also an opportunity to get ahead. In their minds this was an opportunity that they had earned through their service to the country. Federal officials and their surrogates in local communities throughout the nation saw the matter differently. They focused on ensuring that these men became contributing workers as soon as possible. This meant working in economic sectors that were short of workers rather than following individual dreams of advancement.

The subjective decisions of Employment Bureau agents and Veterans Bureau doctors played a large role in determining which rehabilitation programs veterans could enter as well as what disability maintenance allowances they would receive over their lifetimes. Concern over past and present problems shaped policymakers' views on how to handle the challenge of reabsorbing four million returning servicemen. Most officials accepted the prevailing orthodoxy that overly generous financial support of aging and disabled Civil War veterans had drained the treasury, and they were determined to make this generation of wartime veterans as self-sufficient as possible, as quickly as possible. Police and newspapers hysterically warned about a supposed crime wave that veterans unleashed once freed from the constraints of military discipline.[2] Moreover, in the wake of the communist revolution in Russia, fears that U.S. soldiers might return as committed socialists added another dimension of potential political upheaval. Equally disturbing was the evidence of new militancy in the civil rights movement as African American veterans made both political and personal stands against racial discrimination.[3] The racist views of white officials, coupled with the fear that widespread racial rioting might result if black veterans pressed their demands too forcefully, meant that many officials working with ex-servicemen did their best to dampen any expectations that veterans' benefits might become the opening wedge to dismantling Jim Crow.

## Jobs for Veterans

To mobilize the wartime economy, the federal government had intervened in labor conflicts, taken over the railroads, tried to keep able-bodied men on the job with its 1918 "work or fight" order to potential draftees, and channeled resources and labor to defense-oriented industries.[4] Putting veterans back to work continued this wartime pattern of federal management of the economy, as did the insistence on subsuming individual preferences in favor of the national good. War Department employment officials cautioned men to stay away from cities, to resist the impulse to join any radical movement, and to settle back into old jobs as quickly as possible. Those that needed help in securing employment were advised to apply for assistance. By funneling unemployed veterans into sectors of the economy experiencing labor shortages, the government hoped to easily complete the final phase of its war-related management of the economy by ensuring the smooth reintegration of veterans into the job market.

Capt. Paul B. Johnson, a medical officer charged with safeguarding troop morale in Newport News, Virginia, a major port through which many returning veterans would pass, was the first to point out that the U.S. Employment Service had failed to think through the practical implications of the idealistic rhetoric that greeted soldiers upon their return to American soil. Posters, bulletins, and pamphlets throughout the port urged men to write to the War Department if they wanted work, but they were not instructed to indicate their skin color. Pointing out that a man might have the right skills but the wrong complexion for a job, Johnson worried that black soldiers would inadvertently "go to take employment which had been secured for them by mail, only to find that they would not be acceptable on account of their color" or might intentionally withhold information about their race "to be more sure of securing a good job," only to be fired when they arrived.[5] Arthur Woods, the head of the U.S. Employment Service, refused to issue instructions for men to give their race, asserting that he did not know whether it was best for black men to advertise their color or "to say nothing about it."[6] Johnson did not give up, however, sharing his concerns during a camp visit by George E. Hayes, a graduate of Fisk and Yale Universities, who left his position as the first executive director of the Urban League to serve, from 1918 to 1921, as director of Negro Economics in the United States Department of Labor. Having established a working relationship with Hayes, Johnson now saw a way out of this dilemma. In the future, he resolved to simply advise black soldiers to write directly to Hayes when seeking employment.[7]

Still in the early phases of his career as a social worker and educator, Hayes worried about the employment prospects for the increasing numbers of relatively unskilled African Americans migrating to northern cities from the South. The Urban League, where Hayes had previously worked, helped migrants secure jobs and housing. Hoping to foster an image of black migrants as serious-minded, respectable workers, the Urban League also advised to them to join churches, to avoid congregating on street corners, to send their children in school, and not to flit from job to job. While placing a certain amount of responsibility upon the migrant for his employment prospects, Hayes did not ignore the ways that institutionalized racial prejudice denied opportunities to qualified, law-abiding workers. His views on this subject became critical once he agreed to serve as the head of the Labor Department's Office of Negro Economics. Hayes took his charge to foster "harmonious race relations" seriously. Throughout the war and afterward, Hayes discouraged migrants from moving to places where their employment prospects were dim, and he created interracial community committees to provide adequate housing in places experiencing an influx of migrants. Embracing a "push-pull" view of migration, Hayes worried that the disproportionate force of factors "pushing" migrants out of the South (rampant racial segregation, debt peonage, sharecropping, racial violence) meant that blacks would not return even if the "pull" of free transportation to better-paying northern industrial jobs proved more illusionary than real.[8]

"It is impossible to deal with the negro soldier apart from the whole negro question," Woods and Hayes agreed. During the war Hayes constructed "an organization equipped to recruit and ship negro workers to any point at which there is a demand," that he now relied on to find employment for both civilians and ex-servicemen. With industrial demand for labor weakening, the Labor Department initiated a wholesale campaign to try to entice blacks who had recently left the South, either as wartime workers or as soldiers, to return to the South. Federal agents visited and wrote southern chambers of commerce to gather data on the jobs available and negotiated with the railroads so that a prospective employer could pay a laborer's fare when he arrived at his new job.[9] They underscored to southern businessmen and planters the importance of improving working conditions and wages for black workers so that they stayed put. Offers to employ black laborers in turpentine, nitrate, zinc, sawmill, sugar cane, cotton, and logging poured in. The Jacksonville Chamber of Commerce offered their help "in placing these colored men back in the southern states, where they really belong."[10] Further investigation, however, revealed that Jacksonville employers preferred to hire whites for nearly all higher paying factory jobs, underscoring that only the hardest and dirtiest jobs were reserved for African Americans.[11] The Labor Department realized that these racial realities would make relocation an uphill battle. "The negro . . . having migrated north during the war and securing jobs at good wages is reluctant to return to pre-war conditions and wages in the south," one memo correctly noted.[12] Hayes soon discovered that it was nearly impossible to get black veterans who joined this migratory wave to change their minds and accept jobs from southern-based companies and employers.[13]

While mostly content to delegate the issue of black veteran employment to Hayes, on the eve of the Chicago race riots, officials in Woods's office did worry that unemployed black veterans, many of them combat veterans, were becoming a potential source of radical discontent in the city. With the number of unemployed black veterans mounting, federal employment agencies con-tacted thousands of firms with letters, telephone calls, and personal visits urg-ing them to employ black ex-servicemen.[14] In one case, the U.S. Employment Service specifically asked DuPont to halt labor recruiting from Kentucky for its factory in Flint, Michigan, and instead offer jobs to unemployed black veterans in Chicago.[15] Both Hayes and Woods also tackled the question of finding jobs for educated black veterans seeking clerical rather than laboring jobs. Besides providing individual relief, Woods and Hayes wanted to reduce the likelihood of their personal hardships becoming the spark that encouraged these former noncommissioned and commissioned officers to organize civil rights protests. Confronting head-on the limited opportunities available in white-collar oc-cupations, War Department officials unsuccessfully reached out to major em-ployers such as Sears to try to open up jobs.[16]

When racial rioting swept through Chicago from 27 July–3 August 1919, Woods and Hayes blamed the continued unemployment of veterans, along with racial friction at the workplace and over housing, as the main causes for the violence. "Returned discharged soldiers were among those active in stim-ulating the resistance of the Negroes," Hayes reported, noting that constant repetition of stories recounting racial discrimination within the war military stoked community anger.[17] In his overview of the causes of the Chicago riot, Hayes made perhaps an even more astute observation. "There is a general feel-ing among all classes of Negroes that the Federal Government should do some-thing to remedy their condition," he wrote. Hayes's statement echoed the call made by Emmett J. Scott, the former secretary to the now-deceased Booker T. Washington, as he vacated his wartime position as special assistant to the sec-retary of war on issues concerning African Americans. Scott had used his final days in office to argue that the federal government should remain involved in labor relations by removing the general economic barriers that all black workers faced. Proposing that the federal government replicate the temporary role it had assumed after the Civil War as the protector of African American political rights, Scott wanted federal officials to monitor interracial labor relations and living conditions in black neighborhoods.[18] These proposals for an activist government along with Scott's support for a federal anti-lynching bill were in keeping with the vision articulated by the NAACP. Rather than withdrawing from managing the economy now that the war was over, these black civil rights leaders wanted the federal government to redirect its focus to ensuring equal opportunity.

## Mediating Black Veterans' Relationship with the State

Securing the economic rights of disabled black veterans, the only group of African Americans that the federal government had officially pledged to help, became a critical part of this larger campaign to enlist the federal government as an ally in the struggle for civil rights. Disabled veterans, however, maintained a dual identity as both African Americans engaged in the larger struggle for racial advancement and as members of a distinct wartime generation. Membership in veterans' organizations dedicated to helping members secure their legal benefits provided a space where black veterans could cultivate a sense of camaraderie and shared purpose with other ex-servicemen. When E. P. Marrs got word that his physical exam no longer qualified him for hospital care, his role as treasurer of the Disabled American Veterans of the World War in his hometown of Bath, New York, ensured that the president of his chapter wrote directly to Sen. Robert Wagner on his behalf.[19]

Given the crucial role that veterans' organizations played in mediating compensation disputes between disabled veterans and the Veterans Bureau, the limited—but real—ability of black veterans to join the American Legion, either as members of integrated branches or in their own segregated branches, had concrete financial implications. In articulating their reasons for trying to organize a Legion post in Baton Rouge, Louisiana, one group of black veterans emphasized that as a Legion post, they would know "just what the Government is doing for us in the way of benefits for ourselves, our wives, mothers and children."[20] Yet individual state Legion headquarters had the authority to accept or reject applications for "colored posts," and Louisiana was one of several southern states that refused to grant charters for black posts. The desire of southern states to stop black veterans from organizing their own segregated posts was part of an explicit white campaign to prevent black ex-servicemen from organizing to protect their rights, either as ex-servicemen or as citizens. In 1920 Corp. Harry Price, a combat veteran of the 370th Infantry, protested to Legion state officials when he was refused admission to an all-white Decatur, Illinois, post. After showing the reply to local Legion officials, which asked him to send the names of those who refused his application, "in a short time they told him that they would help him to put on a drive for members among the colored ex-soldiers."[21] Such happy endings were rare indeed. Instead "thousands of Negro soldiers are entitled to hospitalization, compensation, vocational training. But who is there to speak and act for them?" asked the organizers of the short-lived Lincoln Legion, an independent veterans organization in Chicago that tried to mount a nationwide membership drive.[22]

Black veterans in southern states not only had few opportunities to join the Legion, but some like Gaines Mundy in Henderson, Kentucky, faced "an organized effort . . . to keep all former colored service men from securing any compensation or other aid and assistance from the government." Mundy's problems also stemmed from his refusal to give the hospital doctor $1.50 to report favorably on his disability claim, the type of illegal fee that other black veterans reported paying so that white doctors would sign necessary forms. While some black veterans negotiated the corrupt Veterans Bureau system on their own by paying bribes when necessary, others tried to enlist help from the NAACP. The organization received numerous letters from disabled veterans seeking help with their claims for disability ratings, allowances, and hospitalization. Mundy, for example, wanted the NAACP to pay for his private legal fees to combat the decision of the local Veterans Bureau, which he suspected of being allied with the Ku Klux Klan (KKK). The best that the financially strapped NAACP could offer in this case was a promise to write to the Veterans Bureau personally.[23] Still, the NAACP undoubtedly performed a useful service for many other disabled veterans by developing a network of "friendly contacts" with white southern lawyers who were willing take on their cases for small fees.

In other rare cases, especially concerning veterans from the famed New York 15th Infantry (a National Guard unit that fought under its federal designation, the 369th Infantry Regiment), veterans could appeal for help from their former white wartime commanders, who often saw it as their duty to continue caring for their men. Col. William Hayward, Col. Arthur Little, and Capt. Hamilton Fish Jr. (who became a congressman from New York after playing leading role in founding the American Legion) all intervened to help veterans of the 369th regiment negotiate the red tape of applying for benefits and appealing unfavorable decisions.[24] Having white benefactors benefited men from New York, but sometimes the interest that whites expressed in helping black veterans simply led to financial exploitation. When Neal Hamilton was confined to an insane asylum, a white lawyer in Temple, Texas succeeded in having the local court appoint him as administrator of Hamilton's affairs. This meant that Hamilton's insurance and disability checks went to the white lawyer rather than his family, an injustice that they were fearful of contesting lest they become targets of the KKK. It took three years for the sister of David Lee, another veteran who suffered a mental collapse, to discover that a city clerk in Greenville, Mississippi, had been appointed her brother's guardian and was drawing his monthly disability allowance. Her concerns went further than money. Living in New York, she questioned the "rather mysterious way" that he had landed in an insane asylum without her family's knowledge or consent. "With the exception of a little nervousness my brother's condition was that of a normal person when he was at home the last time," Rosa Lee contended.[25] Whether or not whites in positions of authority helped or hindered African American veterans in their quest for disability awards, the need for mediation from whites underscored once again the disproportionate power that this racial group held in American society.

## Veteran Rehabilitation

Before a disabled soldier was discharged from the service, the Federal Board for Vocational Education was supposed to collect personal information including age, education, previous line of employment and future vocational aspirations. Once the disabled veteran arrived home, a regional counselor in possession of this card visited to advise him on what training course to pursue. A regional board then had to approve the selection. The actual language of the Vocational Rehabilitation Act of 1918 left unclear who could ultimately decide what program a veteran entered. The law allowed veterans to attend any authorized program of their choosing unless a federal counselor concluded that a particular selection would not lead to actual employment that benefited the economy.[26] Like white veterans, African American veterans soon clashed with the Veterans Bureau over how to define appropriate rehabilitation opportunities. Counselors tended to focus on self-sufficiency, a criteria that put more emphasis on maintaining the economic status quo by putting men in training programs where others with a similar class, ethnic, or racial background typically found jobs. Using the collective findings of army intelligence tests to ascertain whether a disabled veteran could successfully complete a particular training program also became a strong force in favor of maintaining the existing social hierarchy. These culturally biased tests ranked the average mental ages of different ethnic and racial groups, placing native-born white men at the top with an average mental age of 13, Eastern Europeans in the middle, and American-born blacks at the bottom with a dismal average mental age of 10.4.

This "scientific" data offered reassuring evidence that unintelligent blacks and southern European immigrants who held primarily unskilled jobs were working exactly where they should.[27]

Many working-class veterans, black and white, saw rehabilitation training programs as a chance to change their life trajectory by attaining skills previously denied to them. The American Legion and Red Cross supported this view, seeing these programs, in the words of one Red Cross official, as "the duty of the state to repair so far as practicable this former inequality of opportunity."[28] For many disabled veterans, regaining their earning potential was synonymous with retaining their masculine identity, so they shared the federal government's goal of self-sufficiency. At the same time, however, their war wounds attested to some new rights that they had earned for sacrificing their health for their nation. These included adequate medical treatment, a disability allowance, and a chance to work in an occupation of their choosing. Government officials expected veterans to exhibit gratitude for the aid that they received, but veterans instead often complained that the government was not adequately delivering the benefits due them.[29]

The government view of the rehabilitation process was well articulated in the surgeon general's office's glossy magazine, *Carry On*, which tried to demonstrate through words and pictures how veterans could achieve a seamless integration back into their communities. With their missing limbs carefully concealed in empty sleeves or in prosthetic devices, disabled soldiers farmed, repaired automobiles, typed on typewriters, and studied in classrooms. The magazine portrayed black veterans reading or gardening under white supervision, gentle activities intended to help men suffering from tuberculosis recover.[30] Inherent in this image of the proper path to rehabilitation for black veterans lay a conundrum: for many men who had previously worked at hard physical labor, would their wartime injuries require that they receive training in jobs that African Americans had not traditionally held?

As early as 1919, Walter White, the general secretary of the NAACP, wrote to Hayes urging him to use his influence to get black men appointed to the regional federal boards that would determine a man's eligibility for specific rehabilitation programs. White believed that "intelligent colored men . . . will advise the men with regard to their own best interests, instead of forcing them into those lines of employment which the Southern employer of Negro labor or the South in general wishes."[31] White accurately predicted the kind of reception that black disabled veterans would get from federal rehabilitation boards staffed solely with whites. "What's the matter with you? You are able to work aren't you?" was a typical interrogation that applicants in Richmond faced when applying for retraining programs.[32] "Since the war, some of the Southern crackers are using different means to keep we colored soldiers out of the hospitals and from getting vocational training. Their reason for keeping us out of training is to rate us in compensation as low as possible," Joel Moore charged.[33]

By the time that the Veterans Bureau appointed J.R.A. Crossland in 1921 to oversee the effort to provide wounded black veterans with training opportunities in its rehabilitation division, it was clear that these programs had not lived up to their promises. By the early twenties, the frustrations that white and black veterans had encountered with federally sponsored rehabilitation programs had caused most disabled veterans to simply walk away. Only a few thousand men out of the nearly two hundred thousand men eligible for retraining ever completed their courses.[34] Still Crossland worked hard to improve the opportunities for black veterans, making the surely inflated claim that within a year he had increased the numbers of black veterans in training programs from a few hundred to nearly four thousand.[35]

Veterans had the option of several different types of rehabilitation programs, including college degree programs and trade courses at historically black schools or segregated branches of the YMCA. On-the-job placement training was another possibility for those interested in working as an apprentice to gain entry into a skilled trade. While the Federal Board of Vocational Education's official newsletter trumpeted the "highways of progress" made available to the black veteran in "the land he helped to defend," Crossland's private investigations told a different story.[36] Revealing why black veterans had so much trouble getting into their program of choice, a white San Antonio district manager reported that there was no point in putting "the farm negro" into the retraining courses that "we are able to offer him" because most dropped out.[37] Crossland understood immediately that when confronted with the meager retraining opportunities that Southern vocational boards were willing to offer, some disabled black veterans decided they were not worth the trouble. Others tried to game the system, a Richmond official reported, going into these proscribed training programs "not with the view of being rehabilitated, or even ever working at the particular trade, but simply to draw the training pay for the allotted time."[38]

The allure of federal money pouring into their coffers became a tremendous enticement for colleges and vocational schools to offer veteran retraining programs. A petition from fifty African American veterans enrolled in a tailoring course at the A&M State Normal School in Prairie View, Texas, revealed how some white-administered schools enriched themselves at the expense of black veterans. Complaining that they had only one instructor and four machines to use, the veterans also had to bring their own cloth and pay for needles that they broke.[39] Prairie View was the separate campus established "for the Benefit of Colored Youth" when Texas founded the Agricultural and Mechanical College (now Texas A&M) for white students in 1876.[40] Making a visit to Prairie View, Crossland discovered that there were no dormitories available on campus for the veterans, who were instead housed seven miles away in Hempstead, Texas, where the local police harassed them continually.[41] An inspection of the A&M Normal School in Alabama revealed that veterans were living in rotting barracks with a "roof so absolutely leaky that the trainees are forced to move their beds from place to place about the room to avoid sleeping on a wet bed."[42]

Crossland detected a pattern of inattention to veterans' needs at southern black land-grant schools that were closely supervised by white boards and state legislatures. He and his subordinates concluded that white school administrators saw rehabilitation programs mostly as a source of ready cash to exploit. With many traditionally black schools such as Tuskegee Institute, Southern University, and Utica Normal Institute offering successful trade courses for veterans, Crossland saw no reason to continue funding subpar programs. Crossland also recommended removing black veterans from job-placement programs. Many employers, he contended, only wanted to exploit cheap, government-subsidized labor. Instead of receiving comprehensive training that would lead to profitable employment, reports from the field indicated that shops employed the men mainly to sweep and run errands.

The debate between Crossland and his supervisor, Capt. F. O. Smith, over how to address the evident problems in the trade schools and job-placement programs laid bare the competing views over the purpose of rehabilitation programs. Crossland objected to trainees being told they "would take agriculture or nothing," supporting the veterans' effort to use vocational rehabilitation to surmount the poverty and racial discrimination that had hindered their economic advancement. Smith, however, maintained that the bureau's only job was to bring "these men back to an economic status equal to that they would have had had they not seen service in the recent war."[43] Smith was articulating the official Veterans Bureau position, one that considered the extent of a man's physical disability along with his race, social class, and education to determine his eligibility for rehabilitation benefits. Soloman Harper, for example, had no trouble securing permission to complete a preliminary course as an electrician. Setting his sights on advanced training with the goal of becoming a vocational school teacher, he independently got approval from his local electrical workers' union to work as an apprentice so he could get the prerequisite workshop experience the program required. The Veterans Bureau, however, denied his request to obtain further training at government expense, concluding that his eighth-grade education disqualified him from becoming a teacher. Doggedly pursuing this goal, Harper was eventually hospitalized in an insane asylum for harboring delusions about "teacher's training."[44]

Yet the rehabilitation results were not all so bleak. Federal funding offered a few hundred veterans the chance to attend black colleges where they found a supportive environment for their occupational aspirations. Wilberforce accepted 88 veteran trainees in the early 1920s, who were on average eight years older than the rest of the student body and often came with their wives and children.[45] By 1923 Howard University had enrolled 237 federally funded veterans to pursue studies in law, medicine, dentistry, teaching, and business—all programs, university president J. Stanley Durkee assured the Veterans Bureau, with "a definite employment objective."[46] For four years the university accommodated those veterans who, when presented with an unforeseen opportunity to go to college, lacked the required prerequisite schooling to meet Howard's entrance requirements. Temporarily waiving these requirements allowed disabled veterans to take individual courses and gave them time to meet the school's entrance requirements if they wanted to enter degree programs. Federal funding flowing to black universities helped them in their mission to create an educated, vibrant black middle class and supported the aspirations of individual veterans to take advantage of a chance to overcome the limited educational opportunities they had received in the past.

Focusing exclusively on the way that federal aid could help advance the cause of civil rights, however, can obscure the private battles that some disabled veterans waged. Still suffering from the effects of gassing and of foot and abdominal combat injuries, Greenleaf Johnson was carried from class to the hospital several times and missed so many days that he failed his course.[47] Austin Holliday was a shell-shocked veteran who began suffering from seizures on the battlefield of Chateau-Thierry in 1918, and his worsening symptoms forced him to drop out of Howard Law School. He intentionally left Washington, D.C., by car, "hoping to have a seizure and roll off a mountain and be killed"; he eventually ended up in a veterans' hospital in Los Angeles. A government-funded opportunity to pursue a law degree could not resolve his private physical and mental health issues.[48] Another veteran echoed this conclusion, lamenting that "on account of the poor condition of my health and my inability to carry on, all my hopes for doing something in life worth while have been blasted."[49]

The illnesses or wounds that rendered these men disabled also often required medical attention during their stint of vocational rehabilitation, and receiving adequate care posed yet another hurdle for many. Veterans Bureau officials replaced the black doctor charged with caring for veterans attending the A&M School in Normal, Alabama, with a white doctor who was so hostile that many men were afraid to go to him and opted instead to "engage outside doctors at their own expense."[50] James Sanford, a disabled veteran attending a retraining program at Hampton Institute, a vocational high school for African Americans in Hampton, Virginia, complained that when he and his classmates went to the white doctors authorized to treat him, "we are invariabl[y] received and treated as a colored man and not as a disabled soldier."[51] Appealing to Crossland, Sanford reiterated the need for the Veterans Bureau to "send out the 'life lines' to these men and to save them." In writing his letter on behalf of himself and his friends, Sanford retained faith that such help might be forthcoming if he could explain the situation adequately to officials in Washington who "can not see and understand the awful problem . . . ever present . . . in these isolated portions of the South." Perhaps even more importantly, Sanford and other disabled veterans who raised their voice in protest demanded federal protection as a right that they had earned by virtue of their military service, distinguishing themselves as deserving special attention. As one disabled veteran put it, "I know my rights."[52] This became a familiar refrain among disabled men seeking medical care.

## Seeking Medical Care

When most Americans thought of war injuries, they thought of amputations and gas-induced blindness, but these actually accounted for very few of the disabilities that World War I veterans suffered. Men instead brought a wide range of injuries home with them, the full impact of which occasionally took time to materialize. A poorly set broken arm, for instance, could dramatically impact the ability of a manual laborer to earn his living.[53] Far more common were tuberculosis and war neurosis. The mental problems attributable to shell shock, often not visible to the casual observer, were painfully obvious to families. As the child of one 369th veteran sadly concluded, "Some of them come back and they were of no use to their families, mentally and physically."[54]

Seeking care for war neuroses in the poisonous racial climate of the 1920s inflicted additional stress on already ill veterans. Did racism and discrimination affect the psychological well-being of black servicemen and veterans? Many veterans believed that it did. Rayford Logan suggested in his memoir that the shell shock he suffered while in France was only partly due to the shell blast that knocked him unconscious. "My [battle] fatigue resulted from overwork and the trauma of my encounters with Colonel Young [his white commanding officer]," Logan concluded years later.[55] Logan attributed his rapid recovery to French doctors who let him unburden his pent-up anger against white Americans. One veteran's wife concluded that a New York veteran hospital's practice of bringing white patients into the black ward to die "has worked against her husband's health more so than his illness" and described him "as a mental wreck."[56] Black patients in one hospital were threatened with losing their disability rating if they continued complaining about the long waits to see specialists.[57] Nick Wallace, committed to the Marion Military Home in Indianapolis, related how supervisors kept the black patients confined while white veterans had free use of the grounds. "Now this place is suppose to be a mental place . . . lots of them if they would be given a chance I believe they would regain their health but instead of giving them a chance they keep them locked up," Wallace complained. Furthermore, Wallace wrote, "If you hold up for your wrights [sic] you are thrown" into solitary confinement in an annex reserved for violent patients, where "they will try to run you insane" by beating the men with cakes of soap put in socks.[58] His letter prompted the NAACP to ask a member of the Marion chapter to investigate conditions there. Cordelia Lee went to talk to Wallace and discovered that the hospital had put the men to work shoveling coal in the winter, resulting in frostbitten feet on some. Accounts such as Wallace's essentially likened a hospital stay for war-related mental illness to a prison sentence. As Dr. James Crossland concluded, "It is impossible to effect a cure where lack of safety of life everywhere abounds," and patients felt under constant threat of physical violence.[59]

The disability rating schedule determined how much compensation and treatment a veteran received for a war-related injury, rendering a judgment on how much an injury or illness would affect a veteran's potential to earn a living.[60] A disability payment, therefore, was a type of adjusted compensation—a way to compensate veterans for the projected income they would lose (either temporarily or permanently) due to their war wounds. The Veterans Bureau modeled the disability rating schedule on similar charts used to determine workman compensation payments for work-related injuries, hoping to ensure that throughout the nation men with similar disabilities received comparable disability ratings. The process put enormous power in the hands of the doctors who made the initial diagnosis, with predictable consequences for black veterans being examined by white southern doctors. If successful in pressing a claim for disability, because disability payment schedules did not make allowances for race or region, black veterans could potentially receive payments that far exceeded the thirty dollars a month that an average black farm worker received. The potential of federal compensation to give southern disabled black veterans a measure of financial independence from local white employers, therefore, infused a routine medical exam with enormous political and economic significance.

Even though initially the law required proof that disabilities were war related, the large number of claims rejected because veterans lacked this evidence soon became an embarrassing political problem. In 1921 Congress granted exceptions for tuberculosis and war neuroses, presuming that any veteran who developed these illnesses in the immediate postwar period had contracted them while in uniform.[61] Besides accounting for nearly half of the disability compensation awarded to World War I veterans in the 1920s, these two diagnoses guaranteed black veterans eligibility to receive treatment in a government-run hospital.

Finding beds for ill black veterans in existing hospitals posed a significant problem since the Veterans Bureau refused to challenge the "separate but equal" policies maintained in southern and even some northern communities. When a veteran's hospital in Castle Point, New York, agreed to accept Philadelphia resident Lilton Wharton as a patient, the chief medical officer was apparently unaware that Wharton was black. Ignoring the fact that Wharton was running a high fever, the medical officer followed the advice of the regional office and sent him back to Philadelphia. "The reason given for his discharge from your institution would be that there were no available beds," noted the regional officer, suggesting that the medical officer adopt the coded bureaucratic language regularly used to deny blacks care in veterans' hospitals.[62] Segregation by race, like segregation by disease, was an administratively effective way to care for disabled veterans, the Veterans Bureau's acting medical director contended. The idea that "Negro patients are isolated just as diseases are" infuriated local chapters of the NAACP and black American Legion posts.[63]

Albert White's odyssey, which also involved the Castle Point facility, illustrated the unique bureaucratic nightmare that confronted black veterans when trying to find facilities that could address their particular ailment amid the tangle of hospitals that either refused to treat black veterans or would only care for them in separate wards. In 1925 White, who was also a member of the NAACP, began experiencing respiratory problems that his doctor linked to his gas exposure while fighting with the 351st Field Artillery in France. Fading fast, the Veterans Bureau in Pittsburgh sent him, accompanied by a white nurse, to a facility in Dawson Springs, Kentucky. He was allowed to ride reclining in the Pullman car until he reached the Kentucky border but then forced to finish the journey sitting in the "Jim Crow" car. No sooner had he arrived than the hospital informed him that "no Negro soldiers were allowed there," and he returned to Pittsburgh. He fared no better in New York, where hospitals in Beacon and Castle Point refused to take him because they had not established separate wards for black and white veterans. Becoming increasingly desperate as White's condition steadily worsened, the NAACP finally secured a place for him in the National Sanatorium in Dayton, Ohio.[64]

Such stories of racial discrimination in Northern facilities, coupled with tales of abuse in the South, generated a groundswell of support within the black community for establishing an all-black veterans' hospital established in Tuskegee, Alabama. African American civil rights leaders, however, remained divided over whether the hospital helped or hurt veterans seeking care. The NAACP contended that the hospital's existence made it easier for other veterans' facilities to deny beds to black veterans.

Few whites contested the idea of building a hospital just for black veterans, but the question over whether it should be staffed by white or black doctors proved much more explosive. When Maj. Robert Russa Moton (who had become the principal of Tuskegee after Washington's death in 1915) arranged for Tuskegee Institute to donate land to the government for the project, he did it with the understanding that the hospital would employ some black physicians and nurses.[65] The Tuskegee white community had other ideas. The chance to benefit financially from government largesse to veterans caused a flurry of interest in the project, but preserving the racial status quo was also critical. Economic independence, whether through veteran rehabilitation programs or civil service jobs in a government-run hospital, threatened to undermine white supremacy. To gain local white support for the hospital, Treasury Department officials privately agreed to staff it only with whites, and when the newly formed Veterans Bureau inherited the project, it appeared willing to stand by this covert deal.

As the hospital prepared to open in 1923, the staffing question remained unresolved. Following in Washington's footsteps, Moton wanted to cultivate the good will of white philanthropists and politicians by sidestepping controversial questions about racial discrimination. He thus agreed in January 1923 to the appointment of a white "Northern man who would properly consider the interests of colored people" as the temporary superintendant of the hospital, believing this was a necessary concession to begin the process of hiring black doctors and nurses. He soon realized his error when Col. Robert H. Stanley, Alabama born and raised, arrived in Tuskegee and a Veterans Bureau field letter announced that "the medical personnel will be composed of white persons."[66]

Moton now had a choice to make. To fight openly could jeopardize the conservative public image that Tuskegee maintained, but he realized that doing nothing would, "bring down on my head, and on Tuskegee Institute, an avalanche of criticism" from civil rights organizations and the black press "as I have been very active in bringing the hospital here."[67] Moton, along with the NAACP, and the National Medical Association (the professional organization for black physicians) appealed directly to Republican president Warren G. Harding, arguing that if black professionals were denied the chance to compete for these civil service jobs, the president would face "a storm of protest" from African Americans throughout the country that could have serious political repercussions by alienating these usually loyal Republican voters.[68] Aware that the recent wartime influx of African Americans into northern cities had made the black vote crucial in many municipal elections, Harding responded favorably. The president instructed the Veterans Bureau to compile a list of black doctors and nurses qualified to fill civil service positions but stopped short of ordering the appointment of an all-black staff.

Moton now removed himself from the debate, again following the precedent that Washington had set of using proxies to challenge legalized racial discrimination. Worried about permanently damaging the relationship between Tuskegee and the local white community if he openly criticized their insistence on a white-only staff, Moton asked the NAACP to take on the public fight. "It would be disastrous if it was known here that we at Tuskegee Institute had any part, no matter how small, in organizing the colored people from here to protest against this despicable situation," Moton's private secretary acknowledged.[69]

Although the NAACP had opposed creating a segregated hospital in the South, the organization nonetheless willingly took the lead in denouncing plans to exclude black doctors and nurses from the hospital staff. In letters sent to a wide array of newspapers, the NAACP openly mocked whites for their apparent newfound desire to treat black veterans. "Some years ago Alabama passed a law prohibiting white women from nursing Negroes. Now comes this big government hospital with a monthly payroll of $65,000" and delegations of whites travel to Washington, D.C., "to urge the President to permit whites to serve and wait upon Negro patients!"[70] Tuskegee whites had already thought of a way around this conundrum, however. Each white nurse, paid an average annual salary of two thousand dollars would supervise a black maid (paid fifty dollars a month) who would undertake all nursing duties that required actual contact with the patients.[71] Still, as the NAACP and white southerners both fully understood, the battle was about more than money. "'If niggers are put at the head of this hospital, they'll be responsible only to the United States government and we don't want any niggers in Alabama we can't control,'" one white state senator proclaimed.

In April 1923 the steady stream of letters from black citizens to the White House paid off as Harding agreed to an all-black staff. As the Veterans Bureau began recruiting black doctors and nurses, the situation in Tuskegee turned ugly. When Moton's life was threatened, he arranged to leave the school for an extended lecture tour. "I do not see how the situation could be worse as we are really on top of a volcano and can almost literally hear the lava sputtering down below," wrote Albon Holsey, Moton's personal secretary.[72] The day after he composed this letter, the local Ku Klux Klan paid a visit to the hospital grounds. The robed men never violated the gates to the Tuskegee Institute, perhaps aware that students and alumni, who had been streaming onto the campus all day, were ready to take up arms to defend the school.[73] Who would control what happens on federal property, "the 'Invisible Empire' of the Klan or the War Department, through its Veterans' Bureau," asked the *Washington Tribune*, a black newspaper in the nation's capital.[74] Hopeful that the government would crush this attempt to "nullify" federal policy, civil rights activists portrayed the stand-off as a question of respecting federal authority.

The KKK march indeed proved to be the spark that undid local whites' hopes of excluding black staff. The NAACP unleashed a massive letter-writing campaign and urged the federal government to send troops to Tuskegee. "The whole colored population is stirred up, and meetings are beings planned by churches, lodges and other organizations," Crossland reported.[75] Meanwhile major southern newspapers began to ridicule the white Alabamians' sudden desire to care for black patients. By the time Veterans Bureau head Gen. Frank Hines arrived at the hospital for a long-planned visit, this break in the ranks of white segregationists undoubtedly encouraged Hines to broker a compromise. He proposed gradually employing black doctors and nurses while leaving three white supervisors in place for the time being.[76] White Alabamians verbally protested but failed to receive much support from the rest of the white South. By leaving whites temporarily in charge, Hine gave the local white community a way to "save their faces" as they put aside the staffing issue and took up instead the question of where the railroad route to the hospital should go.[77] Moton also agreed to the plan, arousing the ire of the northern-based black press and the NAACP. After learning that Moton had assured the Veterans Bureau that the continued push for an all-black staff was the work of "northern radicals," the NAACP withdrew from the deliberations and returned to its previous stance that creating a segregated hospital had been a mistake.

The National Medical Association refused to step away, however, determined to demonstrate there were indeed enough qualified black medical professionals to fill all available slots. Overcoming some black doctors' reluctance to work at the hospital, either out of concern for their personal safety or anger over the compromise, took time. By 1924, however, the majority of personnel were black. Hines now felt confident enough in the stability of race relations in Tuskegee to appoint Dr. Joseph H. Ward, a black surgeon from Indianapolis, as head of the hospital. Within a few months, the entire hospital was staffed with African Americans. Over the next decade, half of all black veterans who received hospital care were treated at Tuskegee, and all the black doctors employed by the Veterans Bureau worked there.[78]

How would veterans, especially those suffering from mental illnesses, re-cover at the all-black Tuskegee Veterans Hospital located in segregated Ala-bama amid hostile whites when the "environment is certainly an important factor in their care and cure," Dr. W. G. Alexander wondered in a letter to the *Journal of the National Medical Association.*[79] Demeaning treatment from local racist whites was not the only reason black veterans might have found it stressful to receive treatment at Tuskegee. The Tuskegee Institute's ethos of racial uplift through hard work, economic self-sufficiency, and civility meshed well with the general values promoted by Veterans Bureau rehabilitation pro-grams, putting tremendous responsibility on patients to help heal themselves. "You can do even more in behalf of getting well, than can be done for you," one ward supervisor exhorted as he urged patients to eat their meals without using profanity, to scrupulously follow hospital regulations, and to rise each morning repeating the mantra, "every day in every way, I am getting better and better."[80] Patient Claudius M. Pettey echoed this sentiment in the pages of a free hospital newsletter. "We must exercise cleanliness, discipline and perseverance. And this will mean much in bringing us back to life."[81] The insistence on proper decorum and etiquette, not just physical healing, meant that a hospital stay in Tuskegee was a carefully regimented experience.

Did infusing the care of patients, some suffering from mental illness, with larger political goals retard or aid their treatment? Gathered together in hospi-tal wards, the stories that veterans told each other about their wartime exploits became a way to bolster confidence and pride. As Claudius M. Perry boasted in the hospital newsletter, despite "people who predicted that our mental abil-ity was not sufficient to operate artillery," the 349th Field Artillery eventually "won special praise from the French and from our own white artillery; stating that there was none superior to ours."[82] A film extolling their wartime achieve-ments had quite a different effect, however, on another 92nd Division veteran receiving care in Tuskegee. Transported back in time, he saw himself walking to the front past "graves already dug with the American flag waving over them" in anticipation of the large number of casualties that his unit would suffer that day. This veteran had followed his chaplain's advice and written a letter to his parents asking them to pray for him. These preparations for a death that did not come still haunted this man.[83]

In the 1930s the National Medical Association launched an ultimately un-successful campaign to create another government hospital for black veterans located in the North.[84] This time the NAACP refused to budge from its inte-grationist position, arguing that black veterans should receive treatment in existing hospitals. Rather than viewing the hospital as government-sponsored occupational advancement for black professionals, NAACP president Walter

White saw Tuskegee as an example of federally funded segregation. While the debate continued over which approach to veteran care would advance or retard the civil rights cause, the establishment of the *Veterans' Herald*, a newspaper distributed among Tuskegee patients, revealed at least one benefit to placing disabled black veterans in one hospital. It was much easier to ensure that disabled black veterans received informed and accurate information about the potential benefits available to them, especially updates on veteran-related legislation working its way through Congress, including the adjusted compensation certificate that veterans received in 1924.

## Conclusion

The debates over staffing the Tuskegee Veterans Hospital, veteran job placement, and rehabilitation programs revealed the centrality of federal veteran policies to the civil rights movement in the 1920s and 1930s. The government's acknowledgement that disabled veterans, regardless of race, were eligible to receive the same retraining, hospitalization, and maintenance benefits had the potential to undermine the racial status quo. If the civil rights movement had succeeded in persuading the government to stand by this pledge completely, then securing the special privileges awarded to disabled black veterans might have garnered benefits for the entire African American community. By forcing the federal government to offer limited protection of black veterans' economic and medical rights, the struggle over veterans' benefits instead served as the opening gambit for a civil rights strategy that would gain momentum throughout the twentieth century as the movement focused on enlisting the federal government as an ally, rather than a foe, in dismantling Jim Crow.

Yet the disabled black veterans' individual and collective journey home from war necessitated renegotiating more than their relationship with the state. Their desire to access rehabilitation programs and receive medical care was not just an effort to overcome racial discrimination. It was also an attempt to reestablish themselves as self-sufficient breadwinners who could care for their families. These men sought to use veterans' benefits to meet their own needs, not just those of the civil rights movement, by taking control of their lives and their health.

Perhaps most importantly, during the decade that saw the emergence and celebration of the "New Negro" who fought back against racial discrimination, the collective goals of the civil rights movement and the individual aspirations of disabled black men were often completely compatible. Every disabled black veteran who secured hospitalization or compensation was celebrated for achieving a minor victory in the overall campaign for equal rights, helping these men avoid feeling emasculated by their dependence on government aid. With no evident resentment over the special awards given to veterans for medical care and education, civil rights organizations played a key role in helping black veterans reintegrate quickly into the African American community. Rather than viewing them as a special group with unique problems to overcome, the civil rights movement linked the disabled veteran struggle to the obstacles that every person of color faced in the United States. The civil rights movement thus inadvertently helped ensure that one of the major goals of federal veteran policy, the quick reabsorption of veterans into civilian and community life, was achieved.

## Notes

1. David Gerber advanced this argument in a path-breaking essay on disability studies that criticized scholars for assuming that veterans' social identities were mainly a by-product of their interactions with the state. I am suggesting that focusing on how black veterans interacted with the civil rights movement is also only one way of understanding their experiences as disabled men. David A. Gerber, "Disabled Veterans, the State, and the Experience of Disability in Western Societies, 1914–1950," *Journal of Social History* 36, no. 4 (2003): 899–916.

2. Richard Severo and Lewis Milford, *The Wages of War: When America's Soldiers Came Home* (New York: Simon & Schuster, 1989), 240–41.

3. Adriane Lentz-Smith, *Freedom Struggles: African Americans and World War I* (Cambridge, Mass.: Harvard University Press, 2009); Mark Robert Schneider, *"We Return Fighting," The Civil Rights Movement in the Jazz Age* (Boston: Northeastern University Press, 2002); and Chad Williams, "Vanguards of the New Negro: African American Veterans and Post-World War I Racial Militancy," *Journal of African American History* 92, no. 2 (Spring 2007): 347–70.

4. For overviews of the economic mobilization, see David M. Kennedy, *Over Here: The First World War and American Society* (New York: Oxford University Press, 1980); and Robert H. Zieger, *America's Great War: World War I and the American Experience* (Lanham, Md.: Rowman & Littlefield, 2000).

5. Port Morale Officer, Port of Embarkation, Newport News Va. to Colonel Arthur Woods, Special Assistant, Secretary of War, 24 July 1919; "Employment of Negro Ex-Servicemen" folder, Entry 355; RG 165, National Archives and Records Administration [hereafter NARA].

6. Arthur Woods to Paul B. Johnson, 29 July 1919; "Employment of Negro Ex-Servicemen" folder, Entry 355; RG 165, NARA.

7. Paul B. Johnson to Arthur Woods, 1 August 1919; folder "Employment of Negro Ex-Servicemen" folder, Entry 355; RG 165, NARA.

8. James B. Stewart, "George Edmund Haynes and the Office of Negro Economics," in *A Different Vision, African American Economic Thought*, vol. 1 (New York: Routledge, 1997), 216–17.

9. Memo for the Secretary of War, undated, subject: Negro Situation; Memo for Colonel Woods, undated, subject: Negro situation in northern cities; Memo to Maj. John B. Reynolds, 2 May 1919. All in "Employment of Negro Ex-Servicemen" folder, Entry 355; RG 165, NARA.

10. Jacksonville Chamber of Commerce to Arthur Woods, 22 April 1919; "Employment of Negro Ex-Servicemen," folder, Entry 355; RG 165, NARA.

11. Letter to Woods, 22 April 1919; "Employment of Negro Ex-Servicemen," folder, Entry 355; RG 165, NARA.

12. Memo for Colonel Woods, 19 April 1919; "Employment of Negro Ex-Servicemen," folder, Entry 355; RG 165, NARA.

13. Arthur Woods, memo to Major Kobbe, 31 May 1919; "Employment of Negro Ex-Servicemen" folder, Entry 355; RG 165, NARA.

14. Director of Negro Economics to Labor Secretary, 25 March 1919; file #8/102-C; Entry 1; RG 174, NARA.

15. Maj. John B. Reynolds to DuPont Manufacturing, 10 June 1919; folder "Employment of Negro Ex-Servicemen," Entry 355; RG 165, NARA.

16. Memo for Colonel Woods, 17 June 1919; folder "Employment of Negro Ex-Servicemen," Entry 355; RG 165, NARA.

17. Director of Negro Economics to Labor Secretary, 27 August 1919; file #8/102-C, Entry 1; RG 174, NARA.

18. Emmett J. Scott to Grosvenor Clarkson, Director, National Council of Defense, 26 March 1919; file #8/1-2-E, Entry 1, RG 174, NARA.

19. E. P. Marrs to NAACP, 28 December 1932, "Military, Gen'l, 1933-Jan.-Oct." folder, Box C-376, Series I, National Association for the Advancement of Colored People Papers, Library of Congress [hereafter NAACP, LOC].

20. The veterans explained that although some of them were eligible for membership in the more inclusive Veterans of Foreign Wars or Disabled American Veterans, they wanted a Legion post to maximize their numbers. Alex A. Govern to Walter White, 11 October 1934, "Military, General, January-November, 1934" folder, Box C-376, Series I, NAACP, LOC.

21. Marie E. Gray to Mary W. Ovington, 25 January 1920, "Military, General, 1920" folder, box C-374, Series I, NAACP, LOC.

22. Lincoln Legion pamphlet, 24 July 1925, "Military, General, 1925, June–Dec." folder, box C-375, Series I, NAACP, LOC.

23. Gaines Mundy to NAACP, 13 May 1922; Ernest G. Tidrington to James W. Johnson, secretary of the NAACP, 23 May 1922, and reply, 29 May 1992. Both in "Military, Gen'l, 1922, Jan.–June" folder. Undated note on Gaines Mundy case and Press Release on abuses at North Carolina Veterans' Hospital, 2 May 1924, "Military, General, 1924, Jan.–Dec." folder. Assistant Secretary to Dr. M. O. Bousfield, 3 February 1933, "Military, General, 1933, Jan.–Oct." folder. All in box C-374, Series I, NAACP, LOC.

24. See correspondence in "Military, General, 1922, Jan.–June," and "Military, General, 1933, Jan.–Oct." folders, NAACP Papers, LOC. In his autobiography Hamilton Fish talks of receiving a large amount of correspondence from veterans of the 369th Infantry Regiment; Hamilton Fish, *Memoir of an American Patriot* (Washington, D.C.: Regnery Gateway, 1991).

25. Wallace Caldwell to NAACP, 18 January 1924, "Military, General, 1924, Jan.–Dec." folder. Rosa Lee to NAACP, 16 February 1930, and to Rep. Oscar DePriest, 15 February 1930, "Military, General, 1930, Jan.–Dec." folder. All in Box C-375, Series I, NAACP, LOC.

26. Scott Gelber, "A 'Hard-Boiled Order': The Reeducation of Disabled WWI Veterans in New York City," *Journal of Social History* 39, no. 1 (fall 2005): 163–64.

27. Jennifer D. Keene, *World War I* (Westport, Conn.: Greenwood Press, 2006), 46–48.

28. Gelber, "A 'Hard-Boiled Order,'" 165, 168.

29. Ana Carden-Coyne, "Ungrateful Bodies: Rehabilitation, Resistance and Disabled American Veterans of the First World War," *European Review of History* 14, no. 4 (December 2007): 544.

30. Beth Linker, "For Life and Limb: The Reconstruction of a Nation and Its Disabled Soldiers in World War I America," (Ph.D. diss., Yale University, 2006), ch. 4.

31. Memo from Walter White, 4 March 1919; and letter to Hayes, 15 March 1919; both in "Military, General, 1919, March" folder, Box C-374, Series I, NAACP, LOC.

32. James Sanford to J.R.A. Crossland, 10 November 1921, "Misc. file on training of colored men," Entry 63, RG 15, NARA.

33. Joel Moore to NAACP, 29 December 1923, "Military, General, 1924, Jan.–Dec." folder, Box C-375, Series I, NAACP. LOC.

34. Gelber, "A 'Hard-Boiled Order,'" 172; and Mark Meigs, *Optimism at Armageddon: Voices of American Participants in the First World War* (New York: New York University Press, 1997), 202.

35. Assistant Director, Rehabilitation Program to Director, 29 August 1922, "A&T College, Greensboro, NC" folder, Entry 63. RG 15, NARA.

36. *The Vocational Summary* (June 1921), quoted in Gelber, "A 'Hard-Boiled Order,'" 165. Crossland was a prominent physician and public figure who had served as U.S. minister and consul-general of Liberia during the Theodore Roosevelt administration. He had also lost a son in the war and entered office determined to improve educational opportunities for returning veterans. He would end his career with the Veterans Bureau in 1923 when his back-room scheming to become head of the newly created Tuskegee Hospital for black veterans backfired. *The Crisis* (1921): 273; and Pete Daniel, "Black Power in the 1920s: The Case of the Tuskegee Veterans Hospital, *Journal of Southern History* 36, no.3 (August 1970): 384.

37. J.R.A. Crossland to Capt. F. O. Smith, Chief of Training, 3 January 1922, "Training Center for Colored Trainees" folder, Entry 63, RG 15, NARA.

38. Wiley A. Hall to J.R.A. Crossland, 23 January 1922, "Richmond, VA Colored Training Center" folder; Entry 63, RG 15, NARA.

39. Signed petition, 1 May 1922, untitled folder, Entry 63, RG 15, NARA.

40. Schools such as Prairie View that used the land grants provided by the 1861 Morrill Land Grant College Act to create institutions of higher learning were known as land-grant colleges.

41. Inspection of A&M State Normal School, Prairie View, Texas, 2 June 1922, "A&T College, Greensboro, NC" folder, Entry 63; RG 15, NARA.

42. Report on A&M Normal School, 15 March 1923, untitled folder, Entry 63, RG 15, NARA. A&M Normal School was also a black land-grant college.

43. Chief of Training to J.R.A. Crossland, 13 December 1921; and Report on A & M School, Normal, Alabama, 15 March 1923. Both in untitled folder, Entry 63, RG 15, NARA.

44. Letter from Solomon Harper, "Military General, 1923, Jan.–Dec." folder, box C-375, Series I, NAACP, LOC.

45. Inspection Report, 10 June 1922, "A&T College, Greensboro, NC" folder, Entry 63. RG 15, NARA.

46. J. Stanley Durkee, President, Howard University, to Frank Hines, Director, U.S. Veterans Bureau, 7 June 1923; untitled folder; Entry 63, RG 15, NARA.

47. Greenleaf B. Johnson memo, "Military, General, 1924, Jan.–Dec." folder, Box C-375, Series I, NAACP, LOC.

48. Letter from Austin J. Holloday, 1 June 1938. "Military, General, 1938, April–December" folder, box C-376, Series I, NAACP, LOC.

49. E. P. Marrs, letter to NAACP, "Military, Gen'l, 1933, Jan.–Oct." folder, 28 December 1932, box C-376, Series I, NAACP Papers, LOC.

50. Report on A&M Normal School, 15 March 1923, untitled folder, Entry 63, RG 15, NARA.

51. James E. Sanford to J.R.A. Crossland, 10 November 1921, "Mis. file on training of colored men," Entry 63, RG 15, NARA.

52. A. G. Dill, letter to NAACP, 9 May 1922, "Military General, 1922, Jan.–June" folder, box C-374, Series I, NAACP Papers, LOC.

53. Clyde [illegible last name] to NAACP, 25 July 1921, Box C-374, "Military, General, 1921–June–July" folder, NAACP; and George F. Peterson to NAACP, 12 May 1923, "Military, General, 1933 Jan.–Oct." Box C-376, Series I, NAACP

54. K. Nickson, interview in *Harlem Hellfighters*, film by George Merlis and Roscoe Lee Browne (New Video Group, 1997).

55. Rayford Logan, "Woodrow Wilson's War and Logan's War" ch. 6, unpublished autobiography. Rayford Logan Papers, folder 3, box 166–32, Manuscript Department, Moorland-Spingarn Research Center, Howard University, Washington, D.C.

56. W. F. Davis to Walter White, 14 April 1931, "Military General, 1931, Jan.–Oct." folder, box C-374, Series I, NAACP Papers, LOC.

57. Undated petition, untitled folder, Entry 63, RG 15, NARA.

58. Wallace, 22 April 1922; and Cordelia Lee to NAACP, 16 April 1925, "Military, General, 1925, Jan.–May," Box C-375, Series I, Box C-375, Series I, NAACP, LOC.

59. J. R. Crossland to Frank T. Hines, 9 July 1923, file #15.076, Hospital 91, Tuskegee Alabama, Entry 2A NM60, RG 15, NARA.

60. K. Walter Hickel, "Medicine, Bureaucracy, and Social Welfare: The Politics of Disability Compensation for American Veterans of World War I," in *The New Disability History: American Perspectives*, ed. Paul K. Longmore and Lauri Umansky (New York: New York University Press, 2001), 246–56.

61. Ibid., 248.

62. L. M. Pastor, Regional Relief Officer, to Medical Officer-in-charge, U.S. Veterans' Hospital #98, Castle Point, NY, 19 February 1925; Isadore Martin to James Weldon Johnson, 25 February 1925; and reply 27 February 1925. All in "Military, General 1925, Jan.–May" folder, Box C-375, Series I, NAACP, LOC.

63. W. L. Hutcherson to James Weldon Johnson, 23 April 1928; and Winthrop Adams, Acting Medical Director, to Congressman W. A. Ayers, 17 April 1928. Both in "Military, General, 1928, Jan.–Sept." folder, Box C-375, Series I, NAACP, LOC.

64. Multiple correspondence on the Thomas White case is located in "Military, General, 1925, Jan.–May" folder Box C-375, Series I, NAACP, LOC.

65. In 1921 the board of medical experts hired by the Treasury Department to help create a national network of veterans' hospitals strongly recommended creating a segregated hospital. Vanessa Northington Gamble, *Making a Place for Ourselves: The Black Hospital Movement, 1920–1945* (New York: Oxford University Press, 1995), 74.

66. U.S. Veterans Bureau field letter, 2 February 1923, in "Tuskegee Institute, Nov. 3, 1921–June 28, 1923," folder, box C-410, Part I, Series C, NAACP Papers, LOC.

67. Gamble, *Making a Place for Ourselves*, 81.

68. Daniel, "Black Power in the 1920s," 371.

69. A. L. Holsey to J. W. Johnson, Notes on the Tuskegee Hospital Situation, 11 April 1923, "Tuskegee Institute, Nov. 3, 1921–June 28, 1923" folder, Box C-410, Part I, Series C, NAACP, LOC.

70. Letter to the editor, 14 May 1923, "Tuskegee Institute, Nov. 3, 1921–June 28, 1923" folder, box C-410, Part I, Series C, NAACP Papers, LOC.

71. Letter to Walter White, 21 May 1923, "Tuskegee Institute, Nov. 3, 1921–June 28, 1923" folder, box C-410, Part I, Series C, NAACP Papers, LOC. According to Alabama state law, white nurses could refuse to treat black men.

72. Holsey to Emmett J. Scott, 2 July 1923, quoted in Daniel, "Black Power in the 1920s," 377.

73. Daniel, "Black Power in the 1920s," 378.

74. "Ask Troops Guard Tuskegee Negroes," *New York World*, 8 July 1923; "Will Fight Klan on Veterans' Hospital," *New York Herald*, 9 July 1923; and Clippings in "Tuskegee Institute, Nov. 3, 1921–June 28, 1923" folder, box C-410, Part I, Series C, NAACP Papers, LOC.

75. Crossland to Hines, 9 July 1923.

76. Hines soon replaced Stanley with Maj. Charles M. Griffin as head of the hospital and charged him with training black doctors to run the hospital themselves.

77. Gamble, *Making a Place for Ourselves*, 95.

78. Ibid., 102.

79. W. G. Alexander, letter to the editor, *Journal of the National Medical Association* 25, no. 1 (February 1933): 33–34; and Clipping in "Military General 1933, Jan.–Oct." folder, Box C-376, Series I, NAACP Papers. LOC.

80. *Veterans' Herald*, March 1924, 10–11, Library Division, Moorland-Spingarn Research Center, Howard University.

81. *Veterans' Herald*, April 1924, 16.

82. *Veterans' Herald*, March 1924, 14.

83. *Veterans' Herald*, March 1924, 12. Anne C. Rose argues that the focus on staffing Tuskegee with black professionals drew attention away from medical questions such as providing effective treatment for patients battling mental illness. Anne C. Rose, *Psychology and Selfhood in the Segregated South* (Chapel Hill: University of South Carolina Press, 2009), 18–19.

84. Alexander, letter to the editor.

# IV

# Bonuses and G.I. Bills

# 7

## Rethinking the Bonus March

### Federal Bonus Policy, Veteran Organizations, and the Origins of a Protest Movement

STEPHEN R. ORTIZ

Their remedy, obviously, is to pool their political strength . . . and bring irresistible pressure to bear upon the politicians. Various altruistic leaders, eager for the ensuing jobs, already whoop them up to that end. I suspect that they will be heard from hereafter, and in a most unpleasant manner. We are just beginning to pay for the war.

*H. L. Mencken on the veterans' Bonus, December 1931.*

In 1927 the Veterans of Foreign Wars (VFW), the national organization founded in 1899 by veterans of the Spanish-American and Philippine American Wars, appeared destined for historical obscurity. The organization that would later stand with the American Legion as a pillar of the powerful twentieth-century veterans' lobby struggled to maintain a membership of 60,000 veterans. Despite desperate attempts to recruit from the ranks of the nearly 2.5 million eligible World War veterans, the VFW lagged behind both the newly minted American Legion and even the Spanish War Veterans in membership. The upstart Legion alone, from its 1919 inception throughout the 1920s, averaged more than 700,000 members. Indeed, in 1929 Royal C. Johnson, the chairman of the House Committee on World War Veterans Legislation and a member of both the Legion and the VFW, described the latter as "not sufficiently large to make it a vital factor in public sentiment." And yet by 1932, in the middle of an economic crisis that dealt severe blows to the membership totals of almost every type of voluntary association, the VFW's membership soared to nearly 200,000 veterans. Between 1929 and 1932, the VFW experienced this surprising growth because the organization demanded full and immediate cash payment of the deferred Soldiers' Bonus while the American Legion opposed it. Thus, by challenging federal veterans' policy, the VFW rose out of relative obscurity to become a prominent vehicle for veteran political activism. As important, by doing so the VFW unwittingly set in motion the protest movement known as the Bonus March.[1]

In the summer of 1932, more than twenty thousand World War I veterans descended on Washington, D.C., to lobby Congress for immediate payment on their adjusted service certificates, certificates usually referred to as the Bonus. After weeks of mounting tension and the congressional defeat of the Bonus, the U.S. Army forcibly evicted the Bonus Marchers and their families from makeshift encampments on the Anacostia River. The Bonus March and its pitiable denouement figure prominently in the Depression-era historical narrative. In addition to capturing the social dislocation wrought by the Great Depression, the violent conclusion to the Bonus March has come to symbolize the Herbert Hoover administration's perceived disregard for the suffering of average Americans during the Depression's bleakest days. Indeed, despite persuasive evidence exculpating Hoover for the rout of the Bonus Marchers, the episode remains historical shorthand for the failure of the Hoover presidency.[2]

While recent studies have broadened the scope of inquiry into the Bonus March, they do not alter the previous generation of scholarship's depiction of the Bonus March as a spontaneous social protest movement by unemployed veterans, sparked by the Depression yet unsupported by the major veteran organizations.[3] This perspective results in large measure from an overreliance on the American Legion national organization as the voice of organized veteran political activism—an overreliance based on both its stature as the largest veteran organization and its extensive archival material. Thus, while it is true that the American Legion national leadership opposed early payment of the Bonus and condemned the Bonus Marchers, the emphasis on the American Legion has obscured the political milieu from which the Bonus March emerged.[4]

This essay seeks to recontextualize the Bonus March by examining the organized efforts carried out by the VFW for full and immediate payment of the Bonus. In doing so, the essay argues that the supposedly unprompted Bonus Army that moved on Washington in the summer of 1932 actually responded to organized political activism orchestrated by the VFW, an activism that predated the onset of the Great Depression.[5] Moreover, by viewing the origins of the March and the growth of the VFW in tandem, the symbiotic relationships between federal policy and voluntary associations, and the state and civil society can be fruitfully examined.[6] For the federal policy that outlined the Bonus's deferred features inadvertently led to a heady political mobilization by veterans. When the largest of the veteran organizations, the American Legion, failed to challenge federal policy, veterans first flowed into the VFW and then onto the streets of the capital. Federal policies aimed at benefiting veterans instead transformed them into activist citizens.[7] And the attendant rise of the VFW to political prominence would have far-reaching results. As the two major veteran organizations became fierce rivals for veterans' allegiance after 1932, their associational competition would be as responsible as the historical memory of the march itself in leading to the passage of one of the most sweeping pieces of social legislation in U.S. history: the GI Bill of 1944.[8]

■

Prior to 1929 the VFW joined the American Legion in battling three successive administrations over the issue of adjusted compensation, typically called simply "the Bonus." Immediately following World War I, ex-soldiers began to call for an adjustment of their wartime pay. Soldiers complained that wages of thirty dollars a month, minus mandatory war-risk insurance payments, left them with paltry compensation compared to the inflated wartime wages being paid to those not in uniform. The fortunes made in the war industries exacerbated the feelings of inequity. From the start, the VFW echoed soldiers' calls for a Bonus, but the Wilson administration opposed any such payment and found initial support from the newly organized American Legion. While many veterans within the Legion voiced the desire for additional compensation, the Legion suppressed the issue until 1920. Finally, in 1920, Bonus advocates within the Legion forced the organization to back some form of adjusted compensation legislation. Between 1920 and 1924, then, the VFW and Legion fought side by side for some form of Bonus legislation.[9]

In the election year of 1924 Congress passed the Adjusted Compensation Act. The specifics of the legislation proved significant because while veterans would receive a bonus for their soldiering experience, it would not be as an immediate cash payment. Rather, the bonus would be awarded as a deferred interest-bearing certificate payable in 1945 or, at death, to the veteran's beneficiaries. In 1945 veterans would receive compensation of a dollar for every day in service, overseas veterans 1.25 dollars per day, plus the accumulated 4 percent interest. Moreover, as part of the bill, after two years veterans would be allowed to take out a loan from the Veterans Bureau on their certificates' equal to 22.5 percent of face value. Including interest, this total value could reach as high as sixteen hundred dollars. The American Legion leaders supported the insurance policy provisions. The VFW argued against the deferment, but lacking the size and lobbying stature of the Legion, relented, preferring the measure over no Bonus at all. Congress, eager to please this large and vocal constituency, overrode a Calvin Coolidge veto, making the Bonus law and handing veterans a long-sought victory. To the VFW, however, the victory proved insufficient as the organization continued to voice displeasure over what veterans called the "tombstone" bonus.[10]

Between 1926 and 1928 the policies of deferred payment and partial loans against that payment provided the grist for the VFW's challenge to federal veterans' policy. The VFW leadership began to renege on the adjusted service certificates compromise. The leadership offered proposals that chipped away at the Bonus insurance policy by pushing for immediate payment to those rated permanently and totally disabled. In multiple national encampment resolutions, the VFW argued that the "permanent total" invariably suffered a shortened life span and, therefore, should "enjoy the benefits derived from the value of his adjusted compensation during the remaining months of his life." Yet the organization's calls for any adjustments to the Bonus provisions went unheeded by both the Legion and veteran advocates in Congress.[11]

Before 1929 the VFW and the Legion had worked in tandem on most veterans' issues. Both fought diligently for expanded medical benefits and the construction of veteran hospitals and clinics. Each sought to strengthen the existing system of pensions and benefits for ex-servicemen, their widows, and families. Both organizations attempted to make the Veterans Bureau and the War Risk Insurance Board more efficient and more responsive to veterans' needs. On non-veterans' issues, the Legion and the VFW called for a strong national defense and military preparedness, supporting increased defense spending and the maintenance of civilian military training camps. Moreover, both stridently promoted the emotionally charged goal of "Americanism" and fervently opposed Bolshevism in any guise. Notwithstanding these nearly identical political agendas, the two national organizations differed in crucial ways.[12]

The VFW not only lacked the Legion's size and attendant lobbying strength but also its prominent, politically connected leadership. In 1928 the Legion maintained a membership of nearly eight hundred thousand, while the VFW struggled to keep seventy thousand dues-paying members. As important, a group of wealthy and conservative elites known as "the kingmakers" dominated the Legion's national leadership. Never far from the reins of national political power, "kingmakers" such as Theodore Roosevelt Jr., Ogden Mills, and Bennett Champ Clark also exerted tremendous control over the Legion's policies. While rank-and-file veterans complained about this Legion oligarchy, the VFW leadership tended to be less elite in social origins, less entrenched, and ultimately more responsive to the membership than their Legion counterparts. The VFW leadership's lack of economic and political stature also translated into a surprising lack of funds for the organization. Thus, before 1929, the conservative, power-brokering Legion towered over the VFW not just in membership but also in power and prestige, however measured.[13]

In 1929, however, the VFW embarked on a new course of action that would eventually transform the fortunes of the organization. As allowed by the Adjusted Compensation Act, veterans began to draw loans on their adjusted service certificates as soon as they were eligible to do so. Between 1927 and 1929, 1.65 million veterans borrowed $133.4 million against their certificates at the Veterans Bureau and nearly $30 million more at banks. Bolstered by the level of veterans' loan activity, the VFW national leadership began to argue more forcefully that the federal government must uphold its obligations to veterans permanently disadvantaged by their war service. In a *Foreign Service* editorial deriding the "Grave Yard Bonus," the national leadership declared, "The large percentage of loans made on the compensation certificates, since the first of 1927, proves how seriously was—and still is—the need of the average world war veteran."[14]

At the 1929 national encampment in St. Paul, Minnesota, the VFW delegates went on record endorsing the proposal by the populist Iowa senator Smith W. Brookhart to pay the Bonus immediately. The encampment resolution ordered the VFW leadership to "take appropriate action to further the passage and administration of the measure." Thus, prior to the stock market crash and the social dislocation of the Great Depression, the VFW made the government's payment of the Bonus a signature issue based on the rationale that wartime service severely disrupted the economic lives of veterans. The federal policy of a deferred Bonus coupled with the loan provision left the door wide open for future veteran political activism.[15]

The Depression did not trigger the veterans' call for immediate cash payment of the Bonus, but it did impart a new intensity to their demands. While veterans' arguments for immediate payment hinged on the notion that wartime service unfairly disadvantaged them, they—like many Americans—began to bear the additional burdens brought on by the Depression. As early as November 1929, the VFW national leadership witnessed the impact of the stock market crash on veterans' economic livelihoods. VFW national commander Hezekiah N. Duff wired President Hoover asking that he employ the bully pulpit and urge business leaders to provide veterans' additional assistance through preferential hiring programs. On veteran unemployment, the VFW commander reported to the president, "The local units of the VFW throughout the country are being besieged daily with appeals for help from veterans unable to secure employment." Duff painted a grim picture, "Thousands are shuffling along the streets of our cities, thinly-clad and hunger-driven, in futile search for employment and a chance to exist in the country for which they fought and were willing to die on the field of battle." As evidence of the problem, over a nine-day period in January 1930, 170,000 needy World War I veterans applied for first-time loans on their Bonus certificates. Indeed, the scant existing evidence suggests that the Depression disproportionately affected veterans.

Veterans Administration studies in 1930 and 1931 found that veterans experienced a nearly 50 percent higher unemployment rate than non-veterans of the same age cohort. Another Depression-era VA report concluded that veterans experienced longer stretches of unemployment and more dire financial need compared to non-veterans.[16]

As the Depression deepened in 1930, veteran demands for some form of relief intensified. VFW Commander Duff again wrote Hoover asking for federal assistance. Duff explained that the citizenry recognized the federal government's obligation to veterans, noting, "All these citizens know is that these veterans were hale and hearty before they went into service during the World War, and that they are physical and mental wrecks as well as industrial losses today." Congress, eager to please this important constituency, sought to alleviate some of veterans' problems. The 1930 congressional session, however, focused on components of veteran legislation other than the Bonus. In the summer Congress explored and then passed substantial legislation on veteran issues. A considerable portion of the congressional docket was taken up with bills such as the Veteran Relief Act, which granted disability pensions to 150,000 veterans who had been previously unable to prove service connection; several expanded pension adjustments; and the consolidation of the veteran-related federal agencies into the Veterans' Administration. Many commentators suggested that the renewed interest in veteran affairs, although a typical election-year concern, could be seen as an attempt to curtail demands for the Bonus. Indeed, the expansion of disability pensions meant many desperate veterans would now receive some federal financial support. The Bonus remained tabled in Congress for the remainder of the year.[17]

At the 1930 national encampment in Baltimore, the VFW maintained the organization's mandate to fight for immediate payment. Surprisingly, the VFW's relationship with Herbert Hoover proved amicable despite the organization's demands for the Bonus. Indeed, Hoover made the trip to Baltimore to review the VFW's national encampment parade. He declined, however, an opportunity to speak to the VFW delegates. Hoover found no pressing political reasons to discourage the VFW from supporting the Bonus. The larger, more powerful Legion, however, proved a different matter.[18]

When the American Legion met in Boston just weeks after the VFW encampment, the Legion leadership enlisted Hoover to squelch the plans of its most unruly member, the congressional sponsor of immediate Bonus payment, Wright Patman (D-Tex.). Patman publicly announced his intentions of raising the question of the Bonus before the assembled Legion delegates. This so worried administration officials and sympathetic members of the Legion that Hoover, joined by Calvin Coolidge on the dais, gave the first presidential speech to the organization. In the speech, prepared with the aid of Legion lobbyist John Thomas Taylor, Hoover appealed to the legionnaires' patriotism and, pointing to the summer of veteran legislation, explained that the federal government had been very generous to veterans already. Hoover's address enabled Legion leaders to successfully turn back the Bonus tide at the convention. The Legion national leadership's victory over Patman—a legionnaire but ineligible for VFW membership—changed the representatives tactics and further improved the fortunes of the VFW.[19]

In December 1930 Patman made overtures to the VFW national leadership to join forces on the Bonus. By this point, the VFW had been supporting the issue for well over a year. Patman's solicitation of the VFW resulted from his frustration with the intransigence of the Legion leadership. In December, as he wooed the VFW leadership, Patman berated the conservative element in the Legion for opposing the Bonus.[20] Throughout December Patman also spoke with Washington-area VFW posts, often debating with Rep. Hamilton Fish Jr. (R-N.Y.) over the respective merits of the Bonus bills they would submit at the beginning of the new congressional session. Patman's efforts bore fruit as D.C. VFW posts began reporting their endorsement of the Patman plan in the weekly veterans' section of the *Washington Post*. The Federal Post described its members' support for Patman's bill, even though they reported that not one of their members was in need of relief.[21]

In January 1931 at the start of the congressional session, some forty-seven Bonus-related proposals circulated through Congress. Of the forty-seven bill proposals, twenty-eight came from Democrats, eighteen from Republicans, and one from a Farm-Labor congressman. As this broad tripartisan pressure mounted, Congress and the capital witnessed an explosive month of VFW activities. The VFW's aggressive public lobbying tactics, official testimony before both houses of Congress, and Bonus marches to the Capitol by VFW members kept the organization in the spotlight.[22]

On 21 January the VFW ramped up the public pressure for the Bonus. A thousand VFW-led veterans rallied to the Capitol in a procession delivering petitions supporting immediate payment. The 124 members of Congress who publicly supported the Bonus accepted the petitions on the Capitol steps, drawing cheers from the veteran assembly.[23] Three days after the Bonus rally, 200 veterans congregated in Philadelphia's Independence Square and proclaimed their intentions to march to Washington in support of immediate Bonus payment. After speeches by their leaders, VFW members John Alfieri and Terrance B. Cochran of the Cochran VFW post in Philadelphia, and after music from the VFW Darby post band, the marchers began a walk to Washington carrying flags and a handmade sign reading "Philadelphia to Washington."

Only twenty-six of the marchers made it to Washington, but the hungry and exhausted men managed to buttonhole the Pennsylvania congressional delegation and call on Bonus leader Patman. Some of the marchers hoped to appear before the Ways and Means Committee meetings planned for that week. When asked if the march had been a failure, the veterans prophetically explained that, to the contrary, "the hike might serve as a motive to other veterans' groups to actively back the [adjusted] pay bills with similar demonstrations."[24]

Ultimately, however, Legion actions determined the course of legislative action on the Bonus. On 25 January bowing to internal pressure from fifteen state Legion departments and the mounting public pressure for the Bonus, the American Legion national executive committee (NEC) met to review the Legion's position. The Legion NEC made an unexpected reversal and endorsed the principle of immediate payment, noting in the resolution that the Bonus "would benefit immeasurably not only the veterans but the citizenry of the entire country." The Legion did not endorse any specific measure, but the Legion's decision imparted a new weight to the scheduled hearings in the Ways and Means Committee for the next week.[25]

The new Legion position turned the tide in Congress for some liberalization of the Bonus, be it full cash payment or some partial measure. The VFW continued to voice its support for full and immediate payment. However, when a proposal to increase the amount veterans could borrow against their certificates, from 22.5 to 50 percent, received backing from the Legion's chief lobbyist, John Thomas Taylor, Congress jumped at the opportunity to satisfy veteran demands without fundamentally altering the established Bonus policy. This compromise legislation, like the original Adjusted Compensation Act, encountered intense opposition from the administration and business groups. Secretary of the Treasury Mellon assumed the point for the administration, characterizing any Bonus loan or payments as fiscally ruinous. The Republican National Committee released a statement claiming that if the Bonus passed, "we can expect a business depression and a period of acute human suffering the like [sic] of which this country has never known."[26]

On 12 February 1931 Congress took action, passing the 50 percent loan bill despite assurances from the administration that it would be vetoed. Hoover's promised veto message challenged the arguments for the Bonus loan and warned of the financial hardships upon the government. He derided the notion that the loans would stimulate business, calling the money veterans might spend from their loans "wasteful expenditure" and "no assistance in the return of real prosperity." Hoover rejected the moral arguments for the Bonus, noting that "the patriotism of our people is not a material thing." Moreover, he warned that paying the Bonus threatened the moral fiber of the country by eroding the virtues of "self-reliance and self-support." Despite these arguments, Congress quickly overrode the veto. *Time* referred to the decisive vote to override as Hoover's "most serious Congressional reversal." Veterans gladly took advantage of the newly available loans. On the first day, 18,000 veterans applied for loans in the New York City Veterans Bureau offices alone. By January 1932, 2.5 million veterans had borrowed the full 50 percent. Michigan senator Arthur Vandenberg later explained to Hoover that the loan liberalization was the only way to curtail the drive for full payment. Vandenberg wrote, "I shall always believe that if [Congress] had not embraced the loan plan . . . there would have been no escape from the full payment of these compensation certificates at that time."[27]

Yet the federal government's continued reluctance to completely satisfy the admitted obligation only led to further veteran political activism. As it had in 1924, the VFW relented, accepting the compromise measure for practical reasons even though the organization continued to call for full payment. The VFW leadership still bemoaned "the injustice of the tombstone bonus," but they "accepted the compromise measure . . . because we realized this was the best we could hope for under existing conditions." Ironically, the 50 percent loan bill and the political turmoil surrounding it proffered the VFW leadership new ammunition in their fight for full payment. The Hoover administration and business group's overwrought concerns about the catastrophic financial impact of even the 50 percent provision gave the VFW leaders a sharp retort. One month later the editors of *Foreign Service* heaped scorn on those arguments in an editorial titled "No Chaos Yet." The editors dryly noted, "despite gloomy predictions of a terrible calamity, impending bankruptcy, industrial chaos, and a tumultuous financial crisis nothing has actually been exploded but the myths."[28]

The VFW's militant position on the Bonus brought the organization unaccustomed success. In terms of membership growth and the expansion of the organization into new communities, the Bonus struggle paid real dividends for the VFW. From 1929 to 1931 the VFW grew from just less than 70,000 to 138,620 dues-paying members, nearly doubling the membership. As impressive, the VFW expanded its organizational structure into new communities with the formation of 700 new posts, a 43 percent increase. Post growth began to increase dramatically in the late fall of 1930, coinciding with the Legion's stated opposition to the Bonus. In October and November 1930, the VFW chartered 50 new posts each month—setting records for the organization. The growth in 1931 proved most remarkable with 350 new posts being established and 70 more regaining their charter after becoming defunct for nonpayment of dues. By the end of 1931 the VFW's institutional strength surpassed that of any other time in the organization's previous history. To the upper echelons of the organization leadership, their position on the Bonus proved the difference. The VFW legislative committee chairman noted in his annual report, "it is felt that our legislative stand on the bonus . . . provided the working tools for our recruiting drive. It certainly confirms the statement that the Veterans of Foreign Wars truly represent the veterans."[29]

The 1931 national encampment—organized by a VFW member from Independence, Missouri, Harry S. Truman—reflected the organization's new standing. Republican VFW officials wrote to the administration fearing the VFW encampment would turn into a "Democratic Rally" in the friendly confines of the Kansas City Pendergast regime. A VA official with ties to both the administration and the VFW deemed some appearance by a high-ranking administration figure "darn near essential" to stemming a Democratic veterans' "promenade." VA director Frank T. Hines did attend and address the delegates, but his arguments against the Bonus proved futile.[30]

Hines's remarks to the delegates underscored the changing fortunes of the VFW. He congratulated the VFW delegates on their recruiting success but cautioned them in thinly veiled terms about demanding the Bonus. Hines remarked, "You have increased your membership greatly and with that increase comes a greater responsibility, because we must remember that before we were veterans we were citizens of this great country of ours and we are still citizens." He advised the VFW delegates and leaders to tell the next Congress, "because we realize the situation existing in our country and because we are patriotic citizens of this country . . . that we are going to be exceedingly cautious in our demands, because we are not going to be put in the position of asking for something and then be blamed later on because we caused a greater depression or a greater problem in our Nation." Commander Wolman immediately and sharply rebuked Hines in front of the delegates, "we do not think we have ever made any demands as an organization which were unfair, and we certainly pledge that we shall not make any demands that our members believe to be unfair, sir." The encampment promptly and unanimously passed a resolution reaffirming the VFW's commitment to immediate cash payment of the Bonus.[31]

Weeks later the American Legion convention met in Detroit. The NEC decision in January to reverse the official position against the Bonus complicated the matter for those trying to suppress the Patman forces in the Legion. Legion leaders feared the delegates might swing over to a cash payment position, reflecting the NEC decision. To undermine calls for the Bonus, the Legion enlisted a reluctant Hoover to speak to the convention yet again. Despite warnings from Royal Johnson that a riot might ensue during the convention over the Bonus, Hoover accepted the invitation and addressed the legionnaires for the second consecutive year. Hoover appealed to the Legion's "character and idealism" and history of service, asking for "determined opposition by you to additional demands upon the nation until we have won this war against world depression." In response, the Legion delegates passed a resolution voicing almost identical language to Hoover's request and beat back a Bonus vote, 902–507. The Legion resolution called upon "the able-bodied men of America, rich and poor, veteran, civilian, and statesmen, to refrain from placing unnecessary financial burdens upon National, State, or municipal governments." Legion leaders attributed the defeat of the Bonus to Hoover's address. One wrote to Larry Richey, the president's secretary, "I firmly believe the Chief's coming to Detroit changed the vote from two to one for to two to one against payment of the bonus."[32]

In late 1931 as the leadership realized the Legion would not join in the fight during the next congressional session, the VFW started operating more independently, staking an even more vigorous claim to the issue. Moreover, the VFW's Bonus position took on a more edgy ideological cast as the issue began to be conflated with both inflationary economic thinking and the calls for increased "purchasing power" to defeat the Depression. In the process, the VFW made a prophet out of Baltimore's resident cynic H. L. Mencken, who predicted that the fight for the Bonus would turn ugly. In a December editorial, Mencken admitted that "the damage the heroes suffered by being thrust into the war is much under estimated, and that the amount of compensation they have got since they came home is equally over-estimated." He called the Hoover Legion speech and the Legion national leadership's response a "spit in the eye" to veterans. Moreover, Mencken predicted that veterans would "pool their political strength" under "various altruistic leaders" who "already whoop them up to that end." Between December 1931 and May 1932, the VFW would "whoop them up" even more, establishing the immediate context from which the Bonus March would emerge.[33]

■

In late 1931, in response to the Legion leadership's success in squelching a favorable bonus resolution, the VFW national organization undertook a massive publicity campaign to demonstrate veterans' support for the bonus. Cognizant still of the Legion's larger membership and stature, the VFW attempted to demonstrate that the Legion leadership misrepresented the rank-and-file veterans on the bonus issue. The VFW national organization published veteran "bonus ballots" in 162 metropolitan newspapers, newspapers with a combined circulation of 23 million copies. The VFW received 254,324 ballots from veterans in favor of the bonus and only 596 against.[34] *Foreign Service* candidly framed the disconnect between the Legion leadership and veterans' views, "the heart of the American Legion is sound to the core—with the rank and file of its membership wholly in sympathy with the problems of the great mass of veterans who are suffering from economic distress, due to widespread unemployment, and bureaucratic control of agencies that affect their welfare." For proof of the wrong-headedness of the Legion's official stance, the editorial staff pointed to the "thousands of individual Legion posts and members . . . working hand in hand with the VFW in the present crisis of the fight for immediate cash payment of the adjusted service certificates." Thus, even while reaping the benefits of their position and moving aggressively out in front of the issue, VFW leaders needed to confront the perception that the Legion spoke for the average veteran in order to obtain legislative results in the upcoming congressional session.[35]

While the VFW leadership solicited rank-and-file veterans' feelings on the bonus, they did little to squelch veterans' rumblings about a march to Washington to promote the issue. Even in late 1931, small groups of veterans moved on the city, precipitating a specific warning from the leadership in the pages of *Foreign Service*. The leadership did not oppose the lobbying technique; rather, VFW leaders hoped to discourage insolvent veterans from flocking to the District. The warning stated, "all VFW members are urged to refrain from going to Washington to lend their personal influence to the campaign in behalf of cash payment unless they are financially able to take care of themselves during the interim."[36] The VFW leadership discouraged less solvent members from making the trip because the District of Columbia posts already strained to provide relief for local unemployed veterans and for additional down-and-out veterans who journeyed to Washington in order to wrestle with the Veterans Administration bureaucracy. The Washington, D.C., posts told the national leadership they could provide no more assistance to homeless and hungry veterans. That inability determined VFW national policy toward veterans coming to Washington, not disapproval of the lobbying technique. Instead, the VFW steadfastly supported the veterans' right to petition their government and continued to lead veterans in petitioning efforts themselves.

In 1931–32 the VFW's mobilization for the Bonus intensified at both the national and local level. Wright Patman and the dynamic future national commander James Van Zandt began a series of speaking engagements across the country. The Bonus barnstorming tour touched off veteran rallies in cities from Providence, Rhode Island, to St. Paul, Minnesota. *Foreign Service* reported veteran audiences ranging up to 2,500 persons at some of these rallies. The VFW national organization also coordinated a grassroots push by holding four sectional conferences in Washington, D.C., Chicago, Boston, and Kansas

City to train departmental and state leaders in publicity and lobbying tactics. The VFW leadership published petition blanks in *Foreign Service*, furthering the ongoing petition drive. VFW posts around the country reported to the national organization that they had amassed thousands of signatures for the Bonus. Members from Camp Bowie Post No. 78 in Fort Worth, Texas, secured fifty-five thousand signatures in just eighteen days. The national organization published reports highlighting local posts' publicity and recruiting activities for others to emulate, activities that included renting out small storefronts in depressed commercial districts where VFW members combined heavy recruitment of veterans with the aggressive signature drive. Moreover, VFW and Women's Auxiliary national officers called upon members of the local posts and the auxiliaries to write their legislators demanding action on the Bonus. In short, the entire organization mobilized in the election year push for the Bonus.[37]

The VFW national organization also expanded its lobbying efforts into new media platforms. In January the VFW planned a radio program for the NBC network that would combine lobbying for the Bonus, organizational recruiting, and patriotic entertainment. The "Hello America" broadcast featured an address by Wright Patman and a novel recruiting method in which the commander would conduct the induction ceremony's oath of obligation for new members over the radio. Heard in more than fifty radio markets, Patman's speech refuted Bonus opponents' claims and cemented his public affiliation with the VFW. The VFW found the evening an enormous success as more than twenty-one thousand new members joined the organization during the swearing-in ceremony, a number that equaled an overnight 15 percent increase in the existing membership. The VFW leadership found the radio an extraordinary publicity tool, one they would use at both the network level and in local broadcasts for years to come.[38]

From March to May 1932, the VFW lobbied Congress aggressively for the Bonus. The VFW legislative committee offices served as the headquarters for Bonus congressional supporters. The VFW legislative chairman, L. S. Ray, mailed letters asking every representative and senator for their support. Those who wrote back declaring their intentions to vote for the bill went on a public list. Ray kept tabs on the list, periodically releasing it to the newspapers to maintain the pressure. On April 2, prior to the scheduled Committee on Ways and Means Bonus hearings, Ray reported 166 "pledged" legislators supporting the issue, even though the VFW explained "in no instance had the organization threatened any member who refused to support the legislation." The VFW hoped that the committee would rule favorably on the Patman bill, but in case, the VFW also tracked the signatures on a discharge petition that would bring the bill to a House vote regardless of the recommendations in the committee report.[39]

In a key precursor to the Bonus March, three days before the House Ways and Means Committee proceedings on the Patman Bonus Bill, the VFW organized a large rally and march to the Capitol in support of the Bonus. On 8 April 1932 Paul C. Wolman led the Bonus procession with VFW posts from Pennsylvania, Maryland, Virginia, West Virginia, and the District of Columbia taking part. Defiant members of eight Legion posts joined the rally. Between 1,500 and 2,000 veterans marched in a "picturesque" parade up to the Capitol steps led by the VFW band from Clarksburg, West Virginia, and 200 flag-bearers. Members of the House and Senate, including Wright Patman and Elmer Thomas, the respective leaders of Bonus legislation, met with the leaders of the procession and drew loud cheers from the assembled veterans. The VFW leaders presented the members of Congress with twenty packing cases of petitions bearing more than 2 million signatures—281,000 from ex-servicemen—in support of immediate cash payment. Newsreel cameras and photographers thronged around the ceremony on the Capitol steps. Veterans yelled, "Give us cash!" The New York Times noted, "Occasionally there was a shout of 'to the White House' but the mass meeting was an orderly one." Five hundred policemen stood by in case.[40]

When the Committee on Ways and Means finally met on 11 April, VFW national leaders placed the weight of the organization's support behind the Bonus at the hearings. VFW commander Darold D. DeCoe explained to the committee, "The Bonus will be the biggest and best payday this country has had in months." Paul C. Wolman, past-VFW commander and now the chairman of the VFW's cash payment campaign committee, testified that veterans needed the Bonus since they suffered disproportionately compared to the rest of the working population. Legislative chairman Ray submitted to the committee a state-by-state tabulation of the VFW's newspaper ballot results and excerpts from letters written by desperate veterans to the VFW legislative office. The VFW and Patman also called on celebrities to bolster their arguments for the Bonus. The VFW solicited help from Sgt. Alvin York, a popular and highly decorated World War I hero, asking him to testify in person before the committee. However, York, who joined the organization in April as a VFW post reached into the Tennessee hillside, wired a telegram supporting the Bonus instead of appearing in person. The recently retired Marine general Smedley D. Butler also wired the House committee at the behest of his VFW comrades. Father Charles E. Coughlin, the radio priest, offered his opinions on the social and economic merits of the Bonus. Despite the intense VFW activism for the Bonus, on 6 May 1932 the Ways and Means Committee shelved the Patman

Bonus bill with an adverse vote. Both Patman and the VFW vowed to discharge the bill through a petition and continued to press for the measure, even though the congressional calendar afforded little time to complete the necessary parliamentary maneuvers before the end of the session.[41]

While the VFW failed in their Bonus push, the organization collected concrete benefits from their mobilization that was begun in December. The organization's gains in stature and membership relative to the Legion became tangible assets. John A. Weeks, a member of the Minnesota House of Representatives wrote the White House about the differences in VFW and Legion fortunes. He wrote Walter Newton, "A good many of the boys have lost their heads [about the Bonus] because the Legion membership has dropped 25%, while it is claimed that the VFW have doubled their membership."[42] Weeks miscalculated slightly; the Legion lost 162,000 members between 1931 and 1932, a 15.4 percent decline. Weeks did come closer, however, in describing the VFW's success with the Bonus issue. In April, May, and June of 1932, for example, the VFW mustered seventy-one, one hundred, and seventy-four new posts, respectively, shattering all organization records. In May alone, nearly three posts *a day* chartered into the VFW. The leadership clearly recognized that this growth resulted from the organization's more aggressive promotion of veterans' demands compared to the Legion. A May *Foreign Service* editorial touted the VFW's new strength: "Veterans throughout the country are awakening to the fact that they owe their support to a veteran organization that truly represents the rank and file of ex-servicemen." By using a range of aggressive lobbying techniques including rallies and marches to challenge federal Bonus policy, the VFW grew precipitously and set the tone for veterans seeking the Bonus.[43]

In this spirited context of organized veteran political activism, three hundred veterans in Portland, Oregon, set out for the capital, beginning what came to be known as the Bonus March. Leaving on May 10 the veterans rode the rails across the country, encountering widely publicized difficulties with railroad companies and various local authorities. By the time the Oregon contingent made it to Washington on May 29, waves of veterans around the country had joined the trek. While there is no direct evidence that the VFW's Bonus campaign inspired this onslaught of veterans, the organization's refusal to relent on the Bonus and its feverish promotion of the discharge petition as a last-ditch effort both kept the issue in the media and, more important, gave the marchers a concrete goal. Indeed, after the arriving veterans set up camps around the city, they walked to the Capitol daily to convince Congressmen to sign the Bonus discharge petition. Dubbed the Bonus Expeditionary Force (BEF) by the sympathetic district superintendent of police, Pelham D. Glassford, the veteran crowd grew at an astonishing rate.

By June more than twenty thousand veterans, including many with families in tow, had crowded into the capital. A group of communist veterans affiliated with the Worker's Ex-Servicemen League also occupied the capital, but their attempts to recruit the other marchers met with little success. BEF leaders denounced their revolutionary zeal and expelled them from the camps, occasionally with accompanying fists.[44]

As the BEF settled in Washington, congressional Bonus supporters finally gathered enough discharge petition signatures to vault the Patman bill over the Ways and Means Committee and put it before a floor vote. On June 15 the House quickly passed the Patman Bonus measure despite the fact (or possibly because) the bill stood little chance in the Senate and faced a promised veto from Hoover. On 17 June, however, with thousands of veterans awaiting news on the Capitol steps, the Senate decisively defeated the Patman Bonus Bill. Deflated by the loss, more than five thousand veterans took the government's offer for transportation back home. The remaining veterans stayed in the various camps and other abandoned buildings around the city, promising to stay until they got the Bonus, even if that meant waiting until 1945. The Communist Party contingent stayed too, becoming a larger and louder percentage of the veterans in the city but still making little inroads with the larger BEF. For more than a month, the situation simmered as supplies became critically short and sanitation a major concern. Government officials grew increasingly anxious. One source described the situation as "a pile of dynamite on Washington's doorstep."[45]

While the VFW provided an outlet for veterans' Bonus agitation all spring and had set the tone for the subsequent Bonus March, the VFW members also made their mark on the Bonus March itself. Eleven days before the celebrated Bonus Army from Oregon even arrived in Washington—in fact, while they were still in the East St. Louis train yards—twenty-five veterans from VFW Post No. 1289 in Chattanooga, Tennessee, already had arrived in the capital demanding the Bonus. The Chattanooga VFW members parked their truck with "We Want Our Bonus" painted on the side near the White House. One historian of the Bonus March postulates that the Portland group perhaps borrowed the idea that they would not leave the city until they got their money from a statement by the VFW members published in an Associated Press report. A *New York Times* column described a contingent of 125 veterans leaving Hoboken, New Jersey, to join the BEF and bring relief supplies, half of whom belonged to the VFW's Fred C. Hall Post in Jersey City. A group of 450 integrated veterans from the VFW's post in Harlem, the Dorrence Brooks Post No. 528, reported their plans to join the festivities in Washington. By June local VFW leaders close to the situation claimed, much to the dismay of the national leadership, that "60 percent of the veterans in the Capital are members of the VFW waving the colors of their respective posts."[46]

Additional evidence suggests that overseas veterans—the membership pool of the VFW—composed a disproportionately large percentage of the veterans coming to the capital. Using data from District police officers who registered veterans as they came to town, the New York Times reported that 83 percent of the veterans moving into Washington claimed to be overseas veterans. After the Bonus bill's defeat, when the federal government provided transportation to more than five thousand veterans, the Veterans Administration records indicated that 66.5 percent of those who accepted the offer had served overseas during the war. Overall, only half of World War I veterans served overseas. Whether overseas veterans suffered disproportionately from the Depression or rallied more energetically to the VFW's agitation is conjecture, but overseas veterans in Washington for the March far exceeded their proportion of the World War veteran population.[47]

Whatever the percentage of VFW members in the BEF may have been, local posts in Washington and around the country generously provided the Bonus Army with material and moral support. The VFW District of Columbia Council, representing fourteen local posts, donated five hundred dollars to help feed the marchers. The VFW Front Line Post of Washington offered the use of a theater that it had at its disposal. The Front Line Post told a BEF assembly that the theater would be "turned over to the BEF for the purposes of collecting funds for the BEF treasury." The BEF would only need to supply "the talent." On 7 June, when some seven thousand Bonus Marchers paraded up Pennsylvania Avenue, a local VFW band led the procession. Posts from around the nation provided material assistance. One of many examples, VFW members in Asbury Park and Bradley Beach, New Jersey, solicited food and materials for the BEF from local merchants. The New Jersey posts accumulated enough to fill two trucks headed toward Washington, supplemented with twelve veterans eager to join the March. Whether as members of the BEF or as sympathetic supporters, VFW members aligned themselves in solidarity with the Bonus Army.[48]

Adding to the links between the Bonus March and the VFW, key figures from the saga maintained extensive VFW ties. Chief of Police Glassford's personal rapport with the veterans and patient handling of the crisis made him immensely popular with the BEF, so popular that Glassford served as the treasurer of the BEF's funds. Glassford not only belonged to a local VFW post, he had also been a chief recruiter for the VFW in 1931 just prior to taking the police position. Joseph Heffernan, the former mayor of Youngstown, Ohio, and prominent VFW state leader, moved to Washington to begin the publication of *The BEF News*, a weekly newspaper published for the Bonus Army veterans. Heffernan's publication, with its scathing editorials, became the officially sanctioned publication of the BEF, ending its publication run in August at seventy-five thousand copies. Rice Means, publisher of the only national veteran publication unaffiliated with the veteran organizations, the *National Tribune*, supported the Bonus March from the start in print and with coin. Means, a former senator from Colorado, worked extensively with a number of veteran organizations. He was known, however, as the VFW's first national commander and continued to serve on the VFW's legislative committee. Smedley Butler, the popular Marine Corp general who came to Camp Marks to cheer on the men and actually bivouacked overnight in one of the dwellings, belonged to the VFW and would go on in 1933 through 1936 to be the VFW's main recruiting speaker. This is not to say that all of these prominent VFW figures gave the Bonus March VFW sanctioning. But all of these high-profile men publicly supporting the Bonus Army linked the VFW to the episode in visible and important ways.[49]

Clearly, the VFW leadership did not anticipate that their lobbying efforts for the Bonus would spark such a massive demonstration. Yet, given the level of VFW involvement, it is easy to see how the organization that supported the Bonus since 1929 would be associated with the episode. Statements from the VFW leadership reflected their concerns that the March was being viewed as a VFW-sanctioned event. As early as 24 May (five days before the Portland contingent arrived in Washington), the VFW national organization felt compelled to deny any official connection with the demonstrations and discouraged members from coming to the city. In early June, as the BEF grew to nearly twenty thousand members, the national leadership sent communiqués to every post prohibiting members, by threat of expulsion, from taking part in the March. The VFW adjutant general in Kansas City, R. B. Handy Jr., denounced the Communist agitation in the March as an effort "to capitalize upon the unrest and discontent of unemployed veterans." Handy argued that this could only prove counterproductive to the organization's Bonus strategy, "embarrassing existing efforts on the part of our legislative committee and those individual members of Congress who are advocating immediate cash payment." Handy also noted, however, that the goals of most of the Marchers coincided with the VFW's call for immediate payment. Handy explained: "Without doubt, the groups of former service men marching on Washington are inspired by patriotic motives and have no other purpose than assisting in the campaign for cash payment of the Bonus." Handy and the VFW leadership feared those men would set the Bonus drive back, not advance it.[50]

While the VFW national leaders failed to back the Bonus March for pragmatic reasons, VFW officials in close proximity to the veteran encampments blasted the leadership for failing to lead a March that they had unintentionally instigated. In the heat of the Bonus March, the Maryland Department of the VFW met to elect state officers and national encampment delegates. The Maryland delegates became embroiled in a passionate debate over the Bonus March and the failures of the national leadership. The state encampment passed a resolution denouncing the national leadership and requesting an explanation for the national headquarters' actions. Claiming that the VFW had initiated the March as evidenced by the "60 percent" VFW participation, the Maryland VFW decried that "when the big throng moved on Washington nothing was done by way of leadership." Why, they asked, were "no officials sent to lead the 20,000 or more veterans in their fight to urge passage of the Bonus Bill in Congress?" These state leaders suggested that instead of leading the March, the VFW abdicated responsibility for the BEF, giving the Communists the opportunity to commandeer what the VFW had started. Had the VFW appointed leaders to the Bonus Army, the Maryland delegates proclaimed, "the great body of veterans in this country would not be branded radicals." The following day, after VFW chief of staff Joseph Ranken addressed the delegates, cooler and more politic heads prevailed, and the delegates withdrew the resolution. The resolution, however, exposed both the belief that the VFW caused the March and the more troubling proposition that the VFW played into the hands of the Communists by not leading the BEF.[51]

Others echoed the Maryland VFW delegates in making this accusation. An intelligence memorandum circulated to the FBI and the White House explained that the VFW bore responsibility, even though the March was becoming a Communist rally. The memorandum described the situation in terms almost identical to the Maryland accusations. It began, "The present march on Washington is the direct result of Communist agitation, pure and simple." The memo continued, however: "The Communists have taken advantage of Veterans of Foreign Wars internal politics and the urging of the Bonus by the leaders and are trying to turn this agitation to their, the Communists' advantage." Accusations blaming the VFW and the VFW national leadership for causing the Bonus March resounded through other private and public channels that summer.[52]

Prominent figures in veteran circles attributed the descent of the Marchers on the city to the VFW's Bonus agitation. In a private letter, Royal C. Johnson cautioned President Hoover that the Bonus Army might reach one hundred thousand. He explained that perhaps any veteran "who thought [he] had a bonus due would join with them, particularly when they have been excited to such a move by the Veterans of Foreign Wars, members of Congress, newspapers, and even the clergy." Johnson thought the VFW had recognized its mistake, however, claiming, "I feel certain that by this time the Commander of the Veterans of Foreign Wars would also urge them to leave." On 11 June Johnson made similar statements on the House floor, solemnly declaring, "one great organization . . . the Veterans of Foreign Wars, is partially responsible for this migration." He acknowledged that the VFW leadership now sought "to move them out, but they helped get them in." Johnson explicitly linked the VFW's promotion of the discharge petition with the descent of the marchers and proclaimed that "the men who started that [petition] have their share of responsibility." As chairman of the House veterans' committee and a former judge advocate of the VFW national organization, few were in as good of position as Johnson to cast blame for the Bonus March.[53]

On 28 July 1932, the U.S. government moved to expel the Bonus Marchers from the city. When the police tried to disperse the BEF, riots broke out, leaving two veterans dead and several police wounded. Army chief of staff Douglas MacArthur then exceeded his orders and deployed Army troops, including tanks and cavalry, to drive the veterans out of their encampments. In the process, the Army leveled the veteran camps, setting torches to the dwellings. When he heard of the Bonus rout, Democratic presidential candidate Franklin D. Roosevelt reportedly declared to Felix Frankfurter, "Well, Felix, this will elect me."[54]

Barely one month after the rout, the VFW gathered at the annual encampment in Sacramento, basking in the organization's membership success and ready to take the fight to Hoover and Bonus opponents. The organization had a right to boast. Indeed, in 1932 the VFW grew at an amazing clip. Fifty thousand new members joined, raising the membership total to 187,479 overseas veterans. This put the organization at three times the 1927 size and reflected a 35 percent increase in one year. Moreover, post growth broke records just set in 1931. The VFW gained 442 new posts in 1932, by all accounts the most dire year of the Depression and a horrible year for voluntary association membership. Another 186 posts rechartered after being dropped for nonpayment of dues. For the year, the growth averaged 52.3 posts chartered per month, an average that bested the all-time highs for any one month in the organization's history. In other words, in 1932 the VFW's membership and distribution throughout the country simply skyrocketed.[55]

The VFW encampment pointed to the November election as the means to punish the Hoover administration for the rout of the Bonus Marchers. The delegates passed an extraordinary resolution decrying the "criminally brutal, and uncalled for, and morally indefensible" actions of the president. The delegates described the ballot as "the veterans' strongest weapon of defense" against such

Table 7.1 VFW Membership and Post Growth, 1929–1932

|                          | 1929   | 1930   | 1931    | 1932    |
|--------------------------|--------|--------|---------|---------|
| Total membership         | 76,669 | 95,167 | 138,620 | 187,469 |
| Membership gained in year | 6,693 | 18,498 | 43,453  | 48,849  |
| Total posts              | 1,767  | 1,945  | 2,313   | 2,757   |
| Posts gained in year     | 154    | 178    | 368     | 444     |

presidential misdeeds. Then, so that the American people would be aware of the organization's attitude, the VFW delegates commanded that posts should "be urged to mount sandbags and post a military guard from now on until November so that the Washington evacuation begun in July may be fully completed in November."[56]

■

Between 1929 and 1932 the VFW played a crucial role in the Bonus struggle, a struggle that grew to a crescendo with the Bonus March. Based on the Legion national leadership's opposition to both the Bonus and the march, scholars have contended that veteran organizations abdicated their roles as leaders of veteran political activism during the period. Yet throughout the 1931–32 period the VFW led the Bonus struggle, keeping the contentious issue alive for desperate veterans and reaping the institutional rewards that came with their aggressive stance. In the late spring of 1932, as veterans flocked to the capital, they also flocked to the VFW. Indeed, the VFW national organization employed intensive lobbying and marching to the capital as tactics themselves. In this the VFW put its imprint on the Bonus March to the extent that the organization drew blame for instigating the whole affair.

The federal veterans' policy that explicitly recognized a financial obligation to veterans but continually delayed discharging it had given life to an otherwise moribund veteran organization. After 1932 the VFW stood ready to challenge the American Legion as spokesmen for veterans' concerns. The years that the VFW maintained a secondary status helped the organization develop more aggressive lobbying strategies involving radio and direct citizen participation. As the VFW grew in response to its demands and the Legion's recalcitrance, it raised the organization's public profile even further, creating a positive feedback loop for agitation. By the end of 1932 the VFW began to assert itself as an important national political actor, having staked a claim to the Bonus issue that it would hold until its cash payment in 1936. In the period between the Bonus March and the payment of the Bonus in defiance of yet another presidential veto, the VFW continued its spectacular growth, claiming almost 300,000 members in 1935 while the American Legion sunk to a decade-low membership of 700,000, more than 350,000 fewer members than in 1931.[57] Not surprisingly, in 1936 Congress granted the VFW a congressional charter in recognition of the organization's new political clout. For the VFW, Congress's ill-conceived Bonus policy had been the real gift. It made veterans into activist citizens, and the VFW into a pillar of the powerful twentieth-century veterans' lobby.

## Notes

I would like to thank the *Journal of Policy History* and Cambridge University Press for permission to reprint this essay, which previously appeared as "Rethinking the Bonus March: Federal Bonus Policy, the Veterans of Foreign Wars, and the Origins of a Protest Movement," by Stephen R. Ortiz, *Journal of Policy History*, Vol. 18, No. 3 (2006), pp. 275–303 Copyright 2006 © Copyright © The Pennsylvania State University, University Park, PA. Reprinted with the permission of Cambridge University Press. Epigraph from H. L. Mencken, "The Case for the Heroes," *American Mercury* 24 December, 1931: 410.

1. VFW's membership totals in Mary Katherine Goldsmith, "The Veterans of Foreign Wars of the United States: The History of a Veterans' Organization, Its Function in Assisting Veterans, Influencing National Legislation, and Interpreting and Promoting Americanism, 1899–1948," (M.A. thesis, University of Kansas City, 1963), 194. Legion membership totals in *National Tribune*, 7 February 1935. Letter from Royal C. Johnson to Herbert Hoover, dated 1 April 1929, in "World War Veterans—Correspondence, 1929," Box 371, Subject Files Herbert Hoover Presidential Library [hereafter, SFHH].

2. For the two earliest and most thorough studies of the Bonus March, see Roger Daniels, *The Bonus March: An Episode of the Great Depression* (Westport, Conn.: Greenwood Press, 1971); and Donald J. Lisio, *The President and Protest: Hoover, Conspiracy, and the Bonus Riot* (Columbia: University of Missouri Press, 1974), reprinted as *The President and Protest: Hoover, MacArthur, and the Bonus Riot*, 2nd ed. (New York: Fordham University Press, 1994). For selective New Deal narratives, see Arthur M. Schlesinger, *The Age of Roosevelt*, vols. 1–3 (Boston: Houghton Mifflin Co., 1957–60); William E. Leuchtenburg, *Franklin D. Roosevelt and the New Deal, 1932–1940* (New York: Harper and Row, 1963); and David M. Kennedy, *Freedom From Fear: The American People in Depression and War, 1929–1945* (New York: Oxford University Press, 1999). For a recent, yet typical, textbook description of the March, see Paul S. Boyer, et al, *The Enduring Vision* (Boston: Wadsworth Cengage, 2011, 7th ed.), 745–46.

3. See Jennifer D. Keene, *Doughboys, the Great War, and the Remaking of America* (Baltimore: Johns Hopkins University Press, 2001); and Paul Dickson and Thomas B. Allen, *The Bonus Army: An American Epic* (New York: Walker and Co., 2005).

4. On the American Legion, see William Pencak, *For God and Country: The American Legion, 1919–1941* (Boston: Northeastern University Press, 1989); and Thomas A. Rumer, *The American Legion: An Official History, 1919–1989* (New York: M. Evans and Co., 1990).

5. The VFW maintains a limited archive at its national headquarters in Kansas City, Missouri, consisting primarily of the complete catalog of the organization's monthly publication, *Foreign Service* (now *VFW Magazine*). For the sparse literature on the VFW, see Goldsmith, "Veterans of Foreign Wars." For more on the importance of existing organizational struc-

tures to social protest movements, see Aldon D. Morris, *The Origins of the Civil Rights Movement: Black Communities Organizing for Change* (New York: Free Press, 1984); and Charles M. Payne, *I've Got the Light of Freedom: The Organizing Tradition and the Mississippi Freedom Struggle* (Berkeley: University of California Press, 1995).

6. For the "symbiotic relationship" between voluntary associations and the federal government, see Theda Skocpol, with Marshall Ganz, Ziad Munson, Michele Swers, Bayliss Camp, and Jennifer Oser, "How Americans Became Civic," in *Civic Engagements in American Democracy*, eds. Theda Skocpol and Morris P. Fiorina (Washington, D.C.: Brookings Institution Press, 1999); Theda Skocpol, Ziad Munson, A. Karch, and Bayliss Camp, "Patriotic Partnerships: Why Great Wars Nourished American Civic Voluntarism," in *Shaped by War and Trade: International Influences on American Political Development*, eds. Ira Katznelson and Martin Shefter (Princeton, N.J.: Princeton University Press, 2002), 134–80; and Meg Jacobs and Julian E. Zelizer, "The Democratic Experiment: New Directions in American Political History" in *The Democratic Experiment: New Directions in American Political History*, eds. Meg Jacobs, William J. Novak, and Julian E. Zelizer (Princeton, N.J.: Princeton University Press, 2003), 1–19.

7. A number of studies have been dedicated to veterans' relationship with the state. Pioneering studies such as Theda Skocpol, *Protecting Soldiers and Mothers: The Political Origins of Social Policy* (Cambridge, Mass.: Harvard University Press, 1992); and Ann Shola Orloff, *The Politics of Pensions: A Comparative Analysis of Britain, Canada, and the United States, 1880–1940* (Madison: University of Wisconsin Press, 1993) argued that twentieth-century welfare policies were conceived with veterans' welfare as a negative reference. Skocpol's introduction of "policy feedback" to social policy formulation in *Protecting Soldiers and Mothers*, however, has also proven very influential. For the importance of "policy feedback," or the manner in which federal policy helps produce political participation in veterans and their dependents, see Suzanne Mettler, "Bringing the State Back in to Civic Engagement: Policy Feedback Effects of the G.I. Bill for World War II Veterans," *American Political Science Review* 96, no. 2 (June 2002): 351–65; and Suzanne Mettler, *Soldiers to Citizens: The G.I. Bill and the Making of the Greatest Generation* (New York: Oxford University Press, 2005); and K. Walter Hickel, "War, Region, and Social Welfare: Federal Aid to Servicemen's Dependents in the South, 1917–1921," *Journal of American History* 87, no. 4 (March 2001): 1362–91. For an excellent comparative study of European veterans that explores these issues, see Deborah Cohen, *The War Come Home: Disabled Veterans in Britain and Germany, 1914–1939* (Berkeley: University of California Press, 2000). Other important works on how federal policies affect political participation include Andrea Louise Campbell, *How Policies Make Citizens: Senior Political Activism and the American Welfare State* (Princeton, N.J.: Princeton University Press, 2003); Paul Pierson, "When Effect Becomes Cause: Policy Feedback and Political Change," *World Politics* 45 (1993): 595–628; and Joe Soss, "Lessons of Welfare: Policy Design, Political Learning, and Political Action," *American Political Science Review* 93 (1999): 363–80.

8. While the literature on the GI Bill is voluminous, the most recent works are Mettler, *Soldiers to Citizens*; Kathleen Jill Frydl, *The GI Bill* (New York: Cambridge University Press, 2009); and Glenn C. Altschuler and Stuart M. Blumin, *The GI Bill: A New Deal for Veterans* (New York: Oxford University Press, 2009).

9. Daniels, *Bonus March*, 23–28; Pencak, *For God and Country*, 75–77, 197–200; Gustavus A. Weber and Laurence F. Scheckebier, *The Veterans' Administration: Its History, Activities, and Organization* (Washington, D.C.: Brookings Institute, 1934), 229–31; *Foreign Service*, June, 1919: 8 and November, 1920: 1; and *New York Times*, October 16–17, 1920. For the most thorough discussion of war risk insurance, see Hickel, "War, Region, and Social Welfare."

10. Daniels, *Bonus March*, 37–40; Pencak, *For God and Country*, 197–200; and Weber and Scheckebier, *Veterans' Administration*, 231–34.

11. Resolution No. 141, *Proceedings of the 27th Annual Encampment of the Veterans of Foreign Wars of the United States, 1926* (Washington, D.C.: U.S. Government Printing Office, 1927), 264.

12. On the American Legion, see Pencak, *For God and Country*; and Rumer, *American Legion*. On the VFW, see Herbert Malloy Mason, *VFW: Our First Century, 1899–1999* (Lenexa, KS: Addax Publishing Group, 1999), 54–95; Goldsmith, "Veterans of Foreign Wars"; and Stephen R. Ortiz, *Beyond the Bonus March and GI Bill: How Veteran Politics Shaped the New Deal Era* (New York: New York University Press, 2010).

13. Legion membership totals in *National Tribune*, 7 February 1935; and VFW's in Goldsmith, "Veterans of Foreign Wars," 194. On Legion and VFW leadership, see Pencak, *For God and Country*, especially 48–106; Mason, *VFW*, 54–95; and Goldsmith, "Veterans of Foreign Wars," 1–92.

14. Weber and Scheckebier, *Veterans' Administration*, 468; and *Foreign Service*, September 1929, 4.

15. Resolutions, *Proceedings of the 30th Annual Encampment of the Veterans of Foreign Wars of the United States, 1929* (Washington, D.C.: U.S. Government Printing Office, 1930), 267; and Daniels, *Bonus March*, 42. Interestingly, no mention of Wright Patman, the future congressional Bonus leader and then freshman representative from Texas, can be found in the VFW encampment minutes. This is despite the fact that Patman proposed a Bonus bill in the House just days after Brookhart's proposal. For more on Patman, see Nancy Beck Young, *Wright Patman: Populism, Liberalism, and the American Dream* (Dallas: Southern Methodist University Press, 2000).

16. Copy of 22 November 1929 Duff telegram in *Foreign Service*, December 1929, 27; and *Foreign Service*, February 1930, 4. Veteran unemployment data found in Keene, *Doughboys*, 181.

17. Letter from Hezekiah N. Duff to Herbert Hoover, dated 29 January 1930, in "VFW, 1930," Box 359, SFHH. Rumer, *American Legion*, 186–88; and Lisio, *President and Protest* 2nd ed., 26–30.

18. For amicable relationship, see Frank T. Hines to Herbert Hoover, dated 10 September 1930, in "VFW, 1930," Box 359, SFHH. For VFW encampment information, see *Proceedings of the 31st Annual Encampment of the Veterans of Foreign Wars of the United States, 1930* (Washington, D.C.: U.S. Government Printing Office, 1931); and *New York Times* and *Washington Post*, September 1–6, 1930.

19. Daniels, *Bonus March*, 42–43; Lisio, *President and Protest*, 2nd ed., 30–32; and Pencak, *For God and Country*, 200–201. On Taylor's assistance in Hoover speech, Pencak, *For God and Country*, 201.

20. Young, *Wright Patman*, 36; and *Washington Post*, 29 December 1930.

21. *Washington Post*, 21 and 28 December 1930.

22. *Washington Post*, 3 January 1931.

23. Petitions in Daniels, *Bonus March*, 43, 71; and *New York Times* and *Washington Post*, 22 January 1931.

24. Alfieri and VFW marchers in *Washington Post*, 27–28 January 1931.

25. Rumer, *American Legion*, 190–91; *Literary Digest*, 14 February 1931, 5; and *Washington Post*, 25–26 January, 1931.

26. Lisio, *President and Protest*, 2nd ed., 36–39; Daniels, *Bonus March*, 43–45; and *Literary Digest*, 14 February 1931, 5–6

27. Lisio, *President and Protest*, 2nd ed., 38–42; Herbert Hoover Veto Message, 26 February 1931, in "Veterans Bureau Correspondence, 1931, January–February," Box 356, SFHH; "Needy Served First," *Time* 18 (19 March 1931): 11–12; *Literary Digest*, 14 March 1931, 5–6; *Foreign Service*, January 1932, 17; and Letter from Arthur H. Vandenberg to Herbert Hoover, 10 August 1931, in "Trips—1931, September 21, Detroit, American Legion Convention," Box 37, SFHH.

28. *Foreign Service*, March 1931, 5; and *Foreign Service*, April 1931, 4.

29. VFW membership growth in Goldsmith, "Veterans of Foreign Wars," 194; post growth obtained from *Foreign Service*, January 1929 to December 1931. Report in *Proceedings of the 32nd Annual Encampment of the Veterans of Foreign Wars of the United States, 1931* (Washington, D.C.: U.S. Government Printing Office, 1932), 244–46.

30. Internal Memorandum to Walter H. Newton, 8 August 1931, in "VFW, 1931–1933," Box 359, SFHH.

31. Hines' speech and Wolman retort in *Proceedings of the 32nd Annual Encampment of the Veterans of Foreign Wars*, 38–46.

32. Letter from Royal C. Johnson to J. Edgar Hoover, dated 28 August 1931, in "Trips—1931, September 21, Detroit, American Legion Convention," Box 37, SFHH. Address of President Hoover to the Thirteenth Convention of the American Legion, 21 September 1931, in "Congratulatory Correspondence American Legion Address Detroit Sept. 21, 1931, A-D," Box 47, President Personal File, Herbert Hoover Presidential Library [hereafter PPFHH]. Daniels, *Bonus March*, 51. Letter from Gilbert Bettman to Walter [sic] Richey, 25 September 1931 in "Congratulatory Correspondence American Legion Address Detroit Sept. 21, 1931, A-D," Box 47, PPFHH.

33. H. L. Mencken, "The Case for the Heroes," *American Mercury* 24 (December 1931): 409–10.

34. Report of the Director of Publicity, *Proceedings of the 34th Annual Encampment of the Veterans of Foreign Wars of the United States* (Washington, D.C.: U.S. Government Printing Office, 1933), 197–99.

35. *Foreign Service*, January 1932, 17.

36. *Foreign Service*, January 1932, 19–21.

37. Daniels, *Bonus March*, 55; and *Foreign Service*, December 1931 to March 1932.

38. *Foreign Service*, February 1932, 10–12, 24.

39. Daniels, *Bonus March*, 52, 61–64; Young, *Wright Patman*, 45–46; *Foreign Service*, May 1932, 6–8; and *New York Times*, 2–11 April 1932.

40. Of the Bonus March accounts that mention this episode, most downplay its importance as a key precursor. For the most recent example, see Dickson and Allen, *Bonus Army*, 59. For the best coverage of this march, see *Washington Post* and *New York Times*, 9 April 1932; and *Foreign Service*, May 1932, 6–7.

41. For DeCoe, Ray, and Wolman testimony, see House Committee on Ways and Means, "Payment of Adjusted-Compensation Certificates: Hearings Before the House Committee on Ways and Means," 72nd Congress, 1st sess., 1932, 81–83, 188–91, 207–10; *New York Times* and *Washington Post*, 2, 6, 8, 11, 14, and 16 April 1932; Daniels, *Bonus March*, 52, 61–64; and Memorandum from Raymond Benjamin to Larry Richey, 13 April 1932, in "World War Veterans, Bonus Correspondence, 1932, January–June," Box 373, SFHH.

42. Letter from John A. Weeks to Walter H. Newton, 9 January 1932, in "World War Veterans, Bonus Correspondence, 1932, January–June," Box 373, SFHH.

43. Legion totals in Pencak, *For God and Country*, 83–86. See also, *National Tribune*, 7

February 1935. VFW Post total from *Foreign Service*, April–July 1932. Quotation in *Foreign Service*, May 1932, 15.

44. For the most thorough description, see Daniels, *Bonus March*, 65–122; Lisio, *President and Protest*, 51–165; and Dickson and Allen, *Bonus Army*. Keene, *Doughboys*, 179–98 provides an excellent short description. The *Washington Post* coverage from late May until July 1932 is excellent.

45. In addition to the citations in the previous note, see also *Literary Digest*, 25 June 1932, 6.

46. Daniels, *Bonus March*, 80; *New York Times*, 9 and 12 June 1932; and *Washington Post*, 19 June 1932. Ironically, Dickson and Allen's work includes a photograph of the Chattanooga truck without mentioning the clearly legible "VFW" painted on its side panels. See Dickson and Allen, *Bonus Army*, 59.

47. *New York Times*, 8 June 1932. VA records in Frank T. Hines to Herbert Hoover, 2 August 1932, in "World War Veterans-Bonus Reports, Descriptions, and Statements, 1932, August," Box 376, SFHH.

48. *Washington Post*, 4 June 1932; *New York Times*, 12 June 1932. Frontline Post activities in VA Report, Hines to Theodore G. Joslin, 27 July 1932, in "World War Veterans-Bonus Reports, Descriptions, and Statements, 1932, July 26–31," Box 376, SFHH.

49. On Glassford, see Lisio, *President and Protest*, 51–55; and *BEF News*, 13 August 1932, 6. On Heffernan, see obituary in *Youngstown Vindicator*, 21 April 1977. On Rice Means, see *National Tribune*, April–August 1932; and Mason, *VFW*. On Butler, see Hans Schmidt, *Maverick Marine: Smedley D. Butler and the Contradictions of American Military History* (Lexington: University Press of Kentucky, 1987).

50. *New York Times*, 3, 7–9 June 1932; *Washington Post*, 25 May and 3–12 June 1932.

51. *Washington Post*, 19–20 June 1932. Ranken's specific message to the Maryland encampment is unknown, but the passing of the resolution had been hotly contested on 18 June, only to be withdrawn after his address.

52. Letter from Francis Ralston Welsh to J. Edgar Hoover and Lawrence Richey, dated 13 June 1932, in "World War Veterans, Bonus Correspondence, 1932, January–June," Box 373, SFHH.

53. Letter from Royal C. Johnson to The President, 10 June 1932, in "World War Veterans, Bonus Correspondence, 1932, January–June," Box 373, SFHH. Johnson floor speech in *Congressional Record*, 72nd Congress, 1st session, 12716-12717 and *Washington Post*, 12 June 1932.

54. Lisio, *President and Protest*, 139–278; FDR quote at 285.

55. VFW membership data in Goldsmith, "Veterans of Foreign Wars," 194; post data obtained from *Foreign Service*, January 1929 to December 1932.

56. *Proceedings of the 33rd Annual Encampment of the Veterans of Foreign Wars of the United States, 1932* (Washington, D.C.: U.S. Government Printing Office, 1933), 260.

57. VFW data in Goldsmith, "Veterans of Foreign Wars," 194; Legion data found in Pencak, *For God and Country*, 83–86. See also *National Tribune*, 7 February 1935.

# 8

## "Do Something for the Soldier Boys"

### Congress, the G.I. Bill of Rights, and the Contours of Liberalism

NANCY BECK YOUNG

"We are going to have to do something for these soldier boys when they come back," declared Speaker of the House Sam Rayburn (D-Tex.). "They're fighting this war for us, and we're not going to put them on the street corners selling apples when they get back here." A welfare program for soldiers, Rayburn believed, was not the extent of postwar economic reconversion, though. He explained that government policy would be needed to address the economic shifts from war to peace, especially for industries that had converted wholly to military production. As a bridge, Rayburn advocated an expansive program of public works. Yet he never forgot the soldiers. His plan for veterans' benefits projected the outline of what would become the G.I. Bill but also revealed a preference for Jeffersonian social values, including a nation dominated by small yeoman farmers. "We've got to buy them farms, if they want them. Every boy that comes back, if he wants a farm, ought to have one, a good farm with a good house, some cattle," Rayburn explained. "The government will have to finance this program" through loans at cost. "I'll tell you that will build up the backbone in this country and solve a lot of economic problems. You can't beat a good farmer."[1]

In January 1943 Senate Majority Leader Alben Barkley (D-Ky.) told some Philadelphia businessmen about the importance of helping veterans find private-sector employment. His speech typified a deep-seated concern of lawmakers, especially New Dealers, that the Great Depression would return when soldiers reentered the civilian economy, which suggests a much-needed larger context of postwar economic reconversion for understanding the congressional construction of the G.I. Bill of Rights. World War II lawmakers deviated from past practices, urging a veterans' program reliant on private not public jobs. Because the measure enjoyed support from veterans' organizations and passed Congress with relative ease, too many have wrongly assumed that it was not controversial. Instead, it embodied the ideological political wars in Congress: moderates and conservatives used the issue of postwar veterans' policy to advocate a contraction of New Deal liberalism while at the same time liberals hoped the popular G.I. Bill could become a device for expanding the prewar welfare state into a cradle-to-grave system of social benefits. Moreover, while the White House had urged legislative attention to a broad program of economic reconversion very early in the war, Congress still exerted much control over the process, including the G.I. Bill, putting into practice the new institutional and American political realities created and defined by the war. During Franklin D. Roosevelt's twelve years in the White House, moderates and liberals in Congress learned that their most productive moments came when there was a presidential willingness to negotiate; conservatives learned how to practice the politics of obstruction in the modern era. These contradictory tensions helped determine the parameters of postwar liberalism.

Even though the G.I. Bill assumed a foundational role in the moderated welfare state of postwar America, its congressional architects intended that the benefits derived from it would in no way become a tool to advance the New Deal style bureaucracy that they so despised from the 1930s and that they had effectively retarded during the 1940s. As Senate Minority Leader Kenneth S. Wherry (R-Neb.) put it, "The New Deal and this Administration is having its wings clipped and from now on you can expect Congress to continue the clipping."[2] Careful attention to this legislative debate reveals much about the ideology of governance in the period of transition to the postwar. The war years saw Congress become more aware of the global realities of national politics, struggle to find its identity in this new milieu, and craft a more partisan style of operations, all of which threw national politics into turmoil. Nonetheless, lawmakers originated a veterans' policy that departed from the haphazard, costly, and inefficient programs developed for veterans of previous wars. The G.I. Bill, then, was the product of Depression and war-era thinking about the role of the state in the economy. The G.I. Bill's passage revealed the continued importance of Congress to national governance and the direction of liberalism in the postwar era.

Economic reconstruction should not be evaluated by the metric of legislative success or failure. A more complex and more important measurement requires comparative calculations of what was and was not passed against the long-term meanings of each for the future of American politics. Here the legacy of Congress as it moved from the war to the postwar era was much more mixed. Indeed, moderates and liberals in Congress envisioned a much more expansive, state-centered program of reform, including national health care, a full employment program, and national economic planning. The first ultimately fell victim to charges of socialized medicine during the Harry S. Truman presidency, and while legislation implementing full employment and economic planning passed during the Truman presidency, they were but a shadow of what reformers intended.

The politics of economic reconversion provide the perfect prism through which to refract and evaluate the consequences of the World War II policy process, revealing a less experimentally liberal state and a more constrained, moderate approach to reform. These results are highlighted in the decisions made about veterans' benefits and an expanded social security program. It is impossible to separate out any one of these issues for independent analysis, so conjoined were the debates about postwar economic matters. The G.I. Bill, though, is the most studied component of postwar economic reconversion, but the intersection of the congressional intent for the G.I. Bill, congressional involvement in war policy, and the permutations to liberalism and the welfare state have been overlooked.[3]

Ironically, while the G.I. Bill has been termed an unprecedented advance in the federal provision of social welfare, it symbolized the triumph of a more restrained construction of the welfare state because its benefits were targeted to a narrow class. Those left out included southern African Americans and homosexuals, the former having long been a rhetorical target for southern conservatives and the latter the new political straw man.[4] Examining other components of economic reconversion magnifies the failure to expand Social Security and the privileging of capitalists in the various demobilization programs. More important, choices about economic reconversion reflected "lessons" Congress learned in its struggles with the executive branch over the course of the war. The majority of lawmakers had long since deemed Roosevelt's experimental liberalism dangerous and had functioned as a moderating force in national politics between New Deal liberalism and a variegated conservatism that was both economic and racial in composition. Here the vital role of conservatives in the nation's political economy becomes clear. By taking a moderate path between destroying the New Deal and expanding the New Deal, lawmakers cemented a centrist reform tradition into place, one that was compliant with the goals of private industrialists and what Dwight D. Eisenhower termed the military industrial complex approximately a decade and a half later. This shift was not a simple choice in Congress; instead it proved most controversial.[5]

Roosevelt's postwar domestic agenda emerged in 1943 and was fully revealed in his 1944 State of the Union address. He wanted a more activist state, building on and expanding the New Deal. Economic conservatives and some moderates in Congress disagreed. In 1943, the president started talking about the concerns that should occupy the federal government once the war was over. In a December 1943 press conference, Roosevelt advocated expanding Social Security, better employment and housing options, and improved education and health care. The hint of New Dealism in Roosevelt's language even as he suggested Dr. Win the War would replace Dr. New Deal did not please conservative Democrats. For example, Sen. Kenneth McKellar (D-Tenn.) countered,

"Conciliation among Democrats is our best weapon for this fight. We must get every Democrat in line that we can. I think the dropping of the 'New Deal' as a slogan is a good omen." Disregarding McKellar, Roosevelt returned to these proposals in his January 1944 State of the Union address. He both dismissed the New Deal as fixed in past time and past conditions, but he also argued against removing all aspects of the New Deal from the nation's political economy: "Now, in time, there will have to be a new program, who ever runs the government. We are not talking in terms of 1933's program. . . . But that doesn't avoid or make impossible or unneedful another program, when the time comes. When the time comes."[6]

Earlier, when Roosevelt first began talking about his plans for postwar economic security at home, Speaker Rayburn had fought hard behind the scenes to get Roosevelt to rethink his decision. Rayburn argued that Democrats in Congress should focus on the war, but Roosevelt saw it as a program that conservatives could neither support nor oppose, making it a political winner for the presidential election in 1944. Rayburn, though, agreed with the policy recommendations: "This will lie around a long time. Parts of it will be picked up and enacted, others discarded. Congress will move slowly, perhaps over a period of several years. Eventually you'll find that pretty much of this program will become law. It's something to shoot for over the years. And it is popular, or will be when the people understand it." Rayburn worried that the Roosevelt reform agenda would distract Congress from its war work and would ultimately hurt the reform cause. For example, Rep. Robert L. "Muley" Doughton (D-N.C.), chair of the House Ways and Means Committee, refused to hold hearings on the "costly and controversial program" of Social Security expansion, noting "When your house is afire, you don't generally start . . . building an addition to it."[7]

Members of Congress not disposed to Social Security reform or an expanded federal welfare state looked for ways to redirect the national conversation away from Roosevelt's vision for the postwar and toward their own vision of a less activist, moderate state that accepted what remained of the New Deal as status quo but sought otherwise to limit the federal government's involvement in the economy. Raymond Moley, a former New Deal Brain Truster, criticized the trends toward state capitalism, suggesting that war plant workers and soldiers would be a malleable constituency predisposed to supporting a "wide-scale government 'partnership' in industry."[8] Put simply, how much control should the federal government have in a capitalist economy? The contradictory answers lawmakers gave to this question help explain why the G.I. Bill was acceptable but Social Security expansion was not.

Sen. Robert A. Taft (R-Ohio) laid out a conservative philosophy for addressing postwar domestic issues. He expressed happiness that Congress had tried to reestablish the constitutional principles that the New Deal threatened. Taft viewed efforts during the New Deal era that had weakened the role of state and local government in public life as a threat to the sustainability of democracy. The result, he maintained, was a dangerous separation of the federal government from "the folks at home." There a citizen could appeal to city council or the school board, and even "run for office himself. He can be heard. In Washington he is lost in the vast corridors of marble office buildings . . . until he gives up the hopeless search in indignant but useless sputtering." According to Taft, part of the problem resulted from the burgeoning power of federal agencies. Congressional elimination of several New Deal programs, the Civilian Conservation Corps in 1942 and the Works Progress Administration and National Youth Administration in 1943, was positive. "I hope that never again will the federal government operate directly a relief agency," Taft said. "If the federal government is to assist in these fields, it must assist through the state organizations, and not by direct federal operation. The primary obligation is state and local."[9]

When the Republican Post-War Advisory Council met on Mackinac Island in September 1943, it advocated a postwar political agenda different from Roosevelt's. GOP insiders insisted that "without preservation in America of the fundamental principles on which our way of life depends," a victory against the Axis would have no meaning. They called for "individual liberty," states' rights, and congressional and judicial independence vis-à-vis the executive branch. Achieving such goals required scaling back the power and reach of the federal government. After arguing for privileged employment decisions for veterans, policy that required federal intervention, GOP leaders insisted on an end to government "competition with private industry," rationing and price control, and expanded wartime powers for the federal government. Any plan for full employment must be run privately, Republicans argued.[10]

Attendees at Mackinac Island wanted to end "all unnecessary regulation of the individual and of business," especially "small business which has been so recklessly destroyed." They discounted new New Deal social programs, arguing such "would wreck the country because the only remedy it proposes for any problem is unlimited government spending of borrowed money. It would socialize all business, agriculture and the professions. It would extend the power of government until ultimately no man or woman could act, write, speak or work without approval." The council warned that more New Deal laws would result in "Fascism," where a "class-conscious vote-shackled proletariat" acted according to edicts from Washington.[11]

Others in Congress shared Republican concerns about the increased scale and scope of the federal government. Rep. William Lemke (R–N.D.) told a constituent, "With 3,300,000 on the Federal payroll, and I wouldn't be surprised to see it doubled before another four years, there would be little chance for an honest man to be elected . . . I hope not, but, I have my apprehensions." Taft offered a more sophisticated read of the congressional role in the federal government. He attributed negative congressional power to its juridical functions, noting that size and diversity of membership within the institution meant no one group—not the administration and not any political party or faction—controlled it. These facts mitigated against the development of a positive, comprehensive program. While Congress discharged its taxation and fiscal management responsibilities, it did so with "little help from the administration." Whereas Taft argued the National Resources Planning Board, a New Deal–era body that Congress eliminated in 1943, meant a "socialist economy," Roosevelt chided Congress for its shortsightedness in eliminating the planning board.[12]

Some of the issues associated with reconversion were rooted in prewar politics, especially the efforts to expand Social Security and enact some form of national health insurance. Liberals within the Democratic Party had long wanted a cradle-to-grave system of social welfare benefits. Popular support for the old-age provisions within Social Security had resulted in part from the social movement of elderly Americans led by Dr. Francis E. Townsend. Lawmakers then and since, especially those in the leadership hierarchy, were disdainful of a more generalized, bountiful Social Security program. In the summer of 1941 Doughton told a constituent: "You doubtless realize that our Committee is engaged in something more important than Dr. Townsend's proposal—that is, endeavoring to raise revenue to in part finance our National Defense Program."[13]

Entry into the war did nothing to encourage additional legislative support for an expansive Social Security program, but it did cause some in Congress to begin debating reconversion and its meanings for the state. Less than two weeks after the attack on Pearl Harbor, Congress turned its attention to re-conversion—specifically programs to protect soldiers while they were fighting and once the war was over. Previous to passage of the G.I. Bill, Congress constructed other measures to protect the fighting forces—relief from mortgage and debt foreclosure, hospitalization and rehabilitation, national service life insurance, and increased pensions for veterans. These measures passed because they did not challenge capitalism as would an expanded Social Security program did and because the beneficiaries were soldiers.[14] Regardless of ideology, veterans' politics had benefits for lawmakers. Moderates and conservatives used the issue to constrict the New Deal welfare state while liberals relied on veterans' politics to expand it. In this ideological struggle, moderates and conservatives prevailed.

In an August 1942 campaign speech, Rep. John E. Rankin (D-Miss.) touted his work on behalf of soldier compensation. Because of the protracted and messy battle over adjusted compensation for World War I veterans, Rankin contended, "I made up my mind then that if this country should ever engage in another war during my services in Congress, I would do my best to adjust the pay of the men in the service while the war was in progress. So when the soldiers' pay bill came before the House, I offered an amendment to raise the base pay to $50 a month. . . . But, strange as it may seem, when it went to conference my amendment was eliminated." Rankin described the successful efforts he undertook to restore the pay amendment, a morale-boosting measure, and to improve the processing of dependant pay allotments. He bragged to his constituents: "Thus, for the first time in history, we provided for paying the men in the rank and file of our armed forces wages somewhat commensurate with what others were earning in civil life."[15]

Senate Majority Leader Barkley's January 1943 speech to the Real Estate Board of Philadelphia reveals the interconnectedness of reconversion politics for lawmakers. When speaking about programs for veterans, Barkley promised, "We shall be compelled to devise methods by which returning soldiers shall find employment." He reflected key shifts in liberalism away from the experimental 1930s and toward the capitalist postwar era, especially when he recorded a preference that "this employment should be in private industry" as opposed to public sector employment with the federal government. Federal and state veterans' preference laws had been passed as early as the Civil War era, so veterans already had an advantage in public sector employment. More important, even liberals such as Barkley were skeptical about the ever-expanding federal bureaucracy and wanted a postwar reconversion program that encouraged private, not state, capitalism. Nor did they want veterans to become foot soldiers for an expanding New Deal–style bureaucracy. (Soldiers were already suspect in the minds of conservative lawmakers for their New Deal and Roosevelt loyalties.) Furthermore, Barkley promised, "We shall be able to give private employment to most of these returning men in the production of things the world will need and seek."[16]

Jobs for veterans was just one factor. For the United States to win the postwar economic contests, Barkley argued, "we shall be compelled to continue" high taxes "to liquidate the debt which we shall then owe" and to fund reconstruction programs. He warned of the danger of passing on a substantial debt to future generations. Barkley's liberalism connected priorities from the 1930s with the postwar era. He argued that Congress must create "a broader base for the security which we must provide against want and insecurity among the aged and infirm." Convinced that Americans had made a major paradigm shift in the 1930s, he argued, "I think our country is committed to the theory of Social Security in order that the aged and the infirm and the necessarily unemployed may be free from want and the fear of want" and so that job openings will be available to the young.[17]  When beginning to deliberate an appropriate policy for war veterans, lawmakers decided to separate programs for the rehabilitation of former soldiers from rehabilitation programs for the general public. This decision suggested that social welfare programs for nonveterans mattered less. Furthermore, Rep. Graham Barden (D-N.C.), a loyal Roosevelt Democrat who also shared the conservative racial views of his state and his region, told an American Legion official that veterans with service-related disabilities should receive treatment through the Veterans Administration (VA). He also advocated "an over-all rehabilitation program" for all veterans. This program should, Barden argued, cooperate closely with the VA. The more conservative nature of this social welfare program can be found in Barden's argument for its administration: "It was my desire to retain as much control as possible within the states, permitting only the necessary minimum of supervision from Washington except in the field of the veterans." Republicans appeared more generous, at least in their rhetoric, than conservative Democrats. The GOP advocated a veterans' policy not unlike that of the Great War era. According to the Mackinac Declaration of Domestic Policy, issued in September 1943, "Veterans must not come home to be treated as wards of a state or nation, but must find their nation a land of greater opportunity under a free American system."[18]

During 1943 Roosevelt began goading Congress to act on a program of veterans' benefits more akin to the welfare state of the 1930s. He did so despite the fact that lawmakers were already discussing the issue. In July he addressed the nation in a fireside chat. Veterans "must not be demobilized into an environment of inflation and unemployment, to a place on a bread line," Roosevelt explained. "We must, this time, have plans ready—instead of waiting to do a hasty, inefficient, and ill-considered job at the last moment." Minimally, Roosevelt wanted the veterans to receive mustering-out pay, unemployment compensation when necessary, education, credit for their time served toward Social Security, improved medical care for the disabled, and sufficient pensions. In November 1943 Roosevelt sent a detailed message to Congress, linking veterans' policy with other reconversion issues in a way that surely would not please conservatives and moderates in the institution. Roosevelt said, "What our service men and women want . . . is the assurance of satisfactory employment upon their return to civil life. The first task after the war is to provide employment for them and for our demobilized war workers."[19]

Next, the American Legion entered the fray. The Legion had had a formidable working relationship with lawmakers, many of whom were Legion members since its 1919 founding. Moreover, Congress had a long history of voting increased pensions and benefits for veterans. This was true for a variety of reasons, not the least of which was concern for maintaining the soldier vote in elections. The Legion had a reputation for its legislative prowess regarding the drafting and passage of bills; during the fight for the G.I. Bill, Congress relied on the Legion to help with strategy, including the introduction of an omnibus G.I. Bill instead of separate bills for the individual parts of the program. The Legion even gave the G.I. Bill its name.[20]

Moderates and liberals in Congress hoped veterans' benefits would bring expansion of Social Security. Rep. Pat Cannon (D-Fla.) complained that Doughton refused to hold hearings on new Social Security bills. He asked colleagues to demand action: "The first question our soldiers ask all over the world is whether there will be a job for them when they come home. We can answer that question if we can find the way to retire older citizens." Doughton promised a constituent he would oppose the Wagner-Murray-Dingell bill, the most likely vehicle for Social Security reform. Earlier that year, Doughton had observed: "We are deluged with so many crack-pot tax schemes and so many selfish proposals that our work is greatly delayed." He promised that his committee would be "very slow about even considering seriously" Social Security reforms providing for health care reform. "We are having all we can do now to fight this war and put out the fire," Doughton reasoned, "without turning aside to consider and adopt idealistic social reforms or programs."[21]

In speaking before the Washington Medical Society, Rep. Mike Monroney (D-Okla.) carefully delineated between legislative activism and legislative experimentation when he suggested that it was the job of Congress to perform surgery on the nation's body politic. The Wagner-Murray-Dingell bill, which provided for a vast expansion of Social Security to a "truly national social insurance system," attempted just that. Not only did the measure propose national health care, it also included for the first time farmers, farm workers, small businessmen, domestics, professionals, and nonprofit workers in the retirement insurance program. Additionally, Wagner-Murray-Dingell expanded benefits for all categories of workers, equalized benefits for those who retired because of disability with those who retired because of old age, improved unemployment benefits, offered maternity benefits, created a national system of employment offices, provided national health insurance and hospitalization within a system of private medical care, and enlarged public assistance programs for the needy. The Wagner-Murray-Dingell bill was buried in the House Ways and Means Committee and the Senate Finance Committee. The only way to pass a bill was to introduce a "watered down version." In the area of Social Security expansion in 1943, Congress was paralyzed and incapable of action. Said one pundit, "The cradle-to-the-grave social security program is still in the icebox."[22]

Congressional parsimony regarding Social Security was not extended to other economic reconversion issues, specifically programs for veterans. In early January 1944 a bill cleared the Senate providing for generous mustering out payments of $200 to $500 for each soldier exclusive of other federally funded veterans' benefits. With about sixty-five thousand soldiers a month being mustered out of service, the legislation carried an ultimate cost of $9 or $10 billion. According to one Washington observer, "It opens up the field to grab bag veteran politics." Once signed into law, it was only slightly less generous, providing maximum mustering out pay of $300. As lawmakers became more engaged with their work on what became the G.I. Bill, no one recommended policies akin to those developed for veterans after World War I. The initial policies, developed between 1917 and 1923, were viewed favorably by most, but with the passage of soldiers' bonus legislation in 1924, criticism mounted.[23]

Most lawmakers showed but scant interest in FDR's version of the G.I. Bill. "The Congress will be sniping at the White House," argued journalist Frank McNaughton, "and there will be a studied effort to avoid like the plague all controversial legislation." Initially, the costly rehabilitation initiatives for veterans seemed to fit this designation as easily as other more general reconversion proposals like the addition of health care coverage to Social Security. When asked whether he expected an improved mood of the people to translate into more productive legislative behavior, Sam Rayburn replied, "Well, I don't know about that. This is an election year, you know. There'll be a lot of talking in this session. I hope it'll be good talking."[24]

Officials with the leading national veterans' organizations lobbied Congress about the pending G.I. Bill. While the American Legion had begun politicking for a comprehensive program of government assistance for veterans, other veterans' organizations were hesitant. Omar Ketchum for the Veterans of Foreign Wars, Millard W. Rice for the Disabled American Veterans, Frank Haley for the Military Order of Purple Heart, and W. M. Floyd of the Regular Veterans Association told Rankin that while "pressure is being brought to bear on the Congress to force immediate enactment of the so-called G-I Bill of Rights," lawmakers should weigh all options. They introduced a cautionary note into the proceedings, warning that "there is a serious question in the minds of some veteran groups as to whether this so-called G-I Bill of Rights, in its entirety, is a sound and equitable solution."[25]

At issue were the controversial education provisions that "are so broad in scope and potential cost, that its enactment would, in our opinion, probably not only prevent any consideration of several other more equitable proposals to solve such problems, but might also subsequently jeopardize the entire structure of veteran benefits and provoke another Economy Act." Worried about the chance for such unintended and undesirable consequences, Ketchum, Rice, Haley, and Floyd contended that disabled soldiers should receive priority treatment over those seeking a college education, especially "in the light of our tremendous war debt and the ability of the nation adequately to care for its war disabled." They asked Rankin "to consider all proposals . . . now before the Congress, and not to be stampeded into hasty and possibly unwise legislation."[26]

To get the G.I. Bill through the Senate, the American Legion tapped conservative Sen. Bennett Champ Clark (D-Mo.), a former national commander and founder of the Legion, to sponsor the bill and to bring his colleagues on board as cosponsors. After initial hearings before the Senate Finance Committee, Clark became the principal author of the bill, which combined many of the smaller bills other lawmakers had introduced and provided for adequate hospital care; employment services and unemployment benefits; relief for the disabled; assistance in the purchase of homes, farms, and businesses; educational and vocational training; and placement of authority for all veterans' programs with the Veterans Administration in Washington, D.C. Estimated costs for the legislation started at $3 billion.[27]

Meanwhile, lawmakers who wanted an omnibus reconversion program benefiting all Americans, not just veterans, pushed for Social Security reform. When Sen. Robert Wagner (D-N.Y.) received correspondence critical of the health care provisions in Wagner-Murray-Dingell, he responded with detailed information of what the bill did and how physicians retained independence. He did not address how the measure would be funded or how benefits would be administered other than to note that "millions of people" could not pay for medical care but could "afford the service they need and can pay a fair price for it by making small, regular contributions to a fund at the time they earn their incomes." But these questions were not paramount. Instead, the critics charged that health care was being socialized via control of the doctors, and Wagner insisted that doctors could determine who they would treat and how they would be paid. He also explained that medical specialists would garner higher fees, and he noted the research and education funding written into the bill. Finally, he explained that control of the program would fall under the Surgeon General of the Public Health Service.[28]

In mid-March 1944 Sen. James E. Murray (D-Mont.) spoke before the UAW at a health care conference. He argued, "Social security is essential if we are to remain a free and independent people. Social security is not just something it would be nice to have. Social security is not a distant goal toward which we can afford to move slowly and gradually, with due regard for the convenience of vested interests." Murray asserted that nothing less than the continuation of "a democratic society" was at stake. Postponement could bring disaster, he believed. Citing the example of mistakes made after the last world war, Murray insisted, "political freedom alone is not enough to give men real freedom, real security or real stability. Political freedom which is not supported by economic freedom is always in mortal danger. *Social security is essential for economic freedom*."[29]

Murray identified three major obstacles to securing Social Security: the unemployment of individuals and the lack of programs to guarantee full employment, individual catastrophe in the form of debilitating illness or death, and the high cost of health care. He argued that a national standard and a national program were necessary to ensure uniform, universal coverage. Any system left to the states, Murray insisted, would be unequal in benefits and would leave out people in parsimonious states. He also documented how and why voluntary insurance plans were not sufficient to address the nation's health care needs. The costs placed them out of reach for poorer Americans while others were ineligible for coverage. Moreover, such insurance programs included only 5 percent of the population. Conversely, he argued, medical and hospitalization insurance provided under a "national social insurance system" would cover a minimum of 80 percent of the population in its first year.[30]

In answer to critics who suggested a more gradual approach to national social insurance, Murray argued, "The people of this country want security. They do not want only a cash benefit when family income is cut down by unemployment and nothing when it is cut down by sickness. They do not want only a cash benefit in place of wages when they are sick, but no insurance protection against the costs of medical care." The Social Security Act of 1935, Murray said, was "a limited system." "It is high time we stopped experimenting just to please or satisfy some special-interest group." Instead, Murray stressed Social Security must be revamped to include farmers, professionals, small business owners, and other excluded people. Murray linked Social Security reform to postwar economic reconversion because "the inevitable periods of unemployment while industries are converting from war to peacetime production" would make Social Security all the more important. He noted its utility for the sick in need of health care, older war workers looking to retire, and veterans "to help their readjustment to civilian life." "The way in which we demobilize," Murray stated, "will influence the course of events in this country for many years. Thus far, most of the discussion about post war planning has been in terms of planning for business, for the owners of plants and equipment. Our social security bill is a post war plan for human beings."[31]

To a local labor leader in Great Falls, Montana, Murray complained of a postcard campaign criticizing him for his supposed lack of support for Social Security: "Might I point out that it would be far more effective to direct these efforts towards the forces of reaction in your own city and state who are continuously maligning me. . . . The money and effort wasted on me could very well be directed towards those who by their record and public statements show that they need such influence."[32] Murray's poignant arguments failed to generate sufficient support to thwart the tactics of delay and defeat.

A federal government system of health care has been controversial from the first day such a plan was introduced. To date, though, too little attention has been given to the wartime debates about this divisive issue. Because the Wagner-Murray-Dingell legislation was defeated and defeated handily, it has attracted little notice in comparison with Harry S. Truman's presidential initiative a few years later. When viewed in tandem with the contemporaneous G.I. Bill, the demise of Wagner-Murray-Dingell tells a larger, more important story of the fate of liberalism during the war years and the siding of moderates with conservatives in their battle against excessive federal intervention in welfare policies and the economy.

Days before the Senate vote on the G.I. Bill, eighty-one senators supported it, guaranteeing almost certain passage and revealing the very different congressional perceptions for Social Security reform for the whole population and the G.I. Bill, a limited reform for veterans only. Because veterans' politics mattered in an election year, the Senate debate focused on more trivial matters such as provision of benefits for those who did not receive honorable discharges, which Clark explained would not be a problem given the Veterans Administration's discretion over such questions. He stressed, "We certainly have no desire to have any gold-brickers or any habitual dead beats or anyone who is guilty of a crime come under the benefits of the act." Also at issue was whether federalization of unemployment services and compensation would result. Proponents of the bill insisted it would not. The measure passed unanimously and in less than an hour on 24 March 1944.[33]

Conservatives dominated House debates over provisions in the G.I. Bill for education and states' rights. Here the arguments previewed an important civil rights issue that would continue well into the 1960s. The House Committee on Education met in executive session on 28 March 1944 to discuss the G.I. Bill legislation. Barden complained of provisions for educating veterans without safeguarding states' rights. He argued federal bureaucrats should not be empowered to require schools to "revamp" because of this legislation. Rep. Mary T. Norton (D-N.J.) countered that before such sweeping changes were incorporated in the legislation, the full committee should deliberate the problem. Later, when the measure made its way to the House floor, Barden noted that governors from states as diverse as Massachusetts, Ohio, North Carolina, Illinois, Nebraska, Florida, Utah, Maryland, and California all wanted to retain locally controlled education. Furthermore, Barden did not want the legislation to give the federal government authority to create new schools and colleges. While he noted that most Americans approved the outlines of the G.I. Bill, he stressed that "they do not want any Government-issue education." Barden's states' rights rhetoric was far less troubling than what came from other southern Democrats. His purpose was less about racial control and more about education and academic freedom.[34]

During the legislative deliberation over the G.I. Bill, the House Committee on Education and the House Committee on World War Veterans Legislation engaged in a jurisdictional and ideological quarrel with the Education Committee advocating a more moderate bill than the World War Veterans Legislation Committee. Points of disagreement involved how long veterans should be allowed to study under the bill and whether disabled veterans should be granted more years of study. Members of the House Committee on Education met with the World War Veterans Legislation Committee to discuss the pending G.I. Bill. Speaking on behalf of his committee, Barden asked that Rankin's committee incorporate the Education Committee's bill into the one they were debating. Rankin politely refused, arguing that his bill had "substantially the same provisions." Rankin's committee then debated whether the legislation should provide for a wider range of options as to the schools veterans could attend. Most agreed that such a change was in order.[35]

Other controversies included unemployment provisions within the G.I. Bill. Philip Murray, the president of the CIO, complained to members of Congress of a "watered-down version of the bill" that "strikes at the very roots of postwar security for our soldiers and sailors." Most troubling to Murray was the initiative to reduce unemployment compensation for veterans from fifty-two weeks to twenty-six weeks, and to limit compensation to twenty dollars per week, an amount insufficient to support a family in industrial states and less than what could be had with the existing Social Security legislation. Here was an implicit commentary on the politics of race and employment in the United States. Southerners in Congress had long been the loudest proponents of differential wage scales in order to protect the Jim Crow economy. For example, Murray complained when Rankin described more generous G.I. Bill legislation as something that would "'encourage idleness,'" noting that such views were "a gross insult to our servicemen."[36]

Because they were dissatisfied with the Senate bill, Rankin and his colleagues on the World War Veterans' Legislation Committee had spent almost three weeks in executive session pouring over the bill all in an effort to slow its passage and control its content. He denied the presence of political motivation in any of the deliberations. "It is a rather cheap politician," argued Rankin, "who attempts to make political capital out of the physical sufferings of the men who fight the battles of the Nation." He then explained the frugal attitude of his committee toward the question of rehabilitating the veterans. Girding Rankin's thinking was the view that the federal government was less fiscally sound than state or local governments within the United States. He worried that too generous a program would bring too much indebtedness and would generate a constitutional crisis, leading perhaps as far as the break-up of the nation.[37]

An expert parliamentarian, Rankin gained control of the rules that would govern floor debate for the G.I. Bill. The Rankin committee substitute made it more difficult for veterans to access the bill's educational benefits. It tinkered with the home, farm, and business loan features of the bill, raising the maximum amount that could be borrowed by five hundred dollars but also raising the maximum interest rate from 3 to 6 percent. Moreover, authority for the loan program rested with the Veterans Administration as did job placement, all a shift from the Senate bill. Finally, the Rankin committee substitute reduced the time period for readjustment benefits from fifty-two weeks to twenty-six weeks. Since the bill reported came from Rankin's World War Veterans Committee, he controlled the division of time among Democrats for the floor debate. The ranking Republican on his committee, Rep. Edith Nourse Rogers (R-Mass.), an erstwhile ally, controlled the Republican division. Moreover, the rule provided that the House must first vote on the Rankin committee substitute to the Senate bill, making it much harder for moderates and liberals to replace the Rankin bill with the more generous Senate bill.[38]

On 11 May John Rankin began the debate in the House on a defensive tone.

He lambasted the Senate for spending such little time studying the measure before indulging a tirade about the thousands of telegrams and petitions flooding into Congress, many from veterans' groups, noting that only the smallest percentage of signers had any understanding whatsoever of the legislation. He drew an example from his hometown, Tupelo, Mississippi, where some individuals drafted a petition to have the best man in town hanged just to prove the willingness of people to sign such documents. Rankin reported that nearly every person approached, including the person named to be hanged, signed it. "That is just how silly the Congress makes itself when it undertakes to legislate by telegrams and by petition and by resolution coming from people who do not know what is in the legislation," contended Rankin.[39]

Speaking in opposition to Rankin, Barden defended his approach to educational benefits during the first day of floor debate in the House. While his bill gave authority over the veterans-turned-students to the schools where they matriculated, the Rankin bill vested all such authority with an administrator in Washington, D.C. Barden commented, "It is a one-man dictatorship and he can make it rather strong," especially with approximately a million or more former soldiers heading back to the classroom. Rogers disagreed, noting that veterans preferred dealing with an agency that understood their problems rather than the whims of the various schools they might attend.[40]

Thomas G. Abernethy (D-Miss.) argued, "It is my considered judgment that no phase of post-war planning is quite so important" as passage of the G.I. Bill. "These men and women will make up the bulk of the participants in post-war business and unless they are promptly enabled to assume the normal pursuits of a civilian life," stressed Abernethy, "Then all of the post-war planning for business, industry, and agriculture will bear no results." He believed the only solution was a program of "liberal Federal assistance." Despite that assertion, he explained, "this is a veterans' bill. It is also a States' rights bill. It is not a Federal bill, an educators' bill, nor a bill to set up a new agency or bureau." In concluding his remarks, Abernethy stressed that the estimated cost of the G.I. Bill, at least $5 billion, was a pittance in comparison with the service rendered the country by the veterans. "We owe to him these things and many more. Upon return there must be more for the boys than the music of bands and the waving of flags," Abernethy argued. "This bill is the answer."[41]

The unemployment provisions were almost as controversial as the educational benefits. When addressing his colleagues on the House floor, Abernethy argued against a generous program of unemployment assistance, contending it would encourage "idleness." He asserted that a veteran who wished to be lazy could just go fishing and collect eighty dollars a month in unemployment while another more energetic veteran could resume farming for only fifty dollars a month, resulting in a disadvantage for the motivated veteran. Abernethy acknowledged that a majority on the World War Veterans' Legislation Committee disagreed, and he explained that he would defer to the will of the majority, albeit with reservation. In his private correspondence, Rankin came closer to the truth of why conservative southern Democrats disliked this aspect of the G.I. Bill: "We have 50,000 negroes in the service from our State, and in my opinion, if the bill should pass in its present form, a vast majority of them would remain unemployed for at least a year, and a great many white men would do the same thing."[42]

Marion T. Bennett (R-Mo.) declared that the Rankin bill was the "most comprehensive and scientific approach to the problem of veteran rehabilitation." He stressed that the G.I. Bill was not a bonus and would not include adjusted compensation. For example, Bernard William "Pat" Kearney (R-N.Y.), also the former VFW commander in 1937, described the congressional consideration of this measure as "a distinct step forward. It provides assurance that the ghastly mistakes in the treatment of veterans that marked the close of the last war will not be repeated."[43]

While neither the conservative Rankin bill nor the education-oriented Barden bill were liberal in the way that social welfare legislation from the 1930s might have been described, there were significant differences between the two approaches. The Barden bill, in eschewing the Veterans Administration, would have encouraged the development of forty-eight different veterans' programs. Despite Barden's belief that his bill showed Congress as taking responsibility for important questions of public policy, others questioned the merits of his approach. Harry P. Jeffrey (R-Ohio) maintained that the Barden bill took "a lot of paper and ink, and in the end it attempts to function without placing responsibility any place." Rankin, well known for his demagoguery on questions of race and states' rights, nonetheless found himself defending a federal program. On 12 May he told his colleagues: "This is Federal money. Some men talk as if we ought to send the Federal Treasury off down here and have some professors handle it. We are not going to do that. This is Federal money. This is the Congress of the United States. This is the Federal Government."[44]

Veterans' legislation became a flash point for other political issues before deliberations on the G.I. Bill were completed, revealing further the complex ideological wars being fought on the legislative front. On the last day of debate over the G.I. Bill in the House, lawmakers turned their attention to an ad hominem attack against Sidney Hillman and the CIO, especially its political activities. Anti–labor union politics had long been a staple for conservatives, and here it became another vehicle to differentiate the welfare agenda of the G.I. Bill from the New Deal welfare state and advocacy of national health insurance. Rep. Clare Hoffman (R-Mich.) wanted to make sure that no veteran wishing to take an industrial course would also be required to join a union even if he sought a job in a factory with union representation. Vito Marcantonio (AL-N.Y.) fought against efforts to punish veterans for union activity. Howard J. McMurray (D-Wis.) agreed: "I get very angry when I see men in the Congress of the United States, day after day, week after week, month after month, trying to slip into bills that all of us have to support, phrases that are discriminatory against various groups in the population. There is no justification for this." When told that such laws were already operative in several of the states, McMurray countered, "Just because some State legislatures have been stupid is no reason why the Congress of the United States should be likewise." This assertion caused Rankin to mock his Wisconsin colleague: "We would never have known of the stupidity of the State legislatures had it not been for the erudite gentleman from Wisconsin, who presumes to be an authority on that subject."[45]

The Rankin bill ultimately passed the House on 18 May by a vote of 388–0. The House bill differed with the Senate version in several key ways. Lawmakers in the lower chamber included higher loan amounts, up to $2,500 guaranteed by the federal government; an expanded program of educational benefits taking in all who were not over twenty-four years of age; a reduction in the length of time veterans could draw unemployment compensation from fifty-two to twenty-six weeks; and elimination of the staggered weekly unemployment benefits determined by marital status (fifteen dollars for single veterans and twenty-five dollars for married veterans) and replacement with a flat weekly compensation of twenty dollars. Antiunion amendments, which made payment of dues a condition of employment, were defeated.[46]

The Conference Committee fought for three weeks about the House and Senate bills. The Senate conferees were Clark, Walter George (D-Ga.), David I. Walsh (D-Mass.), Scott Lucas (D-Ill.), Robert M. La Follette (R-Wis.), John A. Danaher (R-Conn.), and Eugene D. Millikin (R-Colo.). The House conferees were Rankin, J. Hardin Peterson (D-Fla.), A. Leonard Allen (D-La.), John S. Gibson (D-Ga.), Rogers, Paul Cunningham (R-Iowa), and Kearney. The combined regional and ideological breakdown of the conference committee privileged the so-called conservative coalition of southern Democrats and Republicans. Of the fourteen conference committee members, five were southern Democrats—George, Rankin, Peterson, Allen, and Gibson—and of the six Republicans, only La Follette was not a conservative. Additionally the nonsouthern Democrats on the conference committee were all centrist or conservative in their politics.[47]

Because of a deadlock, efforts to locate Gibson, who had returned home to

Douglas, Georgia, because of illness and who was favorable to the Legion, became a priority for the Legion. Earlier Rankin had sought and gotten Gibson's proxy, but Gibson changed his mind because he preferred the Senate bill's language regarding unemployment. Legion officials, according to one journalist, "began madly telephoning Georgia to locate Gibson." No effort was spared. Local law enforcement and local radio stations were drafted for the manhunt. After finding Gibson, his pursuers pushed him into a car and drove ninety miles per hour to the Jacksonville, Florida, airport. He arrived in Washington in time to vote for the compromise with the Senate, which included more liberal access to educational benefits, location of employment services with the United States Employment Services instead of the VA, and fifty-two weeks of readjustment allowances—all victories for the Senate conferees. The maximum that could be borrowed for home, farm, or business purchases was reduced to $2,000 from $2,500, and the interest rate was lowered from 6 to 4 percent.[48]

Commentary from lawmakers and journalists after the bill's passage reveals the legislative philosophy of the G.I. Bill of Rights, but also its meaning for understanding the war induced contours of liberalism. Sen. Ernest McFarland (D-Ariz.) told an audience of the *American Forum of the Air*, "We worked with the idea of giving the veteran the opportunity to help himself. It was the determination of all that the veterans of World War II should not be the recipients of the neglect and indifference suffered by the veterans of World War I upon their discharge." While the legislation that was passed was not perfect, McFarland stressed his hope that Congress would improve the package with time. Liberal journalists were quick to note its flaws, as the *New Republic* wrote, "The bill does not contemplate making the veteran a permanent ward of the government; it seeks to speed his rapid reintegration into civilian life."[49]

Evaluation of the G.I. Bill in context with the larger program for economic reconversion reveals that liberals do not want veterans' programs when liberalism is ascendant; only when conservatives dominate do liberals use veterans' policy as a Trojan horse to get state expansion back on track, as was the case in 1944. Here liberals succeeded with their immediate but not their larger goals. The role of an independent Congress, one skeptical of an expanded New Deal state, in the creation of the G.I. Bill of Rights and the defeat of Social Security expansion cannot be overestimated. In both, the legislative branch was neither heroic nor demonic but instead reflected the public's growing unease with a 1930s-styled welfare state. The result found in the G.I. Bill of Rights, then, was a mediated and moderated welfare state designed to prevent implementation of cradle-to-grave Social Security and, instead, to reward politically and culturally favored groups. These were the contours of liberalism that carried into the postwar years.

# Notes

1. Sam Rayburn quoted in Frank McNaughton to Bill Johnson, 2 September 1943, in "September 1943," Box 5, Frank McNaughton Papers, Harry S. Truman Library, Independence, Missouri [hereafter HSTL]. McNaughton was a journalist for *Time* magazine; he had the Capitol Hill beat and wrote long memoranda with not-for-attribution, background-only quotations from lawmakers that reveal legislative motivation in ways that no other sources can.

2. David R. B. Ross, *Preparing for Ulysses: Politics and Veterans during World War II* (New York: Columbia University Press, 1969), 91.

3. See, for example, James Stokes Ballard, *The Shock of Peace: Military and Economic Demobilization After World War II* (Washington, D.C.: University Press of America, 1983); Michael J. Bennett, *When Dreams Came True: The G.I. Bill and the Making of Modern America* (McLean, Va.: Brassey's Publishing, 1996); Margot Canaday, "Building a Straight State: Sexuality and Social Citizenship under the 1944 G.I. Bill," *Journal of American History* 90 (December 2003): 935–57; Kathleen J. Frydl, *The G.I. Bill* (New York: Cambridge University Press, 2009); Harold M. Hyman, *American Singularity: The 1787 Northwest Ordinance, the 1862 Homestead and Morrill Acts, and the 1944 G.I. Bill* (Athens: University of Georgia Press, 1987); James E. McMillan, "Father of the G.I. Bill: Ernest W. McFarland and Veterans' Legislation," *Journal of Arizona History* 35 (1994): 357–76; Suzanne Mettler, "Bringing the State Back in to Civic Engagement: Policy Feedback Effects of the G.I. Bill for World War II Veterans," *American Political Science Review* 96 (June 2002): 351–65; Suzanne Mettler, "The Creation of the G.I. Bill of Rights of 1944: Melding Social and Participatory Citizenship Ideals," *Journal of Policy History* 17 (2005): 345–74; Suzanne Mettler, "'The Only Good Thing Was the G.I. Bill': Effects of the Education and Training Provisions on African-American Veterans' Political Participation," *Studies in American Political Development* 19 (Spring 2005): 31–52; Keith W. Olson, *The G.I. Bill, the Veterans, and the Colleges* (Lexington: University Press of Kentucky, 1974); David H. Onkst, "'First a Negro . . . Incidentally a Veteran': Black World War Two Veterans and the G.I. Bill of Rights in the Deep South, 1944–1948," *Journal of Social History* 31 (Spring 1998): 517–43; and Ross, *Preparing for Ulysses*.

4. Canaday, "Building a Straight State," 936; Onkst, "'First a Negro . . . Incidentally a Veteran,'" 517; and David K. Johnson, *The Lavender Scare: The Cold War Persecution of Gays and Lesbians in the Federal Government* (Chicago: University of Chicago Press, 2004).

5. The congressional work on economic reconversion reveals a more nuanced state of affairs on Capitol Hill than suggested by James T. Patterson, *Congressional Conservatism and the New Deal: The Growth of the Conservative Coalition in Congress, 1933–1939* (Lexington: University of Kentucky Press, 1967). Moderating political sentiments in Congress, of which the conservative coalition was an extreme example, reflected overall shifts in public opinion. Closer to the mark, but still not wholly satisfying, is Alan Brinkley, *The End of Reform: New Deal Liberalism in Recession and War* (New York: Alfred A. Knopf, 1995). Brinkley marks the shift in American politics away from the experimental liberalism of the 1930s with the recession of 1937, when in reality it took the wartime conversion to a command economy to end the politics of the 1930s.

6. Franklin D. Roosevelt Excerpts from the Press Conference, 28 December 1943, in John T. Woolley and Gerhard Peters, "The American Presidency Project" [online]. Santa Barbara, CA: University of California (hosted), Gerhard Peters (database). Available from World Wide Web, http://www.presidency.ucsb.edu/ws/?pid=16358 (accessed 6 August 2009); Kenneth McKellar to Roosevelt, 24 December 1943, in PPF 2910, Franklin D. Roosevelt Papers,

Franklin D. Roosevelt Library, Hyde Park, New York [hereafter FDRP, FDRL]; and William L. O'Neill, *A Democracy at War: America's Fight at Home and Abroad in World War II* (New York: Free Press, 1993), 391.

7. McNaughton to McConaughy, 13 March 1943, in "March 1–15, 1943," Box 5, McNaughton Papers, HSTL (quotes); O'Neill, *Democracy at War*, 391–92.

8. Raymond Moley, "State Capitalism after the War," *Los Angeles Times*, 1 April 1943; and "War Contract Law Is Held Beneficial," *New York Times*, 3 January 1943.

9. Address of Robert A. Taft before the Alabama Bar Association at Birmingham, Saturday, 10 July 1943, in "Mackinac Conference—Domestic," Box 158, Robert A. Taft Papers, Manuscript Division, Library of Congress, Washington, D.C. [hereafter MD, LC]

10. Untitled report issued by the Republican National Committee, n.d., in "Republican National Committee, 1944–45," Box 42, Harold Burton Papers, MD, LC.

11. Ibid.

12. William Lemke to J.F.P. Tate, 21 November 1944, in File 9, Box 22, William Lemke Papers, Chester Fritz Library, University of North Dakota, Grand Forks, North Dakota (first quote); Address of Robert A. Taft before the Alabama Bar Association at Birmingham, Saturday, 10 July 1943, in "Mackinac Conference—Domestic," Box 158, Taft Papers, MD, LC (remaining quotes); Roosevelt to Clarence Cannon, 16 February 1943, in PPF 5815, FDRP, FDRL.

13. Robert L. Doughton to Gordon Canfield, 15 July 1941, in Robert L. Doughton Papers, Southern Historical Collection, University of North Carolina, Chapel Hill, North Carolina [hereafter SHC]; Anthony J. Badger, *The New Deal: The Depression Years, 1933–1940* (New York: Hill and Wang, 1989), 227–35. For more on Dr. Francis E. Townsend's plans, see, for example, Edwin Amenta, *When Movements Matter: The Townsend Plan and the Rise of Social Security* (Princeton, NJ: Princeton University Press, 2006).

14. McNaughton to David Hulburd, 18 December 1941, in "December 16–31, 1941," Box 2, McNaughton Papers, HSTL; *Congressional Record*, 78th Congress, 2nd Session, 4513; and Lee E. Cooper, "New Law Gives Draftee the Right to Cancel Lease on Month's Notice," *New York Times*, 18 October 1942.

15. John E. Rankin Speech, 24 August 1942, in 77th Congress, House of Representatives 77A-F39.1, Box 335, House Committee on World War Veterans Legislation, RG 233, Records of the United States House of Representatives, National Archives, Washington, D.C. [hereafter NARA].

16. Post War Reconstruction, Excerpts from address of Sen. Alben W. Barkley before the Real Estate Board of Philadelphia, 23 January 1943, in "January 23, 1943, 'Postwar Reconstruction,' Real Estate Board—Philadelphia, PA," Alben Barkley Papers, University of Kentucky Libraries, Special Collections and Archives, Lexington, Kentucky.

17. Ibid.

18. Letter to Hal, 23 March 1943, in "Civilian Distress Caused by War," 78th Congress, Senate 78A-F10, Box 99, Senate Committee on Finance Papers, RG 46, Records of the United States Senate, NARA; Graham Barden to Roane Waring, 17 February 1943, in 78th Congress, House of Representatives 78A-F8.1, Box 238, House Committee on Education, RG 233, Records of the United States House of Representatives, NARA (first two quotes); Mackinac Declaration of Domestic Policy, 7 September 1943, in "Mackinac Conference—Domestic," Box 158, Taft Papers, MD, LC (last quote).

19. Franklin D. Roosevelt, Fireside Chat, 28 July 1943, in John T. Woolley and Gerhard Peters, "The American Presidency Project" [online]. Santa Barbara, CA: University of California (hosted), Gerhard Peters (database). Available from World Wide Web, http://www.

presidency.ucsb.edu/ws/?pid=16437; Roosevelt, Message to Congress on the Return of Service Personnel to Civilian Life, 23 November 1943, in John T. Woolley and Gerhard Peters, "The American Presidency Project" [online]. Santa Barbara, CA: University of California (hosted), Gerhard Peters (database). Available from World Wide Web, http://www.presidency.ucsb.edu/ws/?pid=16343, both accessed 9 August 2009.

20. Ross, *Preparing for Ulysses*, 98–102.

21. Pat Cannon to Dear Colleague, 6 October 1943, (first quote); Doughton to James W. Davis, 11 October 1943, and Doughton to C. A. Cannon, 13 March 1943, (remaining quotes), all in Doughton Papers, SHC.

22. McNaughton to McConaughy, 23 April 1943, in "April 23–30, 1943," Box 5, McNaughton Papers, HSTL; Address by Sen. James E. Murray of Montana before the CIO Committee for Political Action, New York, 14 January 1944, in File 3, Box 861, Series 2, James E. Murray Papers, K. Ross Toole Archives and Special Collections, University of Montana, Missoula, Montana (first quote) [hereafter KRTASC]; McNaughton to Johnson, 31 January 1944 (second quote); and McNaughton to Johnson, 8 January 1944 (last quote), both in "January–March, 1944," Box 6; and McNaughton to Johnson, 6 July 1943, in "July 1943," Box 5, all in McNaughton Papers, HSTL.

23. McNaughton to Johnson, 8 January 1944, in "January–March, 1944," Box 6, McNaughton Papers, HSTL (quote); *Congressional Record*, 78th Congress, 2nd Session, 4513. See, for example, Roger Daniels, *The Bonus March: An Episode of the Great Depression* (Westport, Conn.: Greenwood Publishing Co., 1971); Paul Dickson and Thomas B. Allen, *The Bonus Army: An American Epic* (New York: Walker and Company, 2004); Jennifer D. Keene, *Doughboys, the Great War, and the Remaking of America* (Baltimore: Johns Hopkins University Press, 2001); Donald J. Lisio, *The President and Protest: Hoover, Conspiracy, and the Bonus Riot* (Columbia: University of Missouri Press, 1974); Stephen R. Ortiz, "Rethinking the Bonus March: Federal Bonus Policy, the Veterans of Foreign Wars, and the Origins of a Protest Movement," *Journal of Policy History* 18 (2006): 275–303; William Pencak, *For God and Country: The American Legion, 1919–1941* (Boston: Northeastern University Press, 1989); Theda Skocpol, *Protecting Soldiers and Mothers: The Political Origins of Social Policy in the United States* (Cambridge, Mass.: Harvard University Press, 1992); and Nancy Beck Young, *Wright Patman: Politics, Liberalism, and the American Dream* (Dallas: Southern Methodist University Press, 2000).

24. McNaughton to Johnson, 8 January 1944, in "January–March, 1944," Box 6, McNaughton Papers, HSTL (first two quotes); and Canaday, "Building a Straight State," 939; Ray Brecht to Johnson, 10 January 1944, in "Ray Brecht Reports, 1944–47," Box 17, McNaughton Papers, HSTL (last quote).

25. Omar Ketchum for the Veterans of Foreign Wars, Millard W. Rice for the Disabled American Veterans, Frank Haley for the Military Order of Purple Heart, and W. M. Floyd of the Regular Veterans Association to John E. Rankin, 16 February 1944, in 78th Congress, House of Representatives 78A-F8.1, Box 238, House Committee on Education, RG 233, Records of the United States House of Representatives, NARA.

26. Ibid.

27. McNaughton to Eleanor Welch, 17 June 1944, in "June 9–30, 1944," Box 6, McNaughton Papers, HSTL; "Veterans' Aid Bill of Legion Revised," *New York Times*, 12 March 1944; and "Committee Votes 'G.I. Bill of Rights' Sweeping Aid Plan," *New York Times*, 18 March 1944.

28. Robert Wagner to James E. Murray, 9 March 1944, in File 3, Box 861, Series 2, Murray Papers, KRTASC.

29. Murray Speech, 10 March 1944, Second Health Conference, Medical Heath Institute,

United Automobile Workers, C.I.O., Book-Cadillac Hotel, Detroit, Michigan, in File 49, Box 945, Series 3, Murray Papers, KRTASC (emphasis in original).

30. Ibid.

31. Ibid.

32. Murray to B. I. Steinmetz, 17 March 1945, in File 3, Box 715, Series 1, Murray Papers, KRTASC.

33. "'G.I. Bill of Rights' Passed by Senate," *New York Times*, 25 March 1944; *Congressional Record*, 78th Congress, 2nd sess., 3075–81 (quote); and C. P. Trussell, "Veterans' 'Bill of Rights' Assured of Quick Passage," *New York Times*, 26 March 1944.

34. Minutes, Committee on Education, House of Representatives, 28 March 1944, HR 78A-F8.3, Box 238, House Committee on Education, RG 233, Records of the United States House of Representatives, NARA (first quote); *Congressional Record*, 78th Congress, 2nd sess., 4340, 4352 (last quote); and Ross, *Preparing for Ulysses*, 112.

35. Minutes, Committee on Education, House of Representatives, 18 April 1944, HR 78A-F8.3, Box 238, House Committee on Education; Executive Session Minutes, (quote); and Committee on World War Veterans Legislation, House of Representatives, 3 May 1944, HR 78A-F39.6, Box 450, House Committee on World War Veterans Legislation, both in RG 233, Records of the United States House of Representatives, NARA.

36. Philip Murray to my dear Congressman, 6 May 1944, Doughton Papers, SHC.

37. *Congressional Record*, 78th Congress, 2nd sess., 4338 (quotes), 4339; and Ross, *Preparing for Ulysses*, 107–8.

38. Ross, *Preparing for Ulysses*, 110–11.

39. McNaughton to Johnson, 25 March 1944, in "January–March, 1944," Box 6, McNaughton Papers, HSTL; "House Member in Wheel Chair Demands Aid to Disabled Veterans be Liberalized," *New York Times*, 13 May 1944; and *Congressional Record*, 78th Congress, 2nd sess., 4337 (quote).

40. *Congressional Record*, 78th Congress, 2nd sess., 4356.

41. Ibid., 4434–36.

42. Ibid., 4435 (first quote); and Ross, *Preparing for Ulysses*, 108 (last quote).

43. *Congressional Record*, 78th Congress, 2nd sess., 4443, 4453.

44. Ibid., 4457, 4449.

45. Ibid., 4635–77 (quotes); and Kathleen McLaughlin, "House by 387 to 0 Approves G.I. Bill," *New York Times*, 19 May 1944.

46. *Congressional Record*, 78th Congress, 2nd sess., 4677–78; and McLaughlin, "House by 387 to 0 Approves G.I. Bill."

47. *Congressional Record*, 78th Congress, 2nd sess., 4698, 5847; "Conferees Agree on G.I. Bill Items," *New York Times*, 9 June 1944; and "Conferees Accept G.I. Bill of Rights," *New York Times*, 11 June 1944.

48. McNaughton to Welch, 17 June 1944, in "June 9–30, 1944," Box 6, McNaughton Papers, HSTL (quote); Ross, *Preparing for Ulysses*, 117–18; and *Congressional Record*, 78th Congress, 2nd sess., 5752–60, 5841–53.

49. "How Adequate Is the G.I. Bill of Rights?" *American Forum of the Air*, 2 January 1945, Box 257, Theodore Granik Papers, MD, LC (first quote); "The G.I. Bill of Rights," *New Republic* 111 (October 23, 1944): 512 (second quote); and Skocpol, *Protecting Soldiers and Mothers*.

# 9

## "A Veteran Does Not Have to Stay a Veteran Forever"

### Congress and the Korean G.I. Bill

MELINDA PASH

On 25 June 1950, seasoned North Korean troops cut through the early-morning drizzle as they filtered south across the border into the American-supported Republic of Korea. Outgunned, outmaneuvered, and inexperienced, South Korean defenders proved not so much a hurdle as a speed bump for the Inmun Gun. The attainment of North Korea's objective, the reunification of the peninsula under communist dictator Kim Il Sung, seemed assured. But, on 27 June, just two days after the invasion began, President Harry S. Truman ordered the U.S. Air Force and Navy to aid the clearly faltering South Koreans, thwarting an easy communist victory and beginning a new chapter in American warfare. That very same day, six thousand miles away from Korea's craggy, barren countryside, a different sort of battle began brewing on Capitol Hill as Rep. John Rankin (D-Miss.), chairman of the House Committee on Veterans' Affairs, introduced legislation to initiate the process of extending to veterans of the current Korean campaign the benefits of the 1944 Servicemen's Readjustment Act, or the G.I. Bill of Rights.[1]

At first blush, Rankin's decision to launch this new fight for veterans' benefits seems oddly ill timed. After all, President Truman had not yet ordered ground troops to the war zone, and it remained unclear whether Korea would blossom into another American war or fizzle into nothing more than a ripple on the pond of postwar peace.[2] However, in a larger sense, it mattered little whether Korea evolved into anything more than a minor dust-up or not. The fact that American servicemen had been compelled to serve there at all and in any strength provided reminder that for the foreseeable future the armed forces would continue to return a steady stream of veterans to civilian society. With that in mind, and with the nearly six-year-old World War II G.I.

Bill's provisions set to expire soon, the question of just what benefits to award this next generation of veterans inevitably surfaced. By mid-1950, then, the time had come for Congress to consider whether servicemen and women in the post–World War II period would earn G.I. Bill entitlements—subsidized education and training, generous unemployment benefits, special loans, and mustering out payments for the able-bodied as well as the service-disabled—or if instead the country would return to giving more traditional, less generous rewards for military service.[3]

Congress wrestled with the issue for more than two years, but after it became clear that Korea was in actuality an old-fashioned ground war and not a short-lived "police action," congressional debate turned less on whether to legislate a Korean G.I. Bill than on what that bill should contain. With millions of veterans among the electorate, no member of Congress wished to appear stingy or unsympathetic to the plight of men and women mustering out of the services, but neither did they want to leave room for accusations of fiscal irresponsibility or discrimination against nonveterans. Thus, despite numerous pleas from soldiers fighting in Korea for Congress to act quickly in giving them a G.I. Bill, both houses of the legislature moved slowly and carefully in their consideration of new G.I. Bill legislation.[4] Finally, after the introduction of scores of resolutions; months of investigations and hearings; and the input of hundreds—perhaps thousands—of individuals, institutions, governmental bodies, veterans' organizations, educational associations, and others, Rankin's proposal to extend the G.I. Bill to Korean veterans finally bore fruit. On 16 July 1952, President Truman signed Public Law 550 of the 82nd Congress, the Veterans' Readjustment Assistance Act.

Often both scholars and the public dismiss the 1952 Veterans' Readjustment Assistance Act, labeled the Korean War G.I. Bill, as little more than the natural and inevitable outgrowth of the World War II G.I. Bill. Indeed, the 1952 legislation looked back to its predecessor, but circumstances and attitudes in America had changed by the early 1950s, bringing new pressures to bear on legislators and making any extension of G.I. Bill benefits an uncertain proposition. In part, the very idea of extending the G.I. Bill to a new generation of veterans brought new concerns to the surface. Public grumblings already accused the G.I. Bill of giving veterans an unfair advantage in society and of allowing disreputable schools and businessmen to loot the public till. If Congress extended the benefits and provisions of the G.I. Bill to a new set of veterans, these problems would carry forward and perhaps become a flawed precedent for American veterans' benefits as a whole. Legislators felt compelled to reevaluate not only the particulars of a new G.I. Bill but also the justifications for veterans' entitlements in general. Thus, the passage of the Korean War G.I. Bill, involving months of debate, hundreds of opinions, and a struggle over what legacy Congress should bequeath to future American veterans, proved a far more complex affair than a simple extension of the World War II G.I. Bill.

The Korean G.I. Bill tendered to Korean veterans the same kinds of benefits that the original bestowed upon those marching home from World War II. Beneath the surface, however, the Korean G.I. Bill differed greatly from its predecessor. Where the 1944 act guaranteed unemployed veterans twenty dollars a week for fifty-two weeks courtesy of Uncle Sam, the Korean bill required veterans to go through state unemployment agencies and promised no more than twenty-six dollars a week for twenty-six weeks. More significantly, the new bill revised the provisions for veteran education and training. Under the original G.I. Bill, the Veterans Administration paid a G.I.'s tuition and related expenses up to five hundred dollars per year directly to the college or institution while sending a monthly stipend to the veteran to cover living expenses. In contrast, the Korean G.I. Bill made no provision for the payment of tuition, instead sending each eligible veteran a monthly check out of which he then had to finance both his education and subsistence. Although Korean War G.I. students received more money each month than did the beneficiaries of the 1944 legislation, it proved insufficient to offset the loss of tuition money and made financing school difficult since many institutions required full payment up front.[5] Also, Korean War veterans had a shorter amount of time after discharge to begin their programs, three years rather than four; fewer subsidized months of training, thirty-six rather than forty-eight; and no extra allowance to help pay for books, supplies, or tools. Furthermore, Korean G.I.s found that a number of new restrictions limited their benefits. No longer would the VA pay for courses it deemed avocational or recreational, such as bartending, nor would it allow a student to change his course of study more than once or attend any school with an enrollment of less than 15 percent non-G.I. Bill students.[6]

Unsurprisingly, since the passage of the Korean G.I. Bill, veterans and others have criticized its seeming lack of generosity in comparison to the original. Seeking an explanation for the differences between the two bills, some critics accuse the 82nd Congress of cost-cutting while others argue that the unpopularity of the Korean War simply filtered down to the men who fought it. The reality, of course, is far more complicated. Hastily hammered out and hustled through Congress, the first G.I. Bill did not signify a permanent shift in veterans' policy. Rather, it represented a one-time effort to forestall the economic collapse and social unrest potentially looming in the return of sixteen million American war veterans.[7] In the Korean War era, these fears and circumstances no longer existed. The national economy had rebounded, even to the point of prosperity, and could be expected to absorb the relatively small number of veterans cycling back into civilian life without much difficulty. Also, Korean War veterans tended to be younger and thus less likely to pose a "veteran problem" or grave danger to the social order upon their return. Congress might have handled their needs easily enough by legislating more conventional benefits. In contemplating a new G.I. bill, then, the task before legislators involved not just deciding which benefits to extend to veterans of the action in Korea but also determining what precedent to set for the future of veterans' benefits in the United States. A single G.I. bill might remain an exception to the general rule, but another could prove the beginning of an expensive new pattern. And, if Congress expected to saddle the American taxpayer with the costs and consequences of another G.I. bill, it needed to be able to explain why such an instrument was necessary and what purposes it would serve. The 81st and 82nd Congresses' answers to those questions provide the key to understanding why the Korean G.I. Bill differs so significantly from the 1944 legislation.

Congress might have chosen any of a myriad of rationales to justify the passage of a new G.I. bill and to help inform its contents. First, despite some well-publicized abuses, the Servicemen's Readjustment Act had proved overwhelmingly successful. As President Truman noted in May 1950, the G.I. Bill had "been of real and lasting service" to those veterans who used its benefits.[8] More than that, though, the title providing for the education and training of veterans could, in the words of Carl Gray, the administrator of Veterans Affairs, "be thought of more as a benefit to the nation than to the individual."[9] In addition to pumping tens of thousands of doctors, scientists, engineers, teachers, and other educated professionals into the work force, the G.I. Bill provided its beneficiaries with the means to repay the government's philanthropy. In 1954 the Veterans Administration estimated that within fifteen years, World War II veterans would reimburse most of the fifteen billion dollar cost of their training through taxes paid.[10] In 1950 or 1951 Congress could have argued convincingly for a new G.I. Bill on the grounds that it would produce an even more capable and highly skilled citizenry prepared to serve and support the country more effectively than ever before.[11]

Even before the outbreak of hostilities in Korea, American institutions of higher education needed something of a lift. For years a steady stream of G.I. Bill students and the federal money they brought with them had bankrolled everything from building projects to faculty expansion. With that program ending and veteran enrollment drying to a trickle, colleges and universities watched helplessly as their budgets crashed. Things only got worse as the Korean War and the draft pulled men out of letter jackets and into olive drab. Some in educational circles feared that if things did not change, "one-half or more of the nation's institutions of higher learning will be in the red" within a year or two.[12] By September 1951 a new G.I. Bill sounded good to educators who urged that one "be adopted to provide educational benefits for the service men now fighting in Korea."[13] President Truman, only recently reluctant to back any more G.I. legislation, now pressured Congress to act by rallying behind the idea of making Korean veterans eligible for government-funded schooling.[14] If Congress wanted to enact a G.I. bill designed to subsidize higher education, many Americans stood ready to offer encouragement and support.

For most legislators, the war itself provided the most persuasive reason to extend a G.I. bill to America's latest crop of veterans. President Truman called Korea a "police action," but representatives and senators, many of whom had performed wartime military duty themselves, quickly realized that "it is a war. . . . a real war in all its horrible aspects and consequences."[15] Still, because the conflict remained undeclared, men fighting from front line foxholes on the Korean peninsula earned nothing more for their service than the trifling benefits allowed peacetime veterans.[16] Men in the war zone wanted to know, "Is it because this is a police action and an unpopular war that the soldiers here have to go without the benefits that were considered only proper for a returning GI of World War II?"[17] Soldiers wrote Sen. Robert Taft (R-Ohio): "They call this a police action, but men are losing their lives the same as in the last war. We are fighting here for freedom of the peoples, the same as in World War II. Why are we any different from the 'G.I.' of the last war?"[18] Pushed to answer, many in Congress concluded that the men dying and bleeding in Korea differed not at all from their World War II counterparts and that under the circumstances the government had a responsibility to "demonstrate the same care and action to the American military personnel which is today seeking to preserve the rights and freedoms which were temporarily made secure on the battlefields of World War II."[19] Rep. Louis Heller (D-N.Y.) argued, "We cannot say that the men who fought for and defended their country in one war are entitled to certain benefits, while those who fought and bled for it in another war are not entitled to the same benefits."[20]

Ultimately, politicians on both sides of the political divide dismissed the idea of using veterans' legislation to either improve society or directly support higher education. As Sherman Adams, President Eisenhower's White House chief of staff, later pointed out to a Harvard graduate student who was eagerly advancing the idea of a post-Korean G.I. Bill to enhance education, improving society and supporting higher education might be important, even desirable outcomes of G.I. Bill laws, but they were "incidental to the primary purpose of the programs." No matter the temptations, veterans' benefits had to speak to the needs of veterans, not to the wants of the nation as a whole.[21] In a 1951 budget message to Congress, President Truman echoed that sentiment, directing that when developing veterans' benefits, "we should provide only for those special and unique needs which arise directly from military service."[22] Such directives swayed Congress, causing those legislators lobbying for a Korean G.I. Bill to ground their arguments on the principle that "only a year and a half has been taken from their lives on the calendar . . . however, we cannot reckon the extent of their displacement. . . . The living who return, with scars on body and spirit, of these we must think and help."[23] Thus, in the early 1950s, Congress embraced veteran readjustment as the driving force of the Korean G.I. Bill. Like the World War II legislation, this G.I. bill would strive to return veterans to civilian life before educational and occupational opportunities passed them by, leaving them unable to readjust or achieve the levels of success attained by their nonveteran counterparts.[24] But this time around, Congress clearly planned to interpret veterans' needs more narrowly, declining to provide veterans with funding or programs to address any issues not directly arising from military service and readjustment.

Even so, there remained a number of details for Congress to work out before voting any of the bills under consideration into law. For instance, legislators needed to determine which veterans would qualify for the new Korean G.I. Bill.[25] Historically, both the legislature and public readily supported major veterans' benefits, such as pensions or educational and occupational rehabilitation, for only those veterans who suffered disability or injury as a result of their military service or who offered compelling evidence of need.[26] Clearly, the first G.I. Bill broke with that tradition.[27] In 1944 Congress reasoned that nearly all World War II veterans had spent years in uniform, many in combat or at least deployed to overseas war theaters, and that the American people had the obligation to ensure that service members "upon return to a civilian life, receive liberal Federal assistance in reaching that place and position which they . . . probably would have achieved, had their service in war not interrupted their careers."[28] With that precedent in mind, members of the 81st and 82nd Congresses likewise argued that wartime service during the "real and bloody and cruel war" in Korea merited benefits beyond the usual for all Americans in uniform.[29]

However, on Capitol Hill, most realized that if a new G.I. bill granted universal benefits, the majority of veterans eligible for its programs would not have participated in combat or even suffered the inconvenience of being posted in the theater of operations. Indeed, of the nearly seven million Americans serving in the military from 27 June 1950 to 31 January 1955, fewer than two million rotated into the war zone for duty.[30] Also, Korean inductees served only about two years, not for the duration of the conflict as had World War II draftees. Certainly, almost everyone agreed with Sen. Styles Bridges (R-N.H.)

that, "There can be no question that these benefits [the G.I. Bill] should be granted to a Korean veteran who has served in the Korean area, on the Korean peninsula, in the waters around it, or in the air above it."[31] But some wondered about the wisdom of extending another G.I. bill to all, including "a man who has served in this country and has never been more than 100 miles away from Washington." They asked, "Should he receive the same type of benefits as are granted to the man who has bled and suffered in Korea? . . . What is the justification for taking everyone, even though some of them may not have gone farther away than Camp Meade?"[32] So, according to critic Sen. Robert Taft (R-Ohio), the question arose whether the G.I. Bill "should not be confined to those who have served abroad, or who have served in Korea."[33]

In addition to wrangling over which veterans deserved to be covered by a new G.I. bill, Congress had to bear in mind the possible ramifications of their decision on the matter. Despite the peace talks in progress since 10 July 1951, no one knew how much longer the conflict in Korea would last or how many more young men would be called to the colors in the meantime. And no one could say for certain that Korea would be the end of the line for American soldiers. Rep. Thomas Abernethy (D-Miss.) wanted to know "whether or not every generation of America's sons is going to have to participate in the mass slaughter, the suffering and heartache that goes with war?"[34] If so, who could reckon the number of Cold Warriors who would march home in the coming years and decades? As President Truman suggested, "before many years nearly all the population may be veterans or the dependents of veterans."[35] Depending on the turn of events, an offer of free schooling for all members of the armed forces serving during wartime might result in the government subsidizing "the education of all able-bodied men for a long time to come."[36]

Perhaps the public would support such legislation, but already some opposition to a G.I. bill as inclusive as the last one had emerged. Within both military and government circles, people worried that granting every ex-serviceman the opportunity to draw unemployment payments or obtain a government-subsidized education would interfere with retention. After all, they reasoned, why would anyone remain in the military once their enlistment expired if it meant giving up a free paycheck or college degree?[37] Also, despite the financial crisis facing institutions around the country, the Association of Land Grant Colleges and Universities advocated a "new approach" to veterans' benefits, saying "when it [military service] is universal no reward should be expected or given."[38] Congress rightly judged that the nation had become more conservative and cost-conscious since World War II, and that qualifying another entire generation of ex-servicemen for G.I. Bill benefits might fuel public resentment. As always, people would support generous treatment for veterans wounded in the line of duty but very well might view it as "something else again to try indiscriminately to tap the public treasury on behalf of men and women who merely served, and suffered no injury in thus doing their simple duty as citizens."[39] Predictably, Congress first moved to provide readjustment assistance to Korean veterans injured or disabled while in service. On 7 December 1950, President Truman requested a new vocational rehabilitation bill, and by the end of the month Congress had Public Law 894 of the 81st Congress, an extension of World War II's Public Law 16, ready for the president's signature.[40] Men and women not visibly harmed during their tours of duty had to wait longer, but advocates of writing the new G.I. bill so as to cover nearly everyone serving in the Korean War–era armed forces pleaded their case convincingly. Speaking directly to the issue of whether men and women serving in the United States deserved or needed any sort of readjustment aid, Sen. Joseph Hill (D-Ala.) noted, "When a man enters the military service . . . he does not determine where he is to serve. He is subject to serving anywhere he may be ordered to serve." Furthermore, Hill argued, "no matter where the veteran may serve, his career is disrupted just the same. Even if he is in the city of Washington . . . he cannot go to school, any more than he could go to school if he were serving in Korea . . . So his career is interrupted the minute he enters the armed services, no matter where he may serve."[41] After relatively little debate, Congress finally settled on eligibility requirements comparable to those of the original G.I. Bill. All veterans serving ninety days or more during the basic service period and discharged from the military "under conditions other than dishonorable" would qualify for the benefits of the Korean G.I. Bill.[42]

But what would those benefits be? This proved a more challenging decision for Congress to make. Several legislators, perhaps influenced by the wishes of the American Legion, pushed for the extension of Public Law 346, the 1944 G.I. Bill, to Korean veterans in its entirety.[43] In fact, by September 1950 a dozen or so bills with the objective of reviving all G.I. benefits found sponsorship in the House of Representatives alone.[44] However, most members of Congress, while agreeing on the success of the original G.I. Bill, also keenly recognized that it possessed serious shortcomings. Public opinion had long since turned against the "52–20 Club" that allowed veterans to draw unemployment for an entire year, and newspaper accounts regularly chronicled incidents of abuse and corruption in the administration of G.I. Bill programs.[45] The General Accounting Office accused the G.I. Bill of declaring "open season" on the Treasury, and some taxpayers deemed its enactment "the signal for a mass ganging up on the public till by dishonest institutions, with the connivance . . . of some veterans who didn't seem to mind looting the Treasury of the country which they risked their lives to defend."[46] Even as they pondered new legislation for the country's latest generation of veterans, lawmakers remained busy churning out amendments to remedy defects in the G.I. Bill created for the last one.[47] As a result, nearly everyone on Capitol Hill reached the same conclusion as President Truman, who, despite urging "prompt" congressional action on the matter of readjustment benefits for discharged Korean veterans, declared, "I do not believe that extension of the Servicemen's Readjustment Act . . . in its present form would be the proper way to meet the new need."[48]

Weighing the various Korean G.I. bills before it, the House Committee on Veterans' Affairs determined that its members could not recommend any new legislation without first sorting through some of the flaws of the original G.I. Bill. Thus, in September 1950 the House created the House Select Committee to Investigate the Educational and Training Program under the G.I. Bill.[49] Chaired by Rep. Olin Teague (D-Tex.), a decorated United States combat soldier of World War II, this special committee spent well over a year conducting research to ascertain the nature of G.I. Bill fraud and to devise methods by which to eliminate it in the construction of a Korean bill. Reporting its findings in February 1952, the Teague Committee charged that "graft, waste, and inefficiency" in the veterans' education and training program wasted "hundreds of millions" of taxpayer dollars.[50] Fly-by-night schools wooed G.I. students and collected government tuition payments but failed to deliver quality instruction. Veterans used their scholarships to pay for classes in dancing, personality development, and calisthenics rather than to obtain degrees that would enable them to begin careers. Trade schools and other institutions padded bills, "jumped" tuition rates, and offered bribes to VA officials responsible for granting tuition contracts. With regard to on-the-job and on-the-farm training, men applied for and received stipends for apprenticing at the businesses or farms at which they had worked before entering the service. Appraisers contracted to determine the value of homes or properties being financed with G.I. loans accepted bribes to inflate appraisals, and inspectors did likewise in exchange for their willingness to overlook deficiencies in quality or workmanship.[51]

Despite these findings, the Teague Committee still supported benefits for Korean veterans but called for a "sharply restricted 'G.I. Bill of Rights,'" one that would preclude the possibility of similar abuses.[52] To this end, and desirous of making the new legislation provide benefits only for the real readjustment needs of Korean veterans, the House Committee on Veterans' Affairs worked to construct an improved G.I. bill. Using the Teague Committee report as a springboard for discussion, the House Committee on Veterans' Affairs held extensive hearings, calling upon educational associations, government agencies, and a multitude of others to provide input. By mid-1952, the committee had ready for presentation to the House a clean Korean G.I. Bill, House Resolution 7656.

This bill reflected the concern of its authors to prevent fraud and waste. Titles granting Korean veterans mustering out pay, employment assistance, and job counseling—programs that generated virtually no accusations of corruption or mismanagement under Public Law 346—remained largely intact. Veterans also retained the same housing benefits as World War II G.I.s except that they gained a one-year warranty on new homes to protect against unethical appraisers and contractors. But the House Committee on Veterans' Affairs dropped the widely unpopular provision for unemployment compensation altogether and shored up veteran training and educational programs against misuse.[53] New terms required the government to pay individual veterans a lump sum each month for tuition and subsistence rather than cutting separate checks for schools and G.I.s. The committee believed that the direct-pay method would deter veterans from enrolling in schools just to get monthly stipends, discourage institutions from raising tuition needlessly, end the role of the government as an educational middleman, simplify the administration of the G.I. Bill, and stop much of the corruption that plagued the old system.[54] In an effort to give veterans a greater stake in their education and less incentive to neglect their studies, the new bill also mandated that students pay for books and supplies out of pocket. Furthermore, H.R. 7656 included provisions to help veterans make sound decisions about how and where to spend G.I. Bill funds. It allowed G.I.s only one change of course (i.e., switching of major or program) and barred them from enrolling in recreational programs, with the result that few veterans could burn three or four years in school and still end up without either a degree or marketable occupational skills. Nor could a G.I. be lured into attending a fly-by-night school since approved institutions had to have been in existence at least two years and possess a minimum nonveteran enrollment of 25 percent. Finally, a number of safeguards incorporated into the bill, including criminal and other penalties, served to ensure that this time around neither veterans nor the schools and agencies involved with the G.I. Bill would betray the public trust.[55]

In an effort to block members of the House at large from undoing its hard work and tacking benefits such as the 52–20 Club back on, the Committee on Veterans' Affairs moved to report H.R. 7656 under a suspension of the rules, barring amendments and limiting debate to forty minutes.[56] The gambit paid off, much to the chagrin of those representatives, such as Laurie Battle (D-Ala.), who felt that some "points have not been clarified and that under the existing rules they cannot be clarified because there is not sufficient time for debate and amendments are not in order."[57] Still, an unexpected and heated controversy over the direct-pay method erupted, threatening to forestall passage of the bill. Fearful that direct-pay would encourage G.I.s to attend cheaper public institutions, a coalition of several private schools led by F. D. Fagg Jr., president of the University of Southern California, formed the Emergency Committee for Amendment of the Korean G.I. Bill and began a letter-writing campaign to force a reversal of policy.[58] Taking up Fagg's cause, Rep. William Springer (R-Ill.) offered up the "Springer Amendment," arguing that the old method of payment "more nearly safeguarded" the veteran's welfare by allowing him to exercise greater freedom of choice in selecting an institution and eliminating discrimination against private schools.[59]

Unimpressed, Teague countered this measure sharply. He labeled Fagg's letter one of the "most unfair and dishonest pieces of lobbying," accused the Emergency Committee of offering the proposal to "insure them a greater take in Federal tuition payments," and charged Springer with dishonesty for introducing his amendment out of committee.[60] A blistering debate ensued with Teague playing lawyer to Springer's witness until Springer finally asked, "All right; are you through?"[61] Teague responded that he was, but now Pandora's Box lay open and legislators who at first had not been certain what all of the fuss was about had questions. Pressed by Rep. Overton Brooks (D-La.) on the issue of whether veterans would be able to attend private colleges in his Louisiana home district under H.R. 7656 without passage of the Springer Amendment, Springer had to concede, "There is nothing to prevent them from going to any school."[62] After that Springer continued to fight for his amendment, but for all practical purposes he already had lost the battle. Then only a few concerns about home warranties slowing down the loan process and minimum nonveteran student enrollment quotas working hardships on segregated institutions stood between the House Committee on Veterans' Affairs and the passage of H.R. 7656. On 5 June 1952 the House approved the measure without the Springer Amendment by a vote of 361 to 1, making any lingering doubts and issues problems for the Senate to work out.[63]

Just shy of a month after receiving H.R. 7656, the Senate Labor Committee reported it out to the full Senate with only a few substantive revisions. Most important, the committee adopted a new approach to G.I. subsistence and tuition payments. Instead of containing two levels of monthly stipends, one for single G.I.s and another for those with dependents, the Senate Labor Committee's version of the bill had three tiers, adding a level for men with more than one dependent, and tacked on an additional payment of up to $360 a year for tuition.[64] On the Senate floor, senators made more changes, generally seeking to bestow fuller benefits on Korean veterans. Sen. Homer Ferguson (R-Mich.) offered an amendment securing unemployment benefits for men and women returning to civilian life, a measure that passed despite concerns that reviving unemployment would result in "the opening wedge in the federalization of the State unemployment compensation systems."[65] Sen. Joseph Hill's (D-Ala.) amendment to prevent some schools, such as state colleges and universities that charged no tuition, from forcing veterans to pay more than civilians also passed.[66] Concerned that schools would have difficulty reaching the House's requirement of 25 percent nonveteran enrollment and that veterans' choices might thereby be limited, the Senate knocked the figure down to 10 percent.[67] Lastly, in an effort to prevent a slow-down in home loans for veterans, the Senate removed the House's provision for a one-year home warranty.[68]

Necessarily, the Senate's revision of H.R. 7656 led to a request for a conference with the House. Working feverishly to give Congress enough time to act before the bill's deadline, conferees put together a compromise bill. Neither house of the legislature got exactly what it wanted. Rep. Hubert Scudder (R-Calif.) complained, "It is my honest belief that the bill as it was originally passed by the House was a much better bill than the one we now have before us."[69] Similarly, a number of senators regretted that the direct-pay method won the day. However, almost everyone agreed that "this is a much better plan and much fairer to the GI boys than the old plan was under the old scheme," that the bill "is sound, . . . moral, and . . . good legislation," and that "we have a bill that each and every Member of this body in good conscience can vote for." As Rep. O'Konski put it, "We have here . . . the best possible bill that could be adopted by this session of the Congress."[70]

With Korean veterans beginning to rotate home by the tens of thousands every month, many on Capitol Hill simply felt time had run out on debating the particulars of a Korean G.I. Bill. Rep. John Vorys (R-Ohio) acknowledged, "While our men fight on and on we cannot pass a law to prevent further mistakes. We can, however, pass this bill to do justice to those who have done the fighting in the struggle."[71] By mid-July, secure in the belief that "we have done the best job that can be done," both the House and Senate approved the Veterans' Readjustment Assistance Act of 1952 and sent it to President Truman for signature into law.[72]

In practice, the Korean G.I. Bill did not always meet its authors' expectations. Instead, it confirmed some legislators' fears that "in the zeal to close all . . . loopholes it well may be that inequities against those of honest purpose and design will develop."[73] Certainly, direct-pay eliminated incentives for schools to raise tuition needlessly and for G.I.s to enroll without a strong commitment to earning a degree or license, but it also worked a great financial hardship on veterans. While some schools, such as Teachers College, Columbia University, revamped payment programs to offer monthly or deferred tuition plans, the vast majority continued to require fees and tuition up front.[74] For G.I.s, who could not collect unemployment or student subsidies until their mustering-out pay expired and whose first educational stipend checks not infrequently ran a month or two behind their enrollment, coming up with school money posed a particular challenge.[75] As Representative Springer and Senator Nixon predicted, a greater percentage of Korean veterans than nonveterans felt compelled to settle for cheaper public universities over pricier private ones.[76]

Furthermore, some private schools declined the opportunity to apply for state approval to train veterans, and many other institutions became victims of the 15 percent nonveteran enrollment rule included in the final legislation.[77] Black schools and colleges in the South, drawing enrollment primarily from a population too poor to afford training or education, especially suffered from the rule, but elsewhere tailoring schools, industrial training centers, and trade schools also had to turn veterans away.[78] Watching their time to begin studies tick away, G.I.s futilely begged Congress to revise the regulations. Both the House and Senate discussed various means to alleviate some of the snags in the Korean G.I. Bill, but aside from extending a few time limits Congress did little. Critics as well as some of the act's intended beneficiaries concluded that Korean veterans got "short-changed" and received a "shabby deal" compared to World War II G.I.s. Consequently, individuals and groups called for expanded benefits. In 1954, for instance, the Association of American Colleges, declared itself "on firm ground in recommending a broadening of the educational benefits for veterans of the war in Korea" on the grounds that "they are not getting treatment as good as that accorded to the veterans of the Second World War and both they and the colleges are suffering."[79]

Still, if "the Korean G.I. Bill of Rights . . . did not go all-out on Government aid as did the earlier law," its limitations had virtually nothing to do with public antipathy toward the "police action," American apathy toward Korean veterans, or the sentiment that perhaps these G.I.s did not measure up to their forebears.[80] Throughout the two years that Congress worked to fashion a G.I. bill for Korean veterans, popular support for the war on the home front dipped as low as 35 percent and never rose above 45 percent. Yet senators and congressmen maintained more than a healthy interest in legislating benefits for Korean veterans, eagerly proposing a proliferation of bills and measures.[81] Rather, the Korean G.I. Bill reflected thousands of hours of congressional debate and compromise as well as the desire of the 81st and 82nd Congresses to devise a bill that would forestall a reprisal of the abuses that accompanied the 1944 act and meet the readjustment needs of the new generation of veterans marching home.[82]

In passing the Veterans' Readjustment Assistance Act of 1952, Congress achieved its goals. Safeguards in the act prevented much of the earlier corruption while allowing 17.8 percent of Korean veterans to collect unemployment; 42 percent, or 2.4 million, to use educational and training benefits; and another 1.5 million to finance their homes with G.I. loans.[83] To be sure, a higher percentage of World War II veterans claimed their benefits. Still Korean War rates of usage are impressive given deferment policies in place to allow men to complete degrees before entering service, the number of Korean veterans already entitled to the first G.I. Bill, the incredible pressure put on men by the military to reenlist, the healthy economy of the 1950s, and the relative youth of Korean veterans.[84] Indeed, although less generous than the original G.I. Bill, Public Law 550 proved life changing for Korean veterans, prompting many to hail its merits. Al Avisato Jr., a former G.I., wrote the senators from his home state of Florida to "express my deepest gratitude to . . . Congress and especially to my fellow Americans, for enabling me to attend . . . [college], under the G.I. Bill. Without it I could not have been able to pursue my present course of study."[85] However flawed, the Korean G.I. Bill provided a model for future G.I. bills and a sustainable veterans' program that, recognizing "a veteran does not have to stay a veteran forever," would acknowledge and reward the service of American soldiers without creating a class apart.[86]

## Notes

1. U.S. Congress, House, "Education and Training and Other Benefits for Persons Serving in the Armed Forces on or after June 27, 1950," 82nd Congress, 2nd Session, 1952, H.R. 1943, 22.

2. President Truman ordered American ground troops to Korea on 30 June 1950. The first of these entered combat on 5 July.

3. Traditionally, Americans favor special benefits for war veterans, especially those with service-connected injuries or disabilities. Before World War II, however, these consisted of income support payments, health care, and preference in jobs for veterans or, in the case of disabled veterans, their spouses. The first steps toward educational benefits came in 1917 and 1918 with amendments to the War Risk Act and the passage of the Vocational Rehabilitation Act, but these offered little to the able-bodied veteran. Not until the 1944 G.I. Bill did Congress offer all veterans, regardless of "need" or disability, sweeping "readjustment" benefits designed to refit the former soldier into civilian society before his failure to readjust resulted in "need." For a discussion of veterans' benefits in the United States, see Sar Levitan and Karen A. Cleary, *Old Wars Remain Unfinished: The Veterans' Benefits System* (Baltimore: Johns Hopkins University Press, 1973); Ilona N. Rashkow, *Veterans Benefits: A Comparison and Analysis* (Washington, D.C.: Library of Congress, Educational and Public Welfare Division, Congressional Research Service, 1975); and and Richard Severo and Lewis Milford, *The Wages of War: When America's Soldiers Came Home—From Valley Forge to Vietnam* (New York: Simon and Schuster, 1989).

4. For examples of such letters, see Extension of Remarks by Rep. Edith Nourse Rogers (R-Mass.), *Appendix to the Congressional Record*, 82nd Cong., 1st sess., vol. 97:13, A3332-A3333. (Hereafter, *Congressional Record* abbreviated as CR).

5. World War II veterans originally received $50 a month, but later the amount increased to $75. Korean veterans got monthly subsistence payments of between $110 and $160 a month, depending upon the number of dependents they had.

6. For comparisons of the World War II and Korean G.I. Bills, see Keith W. Olson, *The G.I. Bill, the Veterans, and the Colleges* (Lexington: University Press of Kentucky, 1974), 105; Rashkow, *Veterans Benefits*, 21–28; Ilona Rashkow, *The G.I. Bill: 1944–1975* (Washington, D.C.: Library of Congress, Educational and Public Welfare Division, Congressional Research Service, 1975); Kenneth Edward Fisher, "A Comparative Analysis of Selected Congressional Documents Related to Educational Benefits Legislated for the Veterans of World War II, the Korean Conflict, and the Vietnam Era Under the G.I. Bill" (Ph.D. diss., Florida State University, 1975); and Congress, House, "Readjustment Benefits: General Survey and Appraisal," report by the President's Commission on Veterans' Pensions, 84th Cong., 2nd sess., 1956, House Committee Print No. 289, 148–60.

7. Representative Thomas Abernethy (D-Miss.), CR, 78th Cong., 2nd sess., vol. 90:4, 4434; Olson, *G.I. Bill*, 27; Fisher, *Comparative Analysis*, 3–4; and Stanley Frank, "We Licked the Veteran Problem," *Saturday Evening Post* 228 (29 October 1955), 20–21.

8. Rep. Joseph Evins (D-Tenn.) quoting President Harry S. Truman, CR, 81st Cong., 2nd sess., vol. 96:5, 6928.

9. Carl R. Gray Jr. quoted in Benjamin Fine, "Education in Review," *New York Times*, 4 February 1951, 131.

10. "10 Years of G.I. Bill Educated a Generation," *New York Times*, 22 June 1954, 6.

11. For an expression of this, see Fine, "Education in Review," *New York Times*, 4 February 1951, 131.

12. Fine, "Education in Review," *New York Times*, 3 December 1950, E9.

13. Benjamin Fine, "College Rolls Drop 250,000 as Financial Worries Mount," *New York Times*, 24 September 1951, 1.

14. "Truman Backs School Aid for Veterans of Korea," *New York Times*, 18 September 1951, 9.

15. Rep. Sidney Fine (D-N.Y.), CR, 82nd Cong., 2nd sess., vol. 98:5, 6643. Given the number of Americans who served in World Wars I and II, it is not surprising that many of those in Congress during the early 1950s had performed wartime military service. A random sampling by this author indicates that nearly half of U.S. representatives in 1952 were veterans, a slightly larger percentage than in the Senate.

16. This fact encouraged Congress to pass a number of bills conferring war veteran benefits, such as hospital and domiciliary care, to Korean veterans long before the 1952 G.I. Bill. Congress did not designate the Korean Conflict as a war until 1958. See Richard K. Kolb, "Korea's 'Invisible Veterans' Return to an Ambivalent America," *VFW Magazine* 85, no. 3 (November 1997): 24.

17. Corp. Henry Orysbal to Rep. Edith Nourse Rogers, quoted in *Appendix to the CR*, 82nd Cong., 1st sess., vol. 97:13, A3333.

18. Sgt. Edward W. Moffett, S.F.C. William H. Bloss, and Sgt. Wade H. Beans to Robert A. Taft, 15 May 1951, Taft Papers, Box 1077, Library of Congress.

19. Sen. Harry Cain (R-Wash.), CR, 81st Cong., 2nd sess., vol. 96:7, 9790–91.

20. Rep. Louis B. Heller (D-N.Y.), *Appendix to CR*, 82nd Cong., 2nd sess., vol. 98:8, A852.

21. Sherman Adams to Lo-Yi Chan, 12 March 1955, Central Files, General Files, GF 125-I 1959 (3), Box 932, Dwight David Eisenhower Library, Abilene, Kansas.

22. "Truman Requests Free G.I. Insurance," *New York Times*, 16 January 1951, 25.

23. Rep. Thomas Lane (D-Mass.), CR, 82nd Cong., 2nd sess., vol. 98:1, 47.

24. Congress, House, "The Historical Development of Veterans' Benefits in the United States," Report by the President's Commission on Veterans Pensions, 84th Cong., 2nd sess., 1956, House Committee Print No. 244, Staff Report No. I, 62.

25. Along with the problem of figuring out how far to go in extending benefits, this question actually led sponsors of G.I. bill legislation to abandon hope, at least temporarily, in September 1950. "Sponsors Abandon G.I. Rights in Korea," *New York Times*, 5 September 1950, 12.

26. See Frank, "We Licked the Veteran Problem," 20–21.

27. Rashkow, *G.I. Bill*, CRS-2.

28. Rep. Thomas Abernethy (D-Miss.), CR, 78th Cong., 2nd sess., vol. 90:4, 4434. Also Rashkow, *G.I. Bill*, CRS-2.

29. Sen. Harry Cain (R-Wash.), CR, 81st Cong., 2nd sess., vol. 96:7, 9790–91.

30. U.S. Department of Veterans' Affairs, Office of Program and Data Analyses, Assistant Secretary for Planning and Analysis, "Data on Veterans of the Korean War," June 2000. http://www.va.gov/Vetdata/docs/SpecialReports/KW2000.pdf.

31. Sen. Styles Bridges (R-N.H.), CR, 82nd Cong., 2nd sess., vol. 98:7, 8412–13.

32. Ibid.

33. Sen. Robert Taft (R-Ohio), CR, 82nd Cong., 1st sess., vol. 97:4, 5179.

34. Rep. Thomas Abernethy (D-Miss.), CR, 82nd Cong., 2nd sess., vol. 98:5, 6388.

35. "Truman Requests Free G.I. Insurance," *New York Times*, 16 January 1951, 25.

36. Benjamin Fine, "Education in Review," *New York Times*, 4 February 1951, 131; and 25 May 1952, E9.

37. Very aware of the problem of military retention, legislators often tried to balance their desire to reward Korean veterans with the military's need to retain experienced troops. Introducing a bill to provide unemployment compensation to Korean War veterans, Rep. Franklin D. Roosevelt Jr. (D-N.Y.) advocated a waiting period so as to not interfere with reenlistment. Franklin D. Roosevelt Jr., "Appendix to the CR," 82nd Cong., 2nd sess., vol. 98:9, A1966-A1968.

38. Quoted in Olson, *G.I. Bill*, 106.

39. "A Nation of Veterans," *New York Times*, 24 April 1956, 30.

40. President Harry S. Truman, CR, 81st Cong., 2nd sess., vol. 96:12, 16242; and Public Law 81–894, United States Statutes at Large, 81st Cong., 2nd sess., vol. 64:1 (Washington, D.C.: U.S. Government Printing Office, 1952), 1121.

41. Sen. Joseph Hill (D-Ala.), CR, 82nd Cong., 2nd sess., vol. 98:7, 8413.

42. "Veterans' Readjustment Assistance Act of 1952," Public Law 82–550, United States Statutes at Large, 82nd Cong., 2nd sess., vol. 66 (Washington, D.C.: U.S. Government Printing Office, 1953), 663. A few legislators did question the idea of allowing men with other than honorable discharges to benefit from the G.I. Bill, but neither the Senate nor the House pursued the matter. Also, because the war in Korea had not ended before Public Law 550 passed, the Korean G.I. Bill had no terminal date. Perhaps responding to complaints after 1953 that "while the shooting war has been over for a long time in Korea, we are still making 'Veterans,' with full wartime rates of compensation, educational and loan benefits, etc. at the rate of 23,000 or more per month," President Eisenhower issued Proclamation 3080 on 1 January 1955 to fix the Korean G.I. Bill's terminal date as 31 January 1955. See N. S. Hathaway to Rep. Edith Nourse Rogers (R-Mass.), 19 July 1954, Record Group (hereafter, RG) 233, Box 2022, National Archives (hereafter, NARA); and President Eisenhower, "Fixing Terminal Date Respecting Service in the United States Armed Forces Entitling Persons to Certain Veterans' Benefits and Services, Preferences, and Other Assistance," 1 January 1955, United

States Statutes at Large, 84th Cong., 1st sess., vol. 69 (Washington, D.C.: U.S. Government Printing Office, 1955), c17.

43. "Legion to Demand G.I. Bill Extension," *New York Times*, 20 January 1952, 13.

44. "Sponsors Abandon G.I. Rights in Korea," *New York Times*, 5 September 1950, 12.

45. Throughout the late 1940s and early 1950s a number of scandals broke concerning the 1944 G.I. Bill. Congress furtively passed amendments in an attempt to curb the abuse. For examples of newspaper accounts of incidents of graft, see "Trade School Closes," *New York Times*, 17 August 1950, 25; "Beauty School Fraud," *New York Times*, 13 January 1951, 1; "13 Veterans Arrested," *New York Times*, 3 August 1951, 22; "Colleges Accused of Treasury Raids," *New York Times*, 21 February 1952, 4; "Widespread Graft in G.I. Housing Seen by Congress Group," *New York Times*, 31 August 1952, 1; and Sidney Shalett, "How Our Tax Dollars Are Wasted," *Saturday Evening Post* 224 (24 May 1952), 12.

46. "Colleges Accused of Treasury Raids," *New York Times*, 21 February 1952, 4; and Shalett, "How Our Tax Dollars Are Wasted," 12.

47. For examples of congressional efforts to clean up the problems of the G.I. Bill, see "School Aid Voted in 'Distress' Areas," *New York Times*, 14 July 1950, 20; "New G.I. Bill Study Rule," *New York Times*, 9 October 1950, 26; "Appendix to the CR," 81st Cong., 2nd sess., vol. 96:18, A7995 and A8002; and Rep. Olin Teague (D-Tex.), CR, 81st Cong., 2nd sess., vol. 96:5, 6921.

48. President Harry S. Truman quoted in "Truman Lists Program for Service Men; Asks Readjusted Aid for Korea Veterans," *New York Times*, 22 January 1952, 21.

49. Carl Esco Obermann, *A History of Vocational Rehabilitation in America* (Minneapolis: T. S. Denison and Company, 1965), 201.

50. John D. Morris, "House Group Finds G.I. Training Graft," *New York Times*, 10 February 1952, 29. See also "Audit of G.I. Bill," *New York Times*, 29 July 1951, 112 in which the Teague Committee estimated that one of every seven hundred dollars spent on the program had been used inappropriately.

51. Rep. Olin Teague (D-Tex.), CR, 81st Cong., 2nd sess., vol. 96:5, 6921; "G.I. Bill Sponsors Ask Drastic Curbs," *New York Times*, 31 December 1951, 6; Morris, "House Group Finds G.I. Training Graft," 29; "Colleges Accused of Treasury Raids," 4; "Widespread Graft in G.I. Housing Seen by Congress Group," *New York Times*, 31 August 1952, 1; "School Aid Favored For Korea Veterans," *New York Times*, 25 December 1950, 3; and "Housing Study Set Under the G.I. Bill," *New York Times*, 14 February 1952, 44.

52. "G.I. Bill Sponsors Ask Drastic Curbs," *New York Times*, 31 December 1951, 6. The Teague Committee made many suggestions. See Morris, "House Group Finds G.I. Training Graft," 29. Teague actually authored a bill based on the special committee's findings. For its provisions, see CR, 82nd Cong., 2nd sess., vol. 98:5, 6376–77.

53. See Congress, House, "Readjustment Benefits: General Survey and Appraisal," 149. See also Rep. Alvin O'Konski (R-Wis.), CR, 82nd Cong., 2nd sess., vol. 98:5, 6391.

54. Contemporary evidence suggests that schools did in fact raise their tuition and fees and pad costs in order to get as much of the G.I.s' tuition allotment as possible. Between 1941 and 1950, tuition rates nearly doubled. Benjamin Fine, "Colleges Disclose Enrollment Loss," *New York Times*, 27 November 1950, 1; "College Rolls Drop 250,000 as Financial Worries Mount," *New York Times*, 24 September 1951, 1; "Colleges Accused of Treasury Raids," *New York Times*, 21 February 1952, 4; and Shalett, "How Our Tax Dollars are Wasted," 12. Even so, many in higher education supported the direct-pay method as well as reduced funding for Korean veterans. They believed many World War II veterans enrolled in school for the sole

purpose of collecting subsistence payments and that requiring Korean veterans to pay part of their way through would weed out those G.I.s not truly interested in earning degrees. Olson, *G.I. Bill*, 106–11.

55. See CR, 82nd Cong., 2nd sess., vol. 98:5, 6366–98; and Benjamin Fine, "Education in Review," *New York Times*, 25 May 1952, E9.

56. "Vote on G.I. Bill Put Off," *New York Times*, 3 June 1952, 3; John D. Morris, "Dispute on Tuition Snags New G.I. Bill," *New York Times*, 28 May 1952, 4; "Korean G.I. Bill Action," *New York Times*, 29 May 1952, 2. Specifically, the committee wanted to prevent of the 52–20 Club as Rep. Edith Nourse Rogers and others wanted. "Veterans Bill Gains," *New York Times*, 27 May 1952, 29.

57. Rep. Laurie Battle (D-Ala.), CR, 82nd Cong., 2nd sess., vol. 98:5, 6391.

58. Rep. Olin Teague (D-Tex.), "Appendix to the CR," 82nd Cong., 2nd sess., vol. 98:11, A3900–3905.

59. Rep. William Springer (R-Ill.), CR, 82nd Cong., 2nd sess., vol. 98:5, 6268.

60. Rep. Olin Teague (D-Tex.), "Appendix to the CR," 82nd Cong., 2nd sess., vol. 98:10, A3231-A3232; and CR, 82nd Cong., 2nd sess., vol. 98:5, 6268–71.

61. CR, 82nd Cong., 2nd sess., vol. 98:5, 6270.

62. Ibid., 6271.

63. Only James P. S. Devereux (R-Md.) voted against the bill, citing disagreement with the decision to suspend the rules. Adam C. Powell Jr. of New York and William L. Dawson of Illinois voted "present" rather than yea or nay in protest of the 25 percent nonveteran enrollment, which they believed would discriminate against black colleges in the South. Notably, Springer voted for the bill. C. P. Trussell, "New G.I. Rights Bill Is Passed by House," *New York Times*, 6 June 1952, 1; and CR, 82nd Cong., 2nd sess., vol. 98:5, 6642.

64. "G.I. Korea Bill Gains," *New York Times*, 25 June 1952, 2. In the Senate, many supported the Nixon Amendment, legislation roughly comparable to the House's Springer Amendment. As he had responded earlier during House debates, Rep. Olin Teague (D-Tex.) came out strong against paying tuition to schools and urged the direct-pay method. Teague, "Appendix to the CR," 82nd Cong., 2nd sess., vol. 98:11, A4298-A4300.

65. Sen. Joseph Hill (D-Ala.), CR, 82nd Cong., 2nd sess., vol. 98:7, 8421. Hill was actually arguing against the idea that unemployment for veterans would lead to the federalization of unemployment benefits in general.

66. Sen. Joseph Hill (D-Ala.), CR, 82nd Cong., 2nd sess., vol. 98:7, 8417.

67. Ibid., 8414.

68. CR, 82nd Cong., 2nd sess., vol. 98:7, 9387.

69. Rep. Hubert Scudder (R-Calif.), CR, 82nd Cong., 2nd sess., vol. 98:7, 9402.

70. Rep. Noah Mason (R-Ill.), Rep. William Springer (R-Ill.), and Rep. Alvin O'Konski (R-Wis.), CR, 82nd Cong., 2nd sess., vol. 98:7, 9398 and 9400–9401.

71. Rep. John Vorys (R-Ohio) in ibid., 9402.

72. Rep. Alvin O'Konski (R-Wis.) in ibid., 9401. Also, Harold B. Hinton, "Congress Rushing to Meet Deadline," *New York Times*, 4 July 1952, 3; Harold B. Hinton, "New G.I. Bill Voted as Congress Works to Adjourn Today," *New York Times*, 5 July 1952, 1; and "New Veteran Bill Signed by Truman," *New York Times*, 17 July 1952, 2.

73. Rep. Harold Donohue (D-Mass.), CR, 82nd Cong., 2nd sess., vol. 98:7, 9405.

74. "College Has G.I. Rate," *New York Times*, 19 July 1952, 15; and Benjamin Fine, "Education in Review," *New York Times*, 27 July 1952, E9.

75. "Dixie Schools to Aid Vets," *Chicago Defender*, 20 September 1952; Paul P. Kennedy,

"Korea G.I.'s Slow in Taking Benefits," *New York Times*, 30 August 1953, 8; "Korean Veterans Due for Benefits," *New York Times*, 9 November 1952, 5; and "Veterans' Aid Extended: Snags in Tuition Pay Removed Korean G.I. Bill," *New York Times*, 14 November 1952, 29.

76. In the fall of 1953 about 44.2 percent of nonveterans enrolled in private schools in comparison to 40.1 percent of veteran students. "Preliminary Data on Enrollment of 'Korean Veterans' and Male Non Veteran Students: Fall 1953," RG 233, Box 2022, NARA. Perhaps a more interesting comparison is that World War II veterans attended private schools at a rate of 50 percent, slightly higher than the general population's 49%, but that only 33 percent of Korean veterans overall attended private schools in comparison to 42 percent of their nonveteran peers. Rashkow, *G.I. Bill*, CRS 8–CRS 9.

77. Charles E. Bennett to House Committee on Veterans' Affairs, 4 December 1952, RG 233, Box 2022, NARA.

78. Trezzvant W. Anderson, editor *Pittsburgh Courier*, to Colonel Karl Standish, chief clerk, Committee on Veterans' Affairs, House, 5 March 1953; Roy Willis to Sen. Charles E. Bennett, 26 March 1953; Nathan B. Spiro, trade school director, to Rep. Edith Nourse Rogers, 16 July 1954; and Carl H. Bowman to Sen. Albert Gore, 5 June 1954, RG 233, Box 2022, NARA.

79. Chancellor William P. Tolley of Syracuse University in Benjamin Fine, "Educators Back Korean Veterans," *New York Times*, 15 January 1954, 2; and "For Korean Veterans," *New York Times*, 16 January 1954, 14.

80. C. P. Trussell, "Bill Extends Aid for G.I. Schooling, *New York Times*, 28 January 1955, 7.

81. George Gallup Jr., *The Gallup Poll: Public Opinion 2000* (Wilmington, DE: Scholarly Resources, Inc., 2000), 194.

82. Congress, House, "Readjustment Benefits: General Survey and Appraisal," 150–54.

83. Fisher, *Comparative Analysis*, 32; Kolb, "Korea's 'Invisible Veterans,'" 30; and Congress, House, "Readjustment Benefits: General Survey and Appraisal," 76–82.

84. Benjamin Fine, "Education in Review," *New York Times*, 24 October 1954, E9; and Congress, House, "Readjustment Benefits: General Survey and Appraisal," 161–72.

85. Al Avisato Jr. to Senators from the State of Florida, 7 January 1954, "Appendix to the CR," 83nd Cong., 2nd sess., vol. 100, A 69.

86. Congress, House, "Readjustment Benefits: General Survey and Appraisal," 157–58.

# 10

## A Price on Patriotism

### The Politics and Unintended Consequences of the 1966 G.I. Bill

MARK BOULTON

In November 1974 author and Vietnam veteran Tim O'Brien wrote an article published in *Penthouse Magazine* titled "The G.I. Bill: Less than Enough." O'Brien summed up the frustrations of a generation of returning service members when he wrote, "their complaints are simple: the 'system' has either ignored or screwed them; the 'bureaucracy' is a hopeless tangle; *they have gone largely unrewarded for their service.*" Specifically, O'Brien disparaged the Vietnam-era G.I. bills for failing to offer the same kind of support offered to World War II veterans. The much-lauded 1944 G.I. Bill had provided World War II veterans with generous education benefits along with a whole slew of other provisions which greatly eased their transition back to civilian life. Vietnam veterans could well have expected to receive similar rewards for their sacrifice. The 1966 G.I. Bill, however, and the subsequent 1972 and 1974 G.I. bills, fell quite short of the Vietnam veterans' expectations and needs. O'Brien quoted one veteran, Forrest (Rusty) Lindley, who slammed the government for offering "old familiar promises" of support only to fail to back them up with positive actions. "For millions of Vietnam vets," claimed Lindley, "the present GI Bill benefits just aren't as good as those our fathers got thirty years ago."[1]

By the time O'Brien wrote his article, criticism of the Vietnam-era G.I. bills had been mounting in the press and within the veteran community. The veterans' complaints focused almost exclusively on the parsimony of the 1966 bill's educational allowances. Veterans attending one Texas community college wrote House Speaker Carl Albert to complain, "We need either increased wages or increased benefits for the services we rendered to our country. In these times of economic adjustment, we have discovered that gainful employment is extremely difficult, if not impossible to obtain."[2] Another veteran wrote Albert, "I am a Vietnam veteran . . . with combat experience. I had to endure a great deal of suffering and all I wish now is to have a fair reimbursement from the government for my education."[3] Others complained to the Speaker of their "considerable difficulty meeting the cost of going to college," or that "the G.I. Bill has been a great help and has enabled us to attend college at night, [but] it is still not enough to live on with the high cost of living."[4]

Tales of veterans' economic hardship mounted in the press. The *Washington Post* carried news of a "Veterans Rights March" in the D.C. area where veterans carried banners with slogans such as "We Demand Decent Living Income for GIs, Vets, and Their Families."[5] Joseph Mulholland, associate dean at Fordham University wrote the *New York Times* to argue that "the disproportionate majority of the deprived and disadvantaged, both black and white, who have fought in Indochina receive stingy handouts; they deserve . . . generous benefits."[6]

Another *New York Times* article contained the testimony from one Air Force veteran who stated, "You want to know what I think of the benefits? I think they stink, man. For the kind of church change they pay you in the service they ought to give you enough for an education when you get out."[7] Frank V. Otto, director of New York State Division of Veterans affairs, used the G.I. Bill after World War II. His G.I. Bill paid his full tuition at Columbia State and gave him sufficient money to live off every month. Surveying the plight of the Vietnam-era veterans his agency administered, Otto told the *New York Times* that "there's no way a vet can go to college on the G.I. Bill today, unless he's got some money of his own."[8] Similarly, John Reavis, assistant dean of the University of New York pointed out, "In 1945, the returning veteran could sustain himself and his family on the G.I. Bill. Today, the cost is astronomical."[9]

The story of the 1966 G.I. Bill is in some ways directly inverse to that of the 1944 G.I. Bill. The original G.I. Bill sits atop the "Good War/Greatest Generation" narrative of World War II. In popular memory, and in the works of historians since, the 1944 bill is revered as a fitting tribute from a grateful public to the nation's warriors who had gallantly set off to fight the dark forces of European fascism and Japanese militarism.[10] By contrast, the Vietnam G.I. bills provided scant reward for soldiers sent to fight in a cause that many American people—and some of the soldiers themselves—had come to question by the early 1970s. The Vietnam War had become "The Bad War," and the soldiers who fought in it were becoming a neglected generation. Numerous books have been devoted to how the Vietnam War became such a national nightmare for the United States. Countless pages have been written to explain the incremental steps taken in the United States' excruciating slide into full involvement in Vietnam and the problems faced on the battlefield leading to the ultimate failure of America's mission in South Vietnam. But the failure of the government to provide the benefits to support the troops it had sent into battle remains understudied.[11] What had gone wrong? Why had the dizzying precedents set by the 1944 bill not been followed? Why was the next generation of warriors not given the same opportunities as their illustrious forbears?

The inadequacies of the Vietnam-era G.I. bills can be attributed to the political battles and unintended consequences of the first piece of legislation, the 1966 G.I. Bill. The insufficient provisions of the bill resulted from a contest between some of the dominant political ideologies of the mid-twentieth century: fiscal conservatism, liberal universalism, and the civic religion of American individualism. Indeed, at the heart of the political debates lay questions about the very nature of American citizenship. Specifically, lawmakers clashed over how much the government owed its citizens for military service—in effect, putting a price on patriotism.

The parsimonious nature of the 1966 bill was dictated in large part by long-standing views of noncombat veterans. Since the founding of the United States, the federal government had argued that veterans who never faced enemy fire or suffered the burden of disability had not earned the right for generous postservice benefits—by serving in the military, they were merely performing what should be considered a natural obligation of democratic citizenship. By declaring peacetime nondisabled veterans unworthy of liberal benefits, the government had long set the precedent that military service was not something requiring recompense but was, instead, an inherent part of living in a participatory democracy. The debates over veterans' benefits in the postwar era challenged this position; they were further complicated by political contests over the expansion of the welfare state during the mid-twentieth century. In his book *The Price of Citizenship*, Michael B. Katz argues that two of the central questions that "lie at the heart of modern debates about the welfare state" are, "What distinguishes those who merit help? . . . [and] What are the limits of social obligation—what do we owe one another?"[12] Such questions ought not have affected Vietnam veterans except for one crucial fact: The 1966 G.I. Bill offered *all veterans*—combat or peacetime—the same benefits, irrespective of whether they served in a war zone, such as Vietnam, or drove a truck in Georgia for their entire military career. The Cold War did not remain cold for every American soldier, and yet those veterans facing fire in global hot spots fell under the same umbrella as those who never stared down a communist foe. By casting such a wide net and incorporating all veterans, the bill failed to provide the appropriate support to those soldiers on the front lines of America's Cold War crusade. Thus, the seeds of the government's neglect of Vietnam veterans were sewn in the 1966 legislation.

The failure to distinguish between the different levels of sacrifice and the different needs of Vietnam conflict veterans (the three million who served in Southeast Asia) and Vietnam-era veterans (some eight million at home or scattered elsewhere across the globe) was among the biggest flaws of the Vietnam-era G.I. bills. Because the 1966 bill did not specifically target the needs and expectations of returning combat veterans, the benefits were not as generous as the 1944 G.I. Bill had been for World War II veterans. Because the 1966 bill covered so many veterans when the nation was not officially at war, the benefits remained low. Consequently, Vietnam combat veterans discovered that their G.I. Bill did not afford them the same quality of education enjoyed by their predecessors. The result was a legacy of bitter resentment and hostility among many combat veterans who believed that the government had neglected their needs. This chapter explores how the framing of the 1966 G.I. Bill due to political compromise and the contests over the obligations of citizenship resulted in a diminished G.I. Bill for veterans of the Vietnam conflict.

Debates over citizenship and veterans' benefits go back to the very founding of the nation. In the aftermath of the American Revolution, Thomas Jefferson opposed the payment of liberal veterans' benefits to those soldiers not injured by their military service, believing that the citizen-soldiers of the virtuous young republic needed no recompense for performing what should be a necessary burden of citizenship.[13] Moreover, some feared that the creation of special privileges for veterans would set them apart from the rest of society and thus undermine the democratic intent of the Revolution. As late as 1818, when Congress debated the passage of the Revolutionary War Pensions act, North Carolina senator Nathaniel Macon warned that offering pensions to those not injured in service was "repugnant to the principles of our Government, and at war with good sense and public justice."[14] Ultimately, the military demands of the War of 1812, combined with widespread press reporting of veterans' hardship overrode such objections, and in 1818 Revolutionary War veterans eventually became the first recipients of a large-scale federal pension program in the United States.[15] Although federal benefits grew more generous thereafter, the issue of veterans' benefits and civic duty resurfaced during and after the nation's wars. The GI Bill of 1944 became the most celebrated and successful reconciliation of these competing visions.[16]

The 1944 Servicemen's Readjustment Act, or G.I. Bill of Rights, made World War II veterans among the most rewarded of any sent into the field. The 1944 bill offered veterans education benefits, home loans, unemployment insurance, and farm and business loans. Yet, compared with previous and future debates over veteran benefits, arguments over the 1944 bill were relatively muted. By placing training and education at the center of the veterans' readjustment needs—instead of a simple cash bonus or an open-ended commitment to a future pension—legislators headed off the charge that veterans would be transformed into a privileged social class. Opponents of government welfare could support the concept of giving veterans an opportunity to better themselves rather than a direct handout. There was, of course, a pragmatic element to the 1944 bill as it eased the problem of accommodating nearly sixteen million returning servicemen and women back into the workforce, abating a widely feared depression. After its passage, this generous approach became the standard, and education and training remained the central features of veterans' benefits offered to Korean Conflict veterans (albeit at slightly reduced amounts) in their G.I. Bill of 1951.

When the Korean G.I. Bill expired in 1955, however, the debate over who should be eligible for benefits gained renewed impetus in the government. Questions arose over whether benefits should be offered to veterans who never faced fire nor suffered any disability from service. In particular, President Dwight Eisenhower's views on the nature of government led him to question the ever-expanding slate of benefits and special privileges offered to veterans after World War II. Despite his military background, Eisenhower was no champion of liberal veterans' benefits. Harking back to the republican spirit of Thomas Jefferson, Eisenhower believed that special interest groups such as veterans should set aside their selfish interests for the sake of the common good, aiming for what one biographer describes as a "corporate commonwealth, . . . a harmonious society free of class conflict, selfish acquisitiveness and divisive party politics."[17] In 1955, to determine which veterans should be eligible for benefits and how much they should receive, Eisenhower brought together a presidential commission under the guidance of Omar Bradley, the decorated World War II five-star general and former head of the Veterans Administration.

When they published their report in 1956, the Bradley Commission argued that the government should direct its benefits only to those veterans injured in military service, and should reduce benefits such as pensions offered to able-bodied veterans.[18] Furthermore, the commission stated, "Military service in time of war or peace is an obligation of citizenship and should not be considered inherently a basis of future Government benefits." It also called for restrictions on the eligibility of veterans for future readjustment benefits. Specifically, the commission warned against providing a full slate of benefits for veterans serving during peacetime. Peacetime veterans should continue to receive medical care and limited reemployment assistance, but the commission argued that "military service does not involve sufficient interruption to the educational progress of servicemen to warrant a continuation of a special educational program for them."[19] Cumulatively, these recommendations posited that the government had no obligation to offer benefits to the millions of veterans being pulled away from civilian life during the Cold War. Since those veterans had never faced hostile fire, they were merely performing their civic responsibility to defend the nation's interests when called upon; no reward was owed, nor should one be expected.

The Bradley Report had an immediate impact on debates over veterans' benefits in the government. In the wake of the release of the report, the House Committee on Veterans Affairs narrowly passed a bill (H.R. 7886) that would have increased pensions for World War I veterans, but the Senate killed the measure. Raising the same questions over the cost and need for such legislation asked by the Bradley Report, the Senate refused to act upon the bill before the adjournment of the 84th Congress. Soon after, Eisenhower submitted a proposal to Congress to tie future pension payments to the economic needs of veterans. With some modification, Congress accepted the president's proposals. Under Public Law 86–211, the new pension system took into account such factors as a veteran's annual income, net worth, and spouse's income in determining eligibility and rates. Washington, it appeared, had reached an agreement that all Americans owed their nation military service without to the subsequent opening up of the government's coffers. But this accord would soon face a significant challenge from a new bill introduced by Texas Democratic senator Ralph Yarborough.

In 1959 Yarborough launched a campaign for the passage of a new Cold War G.I. bill that would give education and other benefits to all veterans, whether they served in times of war or peace, since the expiration of the Korea G.I. Bill in January 1955. For Yarborough, this was a crusade. He was an unreconstructed New Deal liberal with a long career of fighting for worthy public causes. He volunteered for service in World War II when his age would have precluded him from the draft. He pushed for civil rights legislation in Texas and was one of the few southern politicians who refused to sign the Southern Manifesto in 1957 that denounced the landmark *Brown v. the Board of Education* Supreme Court ruling. In the 1960s Yarborough continuously fought for the more progressive elements of the Great Society, including Medicare and Medicaid and the numerous social programs of the War on Poverty. Although his liberal idealism would ultimately cost him his Senate career as Texas politics veered to the right in the early 1970s, Yarborough's activism would leave an indelible mark on American politics and society, and on the lives of millions of the nation's veterans.[20]

Yarborough's bill aimed to reward almost four million veterans who served since the Korean conflict but not during a time of declared war. The bill would have provided higher education benefits at a rate of $110 a month, comparable to the benefits given Korean conflict veterans. Yarborough argued that because of the selective nature of the draft, "it becomes a matter of great national concern when some individuals have to carry a grossly disproportionate share of the burden of citizenship."[21] According to Yarborough, the men and women selected for military service were being placed at a great disadvantage relative to nonveterans because of time lost from civilian life, irrespective of whether they served in wartime or were injured in service. The philosophy behind the bill was directly opposite from that espoused by the Bradley Commission. To a large extent, Yarborough's position reflected America's post–World War II global role. The ongoing threat of war created by the Cold War and America's adoption of a "garrison state" mentality meant that the definition of "peacetime" in the 1950s and 1960s was different from what it might have been in the 1930s.[22] But the main point of departure in Yarborough's bill compared with previous veterans' programs was that the recipients would never have to *earn* their benefits by serving in a time of actual war. If successful, Yarborough's bill had the potential to redefine the meaning of military service and of democratic citizenship in America. If every service member could enter the military with the guarantee of future rewards, the potential arose that military service might now be seen as an avenue to economic advancement rather than a part of living in a democracy. Such concerns over the national character remained secondary to Yarborough. He sought only to provide what he considered to be a fair reward to citizens burdened by military service.

The proposed new G.I. Bill lacked the pragmatic element of previous and future benefits packages. The World War II G.I. Bill boosted the postwar economy, while later veterans' benefits packages offered to the all-volunteer force became an essential recruitment tool for the armed forces. But there was little macroeconomic or military motivation behind Yarborough's bill. Indeed, the Bureau of the Budget (BOB), the Department of Defense (DOD), and the Veterans Administration (VA) all argued strongly against the measure. The Bureau of the Budget argued that soldiers received enough compensation through their basic army pay and through the training and skills attained in service to negate the need for further benefits. BOB officials noted that "compared with wartime, the draft has a lesser impact on the disruption of education and career plans."[23] The Department of Defense opposed the bill on the grounds that it might encourage personnel to abandon a long-term military career in order to use education benefits. According to the DOD, "Programs of educational and vocational assistance encourage personnel to leave military service immediately after accruing the maximum benefits which can be gained. This results in a serious handicap to the Armed Forces in their efforts to attract and retain qualified personnel on a career basis."[24] Even the VA opposed Yarborough's peacetime bill. VA administrator John S. Gleason stated that "service under current conditions does not present on a widespread basis the same rigors and hazards as does wartime service; . . . I do not believe these readjustment programs, education, training and loan, are needed at the present time."[25] In the absence of support from such agencies, the main argument in defense of a new G.I. bill rested on the inequity of removing citizens from civilian life for military service. Requiring some citizens to serve under the terms of selective service draft while others avoided such an imposition represented the kind of social injustice that Yarborough had dedicated his public service to combating.

Yarborough fought hard for his bill on the floor of the Senate. He tried immediately to head off the ubiquitous cries that veterans' benefits verged on selective welfarism by noting that the G.I. Bill, with its provision of training benefits, was "typically American" because of its "emphasis on self-help and individual initiative."[26] Samuel James Ervin, Democratic senator from North Carolina, led the opposition to the bill. His arguments emphasized the considerable costs of Yarborough's bill. Claiming to speak on "behalf of a group of Americans who are sometime[s] forgotten, namely the American taxpayers," Ervin warned of the dangers of creating "the greatest debt ever thrust upon posterity by any generation."[27] Despite its obvious costs, the bill passed the Senate by a vote of 57–31 in July 1959. Forty-eight Democrats and only nine Republicans voted for the bill. Reflecting their different economic philosophies, twenty-one of the more fiscally conservative Republicans and ten (mainly southern) Democrats voted against it.

Outside of the Senate, the rest of the government and much of the veteran community seemed unconvinced by Yarborough's arguments. The House Veterans' Affairs Committee, despite extensive hearings, killed his bill by never reporting it out of committee. In his budget message to Congress in January 1960, Eisenhower reiterated his ideological opposition when he proclaimed: "Peacetime ex-servicemen are recognized as being in a different category from wartime veterans because of the different conditions under which they serve. Those who serve in peacetime undergo fewer rigors and hazards than their usual comrades. . . . I oppose the establishment of special educational and loan guarantee programs for peacetime ex-servicemen. Such benefits are not justified because they are not supported by the conditions of military service."[28] Similarly, veterans associations such as the American Legion, Veterans of Foreign Wars, and the Disabled Veterans of America offered lukewarm or no support for Yarborough's bill. They were more concerned with protecting the privileges of veterans who had fought in actual wars, with World War II veterans being their main priority. In 1956 the Legion had drafted a resolution denouncing the Bradley Report as an "abortive monstrosity" for the threat it posed to veterans' pensions.[29] But Yarborough's bill also threatened the Legion's hard-won gains for World War II and Korea veterans by spreading the government's benefits more thinly. Yarborough attempted to resurrect the peacetime G.I. bill on a couple of occasions at the start of the 1960s but was never able to overcome the weight of long-standing objections in the Executive branch, the House, and the government agencies most affected by the bill. As the nation geared up to send its next generation of citizens off to fight in Vietnam, however, his crusade gained renewed impetus.

In January 1965, citing the deteriorating conditions in Vietnam, Yarborough introduced S.9, another Cold War G.I. bill. Patterned after the Korean conflict G.I. bill, the new legislation offered educational and vocational assistance to all of the nation's veterans who had served since January 1955. He took his message to the press, outlining his hope for "a fair deal for the Cold War soldier" in an article for *Harper's Magazine*. In the article, Yarborough called for public support for the new bill as he urged "a great many Americans to demand it—in the name of both justice and common sense."[30]

By the time of Yarborough's new attempt to pass his bill, the White House had a new occupant, fellow progressive Texas Democrat Lyndon Johnson. But despite a similar ideological and political heritage, Johnson remained unmoved by Yarborough's arguments. Johnson's opposition to the bill differed somewhat from his predecessors. Whereas Eisenhower and—to a lesser extent—John F. Kennedy had opposed the bill (the issue of veterans benefits never gathered much momentum during Kennedy's brief presidency) because they deemed the peacetime veteran's sacrifices as unworthy, Johnson believed that *all* citizens—not just veterans—should be eligible for government assistance.[31]

One internal White House memo laid out the administration's main points of opposition to Yarborough's bill. The first objection raised in the memo was that "an expansive program only for ex-servicemen undercuts the strategy of persuading the Congress to ensure full educational advantages for all."[32] The cost of a new G.I. bill threatened the administration's plans for universal education programs such as grants, loans, and work-study programs that would come to fruition under such measures as the Higher Education Act of 1965. As a cornerstone of his Great Society, Johnson hoped to refocus the nation's resources to help those citizens most greatly in need. He did not count peacetime veterans among them. Heavily influenced by the social programs of the New Deal, Johnson wanted his Great Society to provide every citizen a more equitable share of the nation's considerable wealth. His approach to veterans' benefits was central to what Morton Keller has described as his "qualitative liberalism," that is, a dedication to ensuring that all Americans enjoyed the benefits of the nations' economic prosperity.[33] Johnson saw education as integral to achieving this goal. By directing educational aid to those sectors of society most in need, Johnson aimed to give disadvantaged Americans an opportunity to better their lives, irrespective of their social condition. His administration feared that providing education benefits solely for ex–service members might jeopardize more universal education programs that would benefit those with a greater need than the average peacetime veteran.

The second objection raised in the memo clarified this point further: "The G.I. Bill approach is not selective—not according to need, not according to ability, not according to motivation."[34] The original G.I. Bill had unquestionably turned veterans into a privileged class. But the government and the public accepted the provision of such rewards because those veterans had at least served during a time of war. A peacetime bill might upset Johnson's goal of creating a more equal society by unfairly rewarding those veterans whose lives had not been seriously impaired by service. For Johnson many other sectors of society were far more deserving of federal support. In one speech given in Boca Raton, Florida, Johnson highlighted the success of the original G.I. Bill, but only to illustrate the potential of providing universal education benefits. He praised "The proud achievement of the GI bill," but added,

> It doesn't seem to me that you ought to have to go into uniform and go to boot camp, and spend 2 or 3 years in the service in order for your Government to have an interest in your education. . . . I think we just must not rest until each child—GI or no GI, boy or girl, rich or poor—has the opportunity to get the kind of education that he needs and that his country needs for him to have in order to defend it.[35]

As his legislative agenda soon proved, Johnson was not averse to throwing the weight of the government behind those who needed extra assistance, but he remained unconvinced that peacetime service justified such benevolence.

Veterans Affairs administrator William Driver (Gleason's successor after December 1964) shared Johnson's reservations. However, he did at least raise the possibility of extending benefits for those veterans serving "in a period of hostility, or disabled by such service." Paying benefits to those who served during times of war tended to attract little opposition among the public or in political circles. Driver proposed a far less costly G.I. bill than Yarborough's that would extend only to veterans serving in "warlike conditions" such as those developing in Vietnam or the Dominican Republic.[36] He told BOB director Kermit Gordon, "The immediate situation in Viet Nam creates a climate favorable to enactment of legislation. . . . Realistically and equitably, I believe we must afford some additional recognition by way of wanted veterans' benefits to those members of our armed forces serving in such hot spots as Viet Nam."[37] Limiting benefits chronologically and geographically to areas designated by executive order as "hot spots" would greatly reduce the ideological opposition to enacting a new G.I. bill.

By the middle of 1965, as America's commitment to Vietnam deepened, the battle over Yarborough's bill heated up and the positions of all sides hardened. In May Yarborough wrote the White House and made the emotive plea that "those who are guarding freedom for all of us around the world should come home to classrooms, not to unemployment lines and checks." He also appealed to Johnson's political savvy. Claiming that the bill would likely pass both houses when put to a vote, Yarborough informed the president that the Republicans were positioning themselves as "the Party concerned with helping the fighting man." Support of S.9, he suggested, would allow the Democrats to regain the mantle of "friend to the GI."[38] In June he made his most thorough defense of the bill in his final report of the Committee on Labor and Public Welfare on S.9. Yarborough systematically laid out the reasons why Cold War veterans did indeed suffer disadvantages relative to nonveterans and, therefore, deserved additional compensation. He outlined the potential threats around the globe from the Soviet Union, China, Vietnam, and the Dominican Republic as evidence that the definition of "peacetime" in the early 1960s was far different from the "peacetime" conditions of the 1930s. The presence of the peacetime draft, he claimed, demanded that civilians faced significant disruptions in their lives and were denied the opportunities of the nation's "free enterprise, [and] individualistic way of life."[39] Yarborough accepted the point that Cold War service did not involve comparable sacrifice to wartime service; as a result, the benefits he proposed were not as generous as those offered under the previous G.I. Bills.[40] But by highlighting the very real sacrifices made by Cold War veterans in the report, Yarborough had effectively undercut one of the main tenets of opposition to S.9.

Through the summer of 1965, Yarborough's bill developed a lot of momentum on Capitol Hill. In July the Senate took up the measure. Walter Mondale (D-Minn.) opened the debate by relating how the G.I. Bill had helped him continue his education after service in the Korean conflict. He reiterated Yarborough's argument that the country was not really at peace because of Cold War tensions. Next Hiram Leong Fong (R-Hawaii), cosponsor of S.9, stood and made a statement that challenged the assumption that excessive veterans' benefits might undermine the moral fabric of the republic when he lauded the Cold War G.I.s as "the Minute Men of our times. . . . Every American," proclaimed Fong, "owes a duty to serve his country, but we as Members of Congress know that there is a corresponding responsibility on our part to take care of them."[41]

But following the obligatory patriotic sentiments from cosponsors of the bill, the debate turned more confrontational as several senators attempted to add amendments that would have changed the nature and philosophy of Yarborough's bill. Massachusetts Republican Leverett Saltonstall introduced the most hotly debated amendment, which attempted to limit eligibility for the benefits to only veterans of hot spots or war zones (similar to the VA's proposal). Strom Thurmond spoke up in defense of this measure. He questioned the justice of offering comparable benefits to those who had never faced fire and raised doubts over whether such military service warranted the kinds of rewards being suggested. According to Thurmond, "It is an honor for a man to serve his country in peace or in war. I do not look upon one who serves in peacetime as having his life jeopardized to the extent that his country owes him the same kind of consideration given to veterans of World War II or the Korean conflict."[42] Here again Thurmond resurrected the argument that military service was more of an honor and a democratic obligation than a burden on American citizens. Yarborough and Robert Kennedy (D-N.Y.) launched strongly worded attacks against this proposal and managed to secure its rejection.

In retrospect, Saltonstall's proposal had great merit and would have alleviated many of the readjustment hardships Vietnam veterans would soon face. If Congress had decided to enact a "hot spots" G.I. bill, those veterans who had suffered the heaviest of America's Cold War burdens might have received benefits commensurate with their sacrifice. But Yarborough and his supporters were determined to make sure that all veterans would receive some reward for service. Lacking a forceful advocate for their specific needs, the nation's combat veterans received little separate consideration.

On 19 July 1965, S.9 passed the Senate by a vote of 69–17. Yarborough had done his part, but this was not the first time a Cold War G.I. Bill had left the Senate. Indeed, both the Johnson administration and the House would have to drop their previous opposition if the bill was to become law.[43]

Lyndon Johnson refused to make a strong public stand on the veterans' benefits issue. Instead, "to rack up alternatives," he established an "informal and quiet working group" composed of the agencies most affected by the bill, such as the VA, DOD, and BOB.[44] Their proposed bill limited eligibility to veterans serving in hostile areas.[45] In a cost-saving measure that clearly pleased the Bureau of the Budget, eligibility for benefits would be extended only as far back as 1 October 1963. This date would have left all of the veterans who had served between 31 January 1955 and 1 October 1963 with no recourse to benefits. While the administration refined its plans, the House had also begun to move, albeit rather slowly.

House deliberations were heavily influenced by a third eminent Texas Democrat. In 1960 Olin Teague's House Veterans Affairs Committee killed a previous attempt at a Senate-passed G.I. bill, and he seemed in no rush to pass the newer version in the fall of 1965. The delay resulted in part from Teague's determination to stamp his authority on the proceedings.[46] Teague had a reputation of being "Mr. Veteran" on the Hill since making his name in a House investigation of abuses of the original G.I. Bill, and he exerted considerable sway on veterans' affairs. Indeed, two of the alternative veteran benefits bills in front of his committee came from Teague himself. The White House was aware of Teague's ego. BOB's Charles Schultze warned, "He would like the ball himself. He would just as soon have the Administration make only general statements about this and let his committee work the bill."[47] The problem for the administration was that Teague seemed to be favoring a more expensive bill along the lines of Yarborough's S.9. He had already expressed to the White House his desire to add a provision to the VA's bill to give readjustment benefits to all veterans irrespective of when and where they served.[48] At the end of 1965 Teague visited Vietnam and declared that the peacetime G.I. bill was one of the most important issues raised by the soldiers. Upon his return, he promised that his committee would pass a new G.I. bill "out of committee in January or February." He also claimed to be under "heavy pressure" from BOB and DOD to pass a scaled-down benefits package. He publicly countered DOD's suggestion that a new bill might dissuade career military personnel by claiming that "the bill ought to entice more men into military ranks."[49]

Teague's compromise bill, H.R.12410, reflected his preference for benefits that covered all veterans, but he shared the administration's concerns over the cost of Yarborough's bill. Teague had landed at Normandy with Allied forces in 1944 and was among the most decorated former service members in Congress. His family had suffered considerably during the Great Depression, forcing Teague to pull himself out of poverty through hard work and thrift. The conservative values he internalized from such experiences conditioned the decisions he made during his public career.[50] Although he empathized with the plight of veterans—and invariably supported benefit increases for disabled veterans—Teague sought to place limitations on the government's obligation to able-bodied veterans. His position typified the southern conservative opposition to the expanding welfare state under Johnson's Great Society. For Teague, giving handouts to veterans or any others who had not truly *earned* them ran antithetical to the nation's long-cherished values of self-reliance and individualism. As early as 1953, he outlined his views on veterans' benefits when he wrote,

we can . . . see that those who cannot care for themselves are cared for as long as they shall live.

In addition, I believe that our country owes something to other men and women who were in the service because they were ordered here or there without regard to any of their desires, and certainly their economic situation was not as good as those who saw no service. I do not believe we owe them a world with a fence around it just because they wore a uniform, but surely we can give them some help when they are down and out.[51]

Teague's bill reflected his desire to offer "some help" but stopped well short of generosity. By scaling back the level of benefits offered to only $100 a month and tightening the terms of eligibility, his bill would cost approximately $327 million in its first year compared with $360 million for S.9. Conversely, Johnson's "hot spots" bill would have cost only $150 million for the first year.[52] Teague's bill satisfied neither Yarborough nor the White House, but because it trod the middle ground, many on the Hill viewed it as the best way to reach a compromise.

When Teague's bill went to a vote in the House, a succession of representatives rose in support of the measure. Paul Fino (R-N.Y.) called the bill "a tribute to our veterans, not a grudging concession to national opinion."[53] But the praise was far from universal. Some rose to express their reservations over the low monthly education allowance. Robert Dole (R-Kan.) called the bill "not completely satisfactory."[54] Philip Burton (D-Calif.) spoke for many when he said, "Although I will support it, my one objection to the bill is that it does not go far enough. However, half a loaf is better than none."[55] Despite their reservations, the House passed the bill by a vote of 388–0. In the Senate, Yarborough introduced the House-amended version of his bill and called on his fellow Senators to vote it into law. He did express his disappointment at the "insufficient" benefits but conceded that the reductions were "not yet seriously crippling to the goal of providing a full program of educational and other readjustment benefits."[56] With the a new generation of veterans awaiting some sort of resolution and with the weight of arguments in favor of some kind of new legislation, the compromise bill passed the Senate by a vote of 99–0.

Following the passage of the bill in Congress, the administration moved quickly to distance itself from its earlier opposition. Johnson had hoped for a reduced benefits package, but he appeared to have little enthusiasm to carry the fight any further with a veto. No president had ever vetoed veterans' education benefits legislation, and none would until Gerald Ford in 1974.[57] White House staff members informed Johnson, "Despite its obvious disadvantages, you will want to associate yourself fully with the benefits that will flow from this bill."[58] Therefore, in an effort to garner the political capital that tends to accrue from a pro-veteran stance, Johnson signed the 1966 Cold War G.I. Bill into law on

3 March in a public ceremony in the East Room of the White House. Yarborough and Teague were joined at the ceremony by Secretary of Defense Robert McNamara, Secretary of State Dean Rusk, Vice President Hubert Humphrey, and Gen. William Westmoreland. In his official remarks, Johnson stated, "Because it is for education, I am going to sign this bill, even though it provides hundreds of millions of dollars more than I thought it advisable to recommend or to ask for this year."[59] With the accompanying stroke of a pen, Yarborough's crusade had reached a moderately successful conclusion.

The 1966 Cold War G.I. Bill, Public Law 89–358, ensured that nearly four million veterans who had had their lives interrupted by military service since the end of the Korean conflict could claim benefits to help them further their education or career objectives. For the first time in the nation's history a veteran who had never served in a time of war or suffered perceptible injury from military service could expect rewards from the government. The bill overrode the objections of generations of presidents and politicians concerned with the economic effects on the nation and the moral implications for the nation's soldiers. Although far from generous for combat veterans, the 1966 bill created and greatly expanded the federal benefits system in the United States. Millions of veterans and their dependents could now have access to education, health care, and a host of other benefits without the expectation of having to serve during a time of war.

The 1966 bill created the potential that military service would become less a matter of civic duty and more of a negotiated economic relationship between the citizen and the state. Thereafter, civilians would no longer enter military service without a heightened expectation of some future recompense. After the United States moved toward an all-volunteer force in 1973, benefits became an essential part of the military's attempts to attract new recruits. Since 1973 large majorities of enlistees frequently cite the government's provision of postservice benefits as the primary reason for entering the military.[60] Indeed, opponents of the 1966 G.I. Bill had continued to argue that military service was something for which every citizen should be held accountable and should be a matter of civic pride, and the fear of a more mercenary attitude among servicemen and women died hard. In 1968 the *New York Times* called the concept of peacetime benefits "retrograde in its philosophy" and warned of the "creation of a permanent privileged class of veterans, a postwar mercenary class uncongenial to the national heritage . . . [that would] aggrandize and solidify the specialized status of the veteran and the concept of veteran versus citizen."[61] With the new legislation, citizens entering the military might ask a little less what they could do for their country and expect a little more what their country would do for them.

The 1966 G.I. Bill endured a protracted and contentious gestation. At the heart of the political battles lay questions over whether veterans had earned the right for benefits if they had not fought in a time of war or been injured as a result of service. It took the efforts of one of the most progressive politicians of the 1960s, Ralph Yarborough, combined with the military exigencies of the Cold War to break down the long-standing opposition to peacetime veterans' benefits. Unfortunately, the legislation had tragic unintended consequences. For those veterans who did not face peacetime conditions—particularly those who fought in Southeast Asia—the bill proved scant reward for their sacrifice. The problem was particularly acute for disadvantaged minorities and the underprivileged, who had little additional income to compensate for the benefits' shortcomings.[62] Later attempts to raise the benefits offered to Vietnam veterans offered some relief. A new G.I. bill passed in 1972, which raised the monthly education allowance to $220 a month, and the 1974 G.I. Bill raised it to $340 a month. Yet, even with these increases, neither bill reached the same generous heights as the original 1944 version.[63] Ironically, a far greater percentage of Vietnam veterans used their G.I. Bill education benefits (72 percent) than World War II veterans (51 percent) or Korean Conflict veterans (43 percent). The government poured more than $38.5 billion into higher education under the Vietnam-era bills, almost two-and-a-half times the cost of the World War II G.I. Bill.[64] What these numbers fail to reveal are the problems that many veterans faced trying to pay their way through school. Most recipients of G.I. bill benefits had to supplement their income through additional employment or family support. The veterans clearly had the desire to improve their lives through education, but the government was unwilling to underwrite the costs in the same way they had for World War II veterans. The cause of this shortfall was not a failure of limited imagination. Rather, it was the government's decision to provide such an inclusive, wide-ranging G.I. Bill in 1966.

## Notes

1. Tim O'Brien, "The G.I. Bill: Less than Enough," *Penthouse Magazine* 6, no. 3 (November 1974). Emphasis added.

2. Letter to Carl Albert from the Veterans Club, Tarrant County Junior College, Fort Worth, Texas, Undated (Albert's reply is dated 1 March 1972), Folder 6, Box 142, Carl Albert Legislative Files, Carl Albert Center.

3. Letter to Carl Albert from Michael W. Dubrick, 28 April 1972, Folder 6, Box 142, Carl Albert Legislative Files, Carl Albert Center.

4. Quoted from numerous letters to Carl Albert, Folder 6, Box 142, Carl Albert Legislative Files, Carl Albert Center.

5. "Vietnam Veterans Protest Benefit Cut with Parade, Rally," *Washington Post*, 20 May 1973, B4.

6. Letter to the editor, *New York Times*, 1 June 1972, 42.

7. "Most Veterans of Vietnam Fail to Seek Aid Under the G.I. Bill," *New York Times*, 9 April 1972, 46.

8. Ibid.

9. "Vietnam Veterans in Area Failing to Utilize G.I. Bill," *New York Times*, 4 November 1973, 1.

10. Examples include Katherine Frydl, *The G.I. Bill* (New York: Cambridge University Press, 2009); Glenn Altschuler and Stuart Blumin, *The G.I. Bill: The New Deal for Veterans* (New York: Oxford University Press, 2009); Jennifer Keane, *Doughboys, the Great War and the Remaking of America* (Baltimore: Johns Hopkins University Press, 2001); Keith Olson, *The G.I. Bill, the Veterans, and the Colleges* (Lexington: University Press of Kentucky, 1974); and David B. Ross, *Preparing for Ulysses: Politics and Veterans During World War II* (New York: Columbia University Press, 1969). The bill has received more sanguine analysis in Michael J. Bennett, *When Dreams Came True: The G.I. Bill and the Making of Modern America* (New York: Brassey's Inc., 1996); and Milton Greenberg, *The G.I. Bill: The Law That Changed America* (New York: Lickle Publishing, 1997). Suzanne Mettler's *Soldiers to Citizens: The G.I. Bill and the Making of the Greatest Generation* (New York: Oxford University Press, 2005) and Mettler, "The Creation of the G.I. Bill of Rights of 1944: Melding Social and Participatory Citizenship Ideals," *Journal of Policy History* 17, no. 4 (2006): 345–74, offer long-overdue substantive analysis of the social impact of the 1944 G.I. Bill.

11. Other than several unpublished dissertations written in the early 1970s and a handful of articles, Sar A. Levitan and Joyce Zickler's brief *Swords into Ploughshares: Our G.I. Bill* (Salt Lake City: Olympus Publishing Company, 1973) is the only book to discuss post–World War II veterans benefits. For a more complete analysis of Vietnam-era veterans' benefits, see Mark Boulton, "A Price on Freedom: The Problems and Promise of the Vietnam Era G.I. Bills" (PhD diss, University of Tennessee, Knoxville, 2005).

12. Michael B. Katz, *The Price of Citizenship: Redefining the American Welfare State* (New York: Metropolitan Books, 2001), 341.

13. Jack Resch, *Suffering Soldiers: Revolutionary War Veterans, Moral Sentiment, and Political Culture in the Early Republic* (Amherst: University of Massachusetts Press, 1999).

14. Quoted in ibid., 107.

15. See ibid.

16. See David Bodenger, "Soldier's Bonuses: A History of Veterans Benefits in the United States, 1776–1967" (PhD diss., Pennsylvania State University, 1972).

17. Richard Damms, *The Eisenhower Presidency, 1953–1961* (London: Longman, 2002), 7. For further discussion of Eisenhower's economic and political philosophy, see Eisenhower's memoir, *The White House Years: Mandate for Change, 1953–1956* (New York: Doubleday, 1963), particularly pages 488–89; and Raymond J. Saulnier's "The Philosophy Underlying Eisenhower's Economic Policies" in *Dwight D. Eisenhower: Soldier President, Statesman*, ed. John P. King (New York: Greenwood Press, 1987).

18. *Veterans' Benefits in the United States: A Report to the President by the President's Commission on Veterans' Pensions* (Washington, D.C.: U.S. Government Printing Office, 1956). Hereafter, the Bradley Report.

19. Ibid., 17.

20. Patrick Cox, *Ralph W. Yarborough: The People's Senator* (Austin: University of Texas Press, 2001).

21. 105 Cong. Rec. 13797 (1959).

22. For a discussion of the "garrison state" model, see David R. Segal, *Recruiting for Uncle Sam: Citizenship and Military Manpower* (Lawrence: University Press of Kansas, 1989), 4.

23. Letter from the Bureau of Budget to the Chairman of the Senate Subcommittee on Veterans' Affairs Committee on Labor and Public Welfare, entered into the *Congressional Record* by Strom Thurmond, 108 Cong. Rec. 17524 (1962).

24. Letter from the Department of Defense to the Chairman of the Senate Subcommittee on Veterans' Affairs Committee on Labor and Public Welfare, entered by Strom Thurmond in ibid.

25. Statement of the Administrator of Veterans Affairs before the Subcommittee on Veterans' Affairs Committee on Labor and Public Welfare, United States Senate, 10 April 1963, Folder "The Early Proposals," Box 1, Lyndon B. Johnson Papers, 1963–69, Legislative Background, New G.I. Bill, 1966. LBJ Library.

26. Ibid.

27. 105 Cong. Rec. 13800 (1959).

28. Dwight D. Eisenhower, "Annual Budget Message to the Congress, Fiscal Year 1961," 18 January 1960. *The American Presidency Project*, http://www.presidency.ucsb.edu/ws/index.php?pid=11763&st=&st1= (accessed 21 September 2008).

29. *New York Times*, 22 July 1956, 6.

30. Ralph Yarborough, "A Fair Deal for the Cold War Soldier," *Harper's Magazine*, January 1965, 81.

31. Veterans' benefits were not a major issue during Kennedy's presidency. The few public announcements he made on the subject revealed that he held a similar position to Eisenhower.

32. Memorandum for Bill D. Moyers from Phillip S. Hughes, 15 December 1964, Folder "Initial Administration Opposition and Substitutes," Box 1, Lyndon B. Johnson Papers, 1963–69, Legislative Background, New G.I. Bill, LBJ Library.

33. Morton Keller, *America's Three Regimes: A New Political History* (New York: Oxford University Press, 2009).

34. Memorandum for Bill D. Moyers from Phillip S. Hughes, 15 December 1964, Folder "Initial Administration Opposition and Substitutes," Box 1, Lyndon B. Johnson Papers, 1963–69, Legislative Background, New G.I. Bill, LBJ Library.

35. Ibid.

36. Letter to Lister Hill from the Office of the Administrator of Veterans Affairs, undated, Folder "Initial Administration Opposition and Substitutes-I," Box 1, Lyndon B. Johnson Papers, 1963–69, Legislative Background, New G.I. Bill, LBJ Library.

37. Letter to Kermit Gordon from William Driver, 12 February 1965, Folder "Initial Administration Opposition and Substitutes-I," Box 1, Lyndon B. Johnson Papers, 1963–69, Legislative Background, New G.I. Bill, LBJ Library.

38. Letter to Lyndon Johnson from Ralph Yarborough, 6 May 1965, Folder "Initial Administration Opposition and Substitutes-I," Box 1, Lyndon B. Johnson Papers, 1963–69, Legislative Background, New G.I. Bill, LBJ Library.

39. Report of the Committee on Labor and Public Welfare to Accompany S.9, the Cold War Veterans' Readjustment Assistance Act (Washington, D.C.: U.S. Government Printing Office, 1965), 3.

40. Under previous G.I. bills, veterans had to serve 90 days before becoming eligible for benefits; S.9 decreed that the veterans serve 180 days. The bill also denied business loans and mustering out pay for Cold War veterans. Moreover, S.9 offered only $110 per month to veterans, the same amount offered Korean veterans more than a decade earlier. This amount failed

to take into account the rising costs of tuition and living expenses in the intervening years but perhaps more accurately reflected the lesser readjustment needs of peacetime veterans.

41. 111 Cong. Rec. 17306 (1965).

42. Ibid., 17319.

43. Ibid., 17348.

44. Letter to Lyndon Johnson from Charles L. Schultze, Director of the Bureau of the Budget, 22 July 1965, Folder "Initial Administration Opposition and Substitutes-II," Box 1, Lyndon B. Johnson Papers, 1963–69, Legislative Background, New G.I. Bill, LBJ Library.

45. Memo to Douglass Cater from William Driver, 15 December 1965, Folder "Final Passage," Box 1, Lyndon B. Johnson Papers, 1963–69, Legislative Background, New G.I. Bill, LBJ Library.

46. Memo to Douglass Cater from William Driver, 21 December 1965, Folder "Final Passage," Box 1, Lyndon B. Johnson Papers, 1963–69, Legislative Background, New G.I. Bill, LBJ Library.

47. Recorded telephone conversation to the White House with Charles Schultze, 31 December 1965, Folder "Final Passage," Box 1, Lyndon B. Johnson Papers, 1963–69, Legislative Background, New G.I. Bill, LBJ Library.

48. Memo to Douglass Cater from William Driver, 21 December 1965, Folder "Final Passage," Box 1, Lyndon B. Johnson Papers, 1963–69, Legislative Background, New G.I. Bill, LBJ Library.

49. Quoted in the *Washington Daily News*, 7 December 1965, reprinted in Folder "LE/VA 10/15/65-3/2/66," Box 162, Lyndon B. Johnson Papers, 1963–69, Legislation Ex. LE/VA 2, 11/22/63, LBJ Library.

50. Alec Philmore Pearson Jr., "Olin E. Teague and the Veterans' Administration" (PhD diss., Texas A&M, 1977).

51. Letter to F. B. McElroy from Olin Teague, 9 February 1953, Box 237, Olin Teague Papers, Texas A&M, quoted in ibid.

52. Memo to Lyndon Johnson from Charles L. Schultze, 10 February 1966, Folder "VA Educational Program I," Box 11, Lyndon B. Johnson Papers, 1963–69, Veteran Affairs, General VA3, LBJ Library.

53. 112 Cong. Rec. 2335 (1966).

54. Ibid., 2339.

55. Ibid., 2348.

56. 112 Cong. Rec. 2875 (1966).

57. See Mark Boulton, "Unwilling 'soldiers in the war on brutal inflation': Congress, the Veterans, and the Fight with Gerald R. Ford over the 1974 G.I. Bill." *White House Studies*, 7, no. 4: 313–32.

58. Memo to Lyndon Johnson from Will Sparks and Bob Hardesty, 16 February 1966, Folder "Final Passage," Box 1, Lyndon B. Johnson Papers, 1963–69, Legislative Background, New G.I. Bill, LBJ Library.

59. Lyndon B. Johnson, "Remarks upon Signing the 'Cold War G.I. Bill'" 3 March 1966, *The American Presidency Project*, http://www.presidency.ucsb.edu/ws/index.php?pid=27448&st=&st1= (accessed 25 August 2009).

60. See Segal, *Recruiting for Uncle Sam*; Robert Kaplan and Patricia T. Harris, *The Measurement of High School Students' Attitudes toward Recruiting Incentives* (Fort Sheridan, Ill.: United States' Army Recruiting Command, 1983); Jerald G. Bachman "American High School Seniors View the Military" *Armed Forces and Society* 10, no. 1 (Fall 1983): 86–104; Barbara A. Bicksler,

Curtis L. Gilroy, John T. Warner, and Donald Rumsfeld, eds., *The All Volunteer Force: Thirty Years of Service* (Washington, D.C.: Potomac Books, 2004); and J. Eric Fredland, Curtis L. Gilroy, Roger D. Little, and W. S. Sellman, eds. *Professionals on the Front Line: Two Decades of the All-Volunteer Force* (New York: Brassey's Inc., 1996).

61. "Veterans' Lobby Outdoes Itself," *New York Times*, 23 April 1968, 46.

62. See Mark Boulton, "How the G.I. Bill Failed African-American Vietnam War Veterans," *Journal of Blacks in Higher Education*, no. 58 (Winter 2007–8): 57–61.

63. Indeed, both of these new bills continued to face political opposition, most noticeably from fiscal conservatives Richard Nixon and Gerald Ford. See Boulton, *Price on Freedom*; and Boulton, "Unwilling 'Soldiers in the War on Brutal Inflation': Congress, the Veterans, and the Fight with Gerald R. Ford over the 1974 G.I. Bill." *White House Studies* 7, no. 4: 313–32.

64. *Veterans Administration Annual Report, 1984* (Washington, D.C.: U.S. Government Printing Office, 1984), 81.

# V

## Contemporary Veterans' Politics

# 11

# Conventional and Distinctive Policy Preferences of Early-Twenty-First-Century Veterans

JEREMY M. TEIGEN

What policy preferences does today's veteran population seek, and are they different than those of nonveterans? The policy desires of U.S. military veterans have occasionally appeared very clear. The drive for federal pensions in the late nineteenth century and the push for the G.I. Bill in the twentieth century are obvious successes driven by veterans and their political allies. The educational and civic advantage conferred by these programs for the World War II generation is difficult to overstate.[1] But as the other chapters in this volume demonstrate amply in multiple historical contexts, the politics of veteran-specific policy debates contribute to a complicated, mixed legacy across different issue arenas. In terms of health care, disability benefits, pensions, educational programs, and labor issues, the federal government has occasionally delivered tailored benefits, but the process is hardly the result of a simple reaction to clear preferences held by veterans in the electorate. Democratic governments promise to deliver policies ostensibly based on public opinion, but attributing responsibility for a policy victory simply to "veterans' preferences" is difficult because the organizational influence of pressure groups can be strong, and policies may also be favored by the public at large or other policy elites. Conversely, opposition groups, whether a minority or majority opinion, may confound creation of veteran-specific policy.

Because of the complicated and sporadic nature of veteran policy creation, and the lack of historical polling data, it is difficult to understand past veterans' political attitudes from events such as the G.I. Bill or its antecedents. Extrapolating veterans' preferences from these historical policy victories to understand the veteran population of today is even more difficult. Since the end of conscription in 1973 and the lack of conflicts requiring large conscript armies, the military and the subsequent veteran population have not been the focus of significant political battles, either for candidates or for a particular policy agenda. While veterans' symbolic role in American politics (within policy creation and in electoral politics) may endure, their relative share of the electorate has waned. Still, veterans hold a special role in American electoral politics, both as candidates and as voters, and a frequent presumption about veteran voters is that they differ from the electorate in terms of policy preferences.

To understand veterans' preferences on policy questions, a germane inquiry to supplement the other chapters in this volume lies embedded in our impressions of opinion-driven veteran policy development. This chapter asks and answers a simple corollary question: do today's veterans hold distinctive political attitudes on foreign and domestic policy in the United States? Previous research has explored veterans' civic engagement and political participation, but it is important to expand our understanding of veterans to include policy preferences.[2] After a brief characterization of selected previous research on veterans' political preferences, this chapter tests various hypotheses with extant data: Do veterans hold distinctively hawkish views on foreign policy? Given historical veteran preferences for entitlement programs geared toward veterans, do veterans hold redistributive policy preferences in other arenas of social policy? Does military service color the impressions and evaluation of views on military-specific policies, such as the "don't ask, don't tell" ban on gays in the military?

The short answer, detailed below, is that twenty-first-century veterans hold views that accord closely with the nonveteran population on most political matters. While the veteran population is sometimes presented as more conservative, hawkish, and sympathetic to Republican issue areas, quantitative analysis reveals that the apparent distinctiveness stems from the fact that most vets are male and are older on average.[3] Once one controls for important correlates of political attitudes, including gender, age, race, and partisan identity, veterans resemble nonveterans on most policy preferences. On questions about domestic matters, including fundamental questions of redistribution, veterans hold the same views as nonveterans. On foreign policy questions, including attitudes toward the 2003 war in Iraq, veterans in the electorate do not differ substantially from the nonveterans. One notable exception is veterans' strong negative views in 2004 and 2008 on Defense Department policy toward allowing gays and lesbians to serve openly in the military.

The chapter proceeds in four sections. First is a review of selected examples from germane scholarly literature that have examined political differences between veterans and nonveterans. Next is a description of the data used to evaluate contemporary veteran political attitudes, an explanation of the methodology, and a description of the results of the analyses. Last is a section discussing the results and implications and some possible directions for subsequent attention to the study of veterans attitudes.

## Scholarly Research on Veterans' Political Attitudes

Starting principally after World War II and again after the Vietnam War as a reaction to the large influx of men making the transition from military to civilian life, social scientists in the United States and elsewhere began to investigate veterans' foreign policy views. This group of social psychologists, sociologists, and political scientists posed several hypotheses related to veterans and their attitudes, such as authoritarian leanings, efficaciousness, ideological conservatism, political alienation, cynicism, and other phenomena. Some postulated that military experience directly influenced veterans' foreign policy views. After all, military personnel frequently traveled overseas, and some were involved in combat. The armed forces also exposed members to the more martial and bellicose side of American foreign policy. This exposure may have acclimatized those with service experience to military missions, making them more likely to prefer hawkish views toward American interventions. Conversely, those who share wartime experiences may have seen them as undesirable options for American foreign policy and therefore express less hawkish views. Indeed, some have pointed out how preexisting attitudes might limit the influence of international experiences.[4] This chapter continues this line of investigation into policy preference distinctions of veterans but focuses on both foreign and domestic policy views.

Compared to the relationship between mass opinions and domestic concerns, there is less research on mass attitudes and foreign policy questions because the creation of foreign policy is perceived largely as an elite-driven process. An even smaller body of work examines how service in one of the most important facets of the U.S. government's foreign policy options, the armed services, might affect veterans' views toward foreign policy. Segal and Segal (1976) investigated veteran attitudes about military policy and interventions with a 1973 sample, specifically examining national security views on an isolationism-intervention scale.[5] They found far more similarities than differences, discovering that veterans mirrored nonveterans in their sample on isolationism-interventionism scales. Jennings and Markus looked specifically at Vietnam War veterans using a different 1973 longitudinal sample, comparing them to same-age nonveterans for political attitudinal differences.[6] Their results about veterans indicate both retrospective attitudes toward the decision to go to war in Vietnam and views about the appropriate magnitude of military involvement were distinct from nonveterans, with veterans slightly more likely to view American entry into the war as positive. But they also find that the effect of military service on foreign policy attitudes was mitigated by education levels and the time period of the war service. Another post-Vietnam study saw veterans as slightly more retrospectively hawkish on the war but not by a large magnitude, and differences were based more on frustration rather than ideology.[7] Sharper contrast between veterans and nonveterans was found in views toward the Korean War with earlier data, where military service presaged more hawkish attitudes on the conduct of the war.[8] Another study found few attitudinal differences between veterans and nonveterans on foreign policy questions with 1973 data.[9] A later study with 1980s data discovered that veterans, when controlling for other correlates, were slightly more likely to support spending federal monies on arms.[10] Given the wide array of data and methods used, it is difficult to summarize these findings into a larger conclusive generalization, but the evidence seems to point toward a lack of distinction between those who have served and those who have not when it comes to attitudes toward foreign policy.

Regarding domestic policy, there are few empirical studies of military veteran opinion. This dearth of research is an oversight in the literature, especially given veterans' role as an early policy beneficiary in the process of American state building.[11] We might suspect that veterans exhibit distinctive views on policy matters due to the precedent of benefits and the resulting self-interest that may arise. In the words of Page and Shapiro, groups hold concerns that correlate with their immediate interests: "Black Americans . . . care about civil rights; the elderly about pensions; young men of draft age about military service."[12] A more recent examination of political and civic attitudes among a subset of the civilian veteran population, men who received G.I. Bill benefits after World War II, finds that military service and participation in higher education with governmental assistance fostered lifelong civic participation and positive views toward government.[13] Given that veterans were among the first beneficiaries of federal benefits, it is worth investigating whether today's veterans favor federal redistributive policies that target groups other than veterans.

## Analyzing Veterans and Nonveterans: Methodology and Data

To evaluate contemporary veterans' political attitudes, this chapter employs cross-sectional survey analysis of recent polling data. Using the data released by two survey outfits, the analyses that follow use regression models to contrast veterans' attitudes from nonveterans, ceteris paribus. The two sources are Pew and the American National Election Study, or ANES.[14] Pew is a media-oriented survey organization that fields many polls per year, typically by telephone, and asks many samples a relatively small number of questions on salient news stories of the week. The American National Election Study fields only one survey per election but asks a large number of questions, primarily on domestic policy preferences and voting habits. The comparisons that follow marshal both types of data to test for domestic and foreign policy preferences among veterans in several issue areas. The Pew data serve to evaluate foreign policy views; ANES data are best for the domestic views given the differences between the instruments.

Some conclusions about the distinctive attitudes about veterans attribute the difference in opinions between veterans and nonveterans in survey samples on the veterans' military experience. These inferences are based on the real differences that do appear between responses given by veterans and nonveterans. Yet these efforts overestimate the role of the military service by conflating the effect of previous military service with the distinctiveness of older men in the electorate. Early research on public opinion and foreign policy demonstrated the relationship between socioeconomic status and foreign policy attitudes.[15] Additionally, gender is another important factor in understanding how people feel about the use of force overseas.[16] Because veterans tend to be older and are overwhelmingly male, and because males are more likely to refer to themselves as Republican Party identifiers, multivariate analysis is necessary to distinguish between veterans and nonveterans and empirically convey the substantive differences that America's military veterans possess from the rest of the population as well as to demonstrate where they share views with the rest of the electorate.

Another important control variable for the purposes of understanding military service is level of formal education. Another study of veteran attitudes discovered that education levels drive attitude differences within the veteran population and explain differences irrespective of military service.[17]

Veteran distinctiveness could be generated by one or a combination of two principal influences. Men and women serving in the service might be exposed to institutional socialization, which might take the form of explicit and intentional efforts or by informal processes by peers and direct supervisory personnel. Another way to explain differences between veterans and nonveterans looks not at experiences that the former share in the institution but rather the selection processes that lead some toward service and others away from it. In times without conscription policies, citizens can choose to enlist or forgo service, and there may be attitudinal differences between volunteers and those that choose nonmilitary options. These attitudinal differences, present before the institutional experience, may explain apparent differences between those with military experience and those without it. It is not the intent of this chapter to attempt to unravel the knot of self-selection and socialization, but it assumes that both work toward contributing to possible distinctive attitudes. This self-selection bias would be difficult to contend with from an analytic perspective.

Conscription ended in 1973, and all veterans serving after that year were volunteers while few were before that year, especially during the height of U.S. involvement in World War II, Korea, and Vietnam. As such, by controlling for respondents' age in the subsequent analyses, we are roughly controlling for the possibility of conscription, and by extension, the possibility of self-selection biases.

## Results: Veterans' Foreign Policy Attitudes

The military experience comprises time in an institution geared for possible war. As a study investigating veterans' views on war and peace stated, veterans may exhibit distinctions from nonveterans, perhaps favoring "tough or violent solutions to disagreements (both interpersonal and international)."[18] Having spent time in uniform and exposed intimately to weapons systems (or the support thereof), mission readiness, and countless other martial influences, veterans may be apt to express more hawkish views toward American foreign policy directions. The most salient foreign policy question in the past decade was the invasion of Saddam Hussein's Iraq and the subsequent occupation thereafter, officially named Operation Iraqi Freedom. Because of the situation involving U.S. forces in Iraq, pollsters frequently included a question asking respondents about their retrospective evaluation of whether the United States should have invaded Iraq in the first place. Given the timing and significance of the invasion and subsequent events in Iraq, these analyses used retrospective approval of the operation as the key measure of hawkishness on foreign policy.

Using eleven cross sections of Pew data, fielded sporadically after the start of the Iraq war, we can contrast veterans' views on whether the policy was the "right thing to do," and can compare the results to the nonveterans in the samples. Figure 11.1 demonstrates both groups' percentages across the eleven time points, starting in April 2003, the month following the beginning of combat operations, to February of 2008, almost five years thereafter. As the figure shows, veterans are more likely than nonveterans to retrospectively approve of the invasion for most of the time series. In some months, such as October 2004 and December 2005, veterans' approval exceeds nonveterans' approval by nearly ten percentage points. In other months, however, the differences in this foreign policy attitude between groups are negligible. The generally higher retrospective approval of the Iraq war among veterans is not a narrow artifact of data or the question; veterans do on average exhibit higher levels of approval for the justness of the war's start. Yet it is important to disaggregate the influence of previous military service from the possibly confounding influence of gender and age.

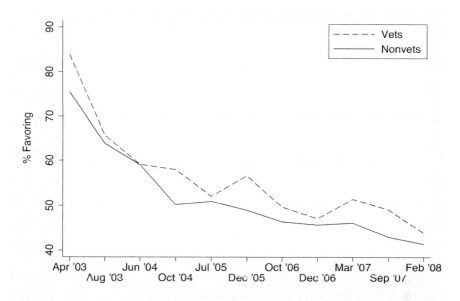

Figure 11.1. Aggregate Retrospective Evaluations of whether 2003 Iraq Invasion was "Right," 2003, 2008. *Source*: Pew Research Center for the People & Press (2009). Question wording: "Do you think the U.S. made the right decision or the wrong decision in using military force against Iraq?" Note: Survey schedule is not measured at equal time intervals.

For this task, multivariate analyses are best suited to evaluate how attitudes toward the war in Iraq relate to past service in the armed forces, irrespective of one's gender or age. Table 11.1 contains results from regression models that predict respondents' hawkish views using their previous military service, party affiliation, race, gender, age, income, and education. Each cell represents a hypothesis test, evaluating whether there is a positive, negative, or statistically insignificant relationship between retrospective feelings toward the Iraq invasion and the correlates listed on the left-hand column.

The results in table 11.1 demonstrate that past military service, despite the aggregate levels seen in figure 11.1, does not drive retrospective evaluations about the war in Iraq one way or the other, except for the first sample in April 2003, while major combat operations still ensued. In other words, once we control for the fact that gender is steeply correlated with past military service—in other words, veterans are mostly men and older than average—the apparent effect of military service on hawkishness disappears.

What drives retrospective evaluations of the justness of the invasion if military service does not? Respondents' partisan proclivities unsurprisingly influence their views on military operation, with Republicans always more likely to approve and Democrats always more likely to disapprove. Women in two of

Table 11.1. Retrospective Evaluations of Whether Iraq Invasion was the "Right Decision," 2003–2008

| | 2003 | | 2004 | | 2005 | | 2006 | | 2007 | | 2008 |
|---|---|---|---|---|---|---|---|---|---|---|---|
| | April | August | June | October | July | December | October | December | March | September | February |
| Veteran | 0.36* | -0.18 | 0.19 | 0.12 | 0.30 | 0.20 | -0.16 | -0.17 | 0.26 | 0.32 | -0.06 |
| | (0.17) | (0.19) | (0.20) | (0.23) | (0.23) | (0.23) | (0.22) | (0.23) | (0.24) | (0.25) | (0.23) |
| Republican | 2.07** | 1.69** | 1.43** | 1.43** | 2.45** | 1.81** | 2.23** | 1.57** | 2.06** | 1.84** | 1.83** |
| | (0.20) | (0.19) | (0.18) | (0.20) | (0.24) | (0.20) | (0.20) | (0.20) | (0.23) | (0.20) | (0.20) |
| Democrat | -0.39** | -0.42** | -0.99** | -1.39** | -0.49** | -0.98** | -0.82** | -1.00** | -0.79** | -0.72** | -0.83** |
| | (0.12) | (0.13) | (0.15) | (0.18) | (0.18) | (0.18) | (0.18) | (0.18) | (0.18) | (0.19) | (0.18) |
| White | 1.00** | 0.73** | 0.76** | 0.71** | 0.52* | 0.57* | 0.54* | 0.37 | 0.56* | 0.80** | 0.59* |
| | (0.15) | (0.14) | (0.19) | (0.22) | (0.22) | (0.24) | (0.21) | (0.24) | (0.22) | (0.22) | (0.25) |
| Female | -0.42** | -0.18 | 0.07 | -0.29 | -0.00 | -0.25 | -0.42* | -0.15 | -0.13 | -0.09 | -0.20 |
| | (0.12) | (0.13) | (0.14) | (0.17) | (0.18) | (0.17) | (0.17) | (0.17) | (0.18) | (0.17) | (0.18) |
| Age | -0.01 | -0.01** | -0.01** | -0.00 | -0.02** | -0.01 | -0.02** | -0.01** | -0.01 | -0.02** | -0.00 |
| | (0.00) | (0.00) | (0.00) | (0.00) | (0.00) | (0.00) | (0.00) | (0.00) | (0.00) | (0.01) | (0.00) |
| Income | 0.04 | 0.06 | -0.04 | -0.03 | -0.01 | 0.02 | -0.02 | 0.04 | 0.03 | 0.03 | -0.04 |
| | (0.03) | (0.03) | (0.03) | (0.04) | (0.04) | (0.04) | (0.04) | (0.04) | (0.04) | (0.04) | (0.04) |
| B.A. | -0.94** | -0.75** | -0.41** | -0.20 | -0.83** | -0.64** | -0.46** | -0.24 | -0.80** | -0.29 | -0.48** |
| | (0.13) | (0.14) | (0.14) | (0.15) | (0.18) | (0.17) | (0.18) | (0.17) | (0.17) | (0.17) | (0.17) |
| Constant | 0.61* | 0.57* | 0.70* | -0.00 | 0.33 | -0.25 | 0.44 | 0.06 | -0.26 | -0.18 | -0.30 |
| | (0.24) | (0.24) | (0.30) | (0.33) | (0.36) | (0.33) | (0.35) | (0.35) | (0.38) | (0.37) | (0.39) |
| N | 2,750 | 2,072 | 1,460 | 1,182 | 1,192 | 1,246 | 1,541 | 1,209 | 1,206 | 1,145 | 1,179 |
| Pseudo-R2 | 0.184 | 0.132 | 0.174 | 0.213 | 0.225 | 0.203 | 0.222 | 0.172 | 0.196 | 0.199 | 0.188 |

*Source:* Pew Research Center for the People & Press (2009)

*Notes:* Logit analyses with robust standard errors in parentheses (** p ≤ 0.01; * p ≤ 0.05) using provided weights. Veteran, Republican, Democrat, White, Female, and Bachelor's Degree are measured as dummy variables; Age measured as an uncoded scale variable with top-coded respondents (97 years) removed; and Income measured as an eight-point ordinal scale. Question wording of dependent variable: "Do you think the U.S. made the right decision or the wrong decision in using military force against Iraq?"

the samples are significantly less likely to view the invasion justly, and eight of samples demonstrate evidence that respondents with a bachelor's degree were also less likely to approve of it. It should be noted that the first sample, taken between the start of the invasion and before George W. Bush's declaration of major combat's end in May 2009, does demonstrate a veteran distinction on views of the war. This finding and the lack of results in the subsequent samples suggest that veterans' evaluation of the conflict may be influenced by the nature and recentness of the conflict.

## Results: Veterans' Domestic Policy Attitudes

If choosing an issue on foreign affairs in the twenty-first century to measure veteran opinion was a rather simple affair with only two options, selecting domestic issues to evaluate potential veteran attitudinal distinctiveness involved far more choices. Rather than rely on several samples with an identical question, the test of the proposition that veterans hold distinct domestic policy positions uses two samples, each taken on the eve of a presidential election and each with an extremely wide battery of questions about domestic political issues. Just as the Pew samples do, the ANES cross-sectional data ask demographic control questions as well as a question about whether respondents had served in the armed forces.

This volume's theme involves questions of veteran-specific policy creation and contexts, which are essentially redistributive political issues. Whether the government should use its finite revenues on a small, targeted group is an essential redistributive discussion frequently debated in democracies. The question posed by this chapter—do veterans in the electorate possess distinct political views?—should therefore examine this matter with redistributive dilemmas in addition to others. Rather than examine what might be interpreted as parochial, self-interested attitudes among veterans, such as "are you in favor of veterans benefits," the analyses below rely upon more general questions about governmental priorities in 2004 and 2008.

The questions on domestic political issues include those on general government spending; government spending on health care; the government's role in employment levels; and governmental spending preferences on highways, combating crime, welfare, child care, Social Security, public schools, and science and technology. Most of these questions were asked with a Likert-style scale ("strongly agree" to "strongly disagree"), and provide an opportunity to see if veterans felt differently in 2004 and 2008 about essential redistributive issues in American politics. Why might veterans think differently about these redistributive domestic political issues? If we conceive of veterans' historical experiences with policy successes, such as the post–Civil War pensions or the post–World War II GI Bill, perhaps veterans may view redistributive governmental policies favorably, in general or for other groups.

Yet veterans in the 2004 and 2008 samples exhibited no meaningful differences from those who had not served in the military. On all the redistributive questions posed by ANES, there was no contrast between veterans and nonveterans. If pensions and educational benefits served as a boon for the veteran populations of yesteryear, their passage guides no precedence for twenty-first-century veterans regarding their views of governmental benefits writ large. Veterans and nonveterans held statistically equivalent views toward the government's role in health care, infrastructure, crime, entitlement programs, and other major redistributive policies.

Another realm of domestic policy preferences involves attitudes toward social and symbolic issues, generally outside the realm of redistributive benefits. These issues include racial and ethnic politics and the related questions of affirmative action and opportunity equality, gender equity questions, and feelings toward people and groups. Specific questions were used for evaluating for potential differences between veterans and nonveterans in 2004 and 2008: feelings toward the traditional family, whether blacks deserve special favors, whether government is fair, women's roles in society, the justness of affirmative action, whether equal rights has "gone too far," feelings toward gays in society, gays' service in the military, and attitudes toward George W. Bush, Barack Obama, John McCain, Joe Biden, and Sarah Palin.

By and large, veterans' views on these questions were statistically equivalent to the nonveterans' views in the sample. Using the same control variables used earlier in the foreign policy tests, including measures of partisan loyalty, gender, age, education, income, and race, veterans voiced views that were no different from the views of those without military service. One exception appears, however, when asking veterans about their views on whether gays and lesbians should be allowed to serve in the military openly.

Using the 2004 and 2008 data, Table 11.2 lists a multivariate analysis of feelings toward two issues related to gays and lesbians. Those with military service were substantially less likely than nonveterans to support gays openly serving in the armed forces in both 2004 and 2008. This difference between veterans and nonveterans remains even when controlling for the other variables listed on the table.[19] While other variables also affect feelings toward gays in the service, such as Republican Party identification (negative), being white (positive), being female (positive), and having a bachelor's degree (positive), military service suppresses the likelihood of approving of open homosexual military service irrespective of these other influences. The mag-

Table 11.2. Feelings toward Gay Military Service and Gay Marriage, 2004 and 2008

| | Gay Military Service 2004 | Gay Military Service 2008 | Gay Marriage 2004 | Gay Marriage 2008 |
|---|---|---|---|---|
| Veteran | -0.76** | -0.48* | -0.49* | -0.05 |
| | -0.28 | -0.21 | -0.25 | -0.19 |
| Republican | -1.39** | -0.60** | -1.40** | -0.75** |
| | -0.25 | -0.19 | -0.22 | -0.18 |
| Democrat | -0.04 | 0.11 | 0.2 | 0.1 |
| | -0.26 | -0.19 | -0.19 | -0.16 |
| White | 0.70** | 0.3 | 0.55** | 0.55** |
| | -0.23 | -0.17 | -0.21 | -0.14 |
| Female | 0.55* | 0.47** | 0.26 | 0.09 |
| | -0.23 | -0.16 | -0.17 | -0.14 |
| Age | -0.01 | -0.02** | -0.03** | -0.03** |
| | -0.01 | 0 | -0.01 | 0 |
| Income | 0.06** | -0.01 | 0.01 | 0 |
| | -0.02 | 0 | -0.02 | 0 |
| B.A. | 0.67** | 0.63** | 0.91** | 0.56** |
| | -0.25 | -0.2 | -0.18 | -0.17 |
| Gay | | 1.26 | | 1.74* |
| | | -0.96 | | -0.84 |
| Constant | 0.85* | 1.75** | 0.25 | 1.45** |
| | -0.36 | -0.27 | -0.33 | -0.24 |
| Observations | 929 | 1,794 | 942 | 1,772 |
| R-squared | 0.11 | 0.071 | 0.119 | 0.083 |

Source: ANES 2004 and 2008. Logit estimates with robust standard errors in parentheses (** $p \le$ 0.01; * $p \le 0.05$) using provided weights. Veteran, Republican, Democrat, White, Female, Gay (2008 only), and Bachelor's Degree are measured as dummy variables; Age measured as an uncoded scale variable with top-coded respondents (91 years) removed; and income as a 23-point ordinal scale. Question wording of dependent variables: "Do you think homosexuals should be allowed to serve in the United States Armed Forces or don't you think so?" and "Should same-sex couples be allowed to marry, or do you think they should not be allowed to marry?"

nitude of the effect is stronger in 2004 than 2008, suggesting that the acceptance of openly gay service increased in the veteran population between the two elections.

It is important to estimate the actual probability of approving of service in the armed forces by homosexuals for veterans and nonveterans in order to convey the results from the multivariate model into more substantively mean-

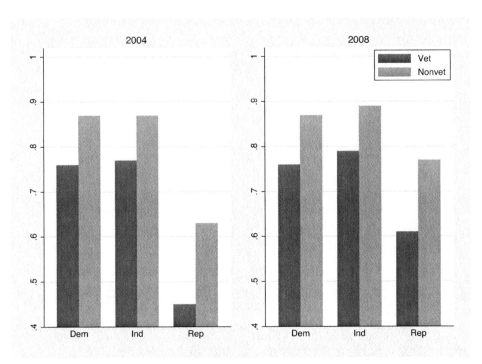

Figure 11.2. Probability of Favoring Gays Openly Serving in the Military. *Source*: ANES, 2004 and 2008. Postestimate probabilities based on models listed in table 11.2, assuming a modal values of the independent variables.

ingful values. Figure 11.2 presents the probability of responding "yes" to the question "Do you think homosexuals should be allowed to serve in the US armed forces" for Republicans, Democrats, and independents among veterans and nonveterans for both years. In all six comparisons, nonveterans were more likely to approve of gay service. Both veterans and nonveterans who call themselves Republicans were less likely than independents and Democrats to favor lifting the ban. Moreover, the gap between veterans and nonveterans was largest among Republican identifiers. This result means that Republicans with military service are the least likely respondents to approve of gay service in both years. It is worth noting that opinion is generally higher than 50 percent for lifting the ban—while veterans were less likely than nonveterans to agree with lifting the ban, all categories except the 2004 Republican veterans were more likely than not to favor the ban's end.

One explanation for these results showing veterans as less open to pro–gay policy is that military service engenders negative feelings toward homosexuals in general. Recent research has investigated the 1993 "don't ask, don't tell" policy, noting that opinions within the military were steeply against lifting the

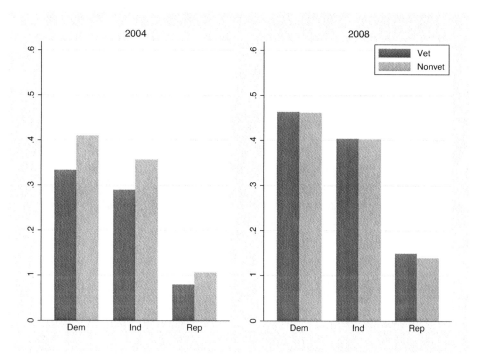

Figure 11.3. Probability of Favoring Legal Gay Marriage. *Source*: ANES, 2004 and 2008. Postestimate probabilities based on models listed in table 11.2, assuming modal values of the independent variables.

ban at the time but have since moderated.[20] As such, to see if veterans have generally anti-gay policy views or only have opinions on homosexuals as it relates to the military institution, table 11.2 also includes analysis of feelings toward gay marriage, a hot-button issue in American politics. The gay marriage models use the same analytic tools as the gay service models and find that while veterans were less likely than nonveterans were to approve of gay marriage in 2004, there was no vet distinction in 2008. Figure 11.3 presents the results using substantive probability form, similar to figure 11.2. As the regression results indicate, the 2004 sample shows that veterans were less likely than nonveterans were to support legal gay marriage in all three party identification groups. Unsurprisingly, Republicans were the least likely and Democrats the most likely to favor legal gay marriage, and independents came in between them. The 2008 sample shows that the veteran distinction disappeared in the intervening four years. Vets in 2008 were statistically identical to nonveterans on the question of gay marriage in all three party identification groups, though the party proclivities remained in force with Republicans most likely to oppose legal gay marriage.

## Discussion: Implications and Future Directions

The results demonstrate that early-twenty-first century military veterans generally share political attitudes with their peers without military service. Using a battery of questions about political issues and attitudes regarding both domestic and foreign policies, this analysis reveals few differences between the two groups when controlling for the confounding effects of age, gender, party, and other correlates of attitudes. Despite the occasionally high interest paid to military veterans during election seasons, veterans in the electorate hold mainstream attitudes and do not constitute a unique group regarding their views on most issues. The findings here, that veterans mirror the population in terms of their views on foreign and domestic policy preferences when viewed against similarly aged nonveteran males, align in broad terms with past scholarly investigations of the veteran population's political attitudes cited herein. While the dramatic civic effect borne from participating in a veteran-specific educational program boosted attitudes toward civic engagement after World War II, there are far fewer veterans from a much smaller army in recent decades. Mettler notes that while the educational benefits have grown over time, the number of recipients has shrunk, and "the program's capacity to grant social opportunity and broaden democratic citizenship is but a glimmer" of what it was for the World War II cohort.[21]

The only unequivocal difference between recent veterans and nonveterans on foreign or domestic policy preferences is the clear demonstration that people with military service are less likely than nonveterans to advocate lifting the ban on homosexuals serving openly in the military, even within a recent 2008 data sample. The debate over gays in the military complicated Bill Clinton's early months in office because of the resistance from Congress and the military to his pledge to lift the ban upon entering office.[22] Opinions from military members at the time of the debate strongly tracked against lifting the ban, though the civilian public was not in favor of lifting the ban either.[23] The results presented herein demonstrate that more than a decade later veterans in the twenty-first century have moved toward a more moderate position on gays in the military along with the rest of the electorate. Yet, although a majority of veterans favor lifting the ban, having served in the military suppresses the likelihood of this attitude irrespective of one's partisan identification, gender, age, and other attributes. Why would veterans be less likely to lift the ban than others? Subsequent research should seek clearer answers, but we can speculate here that the veterans are not different because of a general antigay sentiment given their similarity to the population on other gay policy matters. Other research has investigated homophobia in the military, and recent data suggest that military members have roughly the same levels of homophobia as civilians.[24] Veterans in the population served in the military institutions of times past, during times when attitudes toward gays was more negative than found today, so perhaps the veterans in the 2004 and 2008 sample found to be less likely than nonvets to repeal the ban used frames of their own military experiences to evaluate the contemporary policy question.[25]

Excepting feelings toward the ban on gays and lesbians serving in the military, veterans and nonveterans share attitudes on other policy questions. Perhaps this lack of domestic policy preference distinction among veterans goes against a sense that vets are a recurring and natural target of favorable policy in the form of veteran benefits. They have been the focus of scholarship discussing how veterans' benefits are early predecessors to the American state.[26] Or, similarly, conceptualizing personal experience in an enveloping government institution that provides for its members at a young, formative time in early adulthood as a "camouflaged safety net" might engender sympathy for government benefits in general.[27] Gifford provides a view of the armed forces as a welfare-oriented state agency providing health care, housing, and other benefits to the member and his or her family. However, veterans in recent samples of the electorate exhibit no special affinity toward redistribution policies. The time spent in the armed forces may expose young men and women to a more comprehensive array of governmental benefits than is found in the civilian world, but such experiences does not seem to engender enduring positive (or negative) attitudes toward state benefits for others or in general.

One reasonable explanation of the lack of a distinctive set of veteran policy preferences is the heterogeneity of military experiences. The measure for military service used in the survey analyses discussed here relies on a simple "yes" or "no" to an ordinary "did you serve" question. It, therefore, does not discriminate between different terms of service, combat veterans and support unit service, different branches, or various ranks. Consequently, if there are socialization differences between the different contexts in which one could serve, the way it is being measured by the surveys used here masks these differences.

It is important to remember that demonstrating similarity between veterans' political attitudes and those of the nonveteran population does not refute or devalue their role in American politics nor foretell a future diminishing of veterans in elections. Despite declining numbers in the population, military veterans continue to run for office, presidential candidates always speak at VFW and other veteran conventions, and media attention frequently centers on military and veteran themes during and between elections.[28] Military service has always appeared to engender a special credibility in the American political milieu and may continue to do so despite the smaller number of veterans in the polity.

Future research should continue to monitor the veteran population notwithstanding the similarities found here, probing for what divides those who have served from those who have not. The current veteran population is a reflection of the military population from yesteryear, and, as much of the "gap" literature has indicated, the military of today has become attitudinally distinct from their civilian leaders.[29] If today's military members hold divergent attitudes toward their role, foreign policy, and military policies, then it is likely that future measures of veteran attitudes will reflect those distinctions and potentially influence the relationship between veterans and their nonveteran peers.

## Notes

1. Suzanne Mettler, *Soldiers to Citizens: The G.I Bill and the Making of the Greatest Generation* (New York: Oxford, 2005).

2. M. Kent Jennings and Gregory B. Markus, "Political Participation and Vietnam War Veterans: A Longitudinal Study," in *The Social Psychology of Military Service*, ed. N. L. Goldman and D. R. Segal (Beverly Hills, CA: Sage Publications, 1976); David L. Leal, "It's Not Just a Job: Military Service and Latino Political Participation," *Political Behavior* 21, no. 2(1999): 153–74; Suzanne Mettler, "Bringing the State Back in to Civic Engagement: Policy Feedback Effects of the G.I. Bill for World War II Veterans," *American Political Science Review* 96, no. 2 (2002): 351–65; and Jeremy M. Teigen, "Enduring Effects of the Uniform: Previous Military Service and Voting Turnout," *Political Research Quarterly* 59, no.4 (2006): 601–7.

3. Some examples of journalism that has presented veterans in this way include Karen E. Crummy, "Bush Has Edge with Vets," *Denver Post*, 29 August 2004, A1; and Eric M. Weiss, "Veterans Mostly Support Bush, National Poll Finds," *Washington Post*, 27 August 2004, B1.

4. M. Brewster Smith, "Did War Service Produce International-Mindedness?" *Harvard Educational Review* 15 (1945): 250–57.

5. David R. Segal and Mady Wechsler Segal, "The Impact of Military Service on Trust in Government, International Attitudes, and Social Status," in *The Social Psychology of Military Service*, ed. N. L. Goldman and D. R. Segal (Beverly Hills, CA: Sage Publications, 1976).

6. M. Kent Jennings and Gregory B. Markus, "The Effect of Military Service on Political Attitudes: A Panel Study," *American Political Science Review* 71, no. 1 (1977): 131–47.

7. Jerald G. Bachman and M. Kent Jennings, "The Impact of Vietnam on Trust in Government," *Journal of Social Issues* 31, no. 4 (1974): 141–55.

8. Richard F. Hamilton, *Restraining Myths: Critical Studies of U.S. Social Structure and Politics* (New York: Sage Publications, 1975).

9. Samuel A. Kirkpatrick and James L. Regens, "Military Experience and Foreign Policy Belief Systems," *Journal of Political and Military Sociology* 6, no.1 (1978): 29–47.

10. John S. Butler and Margaret A. Johnson, "An Overview of the Relationships between Demographic Characteristics of Americans and Their Attitudes towards Military Issues," *Journal of Political and Military Sociology* 19 (Winter 1991): 273–91.

11. Theda Skocpol, *Protecting Soldiers and Mothers: The Political Origins of Social Policy in the United States* (Cambridge, Mass.: Belknap Press of Harvard University Press, 1992).

12. Benjamin I. Page and Robert Y. Shapiro. *The Rational Public: Fifty Years of Trends in Americans' Policy Preferences* (Chicago: University of Chicago Press, 1992), 285.

13. Mettler, "Bringing the State Back"; and Mettler, *Soldiers to Citizens*.

14. See The National Election Studies (www.electionstudies.org); THE ANES 2004 Time Series Study [dataset] (Ann Arbor: University of Michigan, Center for Political Studies [producer and distributor]); The American National Election Studies (ANES; www.electionstudies.org); The ANES 2008 Time Series Study [dataset] (Stanford University and the University of Michigan [producers]); and Pew Research Center for the People & the Press (www.people-press.org/about).

15. Andre Modigliani, "Hawks and Doves, Isolationism and Political Distrust: An Analysis of Public Opinion on Military Policy" *American Political Science Review* 66, no.3 (1972): 960–78.

16. Miroslav Nincic and Donna J. Nincic, "Race, Gender, and War," *Journal of Peace Research* 39, no.5 (2002): 547–68.

17. James L. Regens, "Political Attitudes and Vietnam-Era Military Service," *Social Science Journal* 14, no.3 (1977): 83–92.

18. E. M. Schreiber, "Enduring Effects of Military Service? Opinion Differences between U.S. Veterans and Nonveterans," *Social Forces* 57, no. 3 (1979): 824–39.

19. The set of correlates is very similar to the analyses with the Pew data. In 2008, ANES included a measure of whether the respondent was gay, so it was included as a control variable for 2008 but not 2004.

20. Aaron Belkin, "'Don't Ask, Don't Tell': Does the Gay Ban Undermine the Military's Reputation?," *Armed Forces & Society* 34, no. 2 (2008): 276–91.

21. Mettler, *Soldiers to Citizens*, 169.

22. Michael Bailey, Lee Sigelman, and Clyde Wilcox, "Presidential Persuasion on Social Issues: A Two-Way Street?" *Political Research Quarterly* 56, no.1 (2003): 49–58; and Craig A. Rimmerman, "Promise Unfulfilled: Clinton's Failure to Overturn the Military Ban on Lesbians and Gays," in *Gay Rights, Military Wrongs: Political Perspectives on Lesbians and Gays in the Military*, ed. C. A. Rimmerman (New York: Garland, 2003).

23. Laura L. Miller, "Fighting for a Just Cause: Soldiers' Views on Gays in the Military," in *Gays and Lesbians in the Military: Issues, Concerns, and Contrasts*, ed. W. J. Scott and S. C. Stanley (New York: Aldine De Gruyter, 1994); and Clyde Wilcox and Robin M. Wolpert, "President Clinton, Public Opinion, and Gays in the Military," in *Gay Rights, Military Wrongs: Political Persepctives on Lesbians and Gays in the Military*, ed. C. A. Rimmerman (New York: Garland, 1996).

24. Armando X. Estrada and David J. Weiss, "Attitudes of Military Personnel toward Homosexuals," *Journal of Homosexuality* 37, no.4 (1999): 83–97.

25. Randy Shilts, *Conduct Unbecoming: Gays and Lesbians in the U.S. Military* (New York: St. Martin's Griffin, 2005). The ban on gays openly serving in the armed forces ended in September 2011. See Elisabeth Bumiller, "Out and Proud to Serve," *New York Times*, 20 September 2011, A12.

26. See Skocpol, *Protecting Soldiers and Mothers*; Randall G. Holcombe, "Veterans Interests and the Transition to Government Growth: 1870–1915," *Public Choice* 99, no.3 (1999): 311–26; and Laura Smietanka Jensen, *Patriots, Settlers, and the Origins of American Social Policy* (New York: Cambridge University Press, 2003).

27. Brian Gifford, "The Camouflaged Safety Net: The U.S. Armed Forces as Welfare State Institution," *Social Politics* 13, no. 3 (2006): 372.

28. William T. Bianco and Jamie Markham, "Vanishing Veterans: The Decline of Military Experience in the U.S. Congress," in *Soldiers and Civilians: the Civil-Military Gap and American National Security*, ed. P. D. Feaver and R. H. Kohn (Cambridge, Mass.: MIT Press, 2001); and Jeremy Teigen, "Invoking Military Credentials in Congressional Elections 2000–2006," in *Inside Defense: Understanding the U.S. Military in the 21st Century*, ed. D. Reveron and J. H. Stiehm (New York: Palgrave, 2008).

29. Peter Feaver and Richard H. Kohn, *Soldiers and Civilians: the Civil-Military Gap and American National Security* (Cambridge, Mass.: MIT Press, 2001); Ole R. Holsti, "A Widening Gap between the U.S. Military and Civilian Society?: Some Evidence, 1976–96," *International Security* 23, no.3 (1998): 5–42; and Ole R. Holsti, "Of Chasms and Convergences: Attitudes and Beliefs of Civilians and Military Elites at the Start of a New Millennium," in *Soldiers and Civilians: the Civil-Military Gap and American National Security*, ed. P. D. Feaver and R. H. Kohn (Cambridge, Mass.: MIT Press, 2001); and Richard H. Kohn, "Out of Control: the Crisis in Civil-Military Relations," *National Interest* 35 (Spring 1994).

# 12

## Exploring the Effects of Combat Exposure on American Civic Life

### CHRISTOPHER S. PARKER

In democratic societies, citizens are required to serve the republic in many ways. To maintain liberty and stave off external threats to domination, citizens are sometimes required to place the common good ahead of self-interest by placing their lives on the line. While military service is the most demanding duty a citizen performs for the nation-state, many believe that individuals often emerge from military service more educated and dedicated citizens. They evince more loyalty to the nation-state, participate more vigorously in self-governance, and are zealous guardians of the way of life for which they risked everything. But what if the trauma to which many citizens are exposed while fighting for their country affects their civic orientation on returning to civil society? More directly, how might it affect their feelings about the political system for which they were willing to die? This is a question on which social science remains largely silent.

Scholars have shown that war-related trauma affects many aspects of veterans' postservice lives, usually for the worse. For instance, veterans who suffer from posttraumatic stress disorder (PTSD) have a difficult time adjusting to "normal" life on their return to society. The symptoms associated with PTSD, such as flashbacks, emotional numbing, and hyperarousal, affect veterans' ability to retain healthy relationships with spouses and children, to remain gainfully employed and, in some cases, to secure shelter.[1] They are also more likely than veterans who do not suffer from combat stress and civilians in the same cohort to engage in criminal behavior and commit acts of violence.[2]

Veterans who suffer from PTSD and combat-related stress are also likely to be saddled with other issues, most of which are related to mental health in some way. Veterans from World War II and Vietnam afflicted with PTSD are at risk for major depression and substance abuse.[3] Combat-related stress is also related to a feeling of social isolation and to becoming increasingly dissatisfied with life.[4] Veterans who suffer the effects of PTSD are also often afflicted with physical health issues.[5]

In sum, scholars have done much to inform us of the deleterious effects of combat-related trauma on veterans' subsequent health and its impact on their social and family lives and on their mobility. We know nothing, however, about the civic readjustment issues faced by veterans who suffer the debilitating effects of combat stress. Does PTSD, for instance, have similar effects on civic life as it does on social life? In other words, how, if at all, does combat-related stress affect veterans' ability to function as citizens in a democracy?

Drawing on a pilot study based on thirty-one semistructured interviews with veterans, I begin answering these questions by mapping the relationship between combat stress and civic life. In particular, I examine how combat affects civic attitudes. I posit two possible outcomes for participation in combat, both of which draw on the work of Elder and Clipp.[6] The first, and perhaps the most familiar, outcome is called the developmental effect of military service. This is a decidedly positive outcome in which military service transforms individuals into more productive citizens, at least partially by increasing one's sense of confidence as they progress through life. The pathogenic effect, another outcome associated with participation in combat, is commensurate with the mental illness that sometimes accompanies combat trauma. In this scenario, military service produces less allegiant citizens, owing to the symptoms associated with the illness.

To examine the effects of combat exposure on civic attitudes, I investigate veterans' allegiance to the political regime. The effect of military service on allegiance is important because military service is believed to inculcate support for the political system. So strong was this belief that American political elites flirted with the institutionalization of universal military training, that is, compulsory military service, through the 1950s. Allegiance to its institutions and norms, in which the politically allegiant citizen enjoys both a legal and psychological connection to the political system that constitutes the political order, is essential to the stability of the political system.[7] Otherwise, alienation, the flip-side of allegiance, threatens to undermine the stability of the regime by promoting insurgent activity.[8]

The principal import of this essay lies in its timeliness and urgency. The timeliness is related to America's continued involvement in overseas military operations in which it will likely remain engaged for the foreseeable future and the ongoing attention paid to issues surrounding combat stress. As figure 12.1 shows, since the beginning of the war in Afghanistan in 2002, more than 1,700 stories in the print media have touched upon combat stress in some way or another.

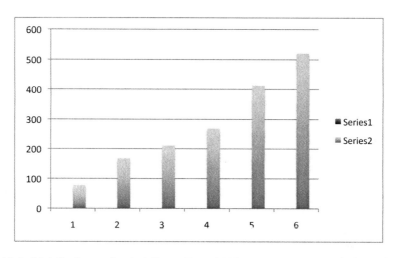

| Year: 2002 | Year: 2003 | Year: 2004 | Year: 2005 | Year: 2006 | Year: 2007 |
|---|---|---|---|---|---|
| 78 | 167 | 211 | 269 | 412 | 521 |

Figure 12.1. Print Stories on Combat Stress. From 2002–7, print stories in which combat stress was discussed increased more than seven-fold, from 78 in 2002 to 521 in 2007.

With the exception of 2005, when print coverage dipped from 2004, media coverage increased every year. From 2002–7, print stories in which combat stress was discussed increased more than sevenfold, from 78 in 2002 to 521 in 2007.[9] Further, if what we know about Vietnam is any indication, the effects from the war in Iraq and Afghanistan will continue to reverberate for many years to come.

Millions of veterans have struggled with PTSD. Currently, more than 215,000 veterans receive disability benefits from the Veterans Administration for PTSD. But this number only represents one-fourth of veterans who actually suffer from PTSD; for various reasons, the remaining 75 percent never seek the benefits to which they are entitled.[10] Of the veterans returning from Iraq who sought treatment at the VA, 31 percent suffered from mental health or psychosocial issues.[11] The potential impact of this high rate of PTSD upon the practice of democracy and equal participation makes addressing the essay's questions urgent. While alienation can lead to insurgent activity, it may also dampen the likelihood for conventional political engagement, including voting and civic activism.[12]

In what follows, I first briefly discuss the background of combat-related stress, particularly combat-related PTSD, after which I detail the urgency of the problem. I then derive theoretical propositions based on the effects of combat exposure that ultimately aim to link combat exposure to civic attitudes. This is followed by a description of the evidence on which I draw, after which I test and predict the positive and negative outcomes associated with combat exposure on political allegiance.

This essay suggests that the developmental effect of military service, an outcome of combat exposure commensurate with a rising sense of self-efficaciousness, is consistent with the attitudes of combat veterans who are not afflicted with PTSD. As a group, such veterans tend to embrace the political regime and political authorities more so than veterans who suffer from the pathogenic effects of combat. The latter group, the results suggest, are less allegiant to the regime and political authorities, particularly the president. More to the point, alienation varies according to combat exposure and the veteran's postwar mental condition: if a person is exposed to combat and suffers no combat trauma, that person will likely embrace the regime and political authorities. Otherwise, that person will become alienated to one or both.

## Background and Theory

Combat-related stress, especially PTSD, is part of the military experience of many veterans. PTSD is a psychobiological syndrome of interlocking symptoms that cohere, forming a prolonged stress reaction to trauma such as war.[13] For a diagnosis to be made, the individual must first be determined to have been involved in a traumatic event. In this case, a traumatic event is characterized by the patient experiencing or witnessing an event in which the threat of death or serious injury occurred to self or others, or in which others died; furthermore, the patient's response is characterized as one of fear, helplessness, or horror. According to the fourth edition of the *Diagnostic and Statistical Manual for Mental Disorders* (DSM-IV), the symptoms of PTSD coalesce around three basic behavioral clusters, the first of which is associated with reexperiencing the trauma in the form of intrusive dreams, thoughts, or perceptions of the trauma and reacting to external cues that symbolize the event. Another symptom of PTSD focuses upon behavior undertaken to avoid thoughts or feelings associated with the trauma. Because of the event, individuals may also lose interest in significant activities, become emotionally distant, perceive that they have no real future, or become alienated from others. Many also turn to drugs and alcohol as a means of dealing with the trauma. The final symptom cluster is drawn together by the patient's increased state of arousal. This often produces insomnia, anger, reduced concentration, persistent alertness, and an increased tendency to become startled. The DSM-IV requires that individuals experience these symptoms for at least one month before a diagnosis of PTSD can be made.

Close to 10 percent of World War II and Korean War veterans suffer the effects PTSD—even after several decades removed from combat.[14] More than 30 percent of Vietnam combat veterans have suffered from PTSD in their lifetime; 15 percent remain afflicted with it.[15] Indeed, Kulka and colleagues estimate that approximately 479,000 Vietnam veterans suffered from PTSD.[16] After the first Gulf War, PTSD affected approximately 10 percent of those who engaged in combat, while the more recent engagements in Afghanistan and Iraq have produced PTSD rates of 11 and 17 percent, respectively.[17] Some argue that these figures are conservative estimates, indicating that these numbers will only increase over time.[18] More to the point, it is likely that the number of Iraq and Afghanistan war veterans who are or will be at risk for PTSD in their lifetimes will reach approximately 510,000. Combined with Vietnam era veterans who remain afflicted with PTSD, more than one million men and women will suffer from it in the near future.[19]

The effects of war on mental health may be divided into at least two broad categories: developmental and pathogenic. The developmental effects of war, according to Elder and Clipp, are those that allow war veterans to cope with adversity and hardships.[20] For some, simply surviving war serves to boost confidence. For many others, however, military service during wartime forces them to think in new and different ways and allows them to take full measure themselves inasmuch as they are pushed to their physical and emotional limit. Successfully performing tasks, highly valued in the political community, leads to a sense of self-mastery and a higher regard for self and one's capabilities.[21]

It takes very little imagination to believe that veterans who grow from military service will transfer this sense of internal control to the political system, perhaps, as normative political theory prescribes, even growing more attached to it as a result of their service.[22] According to this logic, military service activates what sociologist Morris Janowitz called civic consciousness, a positive attachment to the nation-state in which the individual remains committed to its way of life.[23] Moreover, to the extent that the military not only guards but sustains democratic values, it should come as no surprise that many of those who are exposed to its institutional practices emerge from the service with an appreciation for democratic norms and practices.[24] In some cases, this is a function of the civic education received in the military.[25] In other cases, it is the antidemocratic nature of military culture and the restrictions placed on one's liberty that result in more appreciation for freedom and equality.[26] Thus, veterans who benefit from the developmental effects of combat should embrace the political regime and political authorities.

The positive effects of military service during war are all but taken for granted. It is assumed that military service produces citizens who, upon their return from conflict, will care to participate in civic life and remain attached to the political system. But this may not always be the case. It is also conceivable that the psychosocial trauma associated with war, which has proven difficult to overcome in the affected veterans' social and familial life, may also affect their reintegration into civic life. While the pathogenic effect of war is often explored by scores of psychologists, no one attempts to connect the debilitating effects of war directly to politics.

A point at which PTSD and politics may overlap is located in the second symptom cluster: avoidance and emotional numbing in which combat veterans develop "feelings of detachment or estrangement from others," both of which may result in "withdrawal [and] social disengagement."[27] This feeling of isolation and social disengagement in the combat-stressed veteran was not limited to his or her immediate network of friends and family. Often combat veterans also felt alienated from the whole of American society, especially during the Vietnam War, when veterans perceived that the political establishment hindered American forces' ability to effectively prosecute the war.

If a veteran believed this to be true, distrust usually ensued.[28] Likewise, I expect alienation to run deeper among veterans with PTSD and combat-related stress. For them, I contend that their alienation from society spilled over to the political system. In other words, just as the veteran could no longer relate to friends, family, or fellow nationals, he could also no longer relate to a political system in which politicians were permitted to waste lives. These perceptions, then, promote the sense of political normlessness among veterans, the perception that public officials fail to conform the rules of the game, and that these violations are commonplace.[29] Estrangement from the political order and political authorities follows.

Taken together, the developmental and pathogenic effects of combat exposure suggest the following predictions:

H1: Positive experiences with combat exposure, for example, increasing self-confidence and successfully defending the values for which the country stands, should yield veterans who embrace the political system and political authorities.

H2: Emerging from the military with negative experiences associated with combat-stress or PTSD, for example, the feeling that one's life has been disrupted, should result in relative estrangement from the political system and political authorities.

## Data and Method

To help map the proposed relationships, I turn to thirty-one semistructured interviews I conducted with veterans from February 2007 through April 2007.

Participants were recruited through newspaper ads placed in major daily newspapers in California: The *San Francisco Chronicle* and the *Los Angeles Times*. To guard against the possibility of bias associated with location, the interviews drew participants from the Bay Area, Los Angeles, and San Diego. The Bay Area was the site of fourteen interviews, all of which were conducted on the campus of UC Berkeley; eleven were conducted in Los Angeles on UCLA's campus; and six were completed in San Diego. Since there were no institutional arrangements with any campus in the area, I conducted the San Diego interviews in the homes of respondents. The interviews varied in duration from twenty-five minutes to ninety minutes, with a mean of forty-five minutes. Prospective participants were screened to ensure that they understood that this was a research project, not an attempt at outreach of some kind in which I represented an agency. Four prospective respondents were screened out on this basis. Upon determining that the respondents understood the purpose of the project, they were each scheduled for an appointment. Respondents were paid a sum of forty dollars for their time.

Veterans were divided into three cohorts. Six of the participants served during World War II or the Korean War, fifteen served in the military during Vietnam, and ten served after Vietnam, including nine who had served since the first Gulf War. Fifteen of the veterans served in the Army, six are Navy veterans, nine are Marines, and one is an Air Force veteran. Demographically, however, the participants are relatively homogeneous. Twenty-two of the participants are white; twenty-eight are male. Fourteen of the participants have at least a college degree; fifteen are retirees, five of whom retired from the military.

Veterans were also stratified by combat exposure: nineteen served in combat; twelve did not fight. (See the table 12.1 for more details.) Of the nineteen veterans who were exposed to combat, nine reported suffering from symptoms related to PTSD or combat stress. Perhaps the best way in which to assess the presence of PTSD is through a trimodal approach. Through self-reports, clinical interviews, and psychophysiological assessments, clinicians are able to correct the shortcomings of any single mode while simultaneously taking advantage of each mode's strength, allowing them to arrive at fairly accurate diagnoses.[30] In this essay, I rely upon self-reports of PTSD. If veterans conveyed to me that they were currently in treatment for PTSD or if they mentioned elements of the symptom clusters during the course of the interview, I refer to them as PTSD cases. For veterans who mention one or two but not all three symptoms, I refer to them as veterans with combat stress.

This essay attempts to gauge the extent to which exposure to combat affects one's orientation to the political system, specifically political allegiance. To assess allegiance, I asked the veterans whether they support the institutions

Table 12.1. List of Study Participants and Selected Demographics and Military Traits

| Name | Age | Education (years) | Political Party ID | Service Era | Branch | Combat? |
|------|-----|-------------------|--------------------|-------------|--------|---------|
| Ed A. | 54 | 16 | Independent | V/N–Iraq | Army | Yes |
| Willie A. | 78 | 8 | Republican | Korea | Army | Yes |
| Tony A. | 24 | College | Independent | Iraq | Army | No |
| Tom D. | 58 | 18 | Republican | V/N–Gulf I | Marines | Yes |
| Dave E. | 70 | 20 | Republican | Vietnam | Army | Yes |
| Oracio F. | 67 | 18 | Democrat | Korea | Army | No |
| Bill F. | 85 | 16 | Democrat | WWII | Army | Yes |
| Bill H. | 80 | 12 | Republican | WWII–V/N | Marines | Yes |
| Kathleen H. | 27 | 18 | Republican | Iraq | Navy | No |
| Lang I. | 25 | College | Libertarian | Iraq | Marines | Yes |
| Burt J. | 65 | 19 | Republican | Vietnam | Army | No |
| Tia L. | 27 | 16 | Democrat | Iraq | Navy | No |
| Larry L. | 62 | 14 | Democrat | Vietnam | Navy | No |
| Charles M. | 72 | 13 | Independent | V/N–Gulf War | Marines | No |
| Andy N. | 78 | 12 | Democrat | Korea | Air Force | No |
| Dan O. | 36 | 14 | Democrat | Gulf War | Army | Yes |
| Keith P. | 44 | 12 | Independent | Gulf War–Iraq | Marines | Yes |
| Ron R. | 60 | 18 | Republican | Vietnam | Army | Yes |
| Rob R. | 26 | College | Democrat | Iraq | Marines | Yes |
| Les R. | 75 | 18 | Independent | 1954–57 | Navy | No |
| Drew R. | 24 | College | Republican | Iraq | Marines | Yes |
| Bob R. | 62 | 16 | Republican | Vietnam | Army | No |
| Stan R. | 90 | 18 | Independent | WWII | Army | No |
| Mike S. | 59 | 15 | Republican | Vietnam | Army | Yes |
| Art S. | 63 | 16 | Democrat | Vietnam | Navy | No |
| Robert S. | 62 | 13 | Republican | Vietnam | Army | Yes |
| J.W. | 62 | 16 | Republican | V/N–Iraq | Marines | Yes |
| Tonya W. | 45 | 14 | Democrat | 1979–83 | Navy | No |
| Larry W. | 59 | 15 | Democrat | Vietnam | Marines | Yes |
| George W. | 75 | 18 | Democrat | Korea | Army | Yes |
| Carlos Z. | 32 | College | Republican | Iraq | National Guard | Yes |

Note: "College" indicates veterans who are currently enrolled in school. V/N is the abbreviation for Vietnam-era veterans when the individual's service era spanned more than one era. For cells in which service eras are dates instead of wars, these service members did not serve during a designated war.

that comprise the political system: Are the courts fair? Is the legislative branch functioning properly?, and so on. I began each battery of questions requesting a simple "yes" or "no" reply, after which they were asked to explain their responses.

Before embarking on the analyses, a word on some of the limitations faced in this study is necessary. First, it is possible that the veterans who suffer from combat stress do not read the papers in which I advertised. Although I do not discuss it in the present essay, some veterans had no trust for mainstream media. They felt that the media only reported events consistent with its own political agenda. This was especially the case with veterans who had recently seen action in Operation Iraqi Freedom. Perhaps the *L.A. Times* and *San Francisco Chronicle* are too liberal for their respective tastes. For similar reasons (i.e., possible bias), the subjects probably represent those veterans in the upper bound of those who are interested in politics. Even so, I have no reason to believe that the relative differences between veterans with and without combat stress—the principal issue in this study—will be affected.

## Combat Exposure and Allegiance to the Political Regime

The political community notwithstanding, there are two objects to which individuals pledge their allegiance: the political regime and political authorities.[31] I begin the analysis by exploring the ways in which combat exposure affects veterans' allegiance to the political regime, the mix of norms and institutional configurations on which the political system rests.[32] The military seems to be a prime site through which to generate support for the American political regime. Beginning in childhood, citizens are socialized to support the political system and political authorities.[33] Adolescents maintain faith in the political system at least through early adulthood, after which cynicism begins to erode confidence in most things political.[34] However, it is at this juncture that military service may boost flagging confidence in the regime, for it (military service) generally occurs during a time in the life cycle not so far removed from adolescence.

Exposure to combat should only increase one's attachment to institutions and the liberal principles by which they operate, core elements of what constitutes the political regime.[35] Of course, this is more consistent with the developmental effect of military service in which one emerges from the military with a higher regard for both self and country. Thus, we should expect combat veterans without symptoms related to PTSD or combat-stress more generally to be more committed to American institutions than any other group. For those who continue to experience the pathogenic effects of combat such as nightmares, flashbacks, and other symptoms related to PTSD, I expect relative alienation to ensue. Noncombat veterans act as a quasi-control group, serving as a baseline against which to assess responses from the different groups of combat veterans.

## Combat-Stressed Veterans

I begin the examination with veterans who remain affected by the psychosocial trauma associated with war. This group, as we shall see, differs from other combat veterans and veterans with no combat experience in at least one respect: the tone of their responses. Veterans who suffer from combat stress are not only more alienated; they are also angrier than the other groups. One example is Bob. A Vietnam combat veteran who continues to suffer from PTSD, his opinion mirrors other veterans who suggest that the dishonesty of politicians affects the political system. Bob explained, "My opinion has to do with the fact because I paid such a high price to see that our freedoms are put forward. Or a belief that they were put forward, or we were told, and we believed that these were honorable fights that we were in. Of course, that's always hard to tell in the beginning or towards the end if you lose anyway." His distrust of the political system is evident, however, as he alludes to the actions of the political leadership during Vietnam. Bob's anger boils to the surface as he puts the ordeal into perspective. "Whenever you put forth your best, you've paid your price, you would hope that the American political system would see. But they're playing games, often with men's lives," he screams. He added, "It's gone on through history. I don't expect it to stop now. But the fact of the matter is when a political system is not honest about the conflict, they often can cost more lives than what the soldiers have inflicted, and cause them being killed and others being killed because of non-responsibility. They have to be as tough as we had to be!" His rebuke of the system, therefore, has everything to do with his sacrifice and his disappointment with the conduct of politicians during war.

Bob's critique is leveled squarely at American political leadership. His belief in the American political system was shattered by his experience during a war in which political deceit and cowardice led to the needless death of American troops. Political leadership is not the sole reason that some have lost faith in the political system, however. For some, it is the electorate, that is, the people, who are responsible for the failure of the American political system. Dave, a Vietnam veteran and retired police chief who mentioned flashbacks during the course of the interview, shares this view. He readily acknowledges that "a strength of American politics is that the people do have a voice, and that is the absolute essential bottom line in the democracy, and it's one of the strengths that people from time to time get fed up, and throw the rascals out." The problem, according to Dave, is that "people buy a lot of the bullshit that the politicians hand them. There isn't a lot of informed opinion!" Dave holds the educational system responsible for this lack of informed opinion among citizens. He protests that "our educational system doesn't lend itself to the strengthening of democracy. We put people out there that don't understand crap about the history, the democratic process that elects people, or the system of government. They don't know shit, and they go and vote, and that is the fault of the educational system!" Dave offers a rather bleak prognosis for the future of American democracy: "Will there always be stupid people that don't know shit? Yes. Is there anything that we can protect? Look, the worst dictatorships in the history of man have been those that purport to have a utopia at the end of the road." In the end, he has little faith that the problem will be corrected, at least in the near future. "The wrong people sometimes get elected. The right people sometimes get elected, and the people that make those choices aren't as informed as they should be. But, again, I'm an elitist," he sighs with a hint of resignation.

It is clear that for Dave, a principal weakness of the American political system ultimately rests upon education, a pillar of democracy. People are simply uninformed, and this causes problems and will continue to do so for the foreseeable future. Likewise, Bob has little faith in the American political system. However, not all veterans who continue to struggle with the effects of combat stress are pessimistic. Consider Carlos's comments, a national guardsman who has recently returned from Iraq and reports becoming easily agitated and wary of crowds upon his returning, classic symptoms of PTSD. He believes the system "is the best one. Okay, let me rephrase that," he says, upon a moment's reflection. "It may not be great, but it's definitely the best of the alternatives out there right now. It works." He recognizes the presence of corruption but insists that in the American system the "corruption is either better hidden or just less than everywhere else." Among the virtues of the American political system, according to Carlos, is that "it's set up so we don't elect no freaking Hitler or something like that." Thus, another view that veterans seem to have is one in which the American system is simply the best one available; the alternatives are not so attractive.

## Combat Veterans

On the whole, combat veterans who do not suffer from combat stress tend to be a little more optimistic about the political system than veterans with combat stress. This, however, does not mean that they are without criticism of the political system, one of which is the charge that the executive has too much power. In the present case, they are rather upset that President George W. Bush seemed to do whatever he pleased, without regard to the institutional checks intended by the framers. George, a veteran of the Korean War and retired high school teacher, articulates this position the best. "I have a hard time with this," he says. "I taught a course on this in high school, so I have 40 years of opinion on this. I feel that American political institutions need to be reorganized. I think that our President has too much power; not just George Bush, but people before him, taking it [Presidential authority] and using it as they are the king. [It's] like they don't have a Congress, and it doesn't matter what Congress does." He cites the war in Iraq as an example. "The President has the attitude that 'I'm the President, and I can do anything I want.'" George concedes that the president is the commander in chief,

> but [when] the generals in the Pentagon and Congress tell him something, why does he have to think "I know more than they do, so I am going to do it my way." How could he do this when, in fact, he really was not in the military. You talk about veterans; they are guys who actually fought. He [Bush] was in the National Guard, and I don't think he saw a plane and never showed up to his meetings and it was a joke! The military was a joke to him whereas he's sending troops over there and doing all these military things!

George's criticism is as much about flawed institutional design (i.e., too much executive power) as it is of President Bush's dubious character. The implication is that reform lies with making the power wielded by other branches of government more equal to that of the executive. Criticism of the American political system is not limited to its structure, though. Some of the combat veterans believe that individuals inside these institutions cause harm to the political system. Bill, for instance, believes that the "political system's effectiveness is influenced very much by the personalities involved in all the branches." A veteran of World War II, he has had a long time to observe how individuals shape institutions and public policy. He draws on the Supreme Court as an example. "Although they are not supposed to, they bring into the Supreme Court all the prejudices and political leanings, and it has a tremendous effect on us, sometimes very much to our detriment." The decision in *Bush v. Gore*, for Bill, is an ideal example of this. "I think a good, fair-minded court would have said the vote is the key thing. Let the people vote again and decide the issue that way instead of—as I understand it, it was a 5–4 decision, but they agreed to say it was unanimous in trying to unite the country, but it didn't help." He concludes, suggesting that public officials should strive to leave aside personal prejudice and biases and work toward the common good: "There are always some [individuals] that we are unhappy with because they let their prejudices get in the way. I guess that's human nature. But maybe they can try harder to be more fair-minded."

There are, however, some combat veterans who believe the political system to be near flawless. Ed is one of them. A military retiree and veteran of Vietnam, Desert Storm, and Operation Iraqi Freedom, he has unmitigated affection for the American political system. For starters, he highlights the system's ability to overcome potentially fractious divisions and frequent missteps, highlighting its durability. He explained, "Never in the history of mankind have we had the ability to take so many diverse languages, cultures, religions, and belief systems and meld them into one political volume as the glorious experience called America. We have made some tremendous boneheaded stunts that are hard to believe." He illustrates his point by citing a moment at which he educated some of his charges while serving in Iraq: "We were sitting in a country that has been populated for 4 millennia [with people] who are still living in mud huts and fighting inter-village clan battles. We are a country less than 400 years; we have been to the moon and back, and yet in the first half of the 20th Century, we believed that . . . slavery was approvable." According to Ed, the superiority of the American political system is evident in America's ability to "grow and adapt [remaining] melded together even after a major civil war and, where given our land mass, would be twenty countries if this was Europe." He concludes, opining "we have reconstructed the country into one that is the envy of the known world . . . because we are successful at being the body of politics."

## Noncombat Veterans

Noncombat veterans, like their combat counterparts, were also at once skeptical of and enamored with the regime. Burt's opinion is a clear example of the former. A Vietnam-era veteran who served stateside during the war, he reports "not [being] too happy with these institutions, but it's not clear what a better alternative would be." Clearly, he believes there is a need for improvement, especially in reforming the incentive structure for politicians. Burt offered, "I would suggest that if any politicians take let's say more than a dollar from anybody they'd be shot." As an example, he cites the practice of earmarking, a part of the legislative appropriations process in which funds are designated by a legislator to be spent on a specific project, generally in his district. For Burt, it represents another institutional impediment to competent political representation if governing for the collective good is the goal. As for many Americans, earmarking is a source of enduring frustration for Burt. "In my view," he says, "any legislator who proposes any project that that costs government money for his or her own district should be shot." Other noncombat veterans are more impressed with the political system, but they are more impressed with its design versus how it actually works. Art, who served in the Navy in Vietnam, says as much, opining: "I think the forefathers couldn't have [better] written ... the Constitution and the structure of government, to me, it's the best as far as I'm concerned." Asked for specifics, he replies that, "We can amend things; we're supposed to have a balance of power. Those guys were geniuses," he says referring to the Founding Fathers. Kathleen agrees. One of the first female surface line officers to serve aboard a naval combatant, she unabashedly declares: "I believe in the Constitution. Obviously, I've taken an oath to defend it." However, in addition to the system of checks and balances, she is a firm believer "in our system of representative democracy."

With the exception of combat veterans, the majority of whom remain allegiant to the political regime, the interviews suggest that support for it remains in short supply among veterans. More telling, however, is the extent to which estrangement varies with the category to which veterans belong. Each group expresses some degree of alienation, but it is among the veterans who continue to battle the effects of combat stress who seem most distressed about the political order and pessimistic about reform, even angry. Given the well-documented political alienation associated with service in Vietnam, some may question these findings.[36] This possible objection would posit that most veterans who served during Vietnam were alienated, regardless of their postservice condition. Yet, when I account for the postwar condition of veterans, that is, whether or not they suffered the effects of combat stress, a gap emerges among Vietnam-era veterans. Among Vietnam veterans, most of those who remain afflicted by combat stress were far more likely to report feeling alienated than those not bothered by it.[37] While combat veterans cite weaknesses within American political institutions, to them, the flaws do not seem intractable. Since most pledge support to the regime but remain somewhat critical, combat veterans appear to be more supportive than anything else. Similar findings obtain for noncombat veterans. Thus, they too may be classified as allegiant.

We now have an idea of how veterans explain their perceptions of the political system, but we have no idea about the prevalence of their responses. We have noticed that some veterans with combat stress appear more distrustful than other groups of veterans. But as Carlos's example suggests, there are at least some combat-stressed veterans who are willing to embrace the political system. Likewise, we may ask similar questions of combat veterans and veterans who have seen no combat whatsoever. To gain a sense of group trends, I tabulated a few simple frequency distributions. The percentages I report are based upon relatively few observations, a total of thirty-one cases. We must, therefore, remain cautious about the extent to which we may generalize from these results.

Having said that, the results serve the illustrative purpose for which they were intended. The evidence suggests support for the claim that exposure to combat stress is also a factor with which we must contend when the relationship between politics and war, at the individual level, is considered. At 60 percent, more combat veterans, as a group, support the political system than other groups. But this remains true only insofar as the veteran is not haunted by combat stress. Only 44 percent (four out of nine) of those who served in combat and remain affected by it support the system, a general pattern that is repeated in the section that follows. Half of all noncombat veterans, those without the sense of self-regard that comes with surviving combat, remain allegiant to the political system. That more noncombat veterans embrace the system than combat veterans who remain distressed by their military service suggests the debilitating effects of combat stress.

As the interviews indicate, veterans' postwar conditions matter. Veterans who remain stricken with combat-related stress seem more cynical about the political system than the other groups. Moreover, if these findings are any indication, the combat-stressed veterans are also angrier than the other groups. This comports well with the work of psychologists who have found that some veterans with PTSD tend to become angered when they perceive the rules of the game are violated, something that veterans with combat-stress articulated in their comments.[38] And, as the frequency distributions suggest, this disposition is not confined to the veterans who were highlighted; cynicism and anger are carried by most of these veterans. This not to say that noncombat veterans were not cynical; some were. But they remained relatively hopeful about reform. What is more, I failed to detect much anger among this bunch. This distinction is akin to Sniderman's approach to alienation in which he distinguishes between the disaffected and the disenchanted. "Both," he says, "are alienated; yet the judgment of the second is balanced, the first is not."[39] In the present case, the anger and the condemnation of the political regime voiced by veterans with combat stress suggests a relatively unbalanced evaluation of it, one that paints the existing order irretrievably flawed. Combat and non-combat veterans' appraisals of the regime, on the other hand, are balanced by comparison.

## Discussion and Concluding Thoughts

As this essay noted in its introduction, much is known about the effect of combat stress on the social and occupational readjustment of American veterans on their return to civil society. However, until now, there has been no accounting for the civic readjustment of those who were subjected to the horrors of combat. This essay represents a step in that direction, one that seeks to correct this oversight. Toward that end, the essay sought to examine the hypothesized disparate effects of combat exposure, relating them to positive and negative outcomes of military service. The developmental effects associated with positive military experiences in which the service member emerges from war with higher self-regard, part of which is due to surviving combat, were believed to be conducive to support for both the regime and political authorities.

The pathogenic effect of military service, one that indexes, in this case, psychosocial trauma associated with war, portended political alienation. Consistent with expectations, this paper shows that combat-related stress, including PTSD, moderates the effect of war on civic attitudes. More to the point, it illustrates that veterans who must contend with combat stress or posttraumatic stress disorder are less inclined to have faith in politicians or the political regime relative to veterans who claimed not to suffer from the pathogenic effects of military service.

The fact that many veterans appear alienated from the political regime is not entirely new; Frey-Wouters and Laufer's as well as Johnson's work showed similar patterns.[40] What appears new, however, is that alienation varies according to exposure to combat. To the extent that alienation is differentiated between the disaffected and disenchanted, where the former is essentially "one-sided criticism" of authorities and the latter is characterized as a more "even-handed," veterans suffering from combat stress appear to fall more easily into the former category.[41] For, as the interviews indicate, they tend to be more critical than the other groups, their criticism tinged with anger. It seems that when some veterans with PTSD do not believe people are following the rules, they become angry because they had seen buddies die because rules were not followed.[42] These people who had pledged to support and defend the Constitution and obey the orders of the president see George Bush as failing to follow the rules. Perhaps this is the root of their disaffection.

Beyond its ability to affect regard for the political regime, it is possible that combat stress may also affect veterans' ability to participate in politics. Some scholars suggest that mental illness sometimes increases the likelihood of political engagement.[43] Perhaps Lasswell's account in which political symbols serve as an outlet for one's psychological instability is one way to account for increased activism when the political object from which one becomes estranged is the president, arguably the most dominant symbol in American politics.[44] However, none of this work considers the effect of combat stress, particularly PTSD. Links between PTSD and politics, I believe, are located within each symptom cluster. For instance, the first and third symptom clusters may affect political participation.

Many scholars have documented the cognitive difficulties associated with PTSD. Specifically, combat veterans with the syndrome have difficulty with attention, working memory, and verbal learning.[45] Horner and Hamner suggest that the inability to effectively regulate and adapt intrusive memories, such as flashbacks and dreams that affect memory and cognition, are responsible for these deficiencies. It seems that the flash backs associated with re-experiencing the trauma involves "cognitive processing, information storage, and retrieval from memory," taxing these cognitive functions during the process.[46] Hyperarousal and vigilance are implicated to the extent that these symptoms affect problem-solving abilities.[47] If political participation—especially activism—requires some cognitive ability, PTSD could impede the practice of democratic citizenship.

Beyond adding a layer to the literature on alienation and in which political estrangement usually results in decreasing engagement, not the increasing activism that I find, these findings highlight a lacuna in political science. With the exception of Lynn Sanders's work on the connection between politics and mental health, there is nothing, as far as I know, that has touched upon this area in almost forty years.[48] Considering that 26 percent of the adult population suffers from mental disability or engages in substance abuse, often both, mental illness is something to which political scientists should pay more attention.[49]

An obvious limitation of this essay, on which I have already commented, is the number of observations on which findings are based. The results are, therefore, meant to guide future research in which more data maybe gathered to more formally test hypotheses related to the way(s) in which combat-related PTSD moderates the effect of combat on civic attitudes and behavior, controlling for possible confounds and accounting for alternative explanations. Both are needed if we are to have more confidence in the ability of combat stress to explain variation in political outcomes of interest. Therefore, a natural next step includes collecting survey data in which a more representative sample is secured. Another step to be taken is to compare the impact of combat-related PTSD on politics to those who suffer from PTSD that originates with a different type of trauma. One place to start is with victims of PTSD around the terrorist attacks of 9/11, for as Rasinski and his colleagues demonstrate, trauma and politics, particularly confidence in the government, are related.[50]

## Notes

1. Josephina J. Card, *Lives after Vietnam: The Personal Impact of Military Service* (Lexington, Mass.: Lexington Books, 1983); R. M. Kulka, W. E. Schlenger, J. A. Fairbank, R. L. Hough,

B. K. Jordan, C. R. Marmar, and D. S. Weiss, *Trauma and the Vietnam Generation* (New York: Brunner/Mazel Publishers, 1990); R. S. Laufer, "War Trauma and Human Development: The Vietnam Experience," in *The Trauma of War: Stress and Recovery in Vietnam Veterans*, ed. J. Sonnenberg, A. S. Blank Jr., and J. Talbott (Washington, D.C.: American Psychiatric Press, 1985); and M. McCarren, G. R. Janes, J. Goldberg, S. A. Eisen, W. R. True, and W. G. Henderson, "A Twin Study of the Association of Post-Traumatic Stress Disorder and Combat Exposure with Long-Term Socioeconomic Status in Vietnam Veterans," *Journal of Traumatic Stress* 8, no. 1(1995): 111–24.

2. Kulka et al., *Trauma and the Vietnam Generation*; and E. Frey-Wouters and R. S. Laufer, *Legacy of a War* (New York: M. E. Sharpe, 1986).

3. J.R.T. Davidson, H. S. Kudler, W. B. Saunders, and R. D. Smith, "Symptom and Comorbidity Patterns in World war II and Vietnam Veterans with Posttraumatic Stress Disorder," *Comprehensive Psychiatry* 31 (1990): 162–70; Kulka et al., *Trauma and the Vietnam Generation*; and Laufer, "War Trauma and Human Development."

4. Kulka et al., *Trauma and the Vietnam Generation*.

5. T. C. Buckley, B. L. Green, and P. P. Schnurr, "Trauma, PTSD, and Health," in *Assessing Psychological Trauma*, ed. J. P. Wilson and T. M. Keane (New York: Guilford Press, 2004).

6. G. H. Elder and E. Clipp, "Combat Experience and Emotional Health," *Journal of Personality* 57 (1989): 311–41.

7. J. Citrin, "Comment: The Political Relevance of Trust in Government," *American Political Science Review* 68 (1974): 973–88.

8. J. Citrin, "Political Alienation as a Social Indicator: Attitudes and Action," *Social Indicators Research* 4 (1977): 381–419; and Paul Sniderman, *A Question of Loyalty* (Berkeley: University of California Press, 1981).

9. The articles were extracted from a Lexis-Nexus search.

10. "GAO: Few Troops Are Treated for Disorder, Post-Traumatic Stress Risk Gauged," *Washington Post*, 11 May 2006.

11. K. H. Seal, D. Bertenthal, C. R. Miner, S. Sen, and C. Marmar, "Bringing the War Back Home," *Archives of Internal Medicine* 167 (2007): 476–82.

12. L. Johnson, "Political Alienation among Vietnam Veterans," *Western Political Quarterly* 29 (1976): 398–409.

13. J. P. Wilson, "Post-traumatic Stress Disorder and Complex Post-traumatic Stress Disorder," in *Assessing Psychological Trauma and Post-traumatic Stress Disorder*, ed. J. P. Wilson and T. M. Keane (New York: Guilford Press, 2004).

14. D. D. Blake, F. W. Weathers, L. M. Nagy, D. G. Kaloupek, G. Klauminzer, D. S. Carney, and T. M. Keane, "A Clinical Rating Scale for Assessing Current and Lifetime PTSD," *The Behavior Therapist* 18 (1990): 187–88.

15. Kulka et al., *Trauma and the Vietnam Generation*; see also B. P. Dohrenwend, J. B. Turner, N. A. Turse, B. G. Adams, K. C. Koenen, and R. Marshall, "The Psychological Risks of Vietnam for U.S. Veterans," *Science* 313, no. 578: 979–82.

16. Kulka et al., *Trauma and the Vietnam Generation*.

17. H. K. Kang, B. H. Natelson, C. M. Mahan, K. Y. Lee, and F. M. Murphy, "Post-Traumatic Stress Disorder and Chronic Fatigue Syndrome-like Illness among Gulf War Veterans," *American Journal of Epidemiology* 157(2003): 141–48; and C. W. Hoge, C. A. Castro, S. C. Messer, D. McGurk, D. I. Cotting, and R. L. Koffman, "Combat Duty in Iraq and Afghanistan, Mental Health Problems, and Barriers to Care," *New England Journal of Medicine* 351 (2004): 13–22.

18. M. J. Friedman, "Post-traumatic Stress Disorder among Military Returnees from Afghanistan and Iraq," *American Journal of Psychiatry* 163 (2004): 586–93.

19. These figures are based on estimates combining the number of Vietnam era veterans with chronic PTSD with the number of post-Vietnam era veterans who will suffer PTSD during their lifetimes. Iraq and Afghanistan War veterans' estimates are based on the approximately two million veterans who have served in these conflicts since 2001. See L. Korb, P. Rundlet, and M. Bergmann, *Beyond the Call of Duty: A Comprehensive Review of the Overuse of the Army in the Administration's War of Choice in Iraq* (Washington, D.C.: Center for American Progress, 2007); and Institute of Medicine, *Returning Home from Iraq and Afghanistan: Preliminary Assessment of Readjustment Needs of Veterans, Service Members, and Their Families* (Washington, D.C.: National Academies Press, 2010).

20. Elder and Clipp, "Combat Experience and Emotional Health."

21. A. Bandura, "The Assessment and Predictive Generality of Self-Percepts of Efficacy," *Journal of Behavior Therapy and Experimental Psychiatry* 13, no. 3 (1982): 195–99.

22. R. Claire Snyder, *Citizen-Soldiers and Manly Warriors: Military Service and Gender in the Civic Republican Tradition* (Lanham, Md.: Rowman & Littlefield, 1999).

23. Morris Janowitz, *The Reconstruction of Patriotism: Education for Civic Consciousness* (Chicago: University of Chicago Press, 1983).

24. James Burk, "Theories of Democratic Civil-Military Relations," *Armed Forces and Society* 29, no. 1 (2002): 7–29; and Samuel A. Stouffer, *Communism, Conformity & Civil Liberties: A Cross Section of the Nation Speaks Its Mind* (New York: Doubleday & Co., 1955).

25. Janowitz, *Reconstruction of Patriotism.*

26. Klaus Roghmann and Wolfgang Sodeur, "The Impact of Military Services on Authoritarian Attitudes," *American Journal of Sociology* 78, no. 2 (September 1972): 418–33.

27. Wilson, "Post-traumatic Stress Disorder," 25.

28. Frey-Wouters and Laufer, *Legacy of a War*, ch. 2.

29. L. Johnson, "Political Alienation among Vietnam Veterans," *Western Political Quarterly* 29, no. 3 (1976): 398–409.

30. T. M. Keane, "Psychological Effects of Military Combat," in *Adversity, Stress, and Psychopathology*, ed. B.P Dohrenwend (New York: Oxford University Press, 2004). Perhaps the single most common means of assessing combat-related posttraumatic stress disorder is with the Mississippi Scale for Combat-Related PTSD. This scale is a battery of thirty-five Likert-scaled items designed to gauge the presence of the three symptom clusters associated with PTSD: intrusion, avoidance, and arousal.

31. D. Easton, "A Re-Assessment of the Concept of Political Support," *British Journal of Political Science* 5, no. 4 (1975): 435–57; D. Easton and J. Dennis, *Children in the Political System: Origins of Political Legitimacy* (Chicago: University of Chicago Press, 1969).

32. Easton and Dennis, *Children in the Political System*, ch. 3.

33. Ibid.

34. M. K. Jennings and R. Niemi, *The Political Character of Adolescence: The Influence of Families and Schools* (Princeton, N.J.: Princeton University Press, 1974).

35. Easton and Dennis, *Children in the Political System*; and Easton, "A Re-Assessment."

36. For example, Frey-Wouters and Laufer, *Legacy of a War*; and Johnson, "Political Alienation among Vietnam Veterans."

37. To be more precise, 67 percent (four of six) of those with combat stress felt alienated versus 44 percent (four of nine) of those without it.

38. C. M. Chemtob, R. W. Novaco, R. S. Hamada, D. M. Gross, and G. Smith, "Anger

Regulation Deficits in Combat-Related Posttraumatic Stress Disorder," *Journal of Traumatic Stress* 10, no. 1 (1997): 17–36.

39. Sniderman, *Question of Loyalty*, 49.

40. Frey-Wouters and Laufer, *Legacy of a War*; Johnson, "Political Alienation among Vietnam Veterans."

41. Sniderman, *Question of Loyalty*.

42. Chemtob et al., "Anger Regulation Deficits."

43. H. D. Lasswell, *Psychopathology and Politics* (Chicago: University of Chicago Press, 1930); G. E. Marcus, "Psychopathology and Political Recruitment," *Journal of Politics* 31, no. 4 (1969): 913–31; and B. M. Rutherford, "Psychopathology, Decision-making, and Political Involvement," *Journal of Conflict Resolution* 10 (1966): 387–407. Sanders argues that political participation improves mental health. See L. M. Sanders, "The Psychological Benefits of Political Participation," paper presented at the annual meeting of the American Political Science Association, San Francisco, CA, August 30–September 2, 2001.

44. Theodore Lowi, *The Personal President: Power Invested, Promise Unfulfilled*, 2nd, ed. (Ithaca, N.Y.: Cornell University Press, 1985).

45. T. Gil, A. Calev, D. Greenberg, S. Kugelmass, and B. Lerer, "Cognitive Functioning in Posttraumatic Stress Disorder, *Journal of Traumatic Stress* 3 (1990): 29–45; and K. W. Samuelson, T. J. Metzler, J. Rothlind, G. Choucroun, T. C. Neyland, M. Lenoci, C. Henn-Haase, M. W. Lerner, and C. Marmar, "Neuropsychological Functioning in Posttraumatic Stress Disorder and Alcohol Abuse," *Neuropsychology* 20 (2006): 716–26.

46. Wilson, "Post-traumatic Stress Disorder"; and Michael David Horner and Mark B. Hamner, "Neurocognitive Functioning in Posttraumatic Stress Disorder," *Neuropsychology Review* 12, no. 1 (2002): 15–30.

47. Wilson, "Post-traumatic Stress Disorder."

48. Sanders, "Psychological Benefits of Political Participation."

49. R. C. Kessler, W. T. Chiu, O. Demler, and E. E. Walters, "Prevalence, Severity, and Comorbidity of 12-Month DSM-IV Disorders in the National Comorbidity Survey Replication," *Archives of General Psychiatry* 62, no. 6 (2005): 617–28.

50. K. A. Rasinski, A. Matthews, B. L. Albertson, T. W. Smith, and J. Berktold, "The 9/11 Terrorist Attacks: Ethnic Differences in Emotional Response and Recovery," unpublished manuscript, 2002.

# Contributors

Mark Boulton, assistant professor of History, Westminster College–Fulton, Missouri

Carol R. Byerly, independent scholar

Nancy Gentile Ford, professor of History, Bloomsburg University of Pennsylvania

Audra Jennings, coordinator of undergraduate research, Western Kentucky University

Jennifer D. Keene, professor of History, Chapman University

John M. Kinder, assistant professor of American Studies and History, Oklahoma State University

Suzanne Mettler, Clinton Rossiter Professor of American Institutions in the Government Department at Cornell University.

Stephen R. Ortiz, associate professor of History, Binghamton University

Christopher S. Parker, Stuart A. Scheingold Professor of Social Justice and Political Science, University of Washington

Melinda Pash, instructor, Fayetteville Technical Community College

Rosemary A. Stevens, DeWitt Wallace Distinguished Scholar in Social Medicine and Public Policy at Weill Cornell Medical College, Department of Psychiatry

Jeremy M. Teigen, associate professor of Political Science, Ramapo College

Nancy Beck Young, professor of History, University of Houston

# Index

California, 14, 17, 141n1, 212

Camp Beauregard (La.), 45

Camp Lee (Va.), 126

Camp Marks, 190

Camp Sherman (Ohio), 81, 82, 83, 92n54

Cannon, Pat., 207

*Carry On,* 154

Castle Point, N.Y., 160

Chambers of commerce: and Emergency Employment Committee, 132, 133; John F. O'Ryan and, 56; and publicity for employment campaigns for WWI veterans, 131, 132; and race, 149–50; and U.S. Employment Service, 122, 129; Warren G. Harding and, 48

Chattanooga, Tenn., 188

Chicago, Ill.: Army/NRC prosthetics meeting in, 104–5; Forbes indictment in, 58; military hospitals in, 79; race riots in, 139, 150; veterans' groups in, 152, 184; veterans hospitals in, 45, 47–48; WWI veterans in, 125

Chillicothe, Ohio, 81

China, 251

Cholmeley-Jones, Richard G., 46, 52

CIO, 212, 215

Citizenship: children and adolescents and, 289; and education, 291; responsibilities of, 281; scholarship on, 300n43; veterans and, 282, 284, 285–86, 289–97, 299n37; and veterans' benefits, 243, 244, 245–46, 247, 252, 255

Civilian Conservation Corps, 203

Civil rights. *See* African Americans; Jim Crow and segregation

Civil Service Department, 129

Civil War, 69, 120. *See also* Veterans, Civil War

Clark, Bennett Champ, 176, 209, 211, 216

Clarksburg, W. Va., 186

Cleveland, Ohio, 137

Clifford, Edward, 53

Clinton, Bill, 276

Clipp, E., 282, 285

Cochran, Terrance B., 179

Cold War G.I. Bill. *See* G.I. bills, Vietnam-era

Colleges, universities, and trade schools: funding for, 225–26, 228; and G.I. Bill, 230, 231, 238n50; historically black, 234, 239n63; and Korean G.I. Bill, 233–34, 238n50, 239n63; and Vietnam-era G.I. Bills, 242; and WWII veterans, 225. *See also* Vocational rehabilitation and training

*Collier's,* 134

Columbia State, 242

Columbia University, 40, 53, 105, 126, 233

Commission on Training Camp Activities, 92n54

Committee on Prosthetic Devices, 105, 108–9, 110

Committee on Public Information (CPI), 123, 129

Communists and Communism, 124, 125, 188, 190, 191

Congress. *See* U.S. Congress

Connecticut, 133, 141n1

Conroy, Bernard, 25

Conservatives and conservatism, 2, 243, 253

Coolidge, Calvin, 58, 175, 178

Cornell University, 126

Coughlin, Charles E., 186

Council of National Defense, 126, 131. *See also* Emergency Employment Committee for Soldiers, Sailors, and Marines of the Council of National Defense

Cramer, Charles F., 58

Crossland, James, 159, 163, 168n36

Crossland, J.R.A., 155, 156, 158

Crowell, Benedict, 120

Cuba, 16, 17

Cumming, Hugh, 47

Cunningham, Paul, 216

Danaher, John A., 216

Dartmouth University, 126

Daugherty, Harry M., 58

Davis, C. B., 74

Dawes, Charles G., 52, 54, 62n59

Dawes committee, 52

Dawson, William L., 239n63

Dawson Springs Veterans Hospital (Ky.), 46–47, 160

Dayton, Ohio, 74, 160

Dean, Arthur R., 53–54

Decatur, Ill., 152

DeCoe, Darold D., 186

Delaware, 133

Demobilization: facilities for, 66, 120, 128, 133; after WWI, 119–21, 123, 126, 127, 128, 133; after WWII, 94, 107, 201

Democrats and Democratic Party: conservatives and, 202; and gay marriage, 275; and gays and lesbians in the military, 273–74; and G.I. Bill, 213, 216; liberals and, 204; and race, 206; and social welfare system, 204; on war in Iraq, 269

Department of Justice. *See* U.S. Department of Justice

establishment and mission of, 11, 16, 18; facilities at, 21, 25, 28; food at, 11, 12, 21; funding for, 24, 25; historical documentation on, 14–15, 21; location of, 18; as National Historic District, 34n36; and National Home for Disabled Volunteer Soldiers, 14–15, 23, 24; patients' behavior at, 12, 27–28; patients' movement in and out of, 14, 23–24, 26, 27, 28; photos of, 18, 22; population of, 15, 17, 18, 20–21, 22, 23–24, 29, 30, 31; as Public Health Service facility, 30; role of, in veterans' lives, 27; rules at, 11, 12, 21–23, 27, 28; staff at, 18, 20, 23, 24, 25, 26, 27, 28, 29; transfer of patients from, 30; as tuberculosis hospital, 12–13, 14, 16, 17, 18, 21–23, 24; and U.S. Soldiers' Home, 14–15, 17, 23, 24, 25, 28; veterans' benefits at, 23, 24. *See also* Bushnell, George E.

Fort Defiance (Ariz.), 34n32
Fort Logan (Colo.), 19
Fort Lyon (Colo.), 34n32
*Fort Sheridan Recall,* 79
Fort Stanton (N. Mex.), 34n32
Fort Worth, Tex., 185
"Forward to the Farm, Why Not?," 133
Foster, Reginald L., 129–30
Foucault, Michel, 90n11
Frankfurter, Felix, 192
Frey-Wouters, E., 296
Fitzsimons, William Thomas, 30

Gardner, Edward S., 129
Gays and lesbians, 112n7, 201, 264, 272–75, 279n25
General Accounting Office, 229
General Motors, 105
General Staff, 123
General War Times Commission, 131
George, Walter, 216
Georgia, 141n1
Gerber, David, 166n1
G.I. Bill, Korean (1952): amendments to, 234; compared to 1944 G.I. Bill, 224; conference committee on, 233; Congress and, 223–24, 225, 226–27, 229, 234–35, 237n25, 237n37; Dwight D. Eisenhower and, 237n42; eligibility for, 227–28, 229, 237n42; expiration of, 237n42, 245, 246; Harry S. Truman and, 223, 226–27, 228, 230, 233; and higher education, 225–26, 228; House of Representatives and, 230–32, 233, 237n42, 239n56, 239n63; and military retention, 228, 237n37; passage of, 223, 224–25, 233; provisions of, 224, 231, 232–33, 245, 259n41; purposes of,

226–27; results of, 233–34; scholarship on, 223; Senate and, 232–33, 237n42, 239n74; and social welfare, 226–27; use of, 256; Walter Mondale and, 251
"G.I. Bill: Less than Enough" (O'Brien), 241
G.I. Bill of Rights (1944): abuses under, 223, 229, 230, 231, 238n45, 238n50; African Americans and, 201; amendments to, 229–30, 238n45; Conference Committee on, 216–17; Congress's role in, 200, 217; conservatives and, 203, 212, 213; costs of, 209, 214, 256; Democrats and, 213; economic benefits of, 225; eligibility for, 95, 112n7, 201, 227, 229; extension of, 222–23, 229; extent of, 235n3; Franklin D. Roosevelt and, 208; generosity of, 242; House of Representatives and, 212–16, 253; liberals and, 213, 217; Lyndon B. Johnson on, 250; moderates and, 213; as one-time occurrence, 224; passage of, 199–200, 217; philosophy of, 217; as political bellwether, 200; provisions of, 95, 209, 212–13, 214–15, 216, 223, 224, 225, 229, 244–45; public perceptions of, 223, 229, 242; purposes of, 227; and race, 215; reaction to, 217; Republicans and, 213; results of, 225, 241; scholarship on, 3, 195n8, 201, 242; Senate and, 209, 211–12, 213, 214, 216, 217; as social legislation, 175; and U.S. economy, 247; and U.S. Employment Service, 217; use of, 256; Veterans Administration and, 209, 213, 215, 217, 224, 230; veterans' groups and, 207, 208, 209, 214, 217
G.I. bills, Vietnam-era: compared to 1944 G.I. Bill, 241, 242, 243, 244; complaints about, 241–42; congressional debate on, 251–52; costs of, 253, 254, 256; educational allowances of, 241–42; eligibility for, 243, 252, 253; Gerald Ford and, 260n63; and Great Society, 249–50; impact of, 255, 256; passage of, 254; provisions of, 254, 255, 256, 259n41; Richard Nixon and, 260n63; scholarship on, 242–43, 257n11; use of, 256; William Driver on, 250
Gibson, John S., 216–17
Gifford, Brian, 277
Glassford, Pelham D., 187, 189
Gleason, John S., 247, 250
Gobrecht, J. C., 70
Goodyear Tire & Rubber, 105
Gordon, Kermit, 250
Gorgas, William, 16, 19–20, 29
Graham, Hettie, 29
Graham, John L., 29

*Infantry Journal,* 125
Iowa, 141n1
Iraq, 268–71, 283, 285, 288, 291, 293, 299n19. *See also* Gulf War, first; Operation Iraqi Freedom

Jacksonville, Fla., 217
Jacksonville Chamber of Commerce, 149–50
Janowitz, Morris, 285
Jefferson, Thomas, 244, 245
Jeffrey, Harry P., 215
Jennings, M. Kent, 265
Jersey City, N.J., 136, 188
Jewish Welfare Board, 121, 131
Jim Crow and segregation: black veterans and, 146, 148, 160, 163, 165; and Great Migration, 138, 149; and wages, 213
"Jobs for Cripples," 130
*Jobs for Soldiers,* 138
Johnson, Greenleaf, 157
Johnson, Jewell, 25
Johnson, L., 296
Johnson, Linus, 25–26
Johnson, Lyndon B., 249–50, 252, 254–55
Johnson, Paul B., 148
Johnson, Royal C., 49, 173, 182, 191–92
*Journal of the National Medical Association,* 164

Kansas City, Mo., 182, 184–85, 190, 194n5
Kansas State Agricultural College, 86
Katz, Michael B., 243
Kearney, Bernard William "Pat," 215, 216
Keller, Morton, 249
Kelley, Augustine B., 109–10
Kelly, Patrick J., 23, 71, 76
Kennedy, John F., 249, 258n31
Kennedy, Robert F., 252
Kentucky, 141n1, 150, 152
Ketchum, Omar, 209
Kim Il Sung, 222
Kirkbride, Thomas Story, 71
Klopsteg, Paul E., 105
Knights of Columbus, 131
Kobbe, William Hoffman, 127–28
Koch, Robert, 15, 16
Korean War, 222, 223, 226, 228, 234, 268. *See also* G.I. Bill, Korean (1952); Veterans: Korean War
Kraabel, T. O., 103
Kreuz, Frank P., 94, 99–100, 101
Ku Klux Klan (KKK), 152, 153, 163
Kulka, R. M., 285

Labor, 124–25, 136, 137, 141n1
Labor Department. *See* U.S. Department of Labor
La Follette, Robert M., 95, 216
Lake Saranac, N.Y., 21
Lakeville, Minn., 86
"Land and the Soldier, The," 130
Lane, Franklin K., 83–84, 127
Laporte, Ewing, 43–44, 47, 50, 60n22
Lasswell, H. D., 296
Laufer, R. S., 296
Lavelle, M. J., 131–32
League of Nations, 123
Lee, Cordelia, 159
Lee, David, 153
Lee, Rosa, 153
Lemke, William, 204
Lesbians. *See* Gays and lesbians
*Leslie's,* 130, 134
Liberals, 243
Liberia, 168n36
*Life,* 130, 134
Lincoln Legion, 152
Lindley, Forrest (Rusty), 241
Little, Arthur, 152
Logan, Rayford, 158
Los Angeles, Calif., 23, 157, 287
*Los Angeles Times,* 287, 289
Louisiana, 24, 151, 152
Lucas, Scot, 216
Lufkin, Tex., 25

MacArthur, Douglas, 192
MacDonald, John A., 11, 12, 13, 28
Mackinac Declaration of Domestic Policy, 206
Mackinac Island, 203
Macon, Nathaniel, 244
Malisoff, Harry, 108–9
Mallery, Otto T., 135
Mann, James R., 49
Marcantonio, Vito, 216
March, Peyton C., 120
Marcus, Gregory B., 265
Mare Island, Calif., 99
Marines. *See* U.S. Marines
Marion, Ohio, 48
Marion Military Home, 159
Marlow, 135
Marrs, E. P., 151
Marx, Robert S., 81
Maryland, 186, 212
Massachusetts, 141n1, 212

281; WWI veterans and, 30, 42, 46, 48, 49, 54, 55, 77, 78–79, 80, 84, 158–59, 160, 164

New Deal: Congress and, 200, 201–2, 203, 204, 217; FDR's proposals to expand, 201; influence of, on Great Society, 249; opponents of, 103, 200, 201–2, 203–4, 205, 215; scholarship on, 112n7; soldiers and, 205–6; supporters of, 199, 205, 246

New Deal Brain Trusters, 203

New Jersey, 133

New Mexico, 17, 24. *See also* Fort Bayard Army Hospital (N. Mex.)

Newport News, Va., 148

*New Republic,* 217

New York, N.Y., 121, 130, 132, 181

New York 15th Infantry, 152

New York Furniture Exchange Association, 133–34

New York State, 133, 141n1, 152

New York State Division of Veterans Affairs, 242

*New York Times,* 54, 125, 130, 186, 188, 189, 242, 255

*New York Tribune,* 107

*New York World,* 130

92nd Division, 164

Ninth U.S. Cavalry, 18

Nixon, Richard M., 234, 239n74, 260n63

"No Chaos Yet," 181

Norfolk, Va., 45

Normal, Ala., 156, 157

North Carolina, 141n1, 212

North Korea, 222

Northrop, 105, 107

Northwestern Technological Institute, 105

Northwestern University, 105

Norton, Mary T., 212

Noyes, Charles, 24

Obama, Barack, 272

O'Brien, Tim, 241

Oddie, Tasker L., 56

Office of Assistant to the Secretary of War, 123

Ohio, 141n1, 212

Oklahoma, 141n1

O'Konski, Rep., 233

*Old Colony Magazine,* 130

Onamina (farm colony, Minn.), 84

Operation Iraqi Freedom, 268, 289, 293

Ortiz, Stephen R., 112n7

O'Ryan, John F., 56–57, 62n64

Osterman, Roy W., 25

Oteen, N.C., 30

Ott, Katherine, 113n8

Otto, Frank V., 242

Page, Benjamin I., 266

Palin, Sarah, 272

Palmer, A. Mitchell, 124

Pascagoula, Miss., 82

Patman, Wright: and American Legion, 179, 182; and Soldiers' Bonus, 178, 179, 180, 183, 185, 186, 187, 196n15; and Veterans of Foreign Wars, 179, 185

Patman Bonus Bill, 186–87, 188, 189

Peadbody, J.C.R., 132

Pearson, Drew, 105–6

Pennsylvania, 133, 141n1, 186

Pensions: American Legion and, 246; amounts of, 20, 24; budget for, 13; characteristics of recipients of, 15; Civil War veterans and, 2, 13, 70; Congress and, 205, 207, 227; disabled veterans and, 13, 16, 24–25, 26, 30, 39–40, 76, 178, 227; in early modern Europe, 68; eligibility for, 13, 244, 245, 246; during Great Depression, 178; Indian Wars veterans and, 32n5; lawmakers' intentions for, 13; levies against, 25; Mexican war veterans and, 32n5; Philippine Insurrection veterans and, 32n5; public and, 227; qualifications for, 13; Revolutionary War veterans and, 244; sizes of, 21; Spanish-American War veterans and, 32n5; U.S. government and, 68–69; USSH veterans and, 15; veterans' groups and, 176; during WWII, 205, 207; WWI veterans and, 246

Pentagon, 65

*Penthouse Magazine,* 241

Perkins, Frances O., 134

Perkins, Frederick Orville, 139

Perryville, Md., 55, 58

Peterson, Col., 104, 108

Peterson, J. Hardin, 216

Pettey, Claudius M., 164

Pew, 266, 267, 268, 271, 279n19

Philadelphia, Pa., 179

Philippine-American Wars, 173

Philippines, 17, 18, 27

Pittsburgh, Pa., 160

Plattsburgh Barracks, N.Y., 78

Portland, Ore., 121, 187, 188

Posttraumatic stress disorder. *See under* Neuropsychiatric conditions

Powell, Adam C., Jr., 239n63

Thomas, Elmer, 186
Thomas, Jesse O., 138
Thompson, J. W., 58
349th Field Artillery, 164
351st Field Artillery, 160
369th Infantry Regiment, 152, 167n24
370th Infantry, 152
Thurmond, Strom, 252
*Time*, 181, 218n1
Togus Springs, Maine, 71, 72–73
Townsend, Francis E., 204
Trainer, Milton J., 61n39
Trainor, Eugene F., 101–2
*Treat 'Em Rough,* 130
Trudeau, Francis, 21
Truman, Harry S.: administration of, 201; on
    G.I. Bill (1944), 225, 230; initiatives of, 211; and
    Korean G.I. Bill, 223, 226–27, 228, 230, 233;
    and Korean War, 222, 226, 235n2; as Veterans
    of Foreign Wars member, 182; and vocational
    rehabilitation bill, 229
Tuberculosis: African Americans and, 154; Army
    and, 13, 16, 17, 29–31, 42; bacteria causing, 15, 17,
    26; Bureau of War Risk Insurance and, 41; costs
    of treating, 30–31; and disability, 160; effects of,
    15; government concerns about, 15; history of,
    15–16, 26–27, 30–31; legislation on, 16; Public
    Health Service and, 45; susceptibility to, 15, 17;
    transmission of, 13, 15, 26, 31; treatments for,
    12, 14, 15, 16, 17, 21, 26, 31, 35n48, 35n50; and
    vocational training, 92n48; WWI veterans and,
    42–43, 44, 46, 48–49, 80, 84, 86, 158, 160. *See
    also* Fort Bayard (N. Mex.)
Tucson, Ariz., 24
Tupelo, Miss., 214
Tuskegee, Ala., 50, 161, 163
Tuskegee Institute, 156, 161, 162, 163, 164
Tuskegee Veterans Hospital, 161–65, 168n36,
    170n83
Twenty-seventh Army Division, 121

UAW, 210
Unions, 124, 136, 215, 216
United Mine Workers of America, 122
United States: economy of, 39, 94, 120, 122, 123,
    199, 200–201, 224–25, 235; expansion of, 69;
    and isolationism, 123; migration to, 138; popu-
    lation of, 16; race in, 138–39
University of Chicago, 135
University of Minnesota School of Agriculture,
    84, 86

University of New York, 242
University of Pennsylvania, 139
University of Southern California, 232
Urban League, 148, 149
U.S. Air Force, 222
U.S. Army: Aviation Section of, 123; and Bonus
    March, 174, 192; and Bureau of War Risk In-
    surance, 46; civilian attitudes toward, 16; and
    Congress, 107; and Federal Board of Hospi-
    talization, 54; foreign-born soldiers in, 125;
    Medical Corps of, 96; Medical Department
    of, 16–17, 26, 29–31; mission of, 18; and nurs-
    ing, 16; and Public Health Service, 46; Quar-
    termasters Office of, 47; size of, 16, 17; and
    tuberculosis, 13, 16, 17, 18, 21, 29–31, 42; and
    veterans' health care, 12, 13, 17; and WWI-era
    amputations, 96–97; and WWII-era amputa-
    tions, 96–99, 100–101, 102, 103, 104–5, 106,
    107, 108. *See also* Hospitals: military
*U.S. Bulletin,* 134
U.S. Bureau of the Budget (BOB), 54, 95, 247,
    250, 252, 253
U.S. Chamber of Commerce, 129, 131, 133
U.S. Colored Troops, 91n25
U.S. Congress: and active-duty WWII soldiers,
    205; and Fort Bayard, 22; conservaties in,
    200, 218n5; and Franklin D. Roosevelt and
    Roosevelt administration, 200, 201, 206–7;
    and gays and lesbians serving in the military,
    276; and G.I. Bill, 200, 207, 208–9, 238n45;
    and Herbert Hoover, 181; and Korean G.I.
    Bill, 223–24, 225, 226–27, 229, 234–35, 237n25,
    237n37; and Korean War, 226, 236n16; and
    Korean War veterans, 229, 236n16; and Labor
    Department, 121–22; liberals in, 200–201,
    207; and military hospitals, 48; moderates in,
    200–201, 207; and New Deal, 200, 201–2, 203,
    204, 217; on payment of veterans' benefits,
    24; and post-WWII economic reconver-
    sion, 201–3, 204–6, 218n5; and post-WWII
    rehabilitation programs, 206; and public
    works, 136; and Revolutionary War veterans,
    244; role of, in national governance, 200,
    204, 217; scholarship on, 218n5; and Social
    Security, 202, 207; and Soldiers' Bonus, 174,
    175, 176, 178, 179, 180–81, 194; and soldiers'
    homes, 14, 69; southerners in, 213; and U.S.
    economy, 122; and U.S. Employment Service,
    122, 123; and veterans' benefits, 13–14, 48; and
    Veterans Bureau, 56; and veterans' groups,
    194, 207, 208, 209; veterans in, 236n15, 253;

and WWII veterans, 44–45, 46–47, 49, 121, 160, 178; and WWII veterans, 94–96, 206–7

U.S. Court of Appeals, 110

U.S. Department of Agriculture, 126, 130, 131, 133, 135

U.S. Department of Defense (DOD), 247, 252, 253, 264.

U.S. Department of Justice, 58, 110

U.S. Department of Labor: creation of, 121–22; and Emergency Employment Committee, 126; funding for, 122; on industrial wages during WWI, 134; Office of Negro Economics in, 138, 148, 149; Otto T. Mallery and, 135; post-WWI, 121, 124; and publicity, 130, 135; and public works, 136; and race, 149–50; staff of, 135; U.S. Training Service of, 134. *See also* Bureau for Returning Soldiers, Sailors, and Marines

U.S. Department of the Interior, 51, 52, 126–27, 131

U.S. Department of the Treasury: Andrew W. Mellon as secretary of, 50; and black WWI veterans, 161, 169n65; and neuropsychiatry, 54; and tuberculosis treatment, 54; and veterans' benefits, 39; and Veterans Bureau, 51, 52, 53, 62n59; and war risk during World War I, 39

U.S. Department of Veterans Affairs, 38

U.S. Emergency Public Works Board, 136

U.S. Employment Service: Arthur D. Woods and, 127; and class, 146–47; and Congress, 122, 123; and Council of National Defense, 131; criticisms of, 140; and Emergency Employment Committee, 127; and farm labor, 133; funding for, 122; and G.I. Bill, 217; and post-WWI cutbacks, 140; and race, 146–47, 148; and rehabilitation programs, 147; reputation of, 129

U.S. House of Representatives: Committee on Education of, 212; Committee on Labor of, 94; Committee on Veterans' Affairs of, 222, 230–31, 232, 239n56, 248, 252–53; Committee on World War Veterans Legislation of, 173, 212, 213, 215; and eligibility for veterans' benefits, 248, 249, 252–53; and G.I. Bill, 212–16, 229, 230–32, 253; and Harding proposal for department of public welfare, 51; investigations by, 94, 230; and Korean G.I. Bill, 230–32, 233, 237n42, 239n56, 239n63; post-World War I legislation in, 122; rehabilitation legislation in, 95; and Soldiers' Bonus and Bonus March, 185–86, 188, 192; Subcommittee on Aid to the Physically Handicapped of, 107–10; and veterans' hospitals, 46–47; veterans in, 236n15; and Wagner-Murray-Dingell bill, 208; Ways and Means Committee of, 180, 185–86, 188, 204, 207, 208; and WWI veterans, 246; and WWII active-duty soldiers, 205; and WWII veterans, 107–10. *See also* U.S. Congress

U.S. Intelligence Bureau, 137

U.S. Marines, 13, 17

U.S. Navy: and Federal Board of Hospitalization, 54; and Fort Bayard, 24; and health care, 13, 17; and Korean War, 222; and tuberculosis, 34n32; and WWII-era amputations, 94, 99–100, 104, 105, 107, 108

U.S. Pension Bureau, 14, 24, 25

U.S. Pension Office, 21

U.S. Post Office, 127, 131

U.S. Public Health Service (PHS): and Bureau of War Risk Insurance, 46, 52; Dawes committee and, 52; and Edward Hines Junior Memorial Hospital, 48; and Federal Board of Hospitalization, 54; funding of, 44, 45, 50; hospitals run by, 41, 43, 44, 45, 54; during and immediately after WWI, 43, 44, 45–46, 49; legislation governing, 45; and rehabilitation facilities, 79; responsibilities of, 43, 44, 46; and Social Security, 210; and Treasury Department, 43; and tuberculosis, 34n32; and U.S. Army, 46; and Veterans Bureau, 44, 55; and WWII-era amputees, 110, 111

U.S. Railroad Administration, 131

U.S. Senate: Committee on Labor and Public Welfare of, 251; and department of public welfare, 51; Finance Committee of, 208, 209; and G.I. Bill, 209, 211–12; and Korean G.I. Bill, 232–33, 237n42, 239n74; Labor Committee of, 232; and Labor Department, 122; and Red Scare, 122–23; rehabilitation legislation in, 95; and Soldiers' Bonus, 186, 188; and Teapot Dome scandal, 58; and veterans' benefits, 248, 251–52; and Veterans Bureau, 39, 53, 56–57, 58; veterans in, 236n15, 246; and Wagner-Murray-Dingell bill, 208; and WW2 soldiers, 208; and WWI veterans, 246

U.S. Soldiers' Home (USSH, Washington, D.C.): capacity of, 70; Civil War veterans and, 70; on disposition of deceased veterans' belongings, 29; establishment of, 13, 69; and Fort Bayard, 14–15, 23; governance of, 14, 17; leadership of, 11, 12; as medical facilities, 14; movement in and out of, 14, 23; population of, 14, 15, 17, 21–22; as social welfare facilities, 14; and state and territorial homes for veterans, 14; and veterans' pensions, 25

and U.S. political system, 292–93; veterans'
groups and, 248–49. *See also* G.I. Bill of
Rights (1944)
Veterans Administration. *See* U.S. Veterans
Administration
Veterans' benefits: 1917 revisions of, 40; Cold
War veterans and, 243; compulsory contributions toward, 40; and disabilities, 25–26,
38, 40, 41, 44, 159–60, 165, 244; Dwight D.
Eisenhower and, 246; and economic need,
246; eligibility for, 23, 25–26, 38, 41, 44,
159–60; enlisted men and, 40; expansion of,
post-WWII, 95; at Fort Bayard, 23, 24; groups
promoting, 31, 38, 48; history of, 235n3;
John F. Kennedy and, 258n31; legislation
governing, 39, 40–41; liberals and, 217; life
insurance, 38, 40; noncombatants and, 243,
246–48; and Progressivism, 39, 40; as recruitment tools, 247, **255**; and retention, 247, and
social welfare, 217; Treasury Department and,
39–40; WWI veterans and, 38–40, 49. *See
also* Health care; Vocational rehabilitation
and training
Veterans Bureau. *See* U.S. Veterans Bureau
*Veterans' Herald,* 165
Veterans hospitals. *See* Hospitals: military
Veterans of Foreign Wars (VFW): and
American Legion, 175, 176, 183–84; archive of,
194n5; and benefits for noncombatant veterans, 248; black WWI veterans and, 167n20;
congressional charter for, 194; expansion of,
181–82, 187; founding of, 173; and G.I. Bill,
209; and Great Depression, 177; and Herbert
Hoover, 177, 178, 192; influence of, 1, 31, 173,
174–75, 176, 187, 193, 277; leadership of, 176;
as lobbyists, 48; Maryland Department of,
191, 198n50; membership of, 173, 176, 181, 187,
192–94, 215; post-WWI issues addressed by,
176; and 1932 presidential election, 192–93;
Rep. Royal C. Johnson as member of, 173,
192; and Senate investigation of Veterans
Bureau, 56; and Soldiers' Bonus and Bonus
March, 173–74, 175–76, 177, 178, 179–80, 181,
183–87, 188–93; and Wright Patman, 179, 180,
185
Veterans' Readjustment Assistance Act (1952).
*See* G.I. Bill, Korean (1952)
Veteransville (farm colony, Minn.), 84, 85, 86,
88, 92n61
Vietnam War, 242, 250, 251, 268, 286. *See also*
G.I. bills, Vietnam-era; Veterans: Vietnam

Virginia, 141n1, 186
Vocational Rehabilitation Act (1918), 78, 153,
235n3
Vocational Rehabilitation Act (1943), 94–95,
113n12
Vocational rehabilitation and training: activities
associated with, 80, 81; agencies administering,
41; as alternative to higher benefits, 48; black
WWI veterans and, 153–54, 155–56; as component of rehabilitation, 76, 79; courses offered
by, 80, 81; disabled veterans and, 153; eligibility
for, 80–81; experts' agenda for, 46; facilities for,
79–83; funding for, 80; goals of, 80, 82; immigrants and, 153–54; Korean War Veterans and,
229; legislation governing, 40–41, 78; outsourc-
ing of, 79; and reintegration strategy, 67; staff
for, 80, 82; tubercular veterans and, 92n48; as
veterans' benefit, 38; Veterans Bureau and, 79,
80, 82–83, 153; veterans groups and, 154; War
Department and, 134; WWI veterans and, 79,
80–81, 134; WWII veterans and, 100. *See also*
Federal Board for Vocational Education
Vorys, John, 233

Wagner, Robert, 151, 209–10
Wagner-Murray-Dingell bill, 207–8, 209–10, 211
Wallace, Nick, 159
Walsh, David A., 56
Walsh, David I., 216
Walter Reed Hospital (Washington, D.C.), 43, 79,
101, 102, 103
War, definition of, 89n1
War Camp Community Service, 131
Ward, Joseph H., 163
War Department. *See* U.S. War Department
War of 1812, 244
War on Poverty, 246. *See also* Great Society
War Plans Division, 123, 140
War Risk Act (1917), 40–41, 235n3
War Risk Insurance Act (1914), 39
War Risk Insurance Board, 176
Washington, Booker T., 150, 161, 162
Washington, D.C.: Bonus March in, 174, 188–89,
190; civilian hospitals in, 44; disabled black
veterans in, 157; military and veterans hospitals
in, 16, 45, 97; military hospitals and veterans
hospitals in, 79; U.S. Soldiers' Home in, 13;
veterans' marches on, 184; Veterans of Foreign
Wars meetings and posts in, 184, 186, 189;
WWII-era amputees in, 106
Washington Medical Society, 207